BATTLEGROUND

WOMEN, GENDER, AND SEXUALITY

BATTLEGROUND

WOMEN, GENDER, AND SEXUALITY

VOLUME 2 (M–Z)

Edited by Amy Lind and Stephanie Brzuzy

GREENWOOD PRESS
Westport, Connecticut • London

Library of Congress Cataloging-in-Publication Data

Battleground : women, gender and sexuality / edited by Amy Lind and Stephanie Brzuzy.
   p. cm.
   Includes bibliographical references and index.
   ISBN 978–0–313–34037–6 (set : alk. paper) — ISBN 978–0–313–34038–3 (vol. 1 : alk.
paper) — ISBN 978–0–313–34039–0 (vol. 2 : alk. paper)
1. Women—Social conditions—Encyclopedias.   2. Feminism—Encyclopedias.   3. Women's
studies—Encyclopedias.   I. Lind, Amy.   II. Brzuzy, Stephanie.   III. Title: Women and gender.
   HQ1115.B38   2008
   305.403—dcs22   2007029582

British Library Cataloguing in Publication Data is available.

Library of Congress Catalog Card Number: 2007029582
ISBN-13: 978–0–313–34037–6 (set)
          978–0–313–34038–3 (vol. 1)
          978–0–313–34039–0 (vol. 2)

First published in 2008

Greenwood Press, 88 Post Road West, Westport, CT 06881
An imprint of Greenwood Publishing Group, Inc.
www.greenwood.com

Printed in the United States of America

The paper used in this book complies with the
Permanent Paper Standard issued by the National
Information Standards Organization (Z39.48–1984).

10   9   8   7   6   5   4   3   2   1

CONTENTS

GUIDE TO RELATED TOPICS

Education
Equal Rights Amendment
Glass Ceiling
Lesbians and Gays in the Military
Military History
Same-Sex Marriage
Sexual Orientation and the Law
Sports: Professional
Title IX and Women's Sports

GENDER IDENTITIES AND EXPRESSIONS
Femininities and Masculinities
Gender Identity Disorder
Gender Socialization
Intersexuality
Nature versus Nurture
Sex versus Gender
Sex Reassignment Surgery
Third Genders
Transgender and Transsexual Identities

GLOBAL POLITICAL ECONOMY
Colonialism and Imperialism
Environmental Justice
Gender and Globalization: Free Trade Zones
Gender and Globalization: Trends and Debates
Gender and International Development
Human Rights: International Law and Policies
Immigration: Laws and Policies Concerning Entry into the United States
Mail-Order Brides
Mexican Female Migrants
Militarized Prostitution
Terrorism and National Security

MEDIA, VISUAL ARTS, AND COMMUNICATION
Digital Technologies
Feminist Art Practices
Media Images of Women: Advertising
Media Images of Women: Music
Media Images of Women: Television and Film
Sexism in Language

POLITICS AND SOCIAL MOVEMENTS
Leftist Armed Struggle
Lesbian, Gay, Bisexual, Transgender, and Queer Movements

MAIL-ORDER BRIDES

Mail-order brides are chosen by their prospective husbands through self-described advertisements in catalogs, newspapers, Internet sites, or video clips, or through marriage broker services that are paid a fee to make introductions in the hope of a marriage. This practice is viewed by feminists as possible only in a patriarchial society that views women as property and men as owners of that property. Supporters of the practice, in contrast, argue that marriages arranged through a third party, whether through parents or a marriage broker agency, have been a part of most societies historically and can be as fulfilling as non-arranged marriages.

BACKGROUND

Since the 1970s, an increasing number of women in the United States have worked outside their homes, breaking with traditional notions of the nuclear family with a stay-at-home mother and a father who works to support the family. During the 1980s and 1990s, many men from the United States and other Western nations began looking outside their own countries for more "suitable" women to marry, women who would fulfill more traditional roles as stay-at-home wives and mothers. Usually, these men are financially secure individuals who look for wives through the Internet, catalogs, marriage agencies, newspapers, and magazines. The women who marry men from Western cultures through these channels have come to be known as mail-order brides. Mail-order brides advertise themselves or use others to advertise their marriage eligibility and are then "ordered" by men who respond to the advertisements.

THE "CASKET GIRLS": MAIL-ORDER BRIDES IN COLONIAL AMERICA

Since colonial days, mail-order brides have been part of American life. Many people who live in the New Orleans region, for example, claim to be descended from the original "casket girls," a term derived from the chests in which women sent from France by Louis XV to marry Louisiana colonists carried their belongings (Garin 2006).

Thousands of women from all over the world are advertised as available for marriage to strangers. Most of these women are from developing countries such as Vietnam, Thailand, Ukraine, Colombia, Russia, and the Philippines. Women who sign up to become mail-order brides often hope to escape economic poverty and oppression (Sun 1998). Some mail-order brides live happy and successful married lives, while others end up being abused or treated as slaves. The wives in these situations often feel that they are trapped in their marriage arrangements. Language barriers and a lack of resources prevent women from reporting abuse or choosing to leave if domestic violence occurs.

THE DEBATE: SUPPORTERS AND OPPONENTS OF THE MAIL-ORDER BRIDE INDUSTRY

Supporters of the mail-order bride industry feel that marriages set up through international introduction services or marriage broker agencies can be just as fulfilling as nonarranged marriages—or at times even more successful. According to the U.S. Citizenship and Immigration Service (USCIS), mail-order marriages and other forms of arranged marriage have a lower divorce rate, at 20 percent, in comparison to the nation's average of 50 percent for nonarranged marriages. People who support the mail-order bride industry often feel that the mail-order marriage broker services help to preserve family values from further disintegration at the hands of the feminist movement, encourage families to stay together, and maintain the traditional patriarchal societal order. Any regulations imposed on the mail-order bride industry are strongly opposed by the men seeking mail-order brides, especially in the United States, because these men feel that the American government has no right to have any say in how its citizens meet and marry their spouses, whether through a national dating service or international introduction services (Bunagan 2006).

Although 80 percent of the marriages arranged through mail-order services appear to be successful, some brides end up being abused or treated as slaves (for details, see Immigration and Naturalization Service [now USCIS] reports and studies). Many are subjected to all types of abuse from their husbands, who seek out women whom they believe they can control. Because men have paid large amounts of money through agencies and paid for the women's transportation to the country where the potential husbands reside, they feel that they own their wives. The inequity of the relationship is further complicated by the mail-order brides' immigrant status. Even if the wives want to report the battering they experience, they often feel that they are trapped, because they are afraid that if they report any violence in their homes perpetrated by their husbands, they will be deported. They choose instead to tolerate the abuse. Language barriers prevent women from finding out how to report abuse or obtain help in leaving their husbands if domestic violence occurs.

MAIL-ORDER BRIDES AROUND THE WORLD

Asia

The American mail-order bride industry has become a multibillion-dollar business, marketing women from developing countries as potential brides to men in Western nations (Sun 1998). Significant numbers of mail-order brides come from Asia because Asian wives are highly desired by Western men (So 2006). Because Asian women are perceived as more likely to maintain traditional family values than most Western women, some Western men seek out Asian women. Filipinas are often stereotyped as "dream wives" because they are perceived as faithful and as good mothers. Because of this stereotyping, the Philippines are currently the largest exporter of mail-order brides, and Filipinas outnumber prospective mail-order brides from any other country (So 2006). Every year, an estimated 5,000 Filipina mail-order brides marry Americans. Between 1986 and 1997, an estimated 55,000 Filipinas entered the United States to marry Americans (Vergara 2000).

In 1990, Philippines President Corazon Aquino signed a law that outlawed the bride trade but to little effect. To date, women of all social classes continue to be lured by the hope and expectation of better lives and opportunities in the United States. In general, many women from Asian countries opt to become mail-order brides as a way to escape the poverty and hardship of living in a developing country; often, once they are in the United States, they send money home to help support their families. They become mail-order brides to help their families, but the arrangement seldom works out as hoped. Once in the United States, these women generally have little connection to Asian-American communities and often do not know where to go in case of abuse. Asian mail-order brides are often vulnerable to abuse since their husbands feel that they own their wives. Women often feel that they have the obligation to be "perfect" wives because they are indebted to their husbands for rescuing them from the poverty and hardship of their lives back home.

Africa

Although there are no detailed reports on mail-order brides in Africa, trafficking and prostitution in women and children of various ages is believed to be a large-scale problem. In Algeria, for example, during the 1990s, women who were targeted for their ethnicity, religion, or assumed secularism were kidnapped and made into sex slaves by rebels fighting in the name of Islamic revolution (Crossette 1998). Children are the largest group to be at risk of trafficking and prostitution in Africa; in Togo and Benin alone, local nongovernmental organizations (NGOs) have estimated that more than 700 children (both girls and boys) were recaptured on the Benin-Togo border and the Benin-Nigerian border during 1997 and returned to their families (*All Africa News* 1998). In Ghana, a bill was introduced in 1998 stating that anyone involved in the enslavement of others, including Trokosi priests (priests who enslaved girls to become wives of gods), would be punished (Equality Now 1998). Since the introduction of this bill, some Trokosi churches have given up their tradition. Some countries, such as South Africa, have become international transit zones for child pornography and prostitution (Kirmire 1998). In general, women and children throughout Africa tend to be more at risk of forced sexual slavery or forced marriage during periods of civil war.

The Americas

The mail-order bride industry not only affects women in Africa and Asia but women in the Americas as well. With the high demand for foreign brides and the widespread popularity of the internet, the mail-order industry spread to the Americas, especially Latin America, during the 1990s (Miteva 2006). A study conducted by the U.S. Immigration and Naturalization Service shows that mail-order brides from Latin America are often among those who become victims of gendered violence after marriage, with some instances of abuse resulting in murder (Northam 2003).

Scholars and academics focusing on the mail-order bride industry often highlight the exploitation of underprivileged women in developing countries by Western men. But in developed and progressive societies of the Americas, the mail-order bride industry has successfully appealed to middle-class and/or professional Latina women. Many Latina women are drawn into the mail-order bride industry upon answering advertisements after reading success stories of married couples on marriage broker Web sites. For Latina women, American men represent opportunities for a stable, middle-class lifestyle and increased status within their families and communities. In addition, a myriad Latina women report dissatisfaction with the way they are treated in Latin America and feel American men would be more equitable marriage partners (Schaeffer-Grabiel 2006).

American men view Latina women as especially desirable in marriage based on the stereotypes of Latina women as being better mothers and more passionate, feminine, family oriented, willing to please men sexually, willing to put husband and family ahead of themselves, untainted by modern capitalism, seductive, and accustomed to large age differences. Some American men even go as far as to believe that women from Latin America have better genes than American women. A majority of American men seeking foreign brides also cite frustration in relationships with American women, who are often perceived as being dominant, career oriented, selfish, rude, obnoxious, and materialistic. The mail-order industry appeals to men who are interested in submissive women who would permit men increased authority and a central role within the family. In addition, these men blame the disintegration of male-dominated and middle-class family structures on feminism, the increased number of women in the workforce, and women of color who are welfare recipients. Latina women, according to these men, will protect the moral fabric of the family and elevate the men's social capital by accepting the patriarchal notion of a traditional wife and family (Schaeffer-Grabiel 2006). Like Asian and Russian women, who tend to be highly desired in the mail-order bride industry for what are assumed to be their submissive qualities, Latina women are eroticized and desired for their submissiveness. In advertisements, many such women are portrayed as educated, beautiful, and in favor of traditional family values.

Today, in the United States there are as many as 200 mail-order agencies, making the United States a global leader in the industry. Several heartbreaking stories concerning the fate of foreign mail-order brides in the United States have captured the nation's headlines. For example, Anastasia King, a 20-year-old woman from Kyrgyzstan, met her American husband through a mail-order bride service. After she was murdered by her husband in 2000, the investigators discovered that the husband had had a restraining order against him from a former mail-order bride. In 1995, a pregnant Filipina, Susana Blackwell, was shot to death by her husband outside a courthouse in Seattle, Washington, during divorce hearings. In 2003, Alla Barney, a 26-year-old Ukrainian, was stabbed to death by her husband (Garin 2006).

In the light of these tragic events, there have been some recent efforts to regulate the mail-order industry in the United States. Human rights activists, legislators, and others are hoping that criminal background checks will help to protect women's rights and ensure that women are properly informed of their legal rights. President George W. Bush signed into law the International Marriage Broker Regulation Act of 2005, an act that will regulate the mail-order industry by requiring that prospective foreign brides be provided with information about American men's martial and criminal backgrounds, including information obtained from a search of state and federal sex-offender registries (Garin 2006). Earlier, the U.S. Congress passed the Trafficking Victims Protection Act of 2000, which evaluates the efforts to combat trafficking made by governments in other countries. For those governments that fail to meet certain standards, economic sanctions that adversely affect trade will be put in place. Various marriage broker services that set up European tours and put American men in touch with women from other countries, such as Russia or Ukraine, fear that business will be weakened or lost due to increased federal regulation. Supporters of marriage broker services argue that the services help to build strong families by encouraging marriage (Northam 2003).

Europe

There are three main sex trafficking routes in Europe: the Balkan route into Italy or Greece, the Baltic route from Russia and Asia into Finland or Germany, and the Mediterranean route from northern Africa into Spain or Italy. Many women are enticed into the mail-order industry by bogus mail-order bride advertisements placed in newspapers, in magazines, or on the Internet. Men then develop women's trust through constant e-mails and telephone conversations.

When women decide to meet these men in person, they become at risk of being taken as victims in the sex-trafficking industry, where women are forced to participate in sexual activities to repay the costs incurred during transportation to destination countries, the cost of food, housing, and medical expenses, and any other fees (Sulavik 2003).

Marriage broker services often set up European tours to introduce men to prospective brides through lavish social get-togethers, lasting as long as four hours or more, at which the ratio of women to men is at least five to one. Some tours may cost as much as $4,000 for two weeks (Garin 2006). Men are provided with clean hotels, transportation, and translators. During the tour, they hope to find their brides and begin the paperwork needed to bring the brides back to the United States. Among some men, European women, especially those in Ukraine, have a reputation for being wild, uninhibited, and open minded, qualities that are viewed by some as ideal for wives.

European women struggle to find men, often citing population imbalance due to wars and the shorter life expectancy for men. The U.S. Central Intelligence Agency reports that the ratio of men to women in Ukraine is 86 men to every 100 women. In the United States, there are 97 men for every 100 women. As a result of the shortage of men, European women turn to the mail-order bride industry in the hope of finding men of their dreams and having a family (Garin 2006).

CONCLUSION

According to human rights activists, even the strictest regulations fail to address the fundamental problem of the mail-order bride industry. From their perspective, it is a form of sexual exploitation that is no different from prostitution. In fact, it may even be worse than prostitution, because marriage contracts and immigration laws give it a more permanent nature. Impoverished women surrender their lives and sexuality because they hope to obtain economic security—but their dreams for a better life often turn into the cruelest nightmares. Woman are abused and treated as slaves. Often because of language barriers, cultural barriers, and fear, for example, women tolerate the many wrongs that are done to them. This leads to a lifetime of injustice, often unreported or ignored by the government, or even to death.

Despite these criticisms, proponents of the mail-order bride industry continue to view arranged marriage through third parties as an acceptable practice. They view this industry as a modern version of a practice that has existed for centuries in many societies, and they point out that arranged marriages can be strong and lasting. Because the industry has only recently begun to be regulated, little research has been conducted on the practices of the industry, and much has yet to be understood in terms of the positive and negative outcomes of these marriages for the women and men who participate in them.

See also Human Rights: International Laws and Policies; Sex Trafficking.

Further Reading: *All Africa News,* "Child Peddling Serious Problem in Togo and Benin," March 23, 1998; Bunagan, Mae, "Cash on Delivery: The Mail-Order Bride Industry

Exploits Women," *Perspective,* November 2002; Constable, Nicole, *Romance on a Global Stage: Pen Pals, Virtual Ethnography, and "Mail Order" Marriages* (Berkeley: University of California Press, 2003); Crossette, Barbara, "An Old Scourge of War Becomes Its Latest Crime," *New York Times,* June 18, 1998 (city edition); Enss, Chris, *Hearts West: True Stories of Mail-Order Brides on the Frontier* (Guilford, CT: Falcon Press, 2006); Equality Now, "Slavery in Ghana: The Trokosi Tradition," *Equality Now Women's Action,* March 1998; Garin, Kristoffer A., "A Foreign Affair: On the Great Ukrainian Bride Hunt," *Harper's Magazine,* June 2006; Herbst, Robert, *My E-Mail Order Bride: A Trip to Feodosia, Crimea, Ukraine* (Surge Publishing, 2002); Larson, Wanwadee, *Confessions of a Mail Order Bride: American Life through Thai Eyes* (Far Hills, NJ: New Horizon Press, 1989); Kirmire, Merab, "End Child Prostitution, Pornography and Trafficking (ECPAT)," August 7, 1998, press release, Sapa African National Congress; Miteva, Natalia, "Between Mail-Order Brides and Turbo-Folk Women: Eastern Europe's Sexualities in Transition," *Journal of Sex Research* 43, no. 2 (2006): 203–206; Northam, Jackie, interview by All Things Considered for National Public Radio, June 3, 2003, Washington, DC, transcript; Schaeffer-Grabiel, Felicity, "Planet-Love.com: Cyberbrides in the Americas and the Transnational Routes of U.S. Masculinity," *Signs* (Winter 2006): 331–356; So, Christine, "Asian Mail-Order Brides, the Threat of Global Capitalism and the Rescue of the U.S. Nation-State," *Feminist Studies,* Summer 2006; Sulavik, Christopher, "Facing Down Traffickers; Europe Takes on Its Fastest Growing Criminal Enterprise," *Newsweek,* August 25, 2003; Sun, Lena H., "The Search for Miss Right Takes a Turn toward Russia: 'Mail-Order Brides' of the '90s Are Met via Internet and on Romance Tours," *Washington Post,* March 8, 1998; Vergara, Vanessa B. M., "Abusive Mail-Order Bride Marriage and the Thirteenth Amendment," *Northwestern University Law Review,* Summer 2000.

Sara Collins and Arlyn Penaranda

MEDIA IMAGES OF WOMEN: ADVERTISING

Debates about women and advertising concern whether or not advertising directly affects women's identities and roles in society, including their self-esteem, their purported sexualization or objectification, and reported increases in eating disorders and violence against women.

BACKGROUND

Images of women in advertising have been analyzed from various perspectives and span several decades of reforms in the advertising industry. Today, over $266 billion are spent annually on advertising. Average Americans will spend three years of their lives looking at advertisements (Campbell, Martin, and Fabos 2007; Kilbourne 1999). Advertising has crept into some of the most intimate spaces, such as bathroom stalls, and can be seen plastered over bus sides, benches, billboards, grocery carts, magazine covers, and other people's clothing. It seems to be that everywhere one looks there is a label or logo, sometimes with messages, written or symbolic, sometimes just the brand name. Advertisements can be dismissed as silly, inconsequential, sometimes entertaining, and mostly harmless (Kilbourne 1999). Many people do dismiss them in this way. However, some critical theorists disagree, arguing that the effects of advertisements are much greater than simply instilling brand recognition in consumers. They argue that advertisements both construct and reflect reality, and that the reality they create is a damaging one, particularly to women (Cortese 2004).

Advertisers themselves argue that they are only doing their job, that it is what they get paid to do in the mass media marketplace. Depending on whom you speak to, advertising stimulates the economy, provides information to consumers, and provides greater choice and competition among consumer goods. Critics of advertising state that it is deceptive and manipulative, that it raises the prices of consumer goods, that it promotes false and unattainable expectations and realities (Campbell, Martin, and Fabos 2007; Cortese 2004), and that it exacerbates and exploits stereotypes as well as ideals harmful to individuals. Critics of advertising agree that its effects on women's self-esteem and body image are harmful, but it is important to note that different critics view the advertising industry in differing ways. Some critics of advertising believe the advertising industry is unethical because it does not act on the negative effects of advertising that have been found in studies. Others attribute broader, more political motives to advertising, with the idea that its effects are known, intentional, and part of a larger agenda created to weaken women, especially after the rise of the second wave feminist movement.

HISTORY OF THE ADVERTISING INDUSTRY

Advertising has steadily grown over the last hundred years, and now generates a larger amount of revenue and influence than ever before. All mass media outlets are supported by two sources of revenue. The first is user fees, which include items such as subscriptions, the single-copy sale of magazines, and television and Internet fees. The other source of revenue is advertising. Advertisers seek out different media outlets because they target different consumers. Demographic research is conducted on subscribers and hawked to advertisers (Kilbourne 1999). Advertisements are placed in response to the audience for the medium.

Advertising is defined as a "mass mediated attempt to persuade" (Cortese 2004, 3). Persuasion has steadily taken a larger role over the last century. Earlier advertisements were created for the primary purpose of informing. Advertisements announced land sales and stagecoach schedules, for example. Early newspapers and magazines refused to carry advertisements. In contrast, contemporary magazines average about half editorial content and half advertisements (Campbell, Martin, and Fabos 2007; Kilbourne 1999). Paradoxically, although the abundance of advertisements keeps subscription costs low, the advertisements themselves make brand name products more expensive. The first advertising agency, Volney Palmer, was created in 1841. In the first decade of the twenty-first century, there are more than thirteen thousand advertising agencies in existence (Campbell, Martin, and Fabos 2007). These agencies are so numerous and profitable because of the enormous amount of revenue they generate. To cite some contemporary statistics, the average television commercial costs $250,000 to produce, and another $250,000 in payment for airtime. The advertising industry's money pays for more than 60 percent of newspapers' and magazines' costs. Advertising pays $40 billion to television and radio annually and $30 billion to newspapers and magazines (Kilbourne 1999). Many media critics contend that with so much money at stake, contemporary media outlets and their featured content are being influenced in ways profitable to advertisers and deceptive to consumers. Media critics such as Jean Kilbourne state that the advertising agencies and the corporations that back them influence the media in various ways. Kilbourne argues that the editors of magazines, television programs, and newspapers edit content to remove any negative or conflicting information about the products advertised, and that supposedly objective editorials are sometimes not so objective. Kilbourne would argue that the placement of an editorial about how high heels make one feel more empowered next to an advertisement for Gucci shoes is not coincidental.

CURRENT DEBATES ON WOMEN IN ADVERTISING

The debates about gender and advertising involve a series of questions. The first question to consider is: Are there harmful gendered effects from advertising? If yes, what are these effects? And are the effects a result of ignorance on the advertising industry's part, of negligence, or of failure to put things right, or are they the result of malice—that is, is the advertising industry maliciously targeting women with messages the industry knows are harmful, in order to achieve some sort of larger, sexist objectives?

Media critics such as Susan Douglas, Naomi Wolf, and Jean Kilbourne contend that advertising images are in fact harmful to women, that media portrayals of women are sexist, racist, unattainable, and exploitative, and that media portrayals of women have obvious effects, whether intended or unintended. These critics address a range of effects, including negative effects on women's self-image; increased rates of eating disorders; sexualization, objectification, and racialization of women; and increased rates of violence against women. Although these critics have slightly different ideas on how and why advertising functions in its portrayal of women, they universally agree that advertising involving and directed at women impacts women negatively.

THE EFFECTS OF ADVERTISING ON WOMEN'S SELF-IMAGE AND THE OBJECTIFICATION OF WOMEN'S BODIES

In marketing to a general audience, most advertisements use the "association principle." This principle involves associating a product with a positive and usually unrelated image. Potential consumers will see advertisements involving a naked woman draped over a car hood, or a woman with shoes or a purse covering her otherwise naked breasts. The mantra that "sex sells" applies here. While the association principle is not in itself harmful—one cannot blame advertisers for wanting their products to be associated with happiness—media critics argue that the link between commodifying feelings such as happiness or sexual desire and commodifying women as people is harmful. This is commonly referred to as the objectification of women; that is, seeing the women in the advertisements as objects and then treating women in the real world accordingly (Campbell, Martin, and Fabos 2007). Jean Kilbourne contends that the practice of dismemberment, which occurs at a higher rate in advertisements involving women and includes cutting women's body parts out of the frame of the advertisement and showing women as parts of something else, usually an inanimate object, is linked to violence against women. Both Jean Kilbourne and Naomi Wolf argue that the "culture of thinness and perfection," which has evolved from the presentation of atypically thin and conventionally beautiful models in advertisements, is harmful to women, playing a part in their plummeting self-esteem and body image and in the rise in eating disorders. Jean Kilbourne and Susan Douglas also argue that the contradictory messages shown to women through advertisements are harmful and difficult for women and girls to reconcile.

Jean Kilbourne believes that the main fault in the advertising industry is its lack of change and its continued objectification of women. Kilbourne's views reflect the argument that, yes, the intent of advertisements is to sell a product, but the other, maybe unintended, consequences of advertising cannot be ignored. In her book, *Deadly Persuasion: Why Women and Girls Must Fight the Addictive Power of Advertising,* as well as her video lecture series *Killing Us Softly,* first produced in 1979, Kilbourne critiques the advertising industry. In her video lecture "Slim Hopes," she examines in depth the effect of the atypically thin and perfect models on the way women perceive themselves and how they are perceived by others. In Kilbourne's view, the negative effects lie in the cumulative compounding of the advertisements that women see every day. Research studies conducted at Stanford University and the University of Massachusetts found that 70 percent of college women feel worse about themselves after looking at women's

DOVE'S "REAL BEAUTY CAMPAIGN"

In 2005, Dove launched its "Real Beauty Campaign," claiming: "At Dove we believe that every woman's look, shape, and spirit are what creates her own unique beauty." The advertisements for Dove's products show women who are atypical of the models one is used to seeing in advertisements: none of the women in Dove's advertisements is a size 2 or lower. The products marketed in this campaign are firming creams, anti-aging creams, and lotions. While many welcomed the campaign as a step forward, in that it provides some relief from the barrage of waif-like models seen in ads, some feminists and critics dispute this. Jennifer Ponzer, a writer for *Bitch* magazine, claims that despite all its pro-real-women rhetoric, the Dove campaign is still a marketing design, and that it states and exploits a co-opted message of feminism. Many critics feel that the ads are manipulative. Further complicating the debate is the fact that Unilever, which markets Axe body spray in a campaign that many consider blatantly objectifies women, is also the parent company of Dove and its "Real Beauty Campaign." Most critics have mixed feelings, believing that this is a step in the right direction, but that Dove's campaign is insincere.

magazines (Kilbourne 1999, 133). According to the results of this study, the cumulative effect of the advertisements in which we are immersed, all showing the "perfect body," is to lead women to believe that such an unattainable figure is normal, and that they should feel guilty and bad about themselves if they fail to attain it. Kilbourne argues that advertisers use our emotions against us, our desire for happiness and fulfillment—and our guilt (Kilbourne 1999, 132).

GENDER AND RACIAL STEREOTYPES IN ADVERTISING

Stereotyping in advertising spans race, class, and gender, capitalizing on our interpreted desires to try and persuade us to buy the product or service advertised. While it is true that this tactic spans genders, Kilbourne argues that advertisements directed at women are often directly contradictory in ways that men do not experience, and that women are objectified to a much higher degree than men. To give an example, Kilbourne focuses on the way that food is often shown by advertisers as a comfort for women who are upset; that is, women are urged to become obsessed with chocolate, cake, and ice cream. However the twist lies here: women are told by hundreds of advertisements a day that they really should love these foods, but they should not look as if they do. An advertisement for chocolate frosting is followed by a diet ad showing an impossibly thin model in a bikini. This is an example of a double bind, a contradiction that women must reconcile, but one in which there is really no possibility of winning. Women experience double binds in many different messages given by advertising, not just food-related messages. Kilbourne argues that the double binds keep women insecure and looking to products for their solution, products about which advertisers are more than happy to inform us. Kilbourne argues that while the advertisements are probably not designed deliberately to prey, in a hidden fashion, on those who have food addictions or disorders, their creators certainly know about the existence of eating disorders. When it comes to issues of weight and fat, it is important to note the stigma that has resulted from the changing body images presented by advertisers to women. In Kilbourne's words, "In the old days, bad girls got pregnant, in these days, they get fat" (Kilbourne 1999, 120). What is now a $36-billion-a-year diet industry benefits from the stereotype of the ultra-thin woman, although Kilbourne acknowledges that the advertising industry does not directly cause eating disorders; rather, she argues, it promotes abusive and abnormal attitudes toward women's physical selves.

Advertisements present an unattainable and contradictory ideal image of women and girls, the ideal image being someone who both loves sweets and eats them with abandon yet is thinner than 95 percent of women; someone who both is sexually knowledgeable and seductive yet naïve and innocent; someone who is eternally youthful despite the natural aging process. Advertisements also predominantly reflect white standards of beauty, with the norm being lighter-skinned models with straight hair and blue or green eyes. African American women are often portrayed in outdoor scenes, associated with or dressed up like animals. Asian women are portrayed as china dolls, as erotic, passive sex objects, while Latina women are portrayed as seductive, "luscious Latinas" (Cortese 2004, 90, 97, 101, 104).

VIOLENCE AGAINST WOMEN

One of the worst effects of all, Kilbourne argues, is the link between violence against women and portrayals of women in advertising. It is this, she argues, that differentiates portrayals of women and portrayals of men in advertising. Women are objectified passively, and sexuality is mixed with violence. An ad for a bar in Georgetown states, "If your date won't listen to reason, try a velvet hammer." Kilbourne contends that this is disturbing because of the prevalence of alcohol in most date rape cases. She also states that the objectification and dismemberment to which women are subjected in advertisements, particularly alcohol advertisements, contribute to violence against women. The first step in abusing a person is to turn that person into a thing, such as a beer bottle or car (Kilbourne 1999, 274). The advertising industry acknowledges the sexism in alcohol advertisements in a 1991 editorial in the advertising magazine *Advertising Age:* "Clearly, it's time to wipe out sexism in beer ads" (Kilbourne 1999, 278). Yet the ads have continued to proliferate on television and in magazines. Kilbourne points out that the climate that is created and shown as reality has unrealistic and harmful connotations for women. While she does not strongly condemn advertisements as malicious attempts to devalue women, she does critique the lack of action on the part of advertisers to act upon the effects that have manifested themselves.

ADVERTISING AND THE POLITICS OF BEAUTY

Naomi Wolf, author of the 1989 book *The Beauty Myth,* states that advertising's portrayal of women is a direct and malicious response to women's liberation. As in the 1920s, when Marlboro marketed its cigarettes to newly liberated women, Naomi Wolf argues that women are offered beauty as liberation in contemporary times. Wolf argues that women are offered the chance to change the world...with their hairdryer. She calls the advertising world's portrayal of women a "beauty backlash," which she names "the beauty myth," and argues that "images of female beauty are used against women as a political weapon against women's advancement" (Wolf 1989, 10). Wolf contends that beauty pornography, a type of advertising where commodified beauty is linked to sexuality, is used to sell products. Using cultural standards as a means of control, women's empowerment through feminism is being co-opted through advertising promising advancement through nail polish while continuing to objectify women. Wolf compares the contemporary ideal of femininity to the iron maiden, a torture device in medieval times. The iron maiden is pretty and smiling on the outside but hides a painful and terrible interior (1989, 17). Wolf not only criticizes the advertising industry for its unattainable and harmful portrayals of women, but she frames images of women in advertising as part of a larger agenda to combat women's power. Wolf calls beauty maintenance—that is, plucking eyebrows and

TIMELINE

1704: The first newspaper advertisement features land deals and ship cargoes.

1841: The first advertising agency, Volney Palmer, opens in Boston.

1914: The Federal Trade Commission (FTC) is established to monitor advertising abuses, such as false claims.

1920: Women gain the vote; Marlboro markets its cigarettes to women as "liberation."

1960: Second wave feminism organizes for women's rights.

1968: Feminists protest the Miss America Contest in Atlantic City, Georgia.

1971: The tobacco industry agrees to stop advertising on television.

1976: Sociologist Erving Goffman publishes "Gender Advertisements," a deconstruction of advertisements involving men and women.

1979: Jean Kilbourne releases *Killing Us Softly*, a video lecture series deconstructing advertising's portrayal of women.

1989: Naomi Wolf publishes *The Beauty Myth: How Images of Advertising Are Used against Women.*

2005: Dove Launches its "Real Beauty Campaign."

managing hair—a "third shift" on women's time, adding on to the time spent at work and in the home. This, she argues, is in response to women heading out into the workforce in higher numbers. Not only is showing an unattainable ideal as the norm good business for advertisers, but, Wolf argues, it keeps women running on a treadmill of work, spending both their energy and the wage they earn (which is still only three-quarters of what men earn for the same work) on the carrot dangled in front of them—the products that will supposedly end wrinkles, cellulite, weight gain, and so on. Wolf argues that advertisers intentionally keep women in a self-hating, insecure state because it serves dual purposes, both political and economic.

CONCLUSION

Though advertisers and critics have different viewpoints, the manifest effects of advertising are hard to deny. While 50 years ago, advertisers might be able to state that the effects of advertising were unknown, research and vocal critics have publicized the ways in which sexist and racist attitudes in advertisements influence women's opinions of themselves and men's opinions of women. While some critics, such as Jean Kilbourne, have blamed the industry for its failure to act to remove the harmful effects of advertising, other critics, such as Naomi Wolf, argue that the advertisers knew what they were doing all along, and that they continue to act deliberately to benefit the patriarchy. As advertising continues to gain influence in the media and generate more income in our society, it is important to be media literate—that is, to actively deconstruct what we see in the media, in particular advertising, so that we can see what the advertisements are really selling, and what consumers are buying into.

See also Barbie and the Feminine Ideal of Beauty; Beauty Industry; Media Images of Women: Music; Media Images of Women: Television and Film.

Further Reading: Campbell, Richard, Christopher Martin, and Bettina Fabos, *Media and Culture,* 5th ed. (New York: Bedford St. Martins, 2007); Cortese, Anthony, *Provocateur: Images of Women and Minorities in Advertising,* 2nd ed. (Lanham, MD: Rowman and Littlefield, 2004); Douglas, Susan, *Where the Girls Are: Growing Up Female with the Mass Media* (New York: Time Books, 1994; rev. ed. New York: Penguin, 1995); Gallagher, Margaret, *Gender Setting: New Agendas for Media Monitoring and Advocacy* (New York: St. Martin's Press, 2001); Goffman, E., "Gender Advertisements," *Studies in the Anthropology of Visual Communication* 3, no. 2 (1976): 69–154; Gunter, Barrie, and Maggie Wykes, *The Media and Body Image* (Thousand Oaks, CA: Sage, 2005); Hao, Rita, "And Now a Word from Our Sponsors," in *BitchFest,* ed. Lisa Jervis and Andi Zeisler, 111–115 (New York: Farrar, Straus and Giroux, 2006); Kilbourne, Jean, *Deadly Persuasion: Why Women and Girls Must Fight the Addictive Power of Advertising* (New York: Free Press, 1999); Kitch, Carolyn, *The Girl on the Magazine Cover: The Origins of Visual Stereotypes in the Mass Media* (Chapel Hill: University of North Carolina Press, 2001); Wolf, Naomi, *The Beauty Myth: How Images of Beauty Are Used against Women* (New York: HarperCollins, 1989); Zeisler, Andy, "Marketing Miss Right," *BitchFest,* ed. Lisa Jervis and Andi Zeisler, 291–298 (New York: Farrar, Straus and Giroux, 2006).

Laura Turner

MEDIA IMAGES OF WOMEN: MUSIC

Female musicians' roles in the contemporary music industry have been debated in terms of their limited creative and financial access to musical production, ongoing gender biases concerning their musical talent, and gender and racial stereotypes in music videos and lyrics.

BACKGROUND

Though music as an art form has existed for centuries, the role of women within the contemporary popular music industry has changed dynamically since the inception of this industry. In the genres of rock, hip-hop, punk, and Indie music, female musicians have stated that they face many barriers that do not exist for their male counterparts, such as sexism within the industry, having their work and contributions devalued and exploited by the mass media, and hostility from other musicians and fans. Thus while there are now many commercially successful popular female musicians, ranging from Mary J. Blige to Melissa Etheridge, Sheryl Crow, Madonna, and Cristina Aguilera, most female musicians continue to face a set of institutional and cultural barriers when it comes to the way they are represented in the visual media and reviewed by their peers.

Many female musicians have expressed resentment at the current musical environment, and many of those same musicians have increasingly taken a stance against what they feel is sexist and/or racist exploitation by labels and the media, leading them to produce their own music labels and magazines. Some choose to incorporate feminist or pro-woman messages into their music, perform at benefits, or create events that feature female artists, events such as the Lilith Fair and the Michigan Womyn's Music Festival.

HISTORY OF WOMEN IN MUSIC

Earlier Western institutions that taught music professionally catered primarily to male students. In European societies in the fifteenth and sixteenth centuries, musical students either studied at a cathedral school or became apprentices to a master musician. Women did not have access to either of these opportunities. Researcher Eva Rieger has found that churches in the Middle Ages barred women from liturgical rites, keeping them from the high music culture of the time. Women were barred from playing in professional orchestras until the early twentieth century, and then they were only allowed to play the harp, because it was deemed a "feminine instrument" (Lewis 1990). This historical exclusion of women from music can be seen as influencing the sexist attitude many females encounter when they begin to play instruments—the attitude that women are not supposed to do so. In rock, this attitude is particularly pervasive, as driving guitars and drums are two hallmarks of the genre. For example, Kristen Pfaff, the bassist of the band Hole, found that she had to work twice as hard to be taken seriously (Raha 2005).

Rieger also describes the beginning of an assumption many contemporary female musicians fight against, that women are not capable of creating their own work. The few women who were involved in the music culture of the times were invited to perform, not create, and thus were not granted the artistic status that comes with the creation of works. Many men asserted that women had a "natural creative deficiency" (Lewis 1990, 57–58). This false assertion has trickled down through history, causing many successful contemporary female musicians, such as Madonna and Courtney Love, to be accused of having a man write some of their best albums for them (Lewis 1990; Raha 2005). Madonna, in particular, was accused of using her sexuality rather than her musical talent to exploit producers and gain an audience. In an accusatory cover story in *Rolling Stone*, printed in 1984, an article about Madonna snidely states, "She's an unqualified success. But did she exploit people to get there?" (Lewis 1990, 130). Accusations of female artists "sleeping their way to the top" are often voiced in the media, while male musicians are rarely accused of such actions.

ISSUES AND DEBATES CONCERNING WOMEN'S INCREASED VISIBILITY IN THE MUSIC INDUSTRY, 1970s–1980s

Women in the 1970s, empowered by the feminist movement, began taking a larger role in music. While there had been "girl groups" in the 1950s such as the Shirelles and the Supremes, women in the 1970s began taking more creative control of their music and became more assertive in their messages. However, female singers of the early 1970s still had far to go. The mass media promoted female folk singers who expressed an "asexual, feathery [vocal] lightness," and female artists were seen mostly singing and writing, with very few playing instruments (Raha 2005, 5). When mainstream female artists were shown as having a sex drive, it was shown or described in a passive, decorative or demure way. In the male-dominated rock music scene, women were still relegated to the sidelines, in what Maria Raha (2005) calls a strict division of labor, with most women expected to play the role of an adoring, swooning fan or a willing sex-toy groupie. The mass media coverage of female musicians, such as it was, promoted the most sellable, most sexualized, and least threatening version of the female artist.

While women in mainstream music continued to gain ground, one of the most notable movements that influenced women's role in music was the underground genre of punk in the 1970s and 1980s. Punk provided an opportunity for women to adopt the genre's do-it-yourself attitude: pick up an instrument, and join or create a band.

In the rock genre, one of the earliest all-female groups was the Runaways, created in 1975. Featuring five teenage girls, the Runaways briefly switched around the typical gender roles of star (male) and fan (female), and used their music to express their sexuality in a more aggressive way then their predecessors, but they were often represented as sexually tantalizing "jailbait." The media and reviewers were also intensely critical of the band. One review of their 1977 album *Queens of Noise* opened with the line: "These bitches suck" (Raha 2005, 24). In fact, many female or female-fronted bands, up to the 1990s, noted how appalled they felt at the vicious language used to describe their members. It has not been uncommon for editors of magazines and reviewers to use sexist language to describe female bands, referring to members as "bitches, cunts, man haters, and dykes" (Raha 2005, 204), making it particularly difficult for women to succeed in the music industry, despite popular perceptions that women were "making it" as rock and other music stars.

The Runaways, being one of the first female-fronted bands in rock, were plagued by an issue that female musicians continue to struggle with, particularly when they take the main stage, that of their sexuality being valued over their music. Female musicians have tried to overcome this obstacle by making subversive statements, for example, artist Suzie Quatro appearing in *Penthouse* clothed from head to toe, or Plasmatics singer Poly Styrene stating that she would shave her head if she ever became a sex symbol (she eventually felt she had become one and did shave her head: see Raha 2005, 88). Wendy O. Williams, another female artist known for her over-the-top stunts, agreed to pose for *Playboy* on condition that she would skydive in the photo. Women consistently face issues concerning their image that are not exemplified in media interpretations of their male peers. Pat Benatar, an artist in the late 1970s, spoke of her ongoing battle with the media and her image. Female artists such as Benatar found that when the spotlight was on her, every viewed action or press article was framed or interpreted in a way that represented the female artist in a stereotypical, objectified female fashion (Lewis 1990). For instance, a *Rolling Stone* article featured Benatar as the "happy homemaker, cleaning up after the boys" (Lewis 1990, 88). In this way, even female musicians who gained fame or success were undermined in their representation in the media.

In 1982, the Go-Gos became the first all-female vocal and instrumental group to make the Top 10 record charts. Like their female predecessors, Go-Gos' members recall the pressure placed on the group by the media and producers to fit a certain image. Bandmember Margot Olaverra spoke later about the "Go-Go diet" that the group was put on by the manager, stating that it made near anorexics out of the girls, and led some members, such as Jane Widlen, to turn to drugs such as crystal meth to lose weight (Raha 2005). Likewise, Debbie Harry of the 1980s band, Blondie, stated her disgust after seeing a poster of herself in a see-through black shirt, saying that it certainly wasn't her idea, and that record companies exercise their power in multiple ways over the artists themselves, and not just over the music that is produced (Raha 2005).

FEMALE MUSICIANS AND MTV

In 1981, MTV created a revolution in musical broadcasting with the introduction of music videos on television. The creation of MTV had some undeniably positive effects on adolescents, particularly females, who were exposed to music from which they had previously been isolated, and MTV's practice of airing previously unknown bands on the channel increased the visibility of some female musicians. However, the music videos shown on MTV overwhelmingly featured men, and the objectification of women in music videos, an issue that is front and center today, was a common occurrence. Naomi Wolf, author of the influential publication, *The Beauty Myth*, argues that MTV set a negative beauty index and role for women and men to imitate and internalize. Wolf addresses the way that sexual violence against women is portrayed in music videos. She states that, for example, Motley Crue's videos have women as sexual slaves in cages, and in a video by Rick James, he rapes his girlfriend. Wolf states that female beauty is shown by MTV for men as "that which never says no and that which is not really human," citing date rape statistics to show the legacy of such messages (Wolf 1989, 164). Also connected to this message is the abuse that women encounter at rock and roll concerts, including sexual assault.

MEDIA REPRESENTATIONS AND VIOLENCE AGAINST WOMEN

Many scholars would concur that women encounter the most blatant and widespread hostility in the music genres of rock, hip-hop, and rap, although this too depends largely upon factors such as the band, the producers, and the way their music is represented visually. While hip-hop music, sometimes defined interchangeably as rap yet sometimes viewed as a distinct but related genre, was originally intended to reflect the realities of the street culture out of which it was born, African American women often find themselves trying to deal with many hip-hop singers' treatment of women, in both lyrics and video. Patricia Hill Collins, a noted African American scholar, notes that although the messages in rap may not have been originally intended to do so, many songs now operate as "an important site for the spread of sexism and homophobia" (Hill Collins 2005, 82).

For example, in a music video scene of his song "tip drill," rapper Nelly slides a credit card down a scantily clad dancer's butt crack, and in another song, rapper Eminem sings about how he wants to choke to death his now ex-wife Kim. With peers and images like this permeating the hip-hop scenes, the environment created for female artists in hip-hop such as Eve, Missy Elliot, and Mary J. Blige is undeniably hostile.

Female musicians in rock encounter some similar stereotypes in terms of how women are represented in rock music videos. Another disturbing feature, however, is that women as fans within the rock scene encounter assault and abuse at concerts to a frightening degree. This could be due in part to the messages in rock music regarding women. For example, Limp Bizkit, an artist who fuses rap with rock, claims that much of his music is inspired by his lying, cheating ex-girlfriend. While relationships are common subjects for songs, the issue becomes much more relevant when it "bubbles over into a general, sweeping misogyny" on the part of male artists (Raha 2005, 228). At the 1999 Woodstock festival, several sexual assaults were documented, including two in which women were raped while in the crowd during a band's set.

FEMALE MUSICIANS AND INDEPENDENT LABELS: AN ALTERNATIVE IMAGE

Since the 1970s, many female musicians have chosen to abandon the mainstream musical industry, including the accolades and high salaries that go along with it, in order to create their own independent labels, forms of music, and alternative expressions of women's lives. These musicians range from the early feminist protest singers of the "Women's Music" movement, including those on the famous Redwood Records label, to rockers such as Joan Jett, who created her own label in 1980, Blackheart Records, and subsequently released the hit "I Love Rock and Roll"; Indie rocker Patti Smith, who decided to focus on gender-neutral topics with the aim of creating an "artistic androgyny" (Raha 2005); and Indie musicians such as Ani DiFranco, who has produced at least 18 CDs on her Righteous Babes record label.

In the 1990s, two prominent female-led movements emerged: the Lilith Fair and the Riot Grrls. In 1997, Sarah McLachlan, by then a well-established artist, created the all-female music festival, the Lilith Fair, to showcase female artists. With bands including the Indigo Girls, Erykah Badu, Sheryl Crow, Paula Cole, Cristina Aguilera, Queen Latifah, and Natalie Merchant, among many others, the Lilith Fair was an instant success in many cities around the country, albeit a short-lived one, as the last tour took place in 1999. Lilith Fair organizers donated a small percentage of ticket proceeds to local women's organizations in each community they visited. In many ways, the Lilith Fair combined alternative music with the mainstream music industry, thus making it more of a commercial success than the earlier Women's Music movement.

The success of the Lilith Fair, coupled with the increased commercialization of women's rights, led to further examples of female artists who espoused pro-woman agendas through their work. Since the 1990s, many more female artists have donated proceeds to organizations with pro-women agendas (Savage 2003). Some bands have also incorporated their political views into their musical tours. For example, the members of L7, a feminist band founded in 1994, created their own record label, Wax Tadpole, and founded the influential Rock for Choice festival in 1991. Their activism became more radical when, in 1999, L7 arranged to have a banner flown over Warped, a touring music festival with an overwhelmingly male line-up, that stated "Warped needs more beaver....Love L7" (Raha 2005).

One of the most notable movements of women in music was the early 1990s Riot Grrl movement. Riot Grrl was born out of the frustration many women still felt with the punk, rock, and Indie scenes of the time. Partly because of the exploratory do-it-yourself attitude of punk and rock, women were inspired to start their own bands and sing about issues that they felt were important. Because Riot Grrl began as an underground movement, there was little control by record labels and producers and more control by the artists themselves. Though the movement was short-lived, in part due to a media blackout and also due to capitalist co-opting, Riot Grrl participants consistently blended feminist messages with their music and wrote songs protesting sexism, rape, abuse, and violence, quite literally putting the "grr" into "girl" (Fudge 2006, 157). Artists and bands

MICHIGAN WOMYN'S MUSIC FESTIVAL

The Michigan Womyn's Music Festival was born out of 1970s radical feminist activism, as a way to create a women-only space where women were involved in every aspect of the festival's financial, physical, and creative production. Since its inception in 1976, the festival has served as an important space for the promotion of "Women's Music," a genre of music influenced largely by lesbian and radical feminisms. The festival is organized, built, and staffed entirely by women. Many attendees camp out during the event, and there are designated "women of color-only," "chem-free," "scent-free," and "over 50s" spaces. In the 1980s, festival organizers collected enough money to purchase a piece of land in Hart, Michigan, where the festival continues to be held annually. Singers such as Cris Williamson, Meg Christian, and Holly Near all have roots in this festival. Tracy Chapman began her career there.

Almost since its inception, the festival has been faced with controversy. Perhaps the biggest issue concerns whether it should be a woman-only space, defined as a space for "women-born women only" (WBWO). Festival organizers do not allow transsexual women to attend, since they view them as "not real women." Founding organizers Lisa Vogel and Barbara Price have publicly stated that "the Michigan Festival...always has been an event for women, and this continues to be defined as women born women." As a result of this WBWO attendance policy, transsexual and transgender activists, beginning in the early 1990s, organized an alternative protest festival, Camp Trans, which is held on adjacent land. Some musicians have also proclaimed their disagreement with the WBWO policy on stage or have boycotted the festival altogether.

involved in the Riot Grrl movement consistently released albums on their own or on progressive labels, such as the band Sleater-Kinney, which released records on the Riot Grrl–friendly label, Kill Rock Stars. Riot Grrl bands took a hint from other musicians who were not allowed easy access to the mainstream music industry (including, for example, earlier female and African American musicians and contemporary rap musicians), who, fed up with managers and producers parading them around as novelties, started their own labels.

CONCLUSION

More often than not, female musicians of various genres, including rock, hip-hop, folk, and Indie music, face barriers that male musicians do not, including the way they are (re-)presented in public, treated by producers, and reviewed by their peers. The legacy of excluding women from music is historic, but since the rise of second wave feminism, women have made great strides in being taken seriously as musicians instead of being stereotyped as amateurs or groupies. Mainstream female musicians such as Madonna have made a lasting impact on music, not just because of the groundbreaking, main-stage roles that musicians such as Madonna have played in their careers, but because of the autonomy they have wrested away from producers and managers. While not all musicians have been as commercially successful as Madonna, her self-presentation as an empowered female creates a challenge to historical stereotypes about women's gender roles, including their very roles as musical creators and performers. Today, more women are given credit for their work than ever before. However, the representation and sexualization of female artists, specifically in mainstream pop music, is still a pervasive issue, and misogyny in rap, hip-hop, and rock songs is still an issue that needs to be confronted and resolved. Many female artists have found the most success where they have expended their creative energies in creating their own bands, labels, and events, enabling them to enjoy more artistic and creative freedom. The Riot Grrl movement encouraged women to become more aggressive in their music, and to sing, play, and write about controversial issues that had not been discussed before. As women take more control over their art in the historically male-dominated sphere of music, they continue to move forward and counteract the sexism in the music scene.

See also Feminist Art Practices; Media Images of Women: Advertising; Media Images of Women: Television and Film.

Further Reading: Fudge, Rachel, "Girl, Unreconstructed," *BitchFest,* ed. Lisa Jervis and Andi Zeisler, 155–161 (New York: Farrar, Straus and Giroux, 2006); Hill Collins, Patricia, *Black Sexual Politics* (New York: Routledge, Taylor and Francis, 2005); Lewis, Lisa, *Gender Politics and MTV* (Philadelphia: Temple University Press, 1990); Raha, Maria, *Cinderella's Big Score: Women of the Punk and Indie Underground* (Emeryville, CA: Seal Press, 2005); Savage, Ann, *They're Playing Our Songs: Women Talk about Feminist Rock Music* (Westport, CT: Praeger, 2003); Wolf, Naomi, *The Beauty Myth: How Images of Beauty Are Used against Women* (New York: HarperCollins, 1989).

Laura Turner

MEDIA IMAGES OF WOMEN: TELEVISION AND FILM

Since the early twentieth century, representations of women in television and film have changed dramatically, from powerless damsels in distress in the 1940s and 1950s, to butt-kicking, demon-fighting, and financially successful career women in the late 1990s and the early twenty-first century. While many feminists have decried past stereotypical representations of women in popular culture, some have questioned whether current portrayals of women as violent and aggressive are truly leveling the social playing field or whether they continue to represent women through a male gaze.

BACKGROUND

Since the mid-1950s, the women's movement has been one of the most vocal critics of representations of gender roles in television and film. Feminist scholars argue that stereotypical media portrayals of women and men during the early and middle twentieth century kept women in a state of social powerlessness. Popular culture portrayals of women as childlike, passive, dependent, indecisive, physically vulnerable, and emotionally unstable reinforced a social status quo in which men and masculinity are dominant. From the late 1970s through the 1990s, coinciding with the second and third waves of feminism and the women's movement's efforts to diversify portrayals of women in popular culture, gender stereotypes gradually changed. While women in the 1940s and 1950s were predominantly portrayed as housewives, mothers, and victims, from the late 1960s they also began to be shown as independent, assertive, and career minded. Although the mass media continued to frame men within one-dimensional (hegemonic) masculinity, women's portrayals became much broader. This representational diversification was extended to African American women who, historically, had been excluded from or severely marginalized in mainstream television and film. In large part due to the civil rights movement, African American women became less often typecast in roles such as housemaid, mammy, or cook, and were more often seen as independent working professionals.

Much of feminist scholarship has focused on the ways in which women are portrayed in popular culture. Some media scholars suggest that stereotypical media representations of women are harmful because of the sexist political ideologies behind them and the ways in which these reinforce gender inequality in society. Other media scholars contest the notion that media messages have any significant effect on audiences' self-perceptions, on their views of the world, and therefore on society. Instead, they point to debates on the censorship of violence and nudity in popular culture to assert that media effects are not embedded in the messages themselves, but in how society uses these messages. Debates about the alleged effects of violent media on youth, then, fundamentally, serve to mask the true underlying causes behind social problems like youth violence: the damaging effects of hegemonic masculinity or the lack of adequate educational opportunities for many underprivileged young people.

Although the "no-effects" view has its supporters, "direct-media-effects" scholars lean in the opposite direction. A direct-media-effects approach suggests a cause-and-effect relation between media messages, people's self-perceptions, and social problems. Such a link, for instance, is illustrated by studies that suggest a negative correlation between a woman's exposure to gender stereotypes in the media and her levels of self-esteem, potentially leading to eating disorders such as anorexia or bulimia. However, not all media-effects scholars believe this correlation to be direct. Cultural theorist Stuart Hall (1980), for example, believes that individuals do not passively interpret and internalize media messages but actively negotiate a message's meanings. Media messages are intended to be read in accordance with message producers' preferred meanings. Hall suggests that, instead, messages are interpreted within the contexts of audiences' social and national identities and political convictions, and the social networks in which the messages are discussed. An upper-middle-class African American woman in New York, therefore, is likely to have a different interpretation of the spy-series *Alias* than a working-class woman in China.

Whether direct or indirect, media-effects theories are rooted in the idea that social reality is constructed with help of information dispensed by the media. The concept of media-constructed realities rests on the notion that individuals use media messages to supplement their understanding of the world around them and their positions within it. Sociologist Erving Goffman (1974) states that when individuals give meaning to the world, they do so through a framework of interpretation. This framework organizes, positions, and negotiates all of the information an individual receives within previously held beliefs and patterns of interpretation. Through these processes, individuals construct social reality. Stereotypes in mass media, thus, are harmful because they fail to question the patriarchic organization of society. By rendering women's voices invisible, a process that media scholar Gaye Tuchman (1978) calls symbolic annihilation, stereotypical representations of women reinforce dominant, hegemonic ideologies about appropriate gender roles in society.

Symbolic annihilation, or mediated invisibility, does not necessarily mean that women are absent from the mass media altogether. Media scholar Margaret Gallagher (2001) suggests that mediated invisibility also includes the nonrepresentation of women's perspectives or the framing of women within male-constructed, biased, contexts. Perpetuation of gender inequality is, therefore, an interactive process; mass media reflect dominant ideologies in society and society in turn relies on media to represent these ideologies. Tuchman's and Gallagher's views show that because media encourage stereotypes and confer social status on groups and individuals, they are potentially powerful agents of socialization and social change.

HISTORICAL OVERVIEW OF WOMEN IN TELEVISION AND FILM

From the 1950s to the 1970s, men dominated the film and television screens. During this period, less than half of the characters shown were female, and an even smaller percentage of those characters were shown in paid work contexts. (Tuchman 1978) Women were predominantly portrayed as middle-class housewives, mothers, or daughters. African American, Latina, and Asian American women fared even worse; they were hardly represented in the mainstream media at all, except in roles that reflected and reinforced their marginal social status, like Oscar-winning actress Hatty McDaniel's loyal Mammy in the movie *Gone with the Wind* (1939), Rita Moreno's fiery Anita in the *Romeo and Juliet*–inspired film-musical *West Side Story* (1961), or Miyoshi Umeki's placid bride-to-be Mei Li in the first all–Asian American movie, *Flower Drum Song* (1961).

As a rule of thumb, women on television shows were relegated to the situation comedy genre, where their roles as mothers, daughters, and wives revolved around the family. In these roles, women were portrayed as passive, indecisive, emotionally immature, and insignificant in decision-making processes, thereby reinforcing (white) men's "superior" status within the family and society. Some media scholars criticized the portrayals of women during the 1940s and 1950s as narrow, bearing no resemblance to how women really looked or lived their lives. Gender role portrayals certainly were class and race biased and, to a degree, failed to reflect women's social status with accuracy. However, until the second wave of feminism in the 1960s, white middle-class women were mainly confined to the domestic sphere, to home and caregiving roles in the family, and often excluded from major political and economic decision-making processes in society. Also, for many working-class African American women, domestic employment tended to be one of the few available paid labor options in mainstream society. Thus, while representations of women in the 1940s and 1950s certainly were incomplete and helped to reinforce their socially marginal status, these representations also reflected the ways in which women's social and racial status limited their social and economic opportunities.

In the 1960s, women's roles in television programs started to change. The comedy *Father Knows Best* often focused on mother Margaret Anderson's and eldest daughter Betty Anderson's desires to break free from the chains of domesticity, to gain some financial and social independence, and the conflict these desires caused in the family. Other situation comedies such as *The Lucille Ball Show, I Dream of Jeannie,* or *Bewitched* also focused on women's desire for independence, but framed these desires within narrow definitions of rebellion, for example, by showing wives going against the wishes of their husbands or, in the case of *Jeannie,* her "master." While these comedies proved a step in the right direction, they continued to frame women through a male gaze—within contexts of male authority and dominance. Women's rebellion, as often seen in *The Lucille Ball Show,* tended to be used solely for comedic purposes rather than as critique of social patriarchy.

Feminist media scholars generally credit the 1960s *Mary Tyler Moore Show* as the first prime-time television series to strike a significantly feminist tone. For many women, and some men, its lead character, Mary Richards, a newsroom employee of the fictional Minneapolis-based television station WJM, was a breath of fresh air: an independent, single, career-oriented woman in

JULIA, THE FIRST FEMALE AFRICAN AMERICAN WORKING-CLASS CHARACTER ON PRIME-TIME TELEVISION

In September 1968, the comedy series *Julia* premiered on NBC. *Julia* was a milestone in television history for two reasons. Prior to the 1960s, most prime-time television shows featured mostly middle-class white women in predominantly domestic environments. *Julia*, a nurse, was not only a working woman but was also played by an African American actress, Diahann Carroll. For decades, African American women had largely been absent from prime-time television or relegated to stereotypical supporting and extra roles as domestics and cooks. Some critics considered *Julia*, both the series and the lead character, "too white" to make any significant contributions to political debates about racial diversity. However, the fact that Diahann Carroll had not been typecast and played the lead in a prime-time television series did open doors toward more racial diversity in historically race- and class-biased entertainment formats.

paid employment. However, some noted that Richards tended to be a little too deferential to her boss, Lou Grant, and that her single-woman status reinforced the idea that women could not "have it all." Shows like the 1960s *Julia*, the first prime-time sitcom featuring an African American female lead character, Diahann Carroll, the 1970s *Maude*, and the 1980s *Kate and Allie* were representative of the television industry's attempts to include a more feminist consciousness and discourse in their shows—to diversify women's portrayals in popular culture. Furthermore, crime dramas like the 1970s *Police Woman*, the 1980s *Cagney and Lacey*, and *Murder She Wrote* finally broke with the television industry's tradition of placing women predominantly in situation comedies.

The 1980s and 1990s also introduced audiences to series such as *The Cosby Show, Roseanne, Grace under Fire*, and *Murphy Brown*, which featured women who defied most conventional standards of traditional femininity: age, race, social class, family status, and body image. Although gender stereotypes in television shows still prevailed, in the late twentieth century, women were increasingly shown as emotionally, physically, and sexually assertive and autonomous, as in the teen television series *Buffy the Vampire Slayer* or the *Hercules* spin-off, *Xena Warrior Princess*. Representation of women in film largely followed the same pattern as on television. In the 1940s, 1950s, and 1960s, women predominantly were shown as passive, dependent, and emotionally and physically fragile, waiting for men to either rescue or victimize them. In the late twentieth century, like their counterparts on television, movies such as *The Terminator* (1984), *Working Girl* (1988), *Jackie Brown* (1997), *Charlie's Angels* (2000 and 2003), *Aeyon Flux* (2005), *Ultraviolet* (2006), and *The Devil Wears Prada* (2006) increasingly portrayed women as emotionally and physically assertive, independent, and financially successful.

BUFFY THE VAMPIRE SLAYER'S CULT FOLLOWING

The popular television series *Buffy the Vampire Slayer* debuted in 1997 on the Warner Bros. Network. The series followed the trials and tribulations of Buffy Anne Summers and her close circle of friends in the small Southern Californian town of Sunnydale. During the day, Buffy and her friends, like all teenagers, attended high school where they dealt with issues like popularity, self-esteem, and sexual confusion. However, at night, Buffy and her friends battled vampires, demons, and other dark forces. The series quickly garnered a large cult and academic following. Academics from a wide variety of disciplines, ranging from cultural studies to gender studies, used the series' storylines to explore issues of gender, sexuality, and teen angst. The body of scholarly work that emerged from these studies became known as "Buffy Studies." Many academics have credited *Buffy the Vampire Slayer* for its nonstereotypical gender portrayals and frank discussions of issues such as gender role expectations, homosexuality, and popularity.

Nontraditional women's roles in television and film, however, also were systematically defined through frameworks of masculinity. These frameworks suggest that female masculinity as gender performance, its defining elements ranging from sexual and physical assertiveness to financial independence, continued to be seen as deviant, and therefore as (socially) costly. Sexually assertive women, such as Sharon Stone's murder suspect Catherine Tramell in the thriller *Basic Instinct* (1992), Glenn Close's doomed Alex Forrest in the adultery drama *Fatal Attraction* (1987), or Kim Cattrall's sexually liberated public relations woman Samantha Jones in the television series *Sex and the City*, are portrayed as emotion-

ANGELINA JOLIE'S SUCCESS

Both off and on the silver screen, Oscar-winning actress Angelina Jolie is seen by many as the embodiment of a twenty-first-century woman; she displays independence and social awareness, she is financially successful, and, at least according to a plethora of tabloid reports, she is physically and sexually assertive. The daughter of actor Jon Voight and actress Marcheline Bertrand, Jolie shot to fame in her Oscar-winning role as mental hospital patient Lisa in *Girl, Interrupted*. In 2001, the fantasy-action movie *Lara Croft: Tomb Raider*, based on an immensely popular videogame, established her as a female action star. Jolie's 2005 movie collaboration with Brad Pitt, in the action thriller *Mr. and Mrs. Smith*, proved to be her biggest commercial success to date, but also contributed to her controversial off-screen persona as femme fatale. Jolie and Pitt, at the time still married to *Friends* actress Jennifer Aniston, were rumored to have fallen in love during the movie shoot, and their subsequent off-screen romantic involvement attracted much tabloid fascination and public condemnation. While well known for her acting and off-screen romances, Angelina Jolie also is a UN goodwill ambassador, tirelessly campaigning on behalf of land-mine victims and political refugees.

ally unstable. Violent women are represented as either visually masculine, like Sigourney Weaver's alien-hunting Officer Ripley in the science fiction–horror movie *Alien* (1979) or Linda Hamilton's Sarah Connor, a mom fighting androids from the future, in *The Terminator* (1984); or highly sexualized, like Charlize Theron's title character in the science fiction thriller *Aeyon Flux* (2005) or Angelina Jolie's heiress-adventurer Lara Croft in the computer game–inspired action movie *Tomb Raider* (2001). In order to understand the double-edged sword of changing representations of women in popular culture, first, a closer examination of the gendering of violence is warranted.

WOMEN AND VIOLENCE IN TELEVISION AND FILM
A MOVE TOWARD EQUALITY?

The 2005 action thriller *Mr. and Mrs. Smith* was a major international box office success, in large part due to feverish tabloid reports on the rumored off-screen chemistry between its two leading stars, Angelina Jolie and the then still-married Brad Pitt. The movie centers on wife and husband Jane and John Smith who, unbeknownst to each other, lead secret lives as highly skilled assassins and eventually are hired to kill one another. The Dr. Jekyll/Mr. Hyde–like framing of Jolie's Mrs. Smith character, used to represent the double life she leads, is indicative, as discussed earlier, of the ways in which Hollywood tends to justify violence in female characters. Mrs. Smith, the wife and homemaker, acts and looks like a modern-day version of Barbara Billingsley's June Cleaver—the ultimate mother and housewife of the 1960s television series *Leave It to Beaver*. In contrast, Jane Smith, the assassin, is the quintessential twenty-first-century woman, smart, confident, and physically and sexually assertive; a woman whose wit, physical aggression, and skills match those of her husband. While visually, Mrs. Smith, the housewife, is placid and sexually demure, Jane Smith, the assassin, is highly sexualized, often wearing nothing more than a men's dress shirt. Throughout the movie, there exists a positive correlation between the violence performed by Jolie's Jane Smith and the character's visual sexualization.

In Western society, violence is about power, which in turn is associated with masculinity. Gender scholar Edward LaFrance (1995) suggests that media portrayals of violence committed by men have become institutionalized, something that we no longer take notice of. Stephen Whitehead (2002) adds that there seems to be a social dimension to men's violence: a persuasive social discourse that is articulated through the media and pervades most cultures, social and state institutions, and the practices of individual men. This discourse is a set of practices and attitudes that render men's violence as normal, hegemonic, and therefore inevitable. Consequently, Whitehead suggests, men's violence has assumed the status of a cultural arrangement across most societies.

Since violence is culturally defined as a masculine concept, violence in women tends to be portrayed within frameworks that justify this masculinity. As previously illustrated, either the woman is portrayed as masculine and therefore her aggression is an extension of this female masculinity (Halberstam 1998) or her femininity is exaggerated to adjust for the masculinity of her violent disposition.

For instance, in the now defunct ABC spy series *Alias,* Jennifer Garner's character Sidney Bristow—a CIA spy—may know how to use her fists, but she "kicks ass" while wearing a pair of sexy stilettos. Also, the systematic portrayal of financially successful businesswomen as coldhearted, backstabbing, and emotionless helps to reinforce the double standard—rooted in gender stereotypes—that dominate the business world and have traditionally prevented women from climbing the corporate ladder. It perpetuates the idea that business is inherently masculine and that, therefore, women can achieve financial success only at the cost of adopting corporate masculinity.

Because masculinity in women is perceived as unnatural, it is often shown as distorting traditional notions of femininity. Joan Collins's portrayal of ruthless business tycoon Alexis Colby in the television series *Dynasty* or Meryl Streep's demanding and cynical *Runway Magazine* fashion editor Miranda Priestly in the movie *The Devil Wears Prada* are examples of successful women who, therefore, must be portrayed as "bitches." While this may not necessarily be problematic in itself, as traditional femininity is a social construct to begin with, it does reflect the price women are expected to pay for financial success. In popular culture, "bitches," by definition, are portrayed as emotionally dysfunctional. Miranda Priestly is single and emotionally unavailable, and Alexis Colby is a "bad" mother and wife who puts her own success and happiness before that of her family. While these are not necessarily distorted realities—in order to be successful in the male-dominated business world, women are often forced to play by men's rules—such representations do perpetuate the unequal sacrifices women are expected to make to achieve financial success and independence: a loss of femininity, which in the eyes of media producers is tantamount to devaluation of the self, and therefore, inevitably, a deprivation of emotional fulfillment. While the portrayal of women as financially successful is, in itself, a positive development, at the same time, by portraying these women as emotionally dysfunctional it also serves to perpetuate deterministic ideas about the perceived masculinity of the business world and women's place within it.

CONCLUSION

Some scholars believe that the recent trends toward violent women in popular culture aren't such a bad thing after all; that these portrayals help to deconstruct the hegemonic ideologies on which society is built. Since there is no proof that violence is not inherent to femininity and no evidence to link it to gender performance, it can be assumed that violence as a masculine performance is a social construction. Therefore, deconstructing its gendered meaning and hegemonic function in society means that women are given a new voice and more visibility (Gattuso Hendin 2004). At the same time, because of the prevalent assumptions of masculinity inherent in violence, increasing the number of violent women on television or film may not be the most effective way to achieve gender equality, on or off the screen. This establishes a double-edged sword: increasing the number of violent and financially successful women in popular culture challenges the status quo in society, yet it may also reinforce a situation in which women are "allowed" to play in a male-constructed and male-dominated world, by using male rules, rather than in an environment that women and men shape equally.

See also Media Images of Women: Advertising; Media Images of Women: Music; Sexism in Language.

Further Reading: Baehr, Helen, and Ann Gray, *Turning It On: A Reader in Women and Media* (New York: St Martin's Press, 1997); Byerly, Carolyn M., and Karen Ross, *Women and Media: A Critical Introduction* (Malden, MA: Blackwell, 2006); Cole, Ellen, and Daniel Henderson, eds., *Featuring Females: Feminist Analyses of Media* (Washington, DC: American Psychological Association, 2005); Douglas, Susan J., *Where the Girls Are: Growing Up Female with the Mass Media* (New York: Random House, 1994); Gallagher, Margaret, *Gender Setting: New Agenda for Media Monitoring and Advocacy* (London: Zed Books, 2001); Gattuso Hendin, Josephine, *Heartbreakers: Women and Violence in Contemporary Culture and Literature* (New York: St. Martin's Press, 2004); Goffman, Erving, *Frame Analysis: An Essay on the Organization of Experience* (New York: Harper and Row, 1974); Halberstam, Judith, *Female Masculinity* (Durham, NC: Duke University Press, 1998); Hall, Stuart, "Encoding and Decoding," in *Culture, Media, and Language*, ed. Stuart Hall, Dorothy Hobson, Andrew Lowe, and Paul Willis (London: Hutchinson, 1980); Innes, Sherrie A., ed., *Action Chicks: New Images of Tough Women in Popular Culture* (New York: Palgrave Macmillan, 2004); LaFrance, Edward, *Men, Media and Masculinity* (Dubuque, IA: Kendall/Hunt, 1995); Milkie, Melissa A., "Social Comparisons, Reflected Appraisals, and Mass Media: The Impact of Pervasive Beauty Images on Black and White Girls' Self Concepts," *Social Psychology Quarterly* 62 (1999): 190–210; Rodriquez, Clara E., ed., *Latin Looks: Images of Latinas and Latinos in the U.S. Media* (Boulder, CO: Westview Press, 1997); Tuchman, Gaye, "Introduction: The Symbolic Annihilation of Women by the Mass Media," in *Hearth and Home: Images of Women in the Mass Media*, ed. Gaye Tuchman, Arlene Kaplan Daniels, and James Benét (New York: Oxford University Press, 1978); Whitehead, Stephen, *Men and Masculinities* (Cambridge, UK: Polity Press, 2002).

Marc J. W. de Jong

MEDICINE AND MEDICALIZATION: VIEWS ON WOMEN'S BODIES

How does medicine affect women's everyday lives and the feminist struggle for justice? Some scholars assert that medicine liberates women from various physical burdens while others say it is a patriarchal institution that oppresses them.

INTRODUCTION

Medicalization is the process whereby life experiences are defined and treated as medical problems—experiences that were not previously described in medical terms. The concept of medicalization emerged in the early 1970s out of an intellectual movement critical of science and medicine. Prior to this time, most people took for granted medicine's role in society as healer, assuming that it helped people live healthier, longer lives. However, a critical perspective grew among social observers who were becoming leery of what they saw as the increasing power of the medical field. They warned that medicine produced less benign effects.

Many researchers refer to three levels of medicalization, developed by the sociologists Peter Conrad and Joseph Schneider: conceptual, institutional, and interaction. On the *conceptual* level, everyday life occurrences are defined and considered inherently medical in nature, and medical language is used to describe them as illness. On the *institutional* level, the field of medicine attains societal authority and legitimacy to manage these illnesses. And the *interaction* level refers to the contact doctors have with their patients, including consultation, diagnosis, and treatment.

There are two key debates among scholars of medicalization. First, what is the process of medicalization? That is, how did it emerge and how does it proceed today? Second, what effect does it have on individuals? Feminists are particularly concerned about the effects of medicalization on women.

Two main perspectives have arisen and they answer these questions differently. On the one side are scholars who have framed medicine as imperialistic. For them, medicalization is a sign that the medical field is extending its domination and gaining more power over individuals' lives. Meanwhile, individuals are becoming increasingly dependent on it. Medicalization is the result of structural factors and the domineering behavior of doctors, managed care, and the pharmaceutical and insurance industries. For these scholars, the outcomes of medicalization are generally negative, including poorer health and disempowered individuals. However, they acknowledge that medicalization has been beneficial for some patients.

Others have critiqued the passive role patients have played in this framework. Instead of invoking a top-down model, they argue that medicalization emerges through the participation, active involvement, and complicity of the lay populace. Rather than being submissive and compliant, patients are prime movers, in some cases pushing the medicalization process, and in others resisting it. Also, they do not agree that medicalization is necessarily negative, arguing that it can actually empower patients.

HOW MEDICALIZATION HAPPENS

Medical Imperialism

Scholars who frame medicalization as a sort of medical imperialism focus on the expansion of medicine's professional domain on the institutional level. They argue that medicine's jurisdiction continues to expand as more moments in everyday life come to be defined as illness and in need of medical supervision. One example they point to is premenstrual syndrome (PMS). In 1987, a premenstrual syndrome–related condition was classified as a psychiatric disorder when it was included in the American Psychiatric Association's reference book, the *Diagnostic and Statistical Manual of Mental Disorders (DSM)*. This conceptualization of PMS as a medical problem gave physicians the power to diagnose women's behavior, moods, and feelings as illness and to determine how best to manage this illness, usually with drug therapy. The decision to include this condition in the *DSM* was controversial, with opponents arguing that it would stigmatize women. Critics of medicalization see the inclusion as evidence that medicine's dominion continues to grow.

Marxist scholars have noted that capitalism has been central to the spread of medicine's domain. The relatively recent shift toward consumer-oriented health-care has enlarged the bounds of the pharmaceutical industry, which actively pursues patients as potential customers. Since 1997, when the Food and Drug Administration Modernization Act was passed, pharmaceutical companies have created markets for their products by directly advertising to patients. They have been able to increase awareness of conditions, essentially marketing diseases and the drugs to treat them, such as the profitable Viagra for erectile dysfunction (ED).

Medicine's jurisdiction has also expanded, according to critics, through the creation and maintenance of professional boundaries and authority. Largely by gaining the support of the state, medicine has successfully warded off competing professions to become *the* legitimate system of healing available in our society. Licensing laws have required individuals to obtain permission to practice healing from the medical community, in the form of a formal education and license. While official medical history would suggest that these laws logically followed the development of good science and improved medicine, critics argue that they were the result of political maneuvering.

Until the mid-1800s, doctors in the United States were essentially indistinguishable from the many lay healers who were practicing at the time. To separate themselves from the rest, they (mostly white, upper-class men) called themselves "regular" doctors and emphasized their formal training. In those years, however, the education they received was not formal in the way we think of it today. Extensive medical research did not exist then, and some regulars received as little as a few months of training. Many of their practices were generally no better than the potions and cures of their competitors (often female and racial minorities), and some, such as bloodletting, were much more deadly. Between 1915 and 1930, as more women were having babies in the hospital, the rates of infant death due to birth injuries increased substantially.

In spite of evidence that doctors were not the best of healers, they were able to garner the backing of the state and eventually all but eliminate other autonomous healing professions. Feminist scholars argue that this was a tactic to purge women. For centuries women had been the primary healers. As formal medicine took hold, they found their healing practices rendered illegal and were initially barred from entering medicine. Not until the 1970s were women admitted more widely to medical school. In 1970, 11 percent of accepted applicants were women; this rose to one-third in 1984. In 2006, 49 percent of the entering class were female, but segregation within medicine is still prevalent, with women disproportionately underrepresented in higher-paying and prestigious fields such as neurosurgery.

Those healing professions that women do occupy in great numbers, such as nursing and midwifery, are largely directed by and subordinate to the medical field (which is still dominated by men). For example, the state has given medicine the right to approve the practices of these fields and their licensing. Most states require midwives to undergo medically approved state certification. Those who have resisted these laws and practice lay midwifery have been fiercely prosecuted. And physicians often supervise the practice of midwives, overseeing the records of their patients even if the patient never sees the physician in person. Meanwhile, nurses play a submissive role in the hospital, assisting rather than replacing physicians and serving at their request.

Ultimately, medicine has been able to maintain its professional dominance by defining its knowledge as specialized and its technology as sophisticated. Only *experts* possessing extensive formal training can interpret scientific medical data and wield biomedical technology. Such assertions have allowed them to retain control over technical procedures such as surgery and prescription writing. Excluding others from these activities then makes sense to the general public,

A QUESTION OF RACE

The struggle for reproductive freedom has been different for white middle-class women than for poor women of color, who have faced a history of coerced sterilization. In the 1950s, the Puerto Rican government and private agencies waged a campaign to get women on the island to undergo sterilization. By 1968, more than one-third had had *la operación*, the highest rate in the world. Most of these women had not received accurate information about the procedure. In the 1970s, it is estimated that between 60,000 and 70,000 Native American women were sterilized often without informed consent. And many poor African American women were required to "consent" to the procedure before receiving welfare benefits, delivering a baby, or having an abortion. In 1973, a class action lawsuit was filed after two poor African American sisters (12 and 14 years old) had been sterilized without their parents' knowledge. It was revealed that federally funded programs had sterilized 100,000–150,000 poor women. About half were black.

Meanwhile, white middle-class women found it difficult to obtain sterilization. Doctors followed the 120 Formula, which instructed that "if a woman's age multiplied by the number of children she had totaled 120, she was a candidate for sterilization" (quoted in Roberts 1997). A woman with two children would have to wait until she was 60, a woman with three would have to wait until she was 40. Even then, many doctors required the consultation of two other doctors and a psychiatrist.

This disparity of experiences created competing goals among activists. The Committee to End Sterilization Abuse sought informed consent, a 30-day waiting period, and restrictions on consent given during labor or in the postpartum period. The National Abortion Rights Action League (NARAL) and Planned Parenthood, which worked to expand sterilization rights, voted against these guidelines. And other pro-sterilization organizations filed lawsuits against medical facilities for refusing white women elective sterilization.

based on our trust in medical expertise and our suspicion of those who lack it, thereby solidifying medicine's professional dominance.

This largely exclusive power to define, diagnose, and treat illness is dangerous, according to critics. They argue that medical experts have been granted societal influence beyond their expertise, and this exaggerated status has unduly shielded them from external scrutiny. Without supervision, medical professionals have become agents of social control with unchecked power over vast parts of our lives beyond medicine. For example, their power to define illness empowers them to determine who receives jail versus medical attention. Because almost any aspect of daily life could be medicalized, critics warn that medicine has the potential to control more and more of our experiences.

Also of concern, for these scholars, is the loss of individual autonomy associated with medicalization. As medical knowledge and technology become more powerful and legitimate, individuals lose their own sense of capability and authority. This produces widespread dependence on medicine, disempowering individuals and undermining other institutions, such as the family and religion.

Active Participation

Other scholars argue that the imperialism thesis oversimplifies medicalization and overlooks the important role that the laity has played. Proponents of this perspective do not deny that structural factors are important; however, they assert that the active participation of patients is equally important to consider.

On various occasions, lay people have participated in the medicalization process, actively seeking a medical definition for particular conditions. For example, alcoholism became defined as a disease partially through the efforts of Alcoholics Anonymous. Beginning in the 1930s, Activists promoted the idea that alcoholism was an allergy (a physiological disease), not a mental or moral problem. Many doctors initially resisted a physiological explanation for "drunkardness" but the persistence and organization of activists prevailed. In the late 1970s, caregivers for sufferers from "senility" began to form advocacy organizations to support their loved ones. In coalition with neurosurgeons, scientists, and the National Institute of Aging, they pushed for further medicalization of Alzheimer's disease. They have thus increased public awareness of the condition and boosted research funding for it.

In addition to encouraging medicalization, individuals have participated in demedicalization. For example, homosexuality was declassified as a mental disorder by the American Psychiatric Association in 1973, largely in response to lobbying by the gay liberation movement. This victory demonstrates the collective power individuals have developed even to define what is and is not disease. In less public fashion, some women essentially demedicalize artificial insemination by using turkey basters or similar tools themselves at home. These private acts simply dismiss the need for medical practitioners and their technology.

There are also many cases of lay people resisting and questioning medicalization and critically evaluating the risks associated with it. For example, the use of hormone replacement therapy (HRT) has been met with both intrigue and skepticism by women. Many actively research the risks involved, drawing on information from loved ones and the media, as well as searching out medical evidence. Similarly, survivors of ruptured silicone breast implants have shared their stories with one another, publicly rallied for increased awareness of the severe side effects, and called for a moratorium on implant sales. This activism influenced the Food and Drug Administration's (FDA's) decision to restrict the sale of silicone breast implants in 1992. In 2006, the FDA lifted the ban but required manufacturers to conduct follow-up studies.

While acknowledging some of the problematic outcomes of medicalization, scholars who support the active participation of patients tend to focus on its benefits. They assert that medicine offers patients more options and more control over their experiences. For example, various prenatal tests can warn parents if their fetus has genetic maladies. Some parents use this information to choose abortion out of a concern for the child or their ability to raise him/her. Others might use the findings of these tests to gather information about the relevant disease and start to receive advanced support for their new life. Medicalizing problems has also provided for people experiencing stigmatized symptoms a shift in the public eye from deviants to patients. For instance, drunkards who were morally questionable became alcoholics with verifiable medical needs.

Another benefit of medicalization, according to these scholars, is the relief that some patients experience when they are finally able to name their distressing experience and have someone take it seriously. For example, the medicalization of PMS gives credence to real problems associated with it and provides women with the possibility of abating their symptoms.

EFFECTS OF MEDICALIZATION: IS IT HEALTHY FOR WOMEN?

As discussed, the debate about medicalization has taken place on many fronts, including disability, alcohol use, and homosexuality. One of the most controversial of these has been the gender front. At the heart of the debate is how medicalization affects women. Is medicine ultimately healthy for women?

This was the central question of the women's health movement in the 1970s. Of great concern to this second wave of feminists was regaining control of their bodies from men, doctors, and the law. They were acutely aware that women's bodies were more likely than men's to be medicalized and were critical of the effects. They asserted that male doctors, in conjunction with the law, controlled women by restricting their reproductive freedoms and constantly supervising their bodies, behaviors, and relationships.

They also highlighted gender bias in scientific research, noting that its findings were influenced by dominant societal values about women. For example, in the nineteenth century, women's illnesses were generally explained as the outcome of their bodies' inherent defectiveness, or the result of pursuing strenuous activity beyond what their weak constitutions could handle. Women's reproductive organs were thought to compete for energy with the rest of their bodies. Because women's role as mothers was so significant, medical doctors encouraged women to refrain from strenuous activity, especially during important reproductive times, such as menarche, pregnancy, and menopause. Too much studying or physical activity could lead to atrophy of the uterus. This misunderstanding of female physiology was based on the lack of basic knowledge of female anatomy. Until the late eighteenth century, scientists believed that female internal genitalia had the same general structure as male external genitalia. And prior to the nineteenth century, it was believed that women's bodies provided vessels for the life that men deposited there. Feminists asserted that remnants of these historically sexist misperceptions remained prominent in medicine and created an environment hostile to women.

One of the most widespread tactics that members of the women's health movement employed was the collective support of one another. Rather than turning to mainstream medicine, they began to depend on other forms of healing, for example, using self-help groups and drawing on their own experiences as wisdom. The Boston Women's Health Book Collective, for example, was established and published the ever-popular *Our Bodies, Ourselves* as a source of knowledge for women, by women.

Though the women's health movement made many gains, its stated concerns remain among feminists to this day. Feminist scholars continue to critique medical research that is affected by and reinforces cultural assumptions about women, for example. The image of the passive woman and the active, virulent man has been found permeating medical textbooks describing the relationship between the egg and the sperm. And the male body is still largely considered the neutral, generic human body. In 1990, U.S. congressional hearings exposed the fact that women were often not enrolled in research whose findings would eventually be generalized to them. Though heart disease is the number one killer of women, the National Institutes of Health (NIH) study that found aspirin could reduce heart attacks included 22,071 men and no women.

However, the role medicine should play in women's efforts for justice today is debated among feminists. Some maintain that medicine is an inherently flawed system that provides men the tools to control their bodies and corporations the means to profit from their fears and dependence.

Others assert that women can use medicine, even in its current patriarchal state, as a tool of empowerment. They argue that women can counter the patriarchal structures in society by using the power and legitimacy of medicine. They also emphasize that medicine does indeed provide them with greater options central to the freedoms they seek. This debate has emerged in regards to various topics, including contraception, childbirth, and infant feeding, among others.

Contraception

In 1839, the technology of vulcanizing rubber was invented by Charles Goodyear and was soon used to produce condoms, diaphragms, and intrauterine devices (IUDs). By the 1870s, women could purchase a variety of birth control products in the United States from catalogs, pharmacists, and rubber vendors. However, in 1873, Congress passed the Comstock Law, which prohibited the dissemination of "obscene" material (including birth control products and information) through the mail or interstate commerce. In 1916, birth control advocate Margaret Sanger opened a birth control clinic, which was shut down after 10 days. Two years later, the courts ruled that women could use contraception for therapeutic purposes and Sanger soon opened a birth control clinic, launching the birth control movement. Primarily privileged white women joined forces with the medical community in an effort to produce contraceptive devices and legitimize contraception. In 1951, Margaret Sanger petitioned scientist Gregory Pincus to develop a "magic pill" that would be as easy for women to take as an aspirin, a project that he worked on with doctor John Rock for a decade. By 1962, there were 1.2 million American women using the pill. Soon, there were reports of serious, even lethal, side effects. After public pressure, the pill manufactures developed a lower-dose formula that has fewer side effects.

To modern-day feminists, medicalized contraception is a mixed bag. On the one hand, it provides women with more control over their reproductive capacities, which is a central tenet of feminism. The medicalized forms, such as the pill, IUD, and injection, are more effective in avoiding pregnancy and are generally considered convenient, allowing women to focus on other parts of their life.

However, medicalized contraception also has its disadvantages. First there are the side effects, which range from mild discomfort to serious blood clots and infertility. And the fact that women are primarily at risk brings up a second concern: the lack of concern for women's safety. Would the medical establishment be more conscientious about eliminating side effects if they were dealing with men's bodies? Feminists also argue that contraception provides another opportunity for medical supervision and control of women. The pill requires a yearly visit to a physician and prescriptions, and the IUD and Norplant (a device placed under the skin of the upper arm that releases hormones over a five-year period) require a physician for both insertion and removal. And several cases of abuse against women of color have been reported, including the government coercing poor women to use Norplant as a legal punishment and doctors refusing to remove it before the allotted five years.

Also, while some prefer complete authority over their birth control method, other women would prefer their partners to take responsibility. They argue that maintaining birth control as a woman's issue reinstitutes women's place in the home, in charge of the family. Finally, as contraception became a medical, profitable product, its political nature subsided and it is no longer associated with feminist empowerment for most of the women who use it.

In response to these concerns, some feminists have turned to nonmedical forms of birth control including barrier and natural fertility awareness methods. Others find medicalized methods better for their lifestyle. For them, having these options is more empowering than not having the options.

Childbirth

In the early twentieth century, middle- and upper-class women rallied for the availability of anesthesia during childbirth to relieve pain. "Twilight sleep," a combination of morphine and scopolamine, was soon introduced and was widely used through the 1950s. It later became the target of feminist critique as women remained asleep for the entire birth and aftermath. Doctors eventually stopped using it due to its side effects. Since then, pain medication has improved and, when it works properly, women can now remain mentally alert throughout delivery without feeling labor pains.

However, critics disagree with the biomedical model that defines pregnancy as a problematic state in need of constant expert supervision. While most doctors focus on risk management, these feminists argue that pregnancy and childbirth are perfectly normal, natural events that most women can handle with little assistance. While they agree that medical technology is helpful in crisis situations, they argue that constant medical supervision causes more problems than it solves. For example, hospital policies that restrict movement can slow the natural progress of labor and lead to unnecessary induction or cesarean sections. And as women enter the hospital, the domain of medical professionals, their autonomy and authority diminish. They are met with standardized policies that are rigidly enforced, such as restrictions on mobility, food and drink, and visitors. After delivery, various tests, ointments, and shots are automatically given to the baby, often without the parents' explicit permission. Deviations from these policies usually involve fear-filled warnings and liability waivers. Proponents of home birth argue that women control more of their childbirth experience when it takes place in their own domain, attended by midwives. They argue that medicine has focused public attention on pain and convinced women that they cannot handle it. They hope to reclaim women's right to the joy and power of experiencing labor uninhibited by foreign substances or outside authority.

Others emphasize that medicalized birth provides women with the ability to choose the type of birth experience they want to have. For them, there is nothing necessarily heroic about withstanding pain. Rather, a woman should evaluate her situation, beliefs, and feelings to make the best choice for her. Medicine provides her with this possibility. And many women appreciate the option of having a cesarean section or being able to induce labor according to their needs or desires. Birthing in the hospital also provides women with more support, which is especially important to those with partners who do little domestic work. At the hospital, they are able to rest and heal without needing to feed children or wash dishes. They themselves are cared for and have someone available to help with the new baby.

Infant Feeding

Prior to the late nineteenth century, most women nursed their babies, or relied on friends or relatives to nurse them if they were unable to do it themselves. The upper classes often relied on wet nurses, as breastfeeding had become unfashionable among these classes. As science gained prestige, all things "natural," including breastfeeding, were considered debased. At the same time, medical doctors claimed that upper-class women were too delicate to do such things as nurse their babies.

By the 1890s, improved farming and preservation techniques had created a surplus of cow's milk and producers were searching for new markets. Doctors were initially leery of the nutritional quality of cow's milk and preferred breast milk. However, there was also the dominant medical idea that women's bodies were not completely healthy. Around the turn of the century, it was believed that the dysfunctional nature of women's bodies was likely to convert healthy breastmilk into "poison" by the time the baby received it. One of the doctors who prominently asserted this claim, Dr. Thomas Rotch, developed and sold his own formula.

To address nutritional concerns, doctors began to experiment with different ingredients and calculated formulas. With an air of scientific sophistication, they sold these formulas as superior to breast milk. They soon created alliances with milk companies, testing their products and giving them the seal of medical approval. In return, the milk companies put few directions on the containers, encouraging women to seek assistance from their doctors. Some formulas were sold by prescription only.

For many women, the availability of infant formula was a godsend. With industrialization, increasing numbers of women were leaving their babies to work in factories. Formula provided them a means to keep their babies fed while they were away. And upper-class women preferred bottles to wet nurses, who were the objects of their babies' affection. Increased access to milk also helped babies who were unable to be breast-fed because their mothers were ill or had died.

However, various studies dating back to the early twentieth century showed that bottle-fed babies were much more likely to die than those who were breast-fed. This was due to compromised bottle hygiene, which caused diarrhea, and the lack of antibodies obtained through breast milk, which made bottle-fed children more susceptible to communicable diseases. Yet there was little protest by the medical field against the marketing of these products. Soon they were aggressively marketed throughout the world, which ultimately led to the death of millions of babies. In recent decades, infant formula has become safer and more nutritious due to scientific research, but poor babies in third world nations still suffer from its use.

Today the medical community, specifically the American Academy of Pediatrics, endorses breastfeeding and most hospitals have lactation consultants on staff. However, hospitals also provide new mothers with free samples of formula and bottle-feed babies in the nursery, which makes learning to nurse more difficult. And women often find that their doctors and nurses have little helpful advice on nursing problems.

For many feminists, independence from breastfeeding is an important aspect of reproductive freedom. From this perspective, a woman cannot become truly equal to her male partner if there are domestic activities that only *she* can accomplish. This reiterates her "natural" role as caregiver and the logic of retaining women as domestic labor. And as long as she is obliged to nurse her children regularly, she cannot be competitive in the workforce. Finally, a women's body should be her own, and neither her partner nor the world should see it as an object for feeding her baby.

Feminist advocates of breastfeeding, on the other hand, draw on scientific evidence to argue that bottle feeding is less nutritious for babies and denies women various health benefits of breastfeeding, such as reduced rates of some cancers and prolonged infertility. They are critical of multinational corporations interfering with their newborns' nutrition and their relationship with their babies, and profiting from this interference. They also assert that women can attain social freedom and empowerment only when they are proud to be women. Rather than trying to deny their biology and become man-like, these feminists argue that women should embrace nursing and demand that the world around them respect it. Fathers should provide new mothers and babies with quiet time, by cleaning and taking care of the other children. Meanwhile, public spaces, especially the workplace, should be more nursing friendly, providing on-site childcare and nursing breaks.

CONCLUSION

Thus, even among feminists, there is no single clear answer to the question of how medicine affects women. Many see the structured patriarchy of medicine as inherently oppressive and, as such, to be resisted as much as possible. They are also concerned about feminism embracing medicalization because it neutralizes the social and political relevance of injustice. For instance, medicalizing domestic violence has taken attention away from the domineering patriarchal power relationship between men and women that is rampant throughout society.

Others argue that this perspective perpetuates the passive image of women by not acknowledging the active role women have played in bringing about medicalization. They also emphasize that medicine has provided women with important options, allowing them to live as they choose, in spite of its patriarchal tendencies.

Sociologist Catherine Kohler Riessman described medicalization a paradox, a patriarchal structure that some women have been able to use to empower themselves. It has freed women from certain biological limitations and provided them with more choices and opportunities. But, at the same time, women have become dependent on medicine to enjoy these freedoms, thereby losing their own authority.

See also Birthing Practices; Menstruation and Menopause; Mental Health: Gender Bias in Diagnoses of Women; Population Policy.

Further Reading: American Psychiatric Association, *Diagnostic and Statistical Manual of Mental Disorders* (Washington, DC: American Psychiatric Association, 1952, 1987, 1994, 2000); Boston Women's Health Book Collective, *Our Bodies, Ourselves: A New Edition for a New Era* (New York: Touchstone, 2005); Conrad, Peter, and Joseph Schneider, *Deviance and Medicalization: From Badness to Sickness* (Philadelphia: Temple University Press, 1992); Fox, Bonnie, and Diana Worts, "Revisiting the Critique of Medicalized Childbirth: A Contribution to the Sociology of Birth," *Gender and Society* 13, no. 3 (1999): 326–346; Hartmann, Betsy, *Reproductive Rights and Wrongs: The Global Politics of Population Control* (Boston: South End Press, 1995); Martin, Emily, "The Egg and the Sperm: How Science Has Constructed a Romance Based on Stereotypical Male-Female

Roles," *Signs* 16, no. 3 (1991): 485–501; Nechas, Eileen, and Denise Foley, *Unequal Treatment: What You Don't Know about How Women Are Mistreated by the Medical Community* (New York: Simon and Schuster, 1994); Oakley, Ann, *Women Confined: Towards a Sociology of Childbirth* (Oxford: Martin Robertson and Co. and Oxford University Press, 1980); Palmer, Gabrielle, *The Politics of Breastfeeding* (London: Pandora, 1993); Riessman, Catherine K., "Women and Medicalization: A New Perspective," *Social Policy*, Summer 1983, 3–18; Roberts, Dorothy E., *Killing the Black Body: Race, Reproduction, and the Meaning of Liberty* (New York: Pantheon Books, 1997); Schiebinger, Londa, *Nature's Body: Gender in the Making of Modern Science* (Boston: Beacon Press, 1994); Zimmerman, Susan, *Silicone Survivors: Women's Experiences with Breast Implants* (Philadelphia: Temple University Press, 1998).

Andrea Bertotti Metoyer

MENSTRUATION AND MENOPAUSE

The debates on menstruation and menopause center on whether girls and women view these bodily processes positively or negatively. In addition, academic researchers disagree over whether doctors should treat the problems some girls and women experience during menstruation and menopause.

BACKGROUND

How do scholars debate issues of the body, in this case, menarche and menopause? Both certainly occur because of biological and genetic reasons. Menarche refers to the first menses, and in the United States, the mean age of first menstruation is 12.5, but girls can begin as early as 9 and as late as 16. Menopause refers to the last menses, and according to the medical definition, a woman is menopausal when she has not menstruated for 12 consecutive months. Although the average age is 51, women can stop menstruating as early as their late 30s and as late as their mid-50s. Research studies debate how girls and women regard menstruation and menopause, and the role of medicine in treating the difficulties that can occur with both. Some scholars argue that girls view menstruation negatively while others contend that girls can associate menstruation with a sense of empowerment. Similarly, researchers disagree about how to understand the ways in which women undergo menopause. Some focus on physical and psychological changes in women's bodies, such as hot flashes and mood swings. Others argue that those changes must be understood in the context of what else is happening in women's lives as well as whether women associate menopause with aging.

Scholars also dispute whether doctors should treat menstruation and menopause. On one hand, some girls and women *do* suffer, and to ignore their suffering sends the message that their difficulties and therefore their bodies are not important. On the other hand, to define menstruation and menopause as medical conditions supports the cultural view that women's bodies are naturally weaker than men's because of their unique reproductive systems. Overall, the debates focus on how cultural assumptions about girls' and women's roles as well as medical views about the female body influence experiences with menstruation and menopause.

MENARCHE: GIRLS' ROLES, EDUCATION, AND PUBERTY

Research studies indicate that most cultures associate girls' menstrual status with their reproductive ability. However, they present conflicting findings about whether girls view menarche positively or negatively. Most girls in the United States report mixed feelings, but compared to the past, they are more open about their perspectives. Yet studies show a range of experiences: for example, some girls feel confused because of a lack of knowledge about their bodies, some are embarrassed because menarche signals their sexual status, and others feel empowered because it is a sign that they are approaching adulthood.

For example, some studies report that girls look forward to menarche but then express regret or ambivalence after it starts. Research suggests that the limited ways in which girls learn about first menses influence them to view it as embarrassing or as a sign of weakness. When health classes teach about menstruation, many separate boys and girls, which suggests that this topic is private and should not be discussed openly. Classes also focus on the biological causes and do not share stories about how periods feel, and the many different ways in which girls experience periods. Consequently, girls do not know the range of physical and emotional changes that can occur. They also do not have knowledge about their bodies, in particular their genitals, so they are not informed about the sensation of menstrual bleeding or of inserting tampons. Therefore, many experience these occurrences with confusion or fear.

Another issue is that menstruation and puberty are associated with adult female sexuality, which can make girls anxious or self-conscious about their bodies. Menarche and the development of a mature female body can lead adults, especially parents and teachers, to treat girls differently. In particular, they may start talking to girls about sex and the potential for pregnancy. Linking menses with pregnancy can perplex girls. Often they do not understand the biology of pregnancy, and some think that once they begin menstruating, any sexual interaction with a boy can make them pregnant. For example, a girl in one study reported as follows:

> A lot of girls that I hung around with thought as soon as you got your period at any moment you could spontaneously be pregnant.... When kids start getting their periods, they hear all this stuff like, "When you're not pregnant you get this." So they're like, "How do I get pregnant?" and stuff like that. It's scary. (K. Martin 1996, 28)

Girls may also feel embarrassed by the sexual attention that boys give them as a result of their developing bodies. Overall, these studies show that girls associate menstruation with puberty and sexuality, and consequently may view it as confusing, embarrassing, or frightening.

Other studies emphasize the empowering aspects of menstruation, and disagree with research contending that girls view menses only negatively. Some research emphasizes the positive roles that mothers can play. For example, one study finds that girls who have feminist views experience menstruation positively, in part because their mothers have taught them that it is a sign of growing up. Therefore, girls see it as part of their identity as women. Another study suggests that when mothers talk openly and positively about menses as well as provide concrete details about how to use menstrual products like pads and tampons, then girls feel at ease with their first menstruation. This study emphasizes that girls will feel empowered by knowing what to expect and what to do when they menstruate (K. Martin 1996).

Other research indicates that girls use their knowledge about periods to confuse boys and thus to attain power in daily life. In one study, girls talked about bleeding to "gross out" boys as a way to assert themselves and, in doing so, they showed that they would not passively let boys tease and embarrass them at school (Fingerson 2005). Thus they are creatively finding ways to be self-assured in interactions with boys. In sum, these studies argue that girls can be taught to view and therefore experience menarche positively.

MENOPAUSE: WOMEN'S ROLES, MIDLIFE, AND RELATIONSHIPS

Researchers in the United States debate about what type of social-scientific research is best for understanding how women go through menopause. Some favor surveys that quantify the number of times that physical and emotional changes occur for large numbers of women. Others argue that one-on-one interviews provide more detailed information about how women experience menopause, even though such research includes smaller numbers of women. Overall, the two types of research provide different understandings of how women go through menopause.

For example, until recently, much of the sociological and psychological survey research on women in the United States asked women the number of times a particular menopausal change, such as hot flashes, night sweats, and vaginal dryness, occurred. It found that women who no longer menstruate have higher rates of hot flashes and night sweats compared to women who are going through hormonal changes as they approach their last period. Research on the relationship between menopause and moods, however, is conflicted, with some studies finding that the onset of menopause is not associated with an increased risk of depression, while others report that women tend to feel more depressed when the menopause transition begins than after periods cease.

Some scholars disagree with these studies because they ask only about negative changes, and this perpetuates the idea that menopause is only unpleasant. Furthermore, such research implicitly supports the U.S. cultural view that aging itself tends to be primarily bad. These scholars also argue that the word *symptom* is problematic because it presumes that menopause is a disease; therefore, they avoid that term and use menopausal "changes" instead. They point out that few studies ask women about positive changes, and the handful of studies that do ask about these find that some women report increased energy, relief, and a sense of freedom after their last period. Therefore, they argue that researchers should ask women about negative and positive changes in survey research in order to fully understand their experiences (Mansfield and Voda 1997).

Other scholars maintain that surveys do not allow women to explain for themselves what is most important about menopause and, therefore, risk overlooking its range of meanings. These researchers prefer studies based on in-depth interviews so that they can document and analyze women's narratives. For example, one study finds that menopause is not important for some women because of stress. Women do have physical changes like hot flashes and vaginal dryness, but they are also coping with cancer, marital difficulties, or ill parents, so they do not have time to think about how they feel or the fact that they are going through menopause. Therefore, they say menopause is "no big deal" (Winterich and Umberson 1999). Another study that used one-on-one interviews finds that women view menopause positively because it means an end to periods as well as a new stage in their lives. They do not associate menopause with an end to fertility, since most of them stopped having children long before menopause. Also, they do not associate menopause with feeling old, since they will live, on average, 30 more years. Consequently, they see it as a new time in their lives, a time to take care of themselves, to travel or start a new career. Taken together, these studies show why asking about changes in women's bodies is not enough to achieve a full understanding of what they mean in the context of women's lives.

MEDICAL RESPONSES TO MENSTRUATION AND MENOPAUSE

The current debate on menstruation and medicine focuses on whether menstruation is medically necessary. Some argue that since women do not bear as many children as women did historically, frequent menstruation is not necessary. Others maintain that using medication to stop menses could harm women's health. The debate on menopause also centers on the role of drugs in helping women with physical and emotional changes.

In 1999, a controversial book, *Is Menstruation Obsolete?* was published. It argued that regular menses are unique to modern women. The book contends that women throughout history menstruated less often due to frequent pregnancy and lactation, so now medicine should eliminate periods to avoid women's "unnatural" discomfort each month. Four years later, Barr Pharmaceuticals put on the market the drug Seasonale, which reduces periods to four times a year. Since then, increasing numbers of women have been using their hormonal contraceptives without stopping for menstruation. Scholars and doctors who support this use of contraceptives as well as the development of drugs to avoid menstruation altogether argue that allowing periods increases the risks of unwanted pregnancies. Those on this side of the debate agree with the prevalent cultural view that menstruation is a nuisance and thus it should be eliminated.

Those on the other side of the debate do not agree that women's monthly bleeding is unnatural. They argue that the evidence supporting women's infrequent menstruation in the past is sparse; in contrast, an abundance of evidence documents women's menstrual rituals and ceremonies. These researchers contend that ideas about what women's bodies should and should not do are based on culture, not biology. And they are concerned about the lack of scientific evidence on the safety of eliminating menstruation. What are the health risks of not bleeding each month? Scientific studies of the long-term use of contraceptives do not yet exist, and so some researchers caution women to avoid such use of contraceptives until more data are available.

The debates on the medical treatment of menopause have persisted for almost 50 years and, like menstruation, they center on whether women should take medication.

On one hand, until doctors understood how the transition time to the final menses, known as perimenopause, affects women's bodies, they either ignored women's concerns or told them they were imagining their symptoms. This treatment supported the cultural view that women are weaker than men and that women exaggerate their symptoms. Meanwhile, women suffered from physical and emotional discomfort. On the other hand, once doctors prescribed hormone drugs to treat women's symptoms, they viewed menopause as a disease in itself as well as a cause of other diseases like thinning bones (osteoporosis) and heart disease. Academics argue that this medical approach supports the cultural idea that women's bodies are naturally weaker and sicker than men's.

However, scholars agree that the history of medical support of hormone drugs has put women's health at risk. Doctors first promoted estrogen drugs after menopause in the 1960s and early 1970s because they thought the benefits outweighed the risks. In 1980, however, several studies showed an increased risk for cancer of the lining of the uterus, endometrial cancer, in those women who took estrogen. Doctors' prescriptions decreased and most women stopped taking hormones. Meanwhile, medical researchers discovered that by adding a synthetic progesterone, progestin, to estrogen removed the risk of endometrial cancer. So by the mid-1980s, prescriptions soared again for the new drug, called hormone replacement therapy (HRT).

Doctors advised women to take HRT not only to cope with hot flashes and vaginal dryness but also to prevent osteoporosis and to help prevent heart disease. Many women used the drug; between one-sixth and one-fourth of all postmenopausal women took Premarin, the most common form of HRT in 1995. However, this medical advice was based on observational studies. These studies are limited because they examine people's behaviors and, through statistical analyses, make connections between those behaviors and their health. So the federal government initiated the first clinical trial in 1991 to test the benefits and risks of HRT. Clinical trials are the "gold standard" studies in medicine. They are very expensive but they more clearly show the specific role of drugs in people's health because they compare those who take placebos with those who take the drug being tested. Researchers compare those on the drug with those on placebos. in order to understand the specific benefits and risks of the medication.

The preliminary results of the clinical trial of HRT were alarming because they indicated that it actually put some women at an *increased* risk for developing blood clots, strokes, heart attacks, and breast cancer. In other words, doctors

---

DID YOU KNOW?

A type of premenstrual syndrome, premenstrual dysphoric disorder (PMDD), was first classi-fied as a psychological condition in 1987 in the American Psychological Association's *Diag-nostic and Statistical Manual of Mental Disorders (DSM)*. The classification was intended to diagnose women with extreme physical and mental symptoms in the week before menses starts. Women who experienced these symptoms felt relieved that they had options to en-able them to feel better. The Food and Drug Administration approved two medications to treat PMDD: Zoloft and Sarafem. Sarafem is the antidepressant Prozac, but the drug makers repackaged it under a new name to market it for the treatment of PMDD. Women's health activists argue that while the scientific evidence does show that women have premenstrual days, it is inconclusive about whether a psychiatric premenstrual disorder exists. They also contend that even though some women have benefited from antidepressants, research indi-cates that dietary and exercise changes as well as self-help groups can help too. Those who support the *DSM* classification, however, maintain that although PMDD occurs rarely, among from 3 to 8 percent of all women, it significantly impairs a woman's ability to function and thus requires treatment.

---

thought that HRT helped women's hearts but the trial indicated that it actu-ally put some women at an *increased* risk for heart problems. Consequently, the principal investigators stopped the clinical trial in 2002, three years ahead of schedule. Now doctors give the most cautious advice they have ever given since they first promoted hormone drugs: if women must take HRT to help with hot flashes, they should take the lowest dose possible and limit its use. Medical researchers are continuing to explore various combinations of hormone drugs that will alleviate menopausal symptoms without putting women's health at risk. Academics are concerned about how these new drugs will affect women; at the same time they want safe options for those who need medical treatment in order to feel better during menopause. Overall, scholars continue to disagree as to whether doctors should give women medication at all.

CONCLUSION

The debates about menarche and menopause focus on how girls and women experience menstruation and menopause, and whether medical practitioners should play a role in treating these bodily processes. Some argue that the physi-cal and emotional changes that occur with menstruation and menopause need to be taken seriously so that girls and women do not needlessly suffer. Others argue that girls' negative experiences with menarche could be avoided with bet-ter education about what to expect, and women's menopausal experiences could be improved with greater understanding of the context of midlife. Whether medication should play a role in avoiding menstruation and treating menopause is hotly contested as well. Some contend that drugs allow women to avoid dis-comfort, while others maintain that drugs carry risks that can be avoided. As more medications become available for both menstruation and menopause, the debates will undoubtedly intensify.

See also Aging; Birth Control; Birthing Practices; Medicine and Medicalization: Views on Women's Bodies.

Further Reading: Avis, Nancy, "Depression during the Menopausal Transition," *Psychology of Women Quarterly* 27, no. 2 (1993): 91–100; Caplan, Paula J., *They Say You're Crazy: How the World's Most Powerful Psychiatrists Decide Who's Normal* (Addison Wesley, 1995); Coutinho, Elsimar, *Is Menstruation Obsolete? How Suppressing Menstruation Can Help Women Who Suffer from Anemia, Endometriosis, or PMS* (New York: Oxford University Press, 1999); Ehrenreich, Barbara, and Deirdre English, *For Her Own Good: Two Centuries of the Experts' Advice to Women* (New York: Anchor Books, 2005); Fingerson, Laura, "Agency and the Body in Adolescent Menstrual Talk," *Childhood* 12, no. 1 (2005): 91–110; Lee, Shirley, "Health and Sickness: The Meaning of Menstruation and Premenstrual Syndrome in Women's Lives," *Sex Roles* 46, nos. 1–2 (2002): 25–35; Mansfield, Phyllis K., and Ann Voda, "Woman-Centered Information on Menopause for Health Care Providers: Findings from the Midlife Women's Health Survey," *Health Care for Women International* 18 (1997): 55–72; Martin, Emily, *The Woman in the Body: A Cultural Analysis of Women's Reproduction* (Boston: Beacon Press, 2001); Martin, Karen A., *Puberty, Sexuality and the Self: Boys and Girls at Adolescence* (New York: Routledge, 1996); O'Grady, Kathleen, "Contraception/Birth Control," in *An Encyclopedia of Women and Religion,* ed. Serinity Young et al. (New York: Simon and Schuster, 2000); Winterich, Julie, and Debra Umberson, "How Women Experience Menopause: The Importance of Social Context," *Journal of Women and Aging* 11, no. 4 (1999): 57–73.

Julie Winterich

MENTAL HEALTH: GENDER BIASES IN DIAGNOSES OF WOMEN

The diagnosis of mental disorders is seen by health professionals as important for the treatment and care of patients experiencing emotional and behavior difficulties. Critics contend that the mental health system is fraught with gender biases that negatively affect women in the diagnosis and consequent treatment of symptoms.

BACKGROUND

The diagnosing of mental disorders is an age-old practice. Throughout history, philosophers, religious leaders, astrologers, tribal healers, medical doctors, and many others have attempted to explain human behavior. Figuring out what is "normal" and finding the causes of and cures for the "abnormal" have proven to be difficult, often comical, and always imprecise endeavors. Treatments for abhorrent behavior have included lobotomies (disconnecting the two sides of the brain), exorcism (forcing out evil spirits), bloodletting, castration, electric "shock" treatment, incarceration, prescription medication costing billions of dollars, public humiliation, and a great deal of prayer. What is clear is that efforts to explain and treat ailments in the human mental and emotional

PROZAC NATION

In her autobiography, *Prozac Nation: Young and Depressed in America* (1994), Elizabeth Wurtzel documents the debilitating, painful, and stigmatizing aspects of living with depression. Her realistic portrayal of the good, the bad, and the ugly aspects of mental health problems gained her a cult following after the publication of her best-selling book. The book also shed light on the fact that women are twice as likely as men to be diagnosed with clinical depression and to be prescribed antidepressants such as Prozac for their treatment. In 2001, a film based on the book, starring Cristina Ricci, was released at the Toronto Film Festival and greeted with critical acclaim by some and disdain by others. As a result, Miramax Studios shelved the project until 2003, when it was released for a limited run at national theaters with little fanfare.

system have followed closely the political, religious, scientific, and economic realities of the time.

Modern psychology is no exception. The *Diagnostic and Statistical Manual of Mental Disorders (DSM),* published by the American Psychological Association, is the most widely recognized body of work that attempts to scientifically categorize mental illnesses. It is used by psychiatrists, primary care physicians, psychologists, researchers, social workers, and others with an interest in human behavior. It is, however, fraught with controversy regarding the validity of its characterizations of abnormal behavior and the reliability of its use by doctors and therapists who treat patients. First published in 1952, the *DSM* has undergone several revisions, many of the changes being motivated by a growing body of research about psychiatric disorders, others by pressures from the conservative and liberal agendas of the day. Its contributing experts are largely white males, and they arrive at decisions by consensus. Detractors say the classifications and descriptions of mental disorders are inherently biased with regard to women and people of color (Zur and Nordmarken 2006). Still, the *DSM* is the most comprehensive work to date that attempts to make distinctions between various mental disorders and makes possible a common language among behavioral health professionals.

GENDER DIFFERENCES IN DIAGNOSING MENTAL DISORDERS

While there are no differences between men and women in the overall prevalence of diagnosed mental and behavioral disorders, the frequency and type of diagnoses given to men and women are notably different (World Health Organization 2002). For example, women are more than twice as likely to be diagnosed with depression and significantly more likely to experience eating disorders, dissociative identity disorder (formerly known as multiple personality disorder), and somataform disorders (physical complaints and body distortions). While men complete suicide more often than women in almost every developed county, women attempt suicide far more often. The most debilitating of mental illnesses, such as schizophrenia and bipolar disorder, occur equally in men and women; however, men are more likely to have early onset of schizophrenia and women are more likely to experience more severe forms of bipolar disorder. Women carry the diagnosis of borderline personality disorder, characterized by an inability to "regulate" emotions, three times more often than men (Skodol and Bender 2003). Other personality disorders, such as antisocial personality disorder (often associated with criminals and psychopaths), psychopathic gambling, disorders associated with sexual behavior, and intermittent explosive disorder are twice as likely to be associated with men. The same is true for substance use disorders like alcoholism.

Many explanations, both biological and social, have been put forward to account for these differences. Some believe that men are biologically predisposed to violence, while others believe that socialization toward aggressive and sexually acting out behaviors is responsible. Women are often thought to be biologically predisposed to emotionality and problems associated with hormone fluctuation, while others believe that society teaches women to be passive, dependent, and emotional and places strict limits on their roles and autonomy. These expectations can lead to depression, anxiety, and other affective disorders. But what about the definitions of mental disorder themselves? What bias may exist in the assessment and diagnosing of mental problems? What is clear is that the history and current practice of diagnosing and treating mental illness are interwoven with stereotypes and biases that may affect the psychological well-being of both women and men; however, the history and current practice of psychiatry reveal the extent to which women are especially vulnerable.

THE PSYCHOLOGY OF THE OVARY

Throughout the nineteenth century and well into the twentieth century, the ovaries and uterus were thought in the medical profession to be the cause of many physical and virtually all psychological disorders. "Female castration," also known as "ovariotomy" or removal of the ovaries, "cauterization" of (sealing off) the uterus, injections into the uterus, and many other painful and sometimes deadly treatments were thought to be the cures. In 1906 it was reported ovaries were removed from 150,000 women in the United States (Ehrenreich and English 2005, 136). According to historian Barker-Benfield (1972),

> Among the indications were troublesomeness, eating like a ploughman, masturbation, attempted suicide, erotic tendencies, persecution mania, simple "cussedness" and dysmenorrhea [painful menstruation]. Most apparent in the enormous variety of symptoms doctors took to indicate castration was a strong current of sexual appetitiveness on the part of women. (quoted in Ehrenreich and English 2005, 136)

Throughout the development of modern medicine, the treatment of physical and mental illness in women has been infused with religious, social, and patriarchal bias. Women were (and may continue to be) a mystery to the male practitioners of the day. Assumptions about the inner workings of the female body and mind are rooted in answers to the "woman question," painting a picture of the female as innately inferior, primitive, prone to illness, and intensely pathological. Wiping out all manner of problematic behaviors associated with what the ancient Greeks described as the "wandering uterus," known as hysteria and said to gain control of the female personality, was the goal of early psychological interventions. The term *hysteria* appeared in the first version of the *DSM* in 1952. While hysteria could be diagnosed in men, it was overwhelmingly a woman's mental condition. The disorder was later divided into two disorders, hysterical personality disorder and conversion disorder (a neurological-like disorder with no known medical cause, or the "conversion" of intrapsychic distress into physical symptoms). The earlier concept of hysteria would eventually find its way into later versions of the *DSM* disguised as the more palatable histrionic personality disorder, with roots reportedly in the Latin word *histrionicus* or "pertaining to an actor" (Chadoff 1982). With this change in the definition came an evening out of prevalence in the diagnosing of men and women with the disorder, although the diagnosis in men more often is accompanied by gender identity disorder. This is significant because it tells us that only males with stereotypically female traits or what is often labeled "gender role confusion" will likely be given the diagnosis.

Among the leaders of psychiatry in the late nineteenth century and early twentieth century, Sigmund Freud developed his now famous—if not discarded—theories about psychological ailments in women. His work with white, mostly affluent women led Freud to believe women were entirely responsible for their own conditions. He thought of women as a kind of mutilated male, a species that must learn to accept their "deformity" (the "lack" of a penis). This famous doctor is widely thought to have contributed a great deal to the vocabulary of misogyny (hatred, dislike, or mistrust of women: see Ballou and Brown 2002).

During the 1950s and 1960s, there developed a perspective in gynecology that saw pregnancy as in itself a pathological condition that caused women to become temporarily insane (Ehrenreich and English 2005). The root of the problem, it was thought, was the woman's rejection of her femininity caused by the unpleasant changes in her body. Gynecologists at that time began the practice of diagnosing mental illness in women not just during pregnancy but as a routine part of their gynecological care, often using the patient's reaction to the pelvic exam as a way to diagnose problems with sexual adjustment.

In 1986, after a literature review regarding the commonly diagnosed mental illness in women, psychiatrist Paul Chodoff concluded that the hysterical (histrionic) personality is a "caricature of femininity," developing under the influence of cultural forces, particularly male domination, and is not a "natural attribute" of women. It was around that time that psychiatrists finally acknowledged that even though diagnostic criteria do not mention gender, clinicians diagnose women's and men's behavior in different ways (Ford and Widiger 1989).

DID YOU KNOW?

The *Diagnostic and Statistical Manual of Mental Disorders (DSM)*, published by the American Psychiatric Association (APA), is the manual most commonly used to diagnose mental health disorders in the United States. The *DSM* has gone through five revisions and the sixth version is due for publication in approximately 2011. The *DSM* was created to give psychiatrists and other doctors a diagnostic basis for psychiatric research and practice. It has been controversial, however, and some classified disorders have been heavily debated. Critics point out that men and women are often diagnosed according to different criteria, and although the *DSM* is written in gender-neutral language, in practice men and women tend to be diagnosed differently according to gender role expectations.

DIAGNOSING MENTAL ILLNESS IN WOMEN TODAY

One of the most researched mental illnesses in which differences between men and women are evident is depression. The National Institute of Mental Health reports that in any given year, 10 to 14 million people experience clinical depression; women 18–45 years of age account for the largest proportion of this group (National Institute on Alcohol Abuse and Alcoholism 2006). By most accounts, women are twice as likely as men to experience depression and are also far more likely to experience comorbidity with depression. Comorbidity is the occurrence of more than one disorder at the same time and may include physical illnesses as well as other mental disorders and substance abuse. There exists a gender bias in the diagnosing of these comorbid factors as well. For example, women with both depression and substance abuse are more likely to be diagnosed with depression as the primary diagnosis, while the opposite is true for men. Men are more likely to be diagnosed and treated for substance abuse even when the same depressive symptoms are present. This bias could lead to substance abuse issues being taken less seriously in women and depression being taken less seriously in men (Hannah and Grant 1997).

More broadly, some argue that the entire *DSM* is inherently biased, generally coding attributes most often associated with females as pathology, including emotionality and relationship interdependence, but not attributes most often associated with males, such as autonomy and individuality. Clinicians have also been found to have numerous gender biases when treating female patients, such as judging women as more mentally ill than men with the same symptoms, believing what male patients say more than what female patients tell them, prescribing mood-altering drugs more often for women than men, and believing female patients require more monitoring than their male counterparts (Zur and Nordmarken 2006).

BIOLOGICAL FACTORS

There is a vast body of research that documents the presence of mood swings associated with hormone changes as part of the menstrual cycle. Women also experience considerable distress and disorders associated with reproductive health conditions. In direct contrast to earlier beliefs that women are better off without their reproductive organs, infertility and hysterectomy have been found to increase women's risk of mood disorders. Bladder control problems, premenstrual cramping and bloating, and other common gynecological conditions in women are thought to cause symptoms of depression and anxiety. Hormonal fluctuations are linked to antenatal (during pregnancy) and postnatal (after birth) depression.

In 1994 the *DSM* listed a disorder called premenstrual dysphoric disorder (PMDD), characterized by severe emotional and physical symptoms prior to and during menstruation that drastically affect a woman's mood, sense of well-being, sleep, appetite, and so forth. For some, its inclusion as a psychiatric condition legitimized the real mental distress brought about by the female menstrual cycle. For others, it is another example of clear gender bias in the diagnosing of mental illness, pathologizing the normal functions of the female reproductive system. As researchers Zur and Dordmarkin (2006) point out, PMDD's inclusion in the *DSM* was hotly debated among professionals and was decided upon after a vote just before publication. These authors correctly point out that there is no parallel process for men and there are no gender-neutral categories for dysphoria due to hormone imbalance. In their extensive review of the literature on the prevalence of depression in women versus men, Pincinelli and Wilkinson (2000) found that while factors such as adverse experiences in childhood and sociocultural roles likely play a role in the development of depression, the evidence does not support the notion that genetic or biological factors do so. Such findings are likely to discourage some and please others.

GENDER ROLES

It is thought that culturally determined gender roles play a huge part in the prevalence and types of mental disorders diagnosed in females, beginning in childhood and continuing through old age (World Health Organization 2002). Conduct disorders are most often diagnosed in boys during childhood. In adolescence, girls experience lower self-esteem and more anxiety related to body image, both of which are associated with depression and eating disorders. In adulthood, social roles place women more often in situations in which they lack control over their lives. Pressure created by their multiple roles and by gender discrimination resulting in poverty, hunger, malnutrition, overwork, sexual abuse, exposure to violence, and financial insecurity play a role for low-income women in the development of depression. In addition, severe life events that cause a sense of loss, inferiority, humiliation, or entrapment can predict mental illnesses such as depression and anxiety.

SEXUAL VIOLENCE

Globally, sexual violence is experienced by more girls and women than men: an estimated 1 in 4 women in contrast to 1 in 10 men will be victims of sexual abuse or assault in their lifetime (Orsillo 2006). There is a direct correlation between sexual violence and the development of multiple mental health problems later in life, including posttraumatic stress disorder (PTSD). PTSD historically was diagnosed primarily in men who served in combat and was also known as battle fatigue. The evening out of the numbers of men and women diagnosed with this disorder correlates directly with the recognition that the trauma experienced during sexual abuse and violence is equal to the trauma experienced by war veterans as a result of experiences during combat. It is estimated that up to 70 percent of patients diagnosed with borderline personality disorder and dissociative identity disorder were sexually abused in childhood; in addition, these patients are considerably more likely to experience sexual violence as adults than patients without the disorder. Many women with eating disorders, which are diagnosed five times more often in women than men, share the same sexual abuse history.

RESEARCH AND THE DELIVERY OF TREATMENT SERVICES

Historically, the study of mental illnesses and responses to treatment interventions has been largely limited to men, except for the study of disorders, such as postpartum depression, that affect only women. Research subjects for the study of the development of disorders and the response to medications have largely been men, and the results have then been generalized to women. It is important that studies be conducted with both men and women so that gender variables can begin to be sorted out. Research that has done this has yielded some interesting results. For example, women diagnosed with schizophrenia are more likely to have affective (emotional) symptoms compared to men, respond better to certain types of medications, have better outcomes in programs using a psychosocial approach, and have better outcomes overall than men with the disease (Blackshaw et al. 2006).

Complicating the picture of the rates of mental illnesses in women versus men is the fact that women are more likely to seek services for mental health issues than men and are more likely to be referred for mental health services by medical professionals (World Health Organization 2002). Still, the rates of detection, treatment, and appropriate referrals by health professionals are low (Orsillo 2006). Less than half of people meeting the *DSM* criteria for mental disorder are identified by their primary care doctors. Only two in every five people experiencing a mood, anxiety, or substance abuse disorder seek treatment within the first year. These realities make it difficult to identify those who could benefit from treatment, and further complicate the gender bias picture.

CONCLUSION

Diagnosing and treating mental illness has been described by some as "more of an art than a science" (Zur and Nordmarken 2006). Mental health professionals operate under imprecise guidelines that are loaded with cultural and personal gender bias. Because of the status of women and the biased and negative manner in which mental disorders have been and sometimes are addressed, women remain especially vulnerable. It is believed that reducing the overrepresentation of debilitating disorders in women such as depression would drastically reduce the global burden of disability caused by mental health problems. But first, patients and professionals alike may benefit from taking a critical look at the multiple factors involved in the development of definitions of disorder and the gender bias that affects the identification and treatment of women.

See also Depression; Medicine and Medicalization: Views on Women's Bodies.

Further Reading: American Psychiatric Association, *Diagnostic and Statistical Manual of Mental Disorders* (Washington, DC: American Psychiatric Association, 1952, 1987, 1994, 2000); Ballou, Mary, and Laura Brown, eds., *Rethinking Mental Health and Disorder: Feminist Perspectives* (New York: Guilford Press, 2002); Blackshaw, et al., "Teaching on Gender Issues," Canadian Psychiatric Association, position papers, October 29, 2006; Brommelhoff, J., K. Conway, K. Merikangas, B. Levy, "Higher Rates of Depression in Women: Role of Gender Bias within the Family," *Journal of Women's Health* 13, no. 1 (2004): 69–76; Chadoff, Paul, "Hysteria in Women," *American Journal of Psychiatry* 139 (1982): 545–551; Collins, L. H., "Illustrating Feminist Theory: Power and Psychopathology," *Psychology of Women Quarterly* 22 (1998): 97–112; Ehrenreich, Barbara, and Deirdre English, *For Her Own Good: Two Centuries of the Experts' Advice to Women* (New York: Anchor Books, 2005); Ford, M. R., and T. A. Widiger, "Sex Bias in the Diagnosis of Histrionic and Antisocial Personality Disorder," *Journal of Consulting and Clinical Psychology* 57 (1989): 301–305; Hanna, E. Z., and B. F. Grant, "Gender Differences in DSM-IV: Alcohol Disorders and Major Depression as Distributed in the General Population, Clinical Implications," *Psychiatry* 38 (1997): 202–212; Nazroo, James, "Exploring Gender Difference in Depression," *Psychiatric Times* 18, no. 3 (March 2001); Orsillo, Sue, "Sexual Assault against Females: A National Center for PTSD Fact Sheet," 2006, available at: http://www.ncptsd.va.gov/facts/specific/fs_female_sex_assault.html; Piccinelli, Marco, and Greg Wilkinson, "Exploring Gender Difference in Depression," *British Journal of Psychiatry* 177 (2000): 486–492; Skodol, Andrew, and Donna Bender, "Why Are Women Diagnosed Borderline More than Men?" *Psychiatric Quarterly* 74, no. 4 (2003): 349–360; World Health Organization, "Gender and Health, Modules in Review, Gender and Depression, Gender Differences in Diagnosing Depression," 2006, available at: www.genderandhealth.ca/en/modules/depression;World Health Organization, "Gender and Women's Mental Health. Gender Disparities and Mental Health: The Facts," 2002, available at: www.who.int/mental_health/resources/gender/en/; Wurtzel, E. *Prozac Nation: Young and Depressed in America* (New York: Riverhead Books, 1994); Zur, Ofer, and Nola Nordmarken, "DSM: Diagnosing for Money and Power: Summary of the Critique of the DSM," 2006, available at: www.drzur.com/dsmcritique.

Lanai Greenhalgh

MEXICAN FEMALE MIGRANTS

The reasons women migrate from Mexico to the United States are complex and often disputed. The common belief is that women migrate to the United

States primarily to reunite their families. However, the ability to find work plays an important role in migratory patterns.

BACKGROUND

The numbers and proportion (relative to men) of women who migrate to the United States from Mexico are on the rise. They come to reunite their families, but they are able to do this because they can find work here. The longer they live in the United States, the more likely they are to have children who are U.S. citizens. Mexicana (female Mexican) migration and the establishment of families in the United States forge new cultures and identities with implications for our economy and culture. Do women migrate to join their families or for work? Are they likely to settle in the United States, or will they return to Mexico? Who benefits from Mexicana migration?

Beginning in the 1990s, the number of Mexican women migrating to the United States has significantly increased. This is due in part to economic conditions in Mexico, but is also due to labor demand and immigration laws in the United States. The increase in women's migration includes new destinations in the southern, eastern, and midwestern United States, a reflection of changes in the labor market, as demand in California has fallen off and demand has increased in other regions.

The United States has a long history of Mexican migration, dating back to the days when Texas and California were part of Mexico. "Mexican" migration to the United States began in the mid-nineteenth century, when Texas declared its independence and the United States annexed it. The expansion of the railroads in the late nineteenth century opened the rest of the country to the movement of migrants throughout the country. In the first half of the twentieth century, war and economic depression slowed Mexican migration; after 1940, the *bracero* program provided Mexican labor to replace and supplement U.S. labor in the fields. Even when the *bracero* program ended in 1964, Mexican migration continued, although at a lower rate until the 1980s (Massey et al. 1987), when Mexican migration, including female migration, increased (Cornelius 1991; see also LaBotz 2006 and Massey 1995).

Latinos (people of Latin American descent, including Brazilians; Hispanics are people of Spanish-speaking descent, including Spaniards) are the largest minority in the United States, with an estimated population of 40 million. They grow by more than 1.7 million a year. In 2002, Latinos represented 13.3 percent of the total U.S. population; two-thirds (66.9 percent) of these were of Mexican descent. More than one-eighth of the people in the United States are of Latino origin; 10 percent of the population born in Mexico live in the United States. Not only are Latinos an important minority, but they are growing rapidly, accounting for 40 percent of population growth between 1990 and 2000 (United States Hispanic Chamber of Commerce, 2007, http://www.ushcc.com/). By 2006, 44.7 million (or 15 percent) of the U.S. population was Hispanic, accounting for 53 percent of U.S. population growth in the last decade (Pew Hispanic Center 2006). Women represent an even faster-growing proportion

MEXICAN MIGRATION TIMELINE

1836: Battle of the Alamo; Texas declared independence from Mexico.

1845: The United States annexed Texas: Mexicans became *migrants*.

1942–1964: *Braceros* replaced U.S. workers and continued to supply agricultural labor.

1965: The Immigration Law of 1965 emphasized reunification of families.

1980: A total of 300,000 women were recent migrants from Mexico.

1987–1988: The Simpson-Rodini Immigration Reform and Control Act (IRCA) gave legal residence rights to long-term residents of the United States.

1990s: Mexican immigration increased; women's migration increased.

2001: September 11 attack on the World Trade Center.

2004: A total of 1.1 million women were recent migrants from Mexico.

2007: An immigration reform bill was introduced.

Source: LaBotz 2006.

of Mexican immigrants, increasing from 300,000 in 1980 to 1.1 million in 2004 (Fry 2005).

WHY DO THEY COME?

The causes of Mexicana migration lie in the economic and political conditions in Mexico and the United States; these conditions represent the local effects of globalization (the increased and faster links between political, cultural, and economic systems) (Rees and Smart 2001). These effects of globalization can be traced to the world economic crisis that started in the 1970s. The crisis was both economic (falling rates of profit, increasing debt, rising oil prices) and political (legitimacy crises and electoral crises). The crisis began to be felt in the United States and Mexico in the 1980s. In the United States, rates of profit fell and well-paid, unionized jobs disappeared as industrial production migrated to multiple sites with cheaper labor. In the United States, wages have never regained their precrisis levels. New jobs in the United States are mainly in the unskilled and semiskilled sectors (Castells 1980; Portes and Walton 1981). In the United States, the demand for cheap labor brought more migrants and more women into the labor force.

Political and legal measures worked to facilitate the movement of capital by reducing barriers to foreign capital. International financial institutions, plus agreements such as the General Agreement on Trade and Tariffs (GATT) and the North American Free Trade Agreement (NAFTA), forced the Mexican government to freeze wages, float the peso, eliminate agricultural price guarantees, reduce subsidies on basic foods, and open Mexican markets to goods from all over the world. Many internal producers went out of business, the price of maize fell, and unemployment increased. The reform of Article 27 of the Mexican

Constitution privatized land and increased landlessness. These conditions benefited the international sector of the Mexican economy: the incomes of the richest 10 percent of the population increased (de la Garza and Salas 2005), but political resistance was widespread and eventually brought down the governing party. These conditions encourage increased migration to the United States.

Legal mechanisms such as NAFTA facilitate the mobility of capital and products, but workers are constrained by immigration and other laws and local practices, and continue to be, if not controlled, at least penalized for their mobility. Major changes in the organization of production and technology did not eliminate, but rather created, "new world borders" (Rees and Smart 2001) that control the human beings who must cross them. Stepped-up border control and

DISPELLING MYTHS ABOUT MEXICAN MIGRATION

1. *Economic Development.* Migrants do not come from the poorest nations but from growing nations: Mexico is the largest source of immigrants to the United States, with an urban, industrialized economy and an average per capita income of about $9,000 (Massey 2005).

2. *Population Growth.* It isn't overpopulation that fuels migration; women in Mexico have an average of only 2.3 children (Massey 2005).

3. *Wages or Other Resources.* It isn't wages, but a lack of other resources, such as credit, mortgages, and insurance that brings Mexican migrants to the United States (Massey 2005).

4. *Public Services.* Immigrants pay taxes and are not a drain on public services in most cases; immigrants are less likely than others to use public services; 66 percent have Social Security taxes withheld, only 10 percent have sent a child to public schools, and under 5 percent have used food stamps, welfare, or unemployment compensation (Massey 2005). Some data do indicate that, especially with regard to refugees, migrants may be a drain on the public coffers (discussed in Massey 1995). Migrants, however, pay sales taxes and some may subsidize Social Security as they often cannot claim Social Security benefits.

5. *Length of Settlement.* Migrants do not stay long: 75 percent stay less than two years (Massey 2005); Steward, Raub, and Elliott (2006) show that the average stay for Mexican males is 11 years. They all say they would return home if they could.

6. *Criminality.* Mexican immigrant men have a lower rate of incarceration (0.7 percent) than U.S. born Hispanics (5.9 percent) or U.S.-born males (3.5 percent) (Rumbaut, Rubén, and Ewing 2007).

7. *Wage Levels.* Immigrants don't lower wages for native U.S. workers, except for those with less than a high school education. They mainly lower wages for other immigrants (Peri 2007).

8. *Cost of Vegetables.* Undocumented immigrants lower the price of vegetables from 3 to 6 percent (Huffman and McCunn 1996).

new immigration laws have not slowed the flow of migrants, but they have made crossing the border more expensive and more dangerous, especially for women. Migrants have reduced the number of their trips home, and this encourages women to migrate to join their husbands (Donato and Patterson 2004). Mexican women migrate to reunite with their husbands in the United States, often helped by women's networks (Hondagneu-Sotelo 1994). Women join their husbands now more than in the past, because their husbands cannot get back home but also because there are more jobs for women.

WHAT DO THEY DO HERE?

Mexican women migrate to the United States to reunify their families, but most of them work for a living: 51 percent worked at least 47 weeks in 2000 (up from 46 percent in 1980), although more of them work part-time than before. Due to changes in the labor market, jobs are temporary, low-paid, and without benefits. Agricultural employment dropped from 10 percent of female migrant labor in 1980 to 6 percent in 2000; employment in manufacturing dropped from 44 percent to 20 percent. A total of 20 percent worked in food service (Fry 2005). Locally, the makeup of the job market varies. Mexican women migrants have moved from California to other states, where they work in the low-paid service sector.

Latina women earn less than other women, but in some places, they earn more relative to men than other groups. In Butler County, Ohio, for example, Hispanic women's income is 62 percent of men's, higher than that of African American and white women (57 percent). This lesser disparity is due to the fact that all Hispanic workers work in the lowest-paying jobs. Women may earn almost the same as men, but both earn the lowest salaries. High rates of female and male employment may contribute to the anti-immigrant backlash and racial tensions (Massey 1995). In Butler County, Ohio, for example, tension is especially high because (white male) workers have lost well-paid industrial jobs and the only jobs available are assembly and light manufacturing jobs that pay $5/hour. Most of the myths about Mexican migration—criminality, welfare use, remittances as a drain on the U.S. economy, lowered wages, permanent settlement, and so forth—are not supported by the data. Migrant households with women present have more stable housing, more income, and higher church attendance than do households consisting only of men (Rees and Miller 2002; Rees and Nettles 2002).

HOW LONG WILL THEY STAY?

Today, Mexicana migrants are more likely to stay in the United States because crossing the border is particularly dangerous for women, who face harassment and assault by the *coyotes* or border crossing agents (Donato and Patterson 2004). Women's occupations may be less visible and thus women may be less at risk of deportation. Women who work in domestic service do not congregate in large numbers like (mostly male) factory workers. Since women migrate, on average, a few years after their husbands, they are less likely to have immigration documents, a situation that may give their husbands a hold over them. Women may also be less likely to leave because their children are U.S. citizens. Most Mexican migrants do not stay their whole lives—men stay an average of 11 years, according to Steward et al. (2006)—but this may be changing.

Some version of an immigration reform bill is likely to be passed before the end of George W. Bush's presidency by August 2007. Current versions include a guest worker status that prioritizes skills over family, which would increase family separation. Guest worker programs create two categories of workers with different rights—guests and hosts—and are rejected by immigrant rights groups such as the National Alliance of Latin American and Caribbean Communities (www.nalacc.org) and the Coalition for Immigrant Rights and Dignity, a local affiliate in Ohio. Some versions contain a punitive "touch-back" provision that would require the head of the family to return to his home country for a period of time; other versions would simply require him to leave through any border and come back.

Immigration reform may increase the likelihood that Mexicanas will migrate to the United States permanently. They, like women everywhere, make decisions based on their perception of how they can support their family values and survive. Current law and policies make it more likely that women will migrate to the United States and that they will stay and raise their families here.

CONCLUSION

The reasons Mexican women migrate are multiple and dynamic. An analysis of the job market, the history of migrant destinations, and migrant employment indicates that male migrants initially leave Mexico because of economic crisis, and that they go where there are jobs. Mexicanas migrate to reunite their families, but only where they, too, can find employment.

Although most say they want to go home, most cannot support themselves in Mexico, and all are afraid of crossing the border under current conditions. They are likely to stay in the United States, forging a new culture of the twenty-first century, with dynamic identities and new kinds of communities. The anti-immigrant discourse refers to some of the myths about immigrants, but also to the cultural changes that this new majority-minority population has already wrought in language, religion, working style, and neighborhood and household structure. The future points the way toward a global labor market reinforced by local, national, and international barriers, producers, and enclaves. Mexican migration supports the United States' Social Security system and lifestyle.

See also Gender and Globalization: Trends and Debates; Immigration: Laws and Policy Concerning Entry into the United States; Work: Paid versus Unpaid.

Further Reading: Castells, Manuel, *The Economic Crisis in American Society* (Princeton, NJ: Princeton University Press, 1980); Cohen, Jeffrey A., *The Culture of Migration* (Austin: University of Texas Press, 2004); de la Garza, Enrique, and Carlos Salas, eds., *State of Working in Mexico, 2003,* Solidarity Center translation, 2005, available at: http://www.

solidaritycenter.org/content.asp?contentid=506, accessed May 18, 2007; Donato, Katharine M., and Evelyn Patterson, "Women and Men at the Border: Undocumented Border Crossing," in *Behind the Smoke and Mirrors: Research from the Mexican Migration Project,* ed. Jorge Durand and Douglas S. Massey, 111–130 (New York: Russell Sage Foundation, 2004); Fry, Richard, *Gender and Migration* (Washington, DC: Pew Hispanic Center, 2005), available at: http://pewhispanic.org/files/reports/64.pdf, accessed June 2007; Hirsch, Jennifer S., *Courtship after Marriage: Sexuality and Love in Mexican Transnational Families* (Berkeley: University of California Press, 2003); Hondagneu-Sotelo, Pierrette, *Gendered Transitions. Mexican Experiences of Immigration* (Berkeley: University of California Press, 1994); Huffman, W., and A. McCunn, *How Much Is That Tomato in the Window? Retail Produce Prices without Illegal Farmworkers* (Washington, DC: Center for Immigration Studies, 1996); LaBotz, Dan, *Migration of Workers to the United States: A Historical Perspective,* 2006, available at: http://www.floc.com/documents/IRHistory.pdf; Massey, Douglas S., "Five Myths about Immigration: Common Misconceptions Underlying U.S. Border-Enforcement Policy," *Immigration Policy in Focus* 4, no. 6 (August 2005): 1–10; Massey, Douglas S., "The New Immigration and Ethnicity in the United States," *Population and Development Review* 20, no. 3 (1995): 631–652; Massey, Douglas S., Rafael Alarcón, Jorge Durand, and Humberto González, *Return to Aztlán. The Social Process of International Migration from Western México* (Berkeley: University of California Press, 1987); Nash, June, "Global Integration and Subsistence Insecurity," *American Anthropologist* 96 (1994): 7–30; Peri, Giovanni, "How Immigrants Affect California Employment and Wages," *California Counts: Population Trends and Profiles* 8 (2007): 1–20; Pew Hispanic Center, 2006, available at: http://pewhispanic.org/; Porter, Alejandro, and James Walton, *Income, Class, and the International System* (New York: Academic Press, 1981); Rees, Martha W., "Ayuda or Work? Analysis of Labor Histories of Heads of Household from Oaxaca," in *Labor in Anthropology,* Society for Economic Anthropology Monographs, vol. 22, ed. E. Paul Durrenberger and Judith E. Marti, 87–110 (Lanham, MD: Altamora Press, 2006); Rees, Martha W., "How Many Are There? Ethnographic Estimates of Mexican Women in Atlanta, Georgia," in *Latino Workers in the Contemporary South: Proceedings of the Southern Anthropological Society,* ed. Arthur D. Murphy, Colleen Blanchard, and Jennifer A. Hill, 36–44 (Athens: University of Georgia Press, 2001); Rees, Martha W., and T. Danyael Miller, with Gonzalo Saldaña, *Quienes Somos? Que Necesitamos? Needs Assessment of Hispanics in the Archdiocese of Atlanta,* Hispanic Apostolate Office and Staff of the Archdiocese of Atlanta, Report to the Archdiocese of Atlanta, March 15, 2002, available at: asweb.artsci.uc.edu/collegeDepts/anthro/pdfsDocs/; Rees, Martha, and J. Nettles, "Los Hogares Internacionales: Migrantes Mexicanos a Atlanta," in *Migración Femenina,* ed. Hacia Ella, Ofelia Woo, and Sarah Paggie (Mexico: Edamex, 2002); Rees, Martha W., and Josephine Smart, "Plural Globalities in Multiple Localities: New World Borders. Introductory Thoughts," in *Local Responses to Globalization,* ed. Martha W. Rees and Josephine Smart, 1–18 (Lanham, MD: University Press of America, 2001); Rumbaut, Rubén, and Walter A. Ewing, *The Myth of Immigrant Criminality and the Paradox of Assimilation: Incarceration Rates among Native and Foreign-Born Men* (Washington, DC: Immigration Policy Center, 2007); Steward, Dwight, Amy Raub, and Jean Elliott, "How Long Do Mexican Migrants Work in the US?" paper presented at the 2006 meeting of the National Association of Forensic Economics, Boston, MA, 2006, available at: http://www.econone.com/resource/sections/61/Mexican_imigrants_work_in_theUS.pdf, accessed June 2007.

Martha Woodson Rees

MILITARIZED PROSTITUTION

The historical legacy of militarized prostitution has been perceived as natural or acceptable by some and exploitative by others. It is important to understand who benefits from this practice and how different feminist perspectives frame the discussion.

BACKGROUND: OPPRESSION OR LEGITIMATE LABOR?

Long before American women were officially allowed to serve in the U.S. Army, women's lives were militarized. Militarization, according to Cynthia Enloe, "is a step-by-step process by which a person or a thing gradually comes to be controlled by the military *or* comes to depend for its well-being on militaristic ideas" (2000, 3). While most women remained at home during the eighteenth-century wars, some women—known as camp followers—accompanied military forces. These women were wives, relatives, and prostitutes whose duties included laundry, nursing, and cooking in addition to providing companionship and sex for servicemen (Nagel 2003). Joane Nagel notes that "Throughout history local women have been involuntarily 'drafted' in the sexual service of militaries as rape victims and sexual slaves" (2003, 181). While there are clear instances of women being forced into militarized prostitution, some feminists argue that women entered this profession of their own accord.

Other scholars describe all prostitutes as victims and do not believe in the existence of voluntary prostitution. Janice Raymond states that prostitution is

---

KARAYUKI-SAN: COMFORT WOMEN

- A total of 100,000–200,000 Asian women from Korea, China, Thailand, Burma, the Philippines, and Taiwan, and white women from the Dutch East Indies were deliberately and brutally forced by the Japanese Government to work as prostitutes for the Japanese Army during World War II (Enloe 1993).

- Despite earlier representations by comfort women survivors and their allies, it was only after Professor Yoshiaki Yoshimi discovered an official document from the 1930s, "Regarding the Recruitment of Women for Military Brothels," that the Japanese government acknowledged that this occurred (Enloe 1993).

- A Survey of Japanese junior high school textbooks shows that the issue of comfort women receives only one or two lines, and the description does not go further than to say that comfort women were treated badly (Sancho 1998).

- The only charges that have been brought against the Japanese were brought by the Batavia Court, which convicted 13 men of forcing Dutch women into prostitution (Choi 1997). The Tokyo War Crimes Trial heard no cases about the Asian comfort women (Choi 1997).

---

violence against all women and not a type of work (2005). On the other hand, Kamala Kempadoo "view[s] prostitution not as an identity—a social or psychological characteristic of women, often indicated by 'whore'—but as an income-generating activity or form of labor for women and men" (1998, 3). In an effort to combat widespread reluctance to include sex work among other forms of labor, Jill Nagle (1997) offers the argument that sex work is emotional labor, not entirely different from massage therapy, childcare, and psychiatry. In further analyzing resistance to the mainstreaming of sex work, Kempadoo suggests that "Perhaps one of the most confounding dimensions in the conceptualization of prostitution as labor concerns the relation that exists in many people's minds between sexual acts and 'love,' and with prevailing ideas that without love, sexual acts are harmful and abusive" (1998, 4). Here Kempadoo challenges Kathleen Barry's (1995) perception of sex as a sacred, emotional, and psychological act that should only be shared privately. Barry's stance is commonly held among feminists and stems from the stereotypical portrayal of women as overly emotional, caring, and sensitive beings who are unable to have sex for pure physical enjoyment. The opposing feminist perspectives of sex work inform the discussion of militarized prostitution without which military histories would be incomplete.

CONTROVERSY: WHO IS BENEFITING?

Three dollars paid for three minutes of intimacy in Hawaii during World War II, and almost 250,000 took advantage of this great deal each month (Enloe 1993). Prostitutes, however, were not available to all men. The reports that Honolulu brothel managers submitted to Hawaii's military governor tell us something about the racial attitudes of soldiers (Enloe 1993). Prior to the war, both white men and men of color received service from Hotel Street brothels, although they used segregated entrances. With the increase in white males, managers began refusing men of color, as a mixed-race clientele might offend white soldiers and lead to a decrease in revenue (Enloe 1993). From this example, it is evident that militarized prostitution is connected to racial issues.

Militarized prostitution is not limited to Hawaii nor is it limited to wartime (Nagel 2003). Even in times of "peace," military bases—not limited to those of the United States—provide "a convenient and lucrative market for the sex industry" (Nagel 2003, 187). Local women, whose sexual labor services soldiers, describe how their relationships with local men as well as their lack of financial support influence their decision to become prostitutes (Enloe 1992). Military bases are among many environments that allow prostitution to take place. Feminists acknowledge that choice is always constrained by the politics of peoples' histories, locations, and globalized economics, yet still question whether these women are victims or workers seeking employment. As militarized prostitution still exists today, there continue to be divergent perspectives on this and other intersecting institutions such as racism, homophobia, globalization, and imperialism.

See also Colonialism and Imperialism; Mail-Order Brides; Military History; Terrorism and National Security.

Further Reading: Alexander, Priscilla, "Feminism, Sex Workers, and Human Rights," in *Whores and Other Feminists,* ed. Jill Nagle (New York: Routledge, 1997); Barry, Kathleen, *The Prostitution of Sexuality* (New York: New York University Press, 1995); Choi, Chungmoo, *The Comfort Women: Colonialism, War, and Sex* (Durham, NC: Duke University Press, 1997); Davidson, Julia O'Connell, *Prostitution, Power and Freedom* (Ann Arbor: University of Michigan Press, 1998); Enloe, Cynthia, "It Takes Two," in *Let the Good Times Roll: Prostitution and the U.S. Military in Asia,* ed. Saundra Pollock Sturdevant and Brenda Stoltzfus, 22–27 (New York: The New Press, 1992); Enloe, Cynthia, *Maneuvers: The International Politics of Militarizing Women's Lives* (Los Angeles: University of California Press, 2000); Enloe, Cynthia, *The Morning After: Sexual Politics at the End of the Cold War* (Los Angeles: University of California Press, 1993); Kane, Tim, "Global U.S. Troop Deployment, 1950–2005," Heritage Foundation, 2006, available at: http://www.heritage.org/Research/NationalSecurity/cda06–02.cfm, accessed April 1, 2007; Kempadoo, Kamala, ed., "Introduction," in *Global Sex Workers: Rights, Resistance, and Redefinition* (New York: Routledge, 1998); Kempadoo, Kamala, ed., *Trafficking and Prostitution Reconsidered: New Perspectives on Migration, Sex Work, and Human Rights* (Boulder, CO: Paradigm Publishers, 2005); Moon, Katherine H. S., *Sex among Allies: Military Prostitution in U.S.–Korean Relations* (New York: Columbia University Press, 1997); Nagel, Joane, *Race, Ethnicity, and Sexuality: Intimate Intersections, Forbidden Frontiers* (New York: Oxford University Press, 2003); Raymond, Janice, "Sex Trafficking Is Not 'Sex Work,'" *Conscience* 26 (2005), http://action.web.ca/home/catw/readingroom.shtml?x=74355, accessed October 3, 2007; Sancho, Nella, *War Crimes on Asian Women: Military Sexual Slavery by Japan During World War II: The Case of the Fillipino Comfort Women, Part II* (Manila: Asian Women Human Rights Council, 1998); Sullivan, Barbara, "Rethinking Prostitution," in *Transitions: New Australian Feminisms,* ed. Barbara Caine, 184–197 (New York: St. Martin's Press, 1995); Sancho, Nelia, ed., *War Crimes on Asian Women: Military Sexual Slavery by Japan during World War II: The Case of the Filipino Comfort Women* (Manila: Asian Women Human Rights Council, 1998).

Nadia Dropkin

MILITARY HISTORY

Whether women should be allowed to participate in the military and what the nature of their participation should be are questions that have long been debated by men and women alike. Controversies surrounding women's active duty in the military stem from long-held views on traditional gender roles; biological arguments that women are not suited for combat; and historical processes in which women have been viewed as outside the realm of war and battle.

BACKGROUND

Historically, women have accompanied the military in its entourage, as families coming along for support, and to cook or clean for the troops as camp followers. Some have also followed for less "honorable" reasons, seeking to make an income by working as prostitutes, a trend that continues today near military bases around the world. Originally, women who wanted to be members of the military had to disguise their gender and masquerade as men in order to serve their country. Nursing was the primary means for women to aid military causes. During World War II, women were finally allowed to enlist in the military, but as members of auxiliary forces. It was not until the 1970s that women were integrated into the various branches of the military, but there were restrictions on the positions they could fill. Even today, while the roles for women have been expanded, they are still barred from many occupations deemed unsuitable for women due to their close proximity to combat.

EARLY PATRIOTS

During the American Revolution, women were present as camp followers. There were also women in uniform, none suspecting their true identity. Among these women was Deborah Sampson, who, under the name Robert Shurtliff, served with the 4th Massachusetts, performing various duties. She was wounded twice, and her gender was not detected until she came down with a fever. Apparently, she was discreetly discharged from service, and resumed life as a civilian (Leonard 1999, 166–68). During the attack on Fort Washington, Margaret Corbin assumed her husband's position on an artillery piece when he fell wounded. Congress awarded her a pension for her heroism in 1779 (Leonard 1999, 102–3).

In the War of 1812, Lucy Brewer, a farm girl from Massachusetts, served on board the USS *Constitution,* or "Old Ironsides," under the name George Baker. It was many years before the Marine Corps would acknowledge that she may well have been the first woman marine. Women would not be recruited for the Marine Corps until 1918 (Wilson 2007).

During the Civil War (1861–1865), women were allowed to aid the war through efforts with the Sanitary Commission or ladies' aid societies, or as nurses. Others, like Jennie Hodgers, disguised their gender in order to fight in combat. Known as Albert Cashier, Hodgers served the duration of the war, and continued in her male persona even after the war (Leonard 1999, 185). Some women served in the role of vivandière, or "daughter of the regiment." While never officially recognized by the military, these women performed various duties, including cooking, cleaning, carrying water for the troops, and flag bearing. Some even fought alongside the men. Marie Tepe, Kady Brownell, and Annie Ethridge were among the more famous vivandières (Leonard 1999, 106–21). After graduating with a medical degree, Dr. Mary Walker was refused a commission as an army surgeon, but served on a volunteer basis in a hospital in Washington, DC. For almost two years she served as a field surgeon, then was appointed assistant surgeon of the 52nd Ohio Infantry. She received the Congressional Medal of Honor in 1865 (Reeves 1996, 83). Raised a slave in Georgia, Susie King Taylor served as a nurse, cook, and laundress with the First South Carolina Volunteers (an all-black unit) (Leonard 1999, 152–53).

With advancements in medicine, preenlistment physicals became more strict, making it nearly impossible for women to "pass" as men in order to serve in the military. Because of the introduction of physical examinations, women could no longer show their teeth and wear bulky clothes in order to pass as adolescent boys. Now they were forced to find alternative ways to aid the military cause.

WOMEN AS NURSES

Nursing was the way for most women to aid the military. Prior to the American Civil War, medicine had been a largely male occupation, even nursing. But it was obvious that women made good nurses, and there was a need within the military to care for wounded soldiers.

During the Spanish-American War, typhoid epidemics ran rampant through the camps. Congress authorized the procuring of female nurses by the U.S. Army. However, these women would not be given military status: they were hired as "civilian contractors." From 1898 to 1901, over 1,500 women served in the U.S. military, on hospital ships and overseas (Reeves 1996, 88–89).

In 1901, the Army Nurse Corps was established. This was mainly to meet the acknowledged need for educated nurses for the military, as well to provide a way to regulate them. The Navy Nurse Corps was established shortly thereafter, in 1908 (Reeves 1996, 90).

In World War I (1917–1918), nearly 21,500 army nurses served in military hospitals in the United States and overseas. Over 250 military nurses died during the war, most from the "Spanish flu" that swept through military camps. During the war, the army recruited bilingual telephone operators to work switchboards in France. The navy enlisted 11,880 women as yeomen to serve stateside, enabling sailors to go to sea. A total of 305 women marine reservists were recruited to fill positions as clerks and telephone operators on the home front to "free men to fight" (Reeves 1996, 97). In 1930, following the war, the National Defense Act was passed, granting military nurses the status of officers with "relative rank" from lieutenant to major, but not with full rights and privileges (Reeves 1996, 98).

WOMEN IN AUXILIARY GROUPS

During World War II (1941–1945), women found additional ways to serve in the nation's military. In addition to the 60,000 army nurses who served, others joined the WACs, WASPs, and WAVES. The Women's Army Auxiliary Corps (WAAC) was established by the army in 1942, then converted into the Women's Army Corps (WAC) in 1943 (Moore 1996, 116). Of the more than 150,000 WACs, thousands were sent to the European and Pacific theaters. The Women Air Force Service Pilots (WASPs) were organized to serve as civil service pilots, flying stateside missions. Of the more than 14,000 navy nurses, at least 16 were held as prisoners of war. Approximately 80,000 women were recruited into the Navy Women's Reserve, called Women Accepted for Volunteer Emergency Service (WAVES) and established in 1942. The Marine Corps created the Marine Corps Women's Reserve in 1943, and the women who joined it served stateside in a variety of clerical and administrative positions. In 1942, the Coast Guard established its Women's Reserve, known as SPARs (after the motto *Semper Paratus*) and these women were also assigned primarily to clerical and administrative posts. By the conclusion of the war, over 400,000 American military women had served in nearly all noncombat jobs. With the establishment of the United States as a world power, it was forced to maintain the largest peacetime military in the history of the nation, but mustered out all but a few servicewomen (Sadler 1999, 40–41).

When women began joining the military in the 1940s, a woman's character and reasoning were called into question. It was thought that she was joining the military to find a husband or find multiple sex partners, or that perhaps she wished she were a man. Yet the majority of these women served with dedication.

During the Korean War (1950–1953), servicewomen who had joined the reserves after World War II were involuntarily recalled to active duty. Over 500 army nurses served in combat zones and many more were assigned to hospitals in Japan. Navy nurses served on hospital ships in the Korean theater as well as navy hospitals stateside. Air force nurses served stateside, in Japan, and as flight nurses in the Korean theater (Reeves 1996, 106–7). Captain Lillian Kinkela Keil (the inspiration for the film *Flight Nurse*) flew hundreds of air evacuation missions during World War II and in Korea while in the Air Force Nurse Corps She was one of the most decorated women in the U.S. military, earning decorations including the European Theater of Operations Medal with Four Battle Stars, the Air Medal with Three Oak Leaf Clusters, the Presidential Unit Citation with One Oak Leaf Cluster; the Korean Service Medal with Seven Battle Stars, the American Campaign Medal, the United Defense Medal, and a Presidential Citation, Republic of Korea (Wilson 2007).

In 1951, the Defense Advisory Committee on Women in the Services (DACOWITS) was created in order to provide advice on the recruitment of military women for the Korean War. Due to pressure from DACOWITS, Congress removed the ceiling on the number of women who could serve and revised the promotion system (Sadler 1999, 42).

Thousands of American military women served in Southeast Asia during the Vietnam War (1965–1975). Over 6,000 army, navy, and air force nurses and medical specialists served. There were over 500 WACs, and 600 women in the Air force stationed in Vietnam. The women served with MASH units, on medical evacuation flights, in operations groups, and in information offices, as well as in other clerical, intelligence, and personnel positions (Wilson 2007).

INTEGRATION OF THE MILITARY

The 1970s saw a great deal of change for women in the American military. In 1970, the chief of the Army Nurse Corps and the Women's Army Corps director were the first women to be promoted to brigadier general. In 1972, the Reserve Officer Training Corps (ROTC) was opened to women. With the end of the draft and the establishment of the all-volunteer force in 1973, the doors were opened to expand the roles and numbers of servicewomen. Between 1976 and 1978, the separate entities for servicewomen, such as the WAC and SPAR, were disestablished and women were integrated into their respective services (Sadler 1999, 42–44).

In the 1990s, the United States had numerous dealings with the Middle East. During the first war in the Persian Gulf (1990–1991), 40,000 American military women were deployed during Operation Desert Shield and Operation Desert Storm. The 1990s also saw important legislative changes for women, including the National Defense Authorization Acts of 1992 and 1993, which repealed the combat exclusion laws the prohibited women from permanently being assigned to combat aircraft. In 1998, during Operation Desert Fox, a woman fighter pilot delivered a payload of missiles and laser-guided bombs in combat. This was the first time in American history that a woman had served in such a combat role (WIMSA MF 2007).

As of 2003, servicewomen were still barred from several positions. In the army, they are not allowed in the infantry, armored units, special forces, combat engineer companies, ground surveillance radar platoons, and air defense artillery batteries. In the Air Force, they are not allowed to serve as combat controllers, in para-rescue, and in those units and positions that routinely collocate (are embedded) with direct ground combat units. In the navy, they are not allowed in submarines, coastal patrol boats, mine warfare ships, SEAL (Special Forces) units, joint communications units that collocate with SEALs, and support positions (such as medical or chaplain) that collocate with Marine Corps units that are closed to women. In the Marine Corps, they are not allowed in infantry units at the level of regiments and below, artillery units at the level of battalions and below, all armored units, combat engineer battalions, reconnaissance units, riverine assault craft units, low-altitude air defense units, and fleet antiterrorism security teams. In the Coast Guard, all positions are available to women (WIMSA MF 2007).

CONTEMPORARY CONCERNS

In general, the integration of women into the military has been slow and uneven. The need for women's involvement has peaked according to the nation's need, especially in times of war. It was in World War I, World War II, the Korean War, and the Vietnam War that the numbers of women involved, and seeking involvement, reached their highest points. However, there have always been women who have wanted to serve and have been denied. In the twenty-first century, with the United States military stretched across various points around the globe, women could be an asset.

Sexual tension has been cited by many opponents of women's participation to explain why women should not be allowed in the military. The concern is over possible sexual relations that could result in unwanted pregnancy, or cause conflict when facing combat, as in the argument that a man would be more likely to protect his lover than fight for his country. Studies have been conducted, however, showing that gender-integrated combat units are as effective as male-only combat units, and that the members of these units are more likely to develop brother-sister binds than sexual bonds (Peach 1996, 167).

With regard to pregnancy, the historical argument against allowing women in combat was their conflicting roles as mothers, or potential mothers. It is the notion of protecting the nation's childbearers. While the argument remains that women lose more duty time than men due to pregnancy, this may not be accurate if the rates of men's loss of duty time for being absent without leave, for desertion, for drug and alcohol abuse, and for confinement are tallied. While pregnancy does prevent a woman from serving to her fullest capacity, women's potential to be mothers should not prevent all women from serving. (Peach 1996, 170–71). Women still have to contend with the image of women as caregiver and the argument that women are more "naturally" suited to caring for others, and thus that they are best as carers for a child once it is born (Herbert 1998, 28).

Another argument against the inclusion of women in the military has been that women are weaker than men. It is the societal understanding that women, being "feminine," are weaker than and inferior to "masculine" men. (Herbert 1998, 68). The scenario depicted is that of a woman of inferior physical strength leaving a comrade behind. While this might have been a worthy argument in years gone by, the modern age of warfare relies more on technology and button pushing than on physical contact with the enemy (Peach 1996, 168).

Republican members of the House Armed Services Committee pushed a provision (Section 574) in the 2006 Defense Authorization bill (H.R. 1815) that would bar women from serving in "any unit below brigade level whose primary mission is to engage in direct combat on the ground." After objections from the Pentagon and the army, the committee adopted a revised amendment. However, the revised amendment incorporates language from a 1994 memorandum, which excludes women from assignment to forward areas "exposed to hostile fire" and with a "high probability of direct physical contact with the hostile force's personnel." If this wording were to be incorporated into federal law, within the army, more than 20,000 forward support and related positions currently open to women could be closed (Shiozaki 2005).

There are several issues relevant to women beyond their being barred from certain military jobs. In 2006, a survey taken at the Citadel indicated that sexual assault is a problem. Of the 118 female cadets (of whom 114 responded) nearly 20 percent reported having been sexually assaulted since they started classes. A total of 68 percent reported experiencing sexual harassment, usually on campus and involving another cadet. An Associated Press (AP) investigation indicated that in 2005 more than 1,000 potential female recruits were victims of sexual misconduct by recruiters. The Department of Defense has failed to implement a military-wide system of data collection on reports of incidents of sexual assault and harassment. Women like Suzanne Swift, who reported being sexually harassed and raped, have found no justice after reporting the situation to the military authorities. There are reports of U.S. service members sexually assaulting and raping civilian women in the Middle East (Shiozaki 2006).

Women are currently serving with distinction in Iraq and Afghanistan. All soldiers, regardless of their specialty, are "in harm's way." Interestingly, during the Vietnam War, nearly three-quarters of all military women were subjected to combat positions (Peach 1996, 156). The very concept of warfare has changed, since there is no longer a "front line." The mission of the "direct ground combat" (DGC) troops is still the same. Direct ground combat is engaging or attacking the enemy with deliberate offensive action under fire. Current Defense Department regulations require that direct ground combat units be male. Support units that are embedded (collocate) with smaller direct ground combat battalions 100 percent of the time are to bar female soldiers. However, army officials have placed female soldiers in forward support companies (FSCs), which do collocate with all-male infantry/armored maneuver battalions 100 percent of the time, although the secretary of the army and other officials claim that female soldiers will not be present when DGC units are "conducting" direct ground combat. Additionally, the army has dropped multiple launch rocket systems (MLRS) and Reconnaissance Surveillance and Target Acquisition (RSTA) squadrons from the list of DGC units coded to be all male, without Department of Defense authorization or notice to Congress. Therefore, while women may be gaining admission to units from which they were once barred, this is not official or sanctioned. Any changes within the structure of the military need to be formally made so that accountability can be enforced (CMR 2007).

CONCLUSION

Throughout American history, women have shown determination to join the military. When women were barred entirely, and physical exams were lacking, numerous women disguised their gender to join the military. When that was no longer an option, women turned to nursing as a means to aid their nation's military. But this was not enough. Gradually, women gained recognition for their efforts, and in the 1970s women were integrated into the military forces of the United States.

However, there are many positions from which women are barred because of regulations intended to keep women from direct combat situations. In this age of modern warfare, there are no longer certain front lines. Women have proven that they are capable of fighting alongside men and should be allowed admittance to the remaining positions. In light of escalating military involvement around the world, soldiers are needed. Why should qualified women be turned away?

See also Comparable Worth; Equal Rights Amendment; Glass Ceiling; Lesbians and Gays in the Military.

Further Reading: Center for Military Readiness (CMR), "Background and Facts: Women in or near Land Combat," April 10, 2007, available at: http://www.cmrlink.org/WomenIn Combat.asp?DocID=271; Herbert, Melissa S., *Camouflage Isn't Only for Combat: Gender, Sexuality, and Women in the Military* (New York: New York University Press, 1998); Leonard, Elizabeth D., *All the Daring of the Soldier: Women of the Civil War Armies* (New York: W. W. Norton, 1999); Moore, Brenda L., "From Underrepresented to Overrepresented: African American Women," in *It's Our Military, Too! Women in the U.S. Military*, ed. Judith Hicks Stiehm (Philadelphia: Temple University Press, 1996); Peach, Lucinda Joy, "Gender Ideology in the Ethics of Women in Combat," in *It's Our Military,*

Too! Women in the U.S. Military, ed. Judith Hicks Stiehm (Philadelphia: Temple University Press, 1996); Reeves, Connie L., "The Military Woman's Vanguard: Nurses," in *It's Our Military, Too! Women in the U.S. Military,* ed. Judith Hicks Stiehm (Philadelphia: Temple University Press, 1996); Sadler, Georgia Clark, "From Women's Service to Servicewomen," in *Gender Camouflage: Women in the U.S. Military,* ed. Francine D'Amico and Laurie Weinstein (New York: New York University Press, 1999); Shiozaki, Mai, "From the Citadel to Military Recruiting—Sexual Harassment in Military More Pervasive than Ever," September 1, 2006, available at: http://www.now.org/press/09–06/09–01.html; Shiozaki, Mai, "Military Veteran Calls Combat Support Ban Discriminatory, Dangerous," May 24, 2005, available at: http://www.now.org/press/05–05/05–24-b.html; Wilson, Captain Barbara A., "Military Women Veterans: Yesterday—Today—Tomorrow," April 10, 2007, available at: http://userpages.aug.com/captbarb/; Women in Military Service for America Memorial Foundation, Inc. (WIMSA MF), "Highlights in the History of Military Women," April 10, 2007, available at: http://www.womensmemorial.org/Education/timeline.html.

Darla Bowen

NATIONALISM

Debates concerning women and nationalism involve contrasting views on women as biological and cultural reproducers, on whether women should participate in political processes and nationalist movements, and on how nationalist ideologies either exclude or include women as citizens.

BACKGROUND

Nationalism, or national identity, comprises the commonly held beliefs and feelings that unite the members of a nation. Nationalism is mobilized for both positive and negative reasons. Nationalism is constantly shifting and changing, redefined in response to historical legacies, in light of current realities, and with an understanding of future possibilities. Patricia Hill Collins defines a nation as "a collection of people who have come to believe that they have been shaped by a common past and are destined to share a common future" (2000, 229). The people who inhabit nations generally share a common language, cultural practices, a sense of common history, and an identity that makes them different from those outside the national collective. Together, they share a sense of belonging to what some scholars call an "imagined community," since nation-states are human-made constructions that have developed, in elaborate ways, throughout modern history (Anderson 1983). A nation, however, does not require a geographic territory. Rather, multiple nations can occupy one nation-state. For example, Native American nations have national identities distinct from that of the U.S. nation-state. And nations can transcend the boundaries of nation-states; for example, Chicanos/as living in the United States often feel that they are part of the Mexican nation despite their geographic location outside of the Mexican nation-state.

Nationalist ideologies are often mobilized in order to justify processes of war making and militarization: People go to war in the name of the nation. For example, the so-called war on terror is waged in the name of protecting the U.S. nation-state and U.S. nationalistic ideals of freedom and democracy. Anti-state struggles are also often framed by ideas of nationalism and national identity. The antiapartheid struggle in South Africa is an example of a revolutionary movement that mobilized nationalist ideologies in order to resist the nation-state. The Palestinian movement is another example of an ethnic and religious community mobilized on the basis of nationalism; in this case, those who support this struggle wish Palestine to be acknowledged as an independent nation.

While feminist scholars have become increasingly interested in nationalism, traditional scholarship on nationalism and national identity has failed to examine the role of women in the nation. Women have traditionally been seen as marginal to the nation and insignificant in the establishment of national identity, despite their important roles in movements both for and against nation-states, both on the left and on the right. To counter this historical omission, feminist scholars have examined how ideas of citizenship and national belonging are gendered, raced, and classed. By examining how the "ideal" citizen is constructed, feminists have illustrated how nation-states are based on an ideal citizen type that tends to privilege those who fit within that mold while marginalizing segments of the nation deemed inferior, both

FEMALE SUICIDE BOMBERS

The increasing phenomenon of female suicide bombers is an issue of great controversy because according to traditional gender ideologies, women are not expected to play such militant roles in defending a nation or national community. In 1985, the first known female suicide bomber drove a truck into an Israeli Defense Force truck, killing two soldiers (Zedalis 2004). One study documents the fact that between 1985 and 2006, there were 220 female suicide bombers worldwide, comprising nearly 15 percent of the total number of suicide bombings in that time period (Schweitzer 2006, 8). While stereotypes of women as docile and innocent have allowed many female suicide bombers to be successful, some religious leaders and organizations have voiced strong opposition to women's martyrdom through suicide bombings. Because female suicide bombers tend to garner significant media attention, are less likely to be searched at checkpoints, and are increasingly seen as a necessity for nationalist movements with a scarcity of soldiers, some male-based nationalist movements have increasingly supported them (Zedalis 2004). Hamas and the High Islamic Council in Saudi Arabia, among others, use the rhetoric of necessity as a justification for the use of female suicide bombers. They argue that it has become necessary for women to participate in suicide bombings for both tactical and personnel reasons, that is, because of the depletion of male suicide bombers (Zedalis 2004). The entry of women into the role of suicide bomber illustrates how in times of war and conflict women's responsibility to and role in the nation shifts and changes.

formally and informally. For example, many observers have pointed out that people of color, women, and gays and lesbians have been excluded from the citizen rights afforded to those of heterosexual, European/white, male backgrounds.

WOMEN AS BIOLOGICAL REPRODUCERS OF THE NATION

According to scholars of women and nationalism, women are typically viewed in their traditional gender roles, as both biological and cultural reproducers of the nation. Biologically, women are responsible for reproducing the next generation of citizens, thus making their reproductive lives of prime importance to the nation. Within different contexts, women are either encouraged to reproduce or discouraged from reproducing. Nira Yuval-Davis (1997) has identified three primary nationalist discourses that serve to shape how women's reproductive capacity is conceptualized in relation to the nation: the people as power discourse, the eugenics discourse, and the Malthusian discourse.

The people as power discourse is based in the belief that the survival of the nation is dependent upon its continual growth. The need for people can arise for a variety of reasons. For example, the nation may need soldiers to sustain a military struggle, or in order to provide a continuous supply of laborers necessary for economic growth. This discourse generally encourages women to produce new members of the nation, at times admonishing women who choose not to reproduce. Within the context of this discourse, reproduction is women's national duty. The people as power discourse is intimately tied to the eugenics discourse when some citizens or national members are encouraged to reproduce while others are discouraged from reproduction.

The eugenics discourse is more concerned with the "quality" of the nation rather than the size of the nation. The eugenics discourse has been mobilized historically and continues to be used today. Nazi Germany provides the clearest historical example of a nationalist eugenic project. Also of importance to feminists is the historical legacy of sterilizing certain populations in order to prevent the reproduction of certain groups of people. Within the U.S. context, sterilization campaigns have targeted Native American women and women of color. Currently, we can see the eugenics discourse mobilized both in the United States and internationally. Patricia Hill Collins argues that welfare policies that serve to discourage poor women of color from reproducing are fundamentally rooted in a eugenics discourse, continuing the legacy of forced sterilizations (2006). Within an international context, the prime minister of Singapore has deemed it the patriotic duty of highly educated women to reproduce and has offered a cash award to poor, uneducated women who agree to be sterilized (Yuval-Davis 1997, 32). Supporters of eugenicist policies believe in defending a nation's "purity," typically on the basis of race, and in their view women play a central role in either contaminating or purifying the nation.

The Malthusian discourse is focused on decreasing national growth overall. This discourse is rooted in the fear that unregulated population growth will lead to the economic and political collapse of the nation. The Chinese population control policy is the clearest example of the implementation of the Malthusian discourse. The Malthusian discourse tends to have gendered effects. For example, because male children are often more highly valued than female children for social and economic reasons, in many situations where nationalist policies limit women's reproductive capacity we also see high rates of selective abortion and infanticide directed at female children.

Critics of these three approaches argue that policies, laws, and cultural practices should not be directed at women simply because they are responsible for childbearing. Because societal values play important roles in shaping people's ideas about national belonging and about gender roles, these observers argue that women should be viewed as contributors to the public realm of politics, economics, and culture as much as biological reproducers, if not more than as biological reproducers (Yuval-Davis 1997).

WOMEN AS CULTURAL PRODUCERS OF THE NATION

In addition to their role as biological reproducers of the nation, women are also typically viewed as cultural reproducers of the nation. According to this view, women contribute to the cultural reproduction of the nation in two distinct ways. First, women are traditionally responsible for teaching the next generation of citizens the cultural traditions and ideologies of the nation. Through their roles as mothers and caregivers, women have the power to either reinscribe or transform national ideologies. Second, women exist as the symbolic boundary markers of the nation. Through "proper" clothing and "proper" behavior, women embody and perform the collective understanding of national gender identities (Yuval-Davis 1997, 46). When women transgress their traditional position within the nation they are often ostracized by the nation, or in extreme circumstances eliminated from the nation. On the other hand, women who defend "proper" behavior are often rewarded for their efforts and seen as important leaders of change.

Recent demographic changes in the United States, partly catalyzed by immigration patterns, have challenged scholars' understandings of women's role as cultural and biological reproducers. For example, transnational adoption pushes us to question the significance of women as the biological reproducers of the nation. Scholars have begun to question what it means for a nation when the idea of common blood can no longer be imagined. Furthermore, the increasing presence of foreign-born domestic workers and nannies forces us to develop new ways of understanding who can contribute to the reproduction of the nation (Ehrenreich and Hochschild 2002; Hondagneu-Sotelo 2001). Understanding how certain populations actively contribute to the reproduction of other nations and understanding the effects of this transnational reproduction process are increasingly relevant.

FEMALE PATRIOTS: WOMEN AND NATIONALISM DURING TIMES OF WAR AND CONFLICT

Women's relationship to the nation is constantly shifting and changing, particularly during times of war and conflict. Traditionally, women have been defined as those most in need of protection, and men have been defined as those most capable of protecting them: men go to war in the name of the nation in order to protect women and children. History has shown, however, that women are increasingly incorporated into armed struggle, as armed combatants, when the survival of the nation is dependent on their participation. This trend is most clearly seen in nationalist revolutionary struggles, such as the Sandinista revolution in Nicaragua and the antiapartheid struggle in South Africa, and in cases where voluntary service does not fill the necessary ranks, as is currently the case in the United States.

Some scholars have argued that women's incorporation into the military is a precondition for women's achievement of full citizenship. This argument is based on the belief that dying for one's nation is the ultimate citizenship duty and that full citizenship rights are conditional upon one's willingness to fulfill this duty (Yuval-Davis 1997, 93). However, there are two general outcomes of women's incorporation into a nation's armed forces. First, when women are incorporated into armed struggle because of a lack of willing and capable male soldiers, we see a general rolling back of women's roles in the military and in the nation once armed struggle has ended. Women are mobilized when necessary and then expected to retake their marginalized position when their labor is no longer needed. Second, even when women are incorporated into a nation's military, there still generally exists a sexual division of labor. For example, women have been increasingly incorporated into the U.S. military; however, they are still

RADICAL NATIONALIST ORGANIZATIONS AND GENDER IDEOLOGIES

Nationalist organizations focused on creating a "pure" or "ideal" national body exist around the world. Aryan Nations, based in the United States, is one such organization. Founded in 1974 by Pastor Richard G. Butler, Aryan Nations preaches racial and religious purity, wishing to turn North America, and the United States in particular, into a land in which only white Christians reside (Aryan Nations). Their rhetoric is anti-Semitic and often misogynistic.

While Aryan Nations is run by men, many women who share similar ideals have created similar organizations. For example, an organization called Women for Aryan Unity, based in Canada, utilizes traditional female roles to promote Aryan purity in Canada and the United States. These women believe that their roles as wives and mothers are under attack and that the best way women can contribute to the Aryan movement is to "keep [your husband's] home, provide for his comfort and teach your children well" (Women for Aryan Unity). Drawing on the people as power discourse, organizations such as Women for Aryan Unity utilize stereotypical images of women as wives and mothers as part of their campaign to increase the number of national members.

Organizations like Aryan Nations and Women for Aryan Unity utilize nationalist ideologies to create a common understanding among their members. The members of these organizations collectively imagine their "ideal" nation and actively (often violently) work to make it a reality.

prohibited from serving on the front lines and are not fully incorporated into elite forces such as the Green Berets and the Special Forces divisions. Thus, while women give their lives for the nation, we have yet to see an example of a national military that fully incorporates women on equal terms with men for a sustained period of time. Women's incorporation into the armed forces of the nation continues to mirror women's marginalized relationship to the nation in general.

CONCLUSION: GENDER AND NATIONALISM IN A GLOBALIZING WORLD

Demographic changes brought about by global changes, including immigration as well as economic globalization, are challenging scholars to develop new understandings of nationalism and national identity. As people are increasingly crossing borders, nationalism is becoming less tied to citizenship and geographic location. It is becoming more common for individuals to live in a nation-state with which they do not identify or to identify themselves as members of more than one national collective. Furthermore, the rise of transnational economic agreements and global militarization has created a context in which the policies of one nation-state greatly affect the lives of those in other nation-states. For example, transnational trade agreements such as NAFTA (the North American Free Trade Agreement) and CAFTA (the Central American Free Trade Agreement) tie the citizens of North America together in new and complicated ways. The realities of globalization challenge scholars of nationalism to develop new ways of understanding national identity beyond, within, and across borders. Those who study women's relationships to nationalism must take these new transnational processes into account, in addition to continuing to ask important questions about why and how specific groups of women choose to either support or defend their nations, and how and under what circumstances certain women are (or are not) considered full citizens according to the laws and nationalist ideologies that shape their experiences of belonging to a nation.

See also Colonialism and Imperialism; Military History; Terrorism and National Security.

Further Reading: Anderson, Benjamin, *Imagined Communities: Reflections on the Origin and Spread of Nationalism* (New York: Verso, 1993); Aryan Nations, "About Aryan Nations," available at: http://www.aryan-nations.org/about.htm, accessed May 13, 2007; Blee, Kathleen M., *Inside Organized Racism: Women in the Hate Movement* (Berkeley: University of California Press, 2003); Ehrenreich, Barbara, and Arlie Russell Hochschild, eds. *Global Woman: Nannies, Maids, and Sex Workers in the New Economy* (New York: Owl Books, 2002); Grewal, Inderpal, *Transnational America* (Durham, NC: Duke University Press. 2005); Hill Collins, Patricia, *Black Feminist Thought: Knowledge, Consciousness, and the Politics of Empowerment,* 2nd ed. (New York: Routledge, 2000); Hill Collins, Patricia, *From Black Power to Hip Hop: Racism, Nationalism, and Feminism* (Philadelphia: Temple University Press, 2006); Hondagneu-Sotelo, Pierrette, *Doméstica: Immigrant Workers Cleaning and Caring in the Shadows of Affluence* (Berkeley: University of California Press, 2001); Luibhéid, Eithne, *Entry Denied* (Minneapolis: University of Minnesota Press, 2002); McClintock, Anne, *Imperial Leather: Race,*

Gender, and Sexuality in the Colonial Context (New York: Routledge, 1995); Schweitzer, Yoram, "Introduction," in *Female Suicide Bombers: Dying for Equality?* ed. Yoram Schweitzer, 7–12 (Tel Aviv: Jaffee Center for Strategic Studies, 2006), available at: http://www.tau.ac.il/jcss/memoranda/memo84.pdf, accessed May 13, 2007; Smith, Andrea, *Conquest: Sexual Violence and the American Indian Genocide* (Cambridge, MA: South End Press, 2005); Women for Aryan Unity, "Unity and Comradeship!" available at: http://www.crusader.net/texts/wau/, accessed May 13, 2007; Yuval-Davis, Nira, *Gender and Nation* (Thousand Oaks, CA: Sage, 1997); Zedalis, Deborah D., "Female Suicide Bombers," in *Carlisle Papers in Security Strategies*, 2004, available at: http://www.strategicstudiesinstitute.army.mil/pubs/display.cfm?pubID=408, accessed May 13, 2007.

Jill Williams and Damaris Del Valle

NATURE VERSUS NURTURE

Whether individual behaviors, actions, and identities are shaped by innate biological factors (nature) or by environmental factors (nurture) is highly controversial and debated at length in scientific, legal, and popular-cultural arenas. In particular, people are divided over whether gender and sexual identities are acquired through learned behavior or through genes.

BACKGROUND

The phrase *nature versus nurture* refers primarily to the debate on biological determinism versus social constructionism. In this debate, *nature* implies that one is "born that way," whereas *nurture* implies that one is a "product of the environment" that surrounds us. Biological determinism is the belief that a person's genes, as opposed to environmental factors, determine a person's behaviors and actions. There are very few people who strictly adhere to the idea that genetic makeup is entirely responsible for actions because, as scientific studies have shown, there is little research to support such a hypothesis (Fausto-Sterling 1985). However, a number of people believe that certain traits are encoded into our DNA and are then triggered to affect our behavior or identity, including sexual or gender identity.

Theories rooted in social constructionism start from a different point of departure and often present a challenge to theories of biological determinism. Social constructivist theories of identity posit that behaviors or actions are a result of learned environmental factors in a person's specific social or cultural surroundings. Supporters of this approach believe more often than not that the socially constructed environment is the sole factor in shaping actions, behaviors, and the development of identities. In contrast, supporters of biological determinism either believe that "biology is destiny" or there is a combination of influences that include both biology and culture. Most supporters of biological deterministic theories of identity hold mixed views, as it is much harder to prove conclusively that environmental factors have nothing to do with actions, behaviors, or identities, because researchers cannot control for environmental factors

(Fausto-Sterling 1985). Because everyone grows up immersed in culture and society, the mixed view holds, it is hard to control for its effects on individuals. This is one of the reasons why the nature versus nurture debate has continued without any conclusive resolution. It is simply too difficult to prove, one way or the other. However, there are a great many people who believe that while many attributes or behaviors are socially constructed, certain aspects of them may be encoded in our DNA. In both camps, most supporters believe in a combination of nature and nurture, although there is disagreement on which one is more influential in our development.

DEBATES ON NATURE VERSUS NURTURE: GENDER ROLES AND SEXUAL IDENTITY

Current debates on nature vs. nurture have centered primarily on two general issues: gender roles and sexual identities.

Gender Roles: Are Men Naturally Superior to Women?

Gender roles have been one of the most frequently argued issues in the broader nature/nurture debates. Historically, sex and gender were seen as biologically determined and one and the same. Philosophers Simone de Beauvoir (1952) and Michel Foucault (1978), along with several other feminist theorists, have challenged the notion that gender roles are derived entirely from biological sex and that these two categories are inseparable. Generally, contemporary social-scientific and medical theory distinguishes between sex as being rooted in the biological differences between biological males and females, whereas gender encompasses the social roles, norms, and attitudes attributed to the sexes. Especially beginning with second-wave feminism in the 1960s, some traditional arguments, such as the idea that women are "naturally" caregiving, more fit to raise children because they give birth to them, began to be questioned and re-thought.

In contrast, in the nineteenth century, some scientists thought that any women who worked outside the home were setting themselves up for "a struggle against nature" (Bagehot 1879). While the traditional viewpoint of many societies argues that there are natural differences between women and men, such as strength, intelligence capabilities in specific areas, and nurturing and caregiving roles, contemporary feminists questioned the naturalness of these differences. However, recent scholars have pointed out that even these feminists often, ironically, used similar naturalist arguments to assert their points of view. These scholars' arguments hinged on debating *what* was natural, not *whether* anything was (Smith and Carroll 2000). Other more recent feminist arguments have emphasized that biological reasoning has been used historically to attempt to legitimate misogynistic practices, arguments, and structures.

For example, sociobiologists have argued that evolutionary history informs our sexual relationships. They argue that "Man's natural sexuality sends him in search of many sex partners, making him an unstable mate at best, while woman's biological origins destine her to keep the home fires burning, impelling her to employ trickery and deceit to keep hubby from straying" (Fausto-Sterling 1985). In this example of "natural" ideology, men are inherently oversexed, while women are inherently trying to trap a man. Here the stereotypes of women as passive, deceitful, and manipulative and men as aggressive and incapable of commitment are seen as natural instead of resulting from social constructions of men and women's gender roles. These particular stereotypes have been challenged by feminists, who assert that they benefit only men and are used as a justification for violence against women, cheating by men in stable relationships, and retaliation against women who refuse to fulfill their traditional gender roles in the household and elsewhere.

Another focus of feminist debate and controversy concerns women's education, due to the supposedly inherent differences between men and women. Historically, hysteria, in which a woman's womb "wandered," and damage to reproductive organs was believed to be the result of women's attempt to learn (Fausto-Sterling 1985). Women were not allowed to go to college or even to read or write, while men were encouraged to do so for a great deal of modern Western history. Eventually, upper- and middle-class white women secured the right to create women's colleges in the late nineteenth century, and later secured the right to attend "male" colleges. Until the latter part of the twentieth century, women were told to learn different things, even in college, such as home economics or food preparation, instead of math or science. The increasing numbers of women in college and in math and science majors is a direct result of women's rights advocacy for increased opportunities and an acknowledgment that these supposedly inherent differences in ability to learn were in fact a result of stereotypes about gender that manifested themselves in differing relationships between teachers and students rather than a result of natural biological differences. Thus, now, many observers point out that it is not that women are inherently worse at math and science due to brain size or capacity, but instead that women are not given the opportunities to learn math and science at a young age, and are not typically encouraged to study these subjects while young boys are.

The recent emphasis on nature versus nurture by feminist scholars is in response to the second wave of feminist activism that occurred during the 1960s and the 1970s. Betty Friedan's 1963 publication, *The Feminine Mystique,* addressed the question of whether women actually belonged in the home or not. For a great many years, white middle-class women were expected to rear children and be homemakers while their husbands worked for pay in the public sphere. Friedan and several other liberal feminists challenged the idea that women were natural caregivers and should be relegated to the private (versus public) sphere. They explained that this supposedly natural caretaking role was simply a way for society to keep women in positions of servitude and inequality (Friedan 1963). As a result of these feminist arguments, more women began working outside the home and agitating for public recognition of women's equality.

In general, feminists have taken a remarkably wide array of stances on the idea of gender as biologically based or socially constructed. In particular, radical cultural feminists, who believed in biological differences and were sex repressive, were pitted against radical libertarian feminists, who adopted a social construc-tionist approach and were sex positive, as they both tried to interrogate issues of patriarchy as the root of oppression (Tong 1998). Radical cultural feminists noted the biological differences between men and women and held up menstru-ation and childbirth as means with which to acknowledge a "women's culture." They then used this "women's culture" to posit that "women are [inherently] gentler and kinder than men." The strategy for activism would be for a "women's culture" to infiltrate male-dominated spaces to affect change, for example, to eliminate conflicts such as wars and to gain equity in pay and other areas of inequality (Tong 1998). This ideology clearly accepts "natural" biological deter-minism in women's actions and identities, and while it was present in the sec-ond wave of feminism it was also present in many early feminist writings of the first wave, such as the work of Jane Addams in the early years of the twentieth century. Radical cultural feminists, however, did not see a distinct "women's cul-ture" in which all women were inherently more gentle and kind than men. In-stead they viewed patriarchy as encouraging these ideas, which were biologically unfounded, in order to oppress women and keep them in the home.

As feminist thought expanded, the debate over whether or not certain ste-reotypical feminine traits were inborn or socially constructed continued. Ju-dith Lorber, who wrote "Night to His Day: The Social Construction of Gender" (1993), an often-quoted feminist text on these ideas, explains that gender is so endemic in our ways of life, through our gender roles and sex-stereotyping ac-tivities, that most people inherently believe their gender is inborn. However, she argues that the characteristics that seem so inborn are actually gender roles that we attribute to ourselves as a result of our social environment. Lorber shows that different societies do not view men and women in the same way. For example, historically or cross-culturally, third genders, including *hijras,* neither men nor women in Indian society, and *kathoey,* biologically born males who grow up as women in Thailand, exist (Nanda 2000). Showing how gender identity varies by culture calls attention to the ways in which it is a product of culture (nurture) rather than biology (nature).

Sexual Identity: The Causes of Homosexuality

The other current controversy that draws much attention to debates on na-ture versus nurture concerns the cause of homosexuality. Historically, the cause of homosexuality has often been the subject of scientific research studies look-ing for a biological reason for variances in sexual identity. One of the more re-cent and famous studies in this area was conducted by a gay scientist, Simon LeVay, in the late 1980s. LeVay's study of the postmortem brains of 35 men and six women found that a section of the hypothalamus was not as large in the gay men and the women as it was in the heterosexual men studied (LeVay 1991). His research conclusions met with heavy criticism in the medical profession and the media, and gays and lesbians themselves were divided over the issue. Crit-ics argued that LeVay's study sample was not nearly large enough to prove the validity of these results, and that most of the men included in the study had died from complications from AIDS, which was not controlled for in the study. To further complicate matters, in the following year Laura S. Allen and Roger Gorski performed a similar study of the anterior commissure on a larger number of men, with the opposite result (Allen and Gorski 1992). A couple of years later, Canadian researchers found that the corpus callosum was 13 percent thicker in gay men (Hogan and Hudson 1999).

While most of the early studies designed to find the biological cause of homosexuality focused almost entirely on gay men, lesbians were included in the "Finger-Length Ratios and Sexual Orientation" study (Williams et. al. 2000). In this study it was found that lesbians have a more masculinized ring finger to pointer finger ratio than other women. The researchers assert that this is due to prenatal exposure to androgen hormones. The hypothesis is that lesbians are more exposed, in the womb, to androgens than other women, and that these factors vary for homosexual men depending on how many older brothers they have. Marc Breedlove, one of the researchers conducting the study, asserts that nearly 15 percent of homosexual men would not be homosexuals if their mothers had not had as many sons before they were born (Williams et al. 2000).

More recent studies involving twins, and studies carried out to isolate gene traits, have been less ridiculed than some of the previously mentioned studies. Twin studies find higher rates of homosexuality between identical twins than between fraternal twins or single sisters or brothers, but the correlation is still far from 100 percent. While they are still looking to prove causation, most studies now hold that there may be a genetic predisposition to homosexuality, but that genes do not work in isolation from the environment, as the identical twin studies reveal (Hogan and Hudson 1999).

In contrast, many other researchers have focused more on the question of the environment and its role in shaping gay, lesbian, or heterosexual identities. One issue concerns the fact that scientists tend to focus on genetic makeup or biology whereas social scientists and humanities scholars tend to focus on studies of culture and environment. It is often difficult to bring together these disparate fields of study. Furthermore, gays and lesbians themselves are divided on whether their identification as gay stems from biology or culture, just as many women are divided on where their desire (or lack thereof) for parenting and household responsibilities stems from, nature or nurture. Recent examples from queer studies and transgender studies illustrate the complexities involved in arguing for a purely nature or a purely nurture approach to identity, roles, and expectations.

ADDITIONAL RECENT DEBATES

Generally speaking, both queer and transgender studies scholars have provided important critiques of earlier feminist, medical, and sociological views on nature versus nurture. Queer theory, which is founded on the premise that gender and sexual identities are socially constructed and regulated, has challenged heteronormativity, or the centrality of the heterosexual experience, in feminist understandings of men's and women's gender roles and biologies. Philosopher Judith Butler, author of *Gender Trouble* (1990), explicitly challenges assumptions about "biology as destiny" in her examination of gender as performance. In this widely cited publication, Butler identifies gender as performative, meaning that it is remade in an image of itself over and over again, supporting the idea that there is no true gender. As queer theory is heavily influenced by poststructuralist and postmodernist thought, the foregrounding ideology is the idea that gender is first and foremost constructed.

Drawing from queer theory yet in contrast to it, transgender theory is divided on whether identities are socially constructed or are inherent in the person and therefore biologically based. Some transsexuals believe that they are "trapped in the wrong body" and support the idea of biological foundations for their gender and sex identities. However, some transgender and genderqueer people believe the opposite, that their identities are more fluid than that, and they exhibit themselves as proof. Many of these differences are demarcated by generation: the younger the transidentified person is, the more often s/he will view sex and gender in less scientific, binary terms (Beemyn and Rankin forthcoming).

Intersexed people (formerly known as hermaphrodites), who are born as not only male or female, have made visible their political struggle for a rethinking of the medical codification of sex as rooted in dichotomous biological terms. Since the 1950s, individuals born with ambiguous genitalia (genitalia being the marker for male or female in current Western medical practice) have often undergone sex assignment surgeries shortly after birth in order to make their genitalia conform to a male or female sex category. Some intersexed adults who have survived these surgeries have grown up to discover that their medically assigned gender is incorrect; they have then chosen to switch genders, going against the medical advice originally given to their parents. The individuals who have chosen to make public their struggle are advocating for a different medical protocol, one that is not based on biology but rather on socialization; they are asking doctors to wait for children to grow to a certain age and to decide upon their own gender before having to undergo invasive medical procedures. In essence, then, these advocates are making visible the fact that even sex is socially constructed, in the sense that the medical and psychological fields have socially defined the medical protocol for treating individuals based on genitalia and other body parts, rather than on people's own ways of identifying themselves in terms of gender and/or sexual identity (Chase 1998).

CONCLUSION

Most contemporary feminist and queer theorists emphasize nurture or social constructionism as the prominent explanation for individual action, behaviors, and identities. Often it is argued that searching for a biological cause of gender and sexual identities should not matter. What should matter is the elimination of the social inequalities that exist based on sex, gender, and sexual identity. There is a great deal of literature and a general understanding in many communities that society has at least a modicum of influence on identities and actions. Essentially, in the struggle for human rights, it should not matter whether some identity or action is biologically based or caused by environmental factors. Yet the source of gender and sexual difference continues to be much debated in cultural, political, scientific, and religious terms, and will surely continue to influence the policies and laws concerning those who do not fit within prescribed gender and sexual roles, including gay men, lesbians, bisexuals, and transgendered people. Those who believe that we should be asking a different kind of question, instead of the question of how nature shapes us, argue that people should be treated equally regardless of the reasons for differences between them. However, the nature versus nurture debates surrounding gender and sexual roles, expectations, and identities are likely to continue without resolution for quite some time.

See also Femininities and Masculinities; Gender Socialization; Sex versus Gender; Sexual Identity and Orientation.

Further Reading: Allen, Laura S., and Roger Gorski, "Sexual Orientation and the Size of the Anterior Commissure in the Human Brain," *Proceedings of the National Academy of Sciences of the U.S.A.* 89, no. 15 (1992): 7199–71202; American Psychiatric Association, *Diagnostic and Statistical Manual of Mental Disorders*, 4th ed., text revision (Washington, DC: American Psychiatric Association, 2000); Bagehot, W., "Biology and 'Woman's' Rights," *Popular Science Monthly* 14 (1879): 201–213; Beemyn, Brett-Genny, and Sue Rankin, *Understanding Transgender Lives* (forthcoming), preliminary data from study available at: http://www.umass.edu/stonewall/uploads/listWidget/9002/Understanding%20Transgender%20Lives.pdf, accessed May 24, 2007; Butler, Judith, *Bodies That Matter: On the Discursive Limits of "Sex"* (New York: Routledge, 1993); Butler, Judith, *Gender Trouble: Feminism and the Subversion of Identity* (New York: Routledge, 1990); Butler, Judith, *Undoing Gender* (New York: Routledge, 2004); Chase, Cheryl, "Hermaphrodites with Attitude: Mapping the Emergence of Intersex Political Activism," *Gay and Lesbian Quarterly* 4, no. 2 (1998): 189–211; de Beauvoir, Simone, *The Second Sex* (New York: Alfred A. Knopf, 1952); Fausto-Sterling, Anne, *Myths of Gender: Biological Theories about Women and Men* (New York: Basic Books, 1985); Fausto-Sterling, Anne, *Sexing the Body: Gender Politics and the Construction of Sexuality* (New York: Basic Books, 2000); Foucault, Michel, *The History of Sexuality: An Introduction* (New York: Random House, 1978); Friedan, Betty, *The Feminine Mystique* (New York: W. W. Norton, 1963); Hogan, Steve, and Lee Hudson, *Completely Queer: The Gay and Lesbian Encyclopedia* (New York: Owl Books, 1999); LeVay, Simon, "A Difference in Hypothalamic Structure between Heterosexual and Homosexual Men," *Science* 253, no. 5023 (1991): 1034–1037; Lorber, Judith, *Paradoxes of Gender* (New Haven, CT: Yale University Press, 1993); Nanda, Serena, *Gender Diversity: Cross-Cultural Variations* (Long Grove, IL: Waveland Press, 2000); Smith, Hilda L., and Bernice A. Carroll, *Women's Political and Social Thought: An Anthology* (Bloomington: Indiana University Press, 2000); Sullivan, Andrew, *Virtually Normal: An Argument about Homosexuality* (New York: Alfred A. Knopf, 1995); Tong, Rosemarie, *Feminist Thought: A More Comprehensive Introduction* (Boulder, CO: Westview Press, 1998); Williams, Terrance J., Michelle E. Pepitone, Scott E. Christensen, Bradley M. Cooke, Andrew D. Huberman, Nicholas J. Breedlove, Tessa J. Breedlove, Cynthia L. Jordan, and Marc S. Breedlove, "Finger-Length Ratios and Sexual Orientation," *Nature* 404 (2000): 455–456.

Kai Kohlsdorf

PLASTIC SURGERY, TATTOOING, AND PIERCING

Women's decisions to modify the external appearance of their bodies through plastic surgery, tattooing, or piercing have been promoted by some as expressions of women's freedom to control and enhance their physical appearance. Opponents contend that they can be socially coerced forms of self-mutilation used by women who feel pressure to conform to societal stereotypes of the "ideal" physical appearance.

BACKGROUND

In 1959, the first Barbie doll was introduced; it would signify to many the ideal look of the female body for many years to come. Women such as Marilyn Monroe would be idealized by men as the "perfect woman." On the other hand, the fashion industry would set the feminine ideal as being that of a little, thin girl lacking adult female characteristics (Thesander 1997). By 1965, this would change, with the introduction of the miniskirt, which changed the female look by once again aiming to sexualize and objectify women. The women's liberation movement rejected the ideals of femininity found in magazines and moved to have clothes desexualized. Women began to rebel against the feminine ideal, which they felt contributed to sex discrimination and inferior roles in society. Some women stopped using makeup and stated that the body was to be accepted as it was and didn't need to be "improved" (Thesander 1997).

During the 1970s, the natural ideal blossomed, with a lessening in the use of corsets and bras. In the 1980s, the body ideal changed with the introduction of physical fitness as the new standard. More demands were placed on the look of the physical body than on clothing. Women used exercise to obtain firm bodies, slim waists, and narrow hips (Thesander 1997). The shaping of women's breasts made a comeback with the use of underwire bras. Women began to wear male-inspired clothing, such as suits, in the workplace. Many believed that looking younger and more physically attractive would enhance their social lives. For women who could not meet the new body standards, plastic surgery became a new way to meet this ideal.

In the late 1980s, a new curvy and full-busted woman was introduced into fashion as the ideal. Many women now had established jobs and were able to pay for plastic surgeries, and many felt that this ability empowered them. They could now change their bodies with the aim of increasing their self-esteem and self-confidence. Body modification, including plastic surgery and the more recent tattooing and piercing trends, all represent ways in which women of particular age groups and socioeconomic backgrounds have developed forms of expression related to beauty. Whereas plastic surgery has become more culturally acceptable over time (although still controversial), and many women undergo this type of body modification as a way to acquire normative, traditional beauty standards, tattooing and piercing have been adopted by younger generations as a means to call traditional beauty standards into question. Debates continue as to whether these forms of body modification are culturally acceptable, and much depends upon the socioeconomic and cultural context within which each type of modification occurs.

HISTORY OF PLASTIC SURGERY

Today there are a number of readily available procedures for permanently modifying the external appearance of the body. These procedures include semipermanent liposuction to reduce body fat; botox and collagen injections to reduce wrinkles; minimally invasive but permanent tattoos and makeup; body piercing; and more invasive procedures such as outpatient surgery, required for face and body tightening and face, breast, and buttock implants, and major surgery required for gender reassignment.

The contemporary word *plastic* comes from the Greek word *plastikos,* which means "to mold" or "to give form." The term was first coined in 1818 by Carl Ferdinand Von Graefe, who developed surgical remedies for certain eye disorders. Plastic surgery can be traced back to over 2,600 years ago in Egypt and India. Hindu texts of that time describe nose, ear, and lip reconstruction techniques. These would use skin grafts and pedicle flaps to change the form of the body. In Egypt, the "Edwin Smith Papyrus" provides descriptions of surgeries used to manage facial trauma. Later on, both the Greeks and Romans created texts, such as *De Medicina* and *Synagogue Medicae,* that would detail the use of reconstructive surgery. The use of surgery as a way to reconstruct damaged and/or altered anatomy would continue through the Middle Ages and the Renaissance, even though there were few surgical developments over these years.

By the late 1890s, there was a shift from performing plastic surgery for reconstructive reasons only to what is now called cosmetic surgery. The introduction of anesthesia and sterilization techniques created a shift to more modern forms of surgery. Cleft lip repair, palate repair, and skin grafting became an option for those seeking the physical enhancement of their bodies. The development of microinstruments in the 1950s would change the range of possibilities for both reconstructive surgery and cosmetic surgery. While facelifts and other forms of cosmetic surgery were commonly undergone by American film stars and the wealthy during the second half of the twentieth century, in the 1980s increasing numbers of ordinary people were opting for such surgery. There was a 175 percent growth rate in cosmetic surgery during the 1990s (Ciaschini and Bernard 2007). Currently, liposuction is the most common cosmetic surgery performed, followed by breast augmentation. Women most commonly have liposuction and breast operations, while men most commonly opt for nose and/or eyelid surgery (Thesander 1997).

TATTOOING AND PIERCING

In contrast to plastic surgery, tattooing and piercing have emerged more recently in many U.S. subcultures. Tattooing, creating permanent designs on the body by applying dyes through punctures in the skin, is probably the most popular form of body adornment in America today (UPM, "Tattooing," 2007). Tattooing is commonly practiced in cultures around the world and has a history that dates as far back as ancient Egypt. This cultural history, however, also highlights the gender issues associated with tattoos and other body modifications. Until contemporary times, Maori men in New Zealand had extensive, painfully applied facial tattoos that were meant to impress and intimidate opponents in battle, while Maori women had tattoos only on the lips and chin. Meanwhile, even today throughout Africa, girls' faces are extensively and painfully scarified to create patterns of scar bumps, sometimes dyed, that are considered attractive, both to look at and to touch, by male suitors (UPM, "Tattooing," 2007). As with piercing, tattooing has become increasingly popular among American teenagers since the 1990s. Permanent makeup, an increasingly popular form of body modification particularly for women, involves the use of techniques similar to those used for tattooing.

Piercing, involving cutting a hole through the skin or a body part and inserting an ornament of metal, bone, glass, and so forth, also has a long history and

---

BODY TATTOOING: DID YOU KNOW?

According to a survey of over 1,000 people conducted by the Scripps Howard News Service and Ohio University, about one in every seven adults in the United States has a tattoo; 30 percent of people between the ages of 25 and 34 have tattoos; about 28 percent of adults younger than 25 have tattoos; and in all, the members of the post–baby boomer generation are more than three times as likely than boomers to have tattoos.

Source: American Tattooing Institute, http://www.tatsmart.com/tattoo_statistics.

---

is commonly practiced around the world (UPM, "Piercing," 2007). Throughout history, and still today, the most commonly pierced body parts have been the ear lobes, with the number of ear holes and earrings often signifying social status for both men and women. A recent variation on this practice in the United States is the stretching of ear lobes through the insertion of large disks or weights. Lip and nose piercings and rings are also commonly found in various cultures around the world today. Starting in the early 1990s, a body art movement that espoused extensive body piercing and tattoos has grown in popularity particularly among American teenagers as a form of self-expression and rebellion against conventional social norms (Pitts 2003). More extreme piercings now include piercing of tongues, navels, nipples, and genitals.

FEMINIST DEBATES ON BODY MODIFICATION: EMPOWERMENT AND SELF-ENHANCEMENT VERSUS MISOGYNY AND SELF-MUTILATION

Feminist scholars have long debated whether (especially extreme forms of) body modification are beneficial or detrimental to women. Feminist scholars of the 1970s criticized beauty practices that caused women to diet and use makeup; they viewed these practices as conforming to masculine aesthetic standards that ultimately caused women to feel that their bodies were somehow inadequate in their natural state. By the 1980s and 1990s, however, this critique itself came under attack by newer generations of feminist scholars, who argued that feminism had given women the choice of using makeup and body modification technologies to feel good about themselves, not just to conform to the standards of men in their lives or to a male-dominated society. Postmodern feminists, influenced by discourse analysis, pointed out that the body was merely a text that

THE BOTOX REVOLUTION

In 2002, the Food and Drug Administration accepted the use of Botox in minimizing the appearance of glabellar lines, otherwise known as wrinkles, paving the way for the much-publicized Botox parties held in cities around the country. With new, easy access to a relatively inexpensive form of body modification, women as well as men have undergone Botox injections as a way to get rid of unwanted wrinkles, bags under their eyes, or sagging skin related to aging. Especially in upper-middle-class communities, Botox parties have been held in salons and individual women's homes, where a licensed cosmetic surgeon is called in for the day to administer injections to women, while the remaining attendees enjoy elaborately presented food, wine, and conversation. Unlike earlier days, when women (and men) often retreated to special spas in places such as Palm Springs, California, to recover, sometimes for weeks at a time, from invasive cosmetic surgeries, today, Botox allows women the freedom to acquire a sense of beauty quickly, with less bodily invasion, and less expensively than surgery. Now that many salons offer Botox and chemical peels alongside hairstyling and manicures, these forms of modification have become normalized by those who use them.

could be modifiable at will. Extreme modifications through extensive tattoos and piercings and through surgery were thus idealized as a form of creative self-expression (Jeffreys 2005).

Some scholars also consider weight lifting and exercise routines as expressions of body modification, although weight lifters' and exercise practitioners' bodies are often seen as works of nature, despite the very active modification taking place as people train. Eric Gans points out that all of these types of body modification—weight lifting, tattooing, piercing, and surgery—are ways in which people turn their bodies into created exhibits of "the arbitrary and painful meaningfulness of the inscribed sign" (Gans 2000, 160). According to this view, body modification becomes a narrative, where each succeeding modification creates both significance for and a historical record of the person's life. Such modifications are particularly attractive to a youth culture rebelling against conventional social norms and exalting their freedom and mastery to achieve "the gratuitous and unproductive extremes of physical and spiritual experience" (Gans 2000, 165). While erotic needs are clearly a major motivation for body modifiers, Gans also notes that the self-description of many body modifiers as "modern primitives" reflects a desire to "humiliate the flesh," a harkening back to ancient self-sacrificial, self-flagellating practices in the name of spiritual enlightenment.

While Victoria Pitts' (2003) interviews with body modifiers confirm many of the emotional and political motivations and fulfillments described by Gans (2000), Pitts is ultimately not entirely comfortable with the postmodern feminist idea of the body as a purely created object. She sees mixed messages in the meanings women ascribe to their body modifications, wonders about the extent to which such ascribed meanings are merely reactions to conventional social norms, and is concerned that important distinctions of race, gender, sexual orientation, social class, and so forth are glossed over by an emphasis on the created body. Finally, she asks, where does the emphasis on individual control of the body fit in with a feminist perspective on social reality that emphasizes the relationships and interconnections between people?

In contrast, Sheila Jeffreys (2005) argues that beauty practices in Western societies, ranging from the use of cosmetics to cosmetic plastic surgery, are "harmful cultural practices." In this view, the culture of Western male dominance causes the common occurrence of socially accepted practices that harm women. The idea of harmful cultural practice has already been recognized by international human rights organizations with regard to the brutal body modification of female genital mutilation, practiced in various African, Middle Eastern, and Asian countries. Such mutilation includes but is not limited to the cutting off of the clitoris of girls to deliberately reduce sexual pleasure and ostensibly ensure marital fidelity. Jeffreys argues that in Western societies women have in the past been willing to put toxic chemicals on their faces and force restrictive diets on themselves to conform to male conceptions of the ideal physical form for women. She is alarmed that now women are demonstrating an increased willingness to have their bodies cut into, with body parts removed or implants inserted, as a response to this societal coercion.

WHAT IS BODY DYSMORPHIC DISORDER?

Body dysmorphic disorder (BDD) is a psychiatric diagnosis (American Psychiatric Association 2000) characterized by a preoccupation with minor or imaginary physical flaws usually of the skin, hair, and nose, such as acne, scarring, facial lines, marks, pale skin, thinning hair, excessive body hair, and a large or crooked nose. There can be intense anxiety and stress about the perceived flaw, and a large amount of time will be spent focusing on it. People with BDD tend to have various types of cosmetic surgeries to try to correct the "flaw(s)." Even if the surgeries are successful, many are unhappy with the outcomes.

Source: MedicineNet.com, 2007.

Jeffreys (2005) describes the ancient Chinese body modification practice of foot binding, in which girls' feet were crushed and the girls consequently crippled, so that when they were adults they could wear tiny pointed shoes, considered erotic by Chinese men. She then compares this brutal practice with the crippling injuries suffered by contemporary Western women wearing fashionable pointed, stiletto-heeled shoes. Her analyses include a discussion of how the increased practice and exhibition of male transvestism/transsexualism, starting in the 1970s, in which men adopted "feminine" beauty practices, demonstrated that such practices were not, in fact, "natural" to women and that in men's minds such practices were about sexual subordination. She argues that the growth of the pornography and prostitution industries during the 1970s also helped influence new fashion norms for women, which, in some cases, involved increasing amounts of flesh being exposed. Jeffreys concludes by arguing that, in such a coercive society, the idea that women have the ability to freely "consent" to the self-mutilation inherent in body modification procedures is dubious at best.

Psychiatrist Armando Favazza (1996) provides clinical support for Jeffrey's argument by drawing parallels between body modification and clinically defined self-mutilation, a syndrome involving repeated self-injury. He argues that what often drives both self-mutilators and those who engage in body modification is the desire to relieve troublesome symptoms of overwhelming anxiety, racing thoughts, and depersonalization. Self-mutilation relieves such symptoms by creating the illusion of control. Also consistent with Jeffrey's argument is the higher incidence of self-mutilation among women as compared to men and the association of self-mutilation with eating disorders, which are also heavily female biased. Surveys of college students have found that having body modification is associated with psychopathic tendencies, nonconformity, and low self-esteem (Nathanson, Paulhus, and Williams 2006), while approval and reported future likelihood of cosmetic surgery in college women was associated with greater media and family/friends' exposure to such procedures and with greater self-reported importance of appearance for self-worth (Delinsky 2005).

CONCLUSION

In Western societies, advances in medical technology and in women's economic resources and personal freedom have spurred a large increase in women's use of body modifications ranging from tattooing and piercing to cosmetic plastic surgery. While some feminist theorists and many women who have such body modifications done argue that such modification is personally empowering, there is evidence to suggest that these modifications are quite possibly unconsciously coerced reactions to ideals of the feminine form set by a still male-dominated society. At the very least, women will continue to hold a variety of views on their own participation in cosmetic surgery, tattooing, or piercing, and observers remain divided on whether these cultural practices are empowering or harmful to women, or perhaps a bit of both.

See also Barbie and the Feminine Ideal of Beauty; Beauty Industry; Self-Injury and Body Image.

Further Reading: American Psychiatric Association, *Diagnostic and Statistical Manual of Mental Disorders,* 4th ed., text revision (Washington, DC: American Psychiatric Association, 2000); American Society of Plastic Surgeons (ASPS), "Cosmetic Surgery: Procedures at a Glance," 2007, available at: http://www.plasticsurgery.org/patients_consumers/procedures/CosmeticPlasticSurgery.cfm?CFID=78213228&CFTOKEN=44248911, accessed May 12, 2007; Ciaschini, Michael, and Steven L. Bernard, "History of Plastic Surgery," 2007, available at: http://www.emedicine.com/plastic/topic433.htm, accessed May 18, 2007; Delinsky, Sherrie S., "Cosmetic Surgery: A Common and Accepted Form of Self-Improvement?" *Journal of Applied Social Psychology* 35 (2005): 2012–2028; Favazza, Armando R., *Bodies under Siege: Self-Mutilation and Body Modification in Culture and Psychiatry* (Baltimore: Johns Hopkins University Press, 1996); Gans, Eric, *The Body Aesthetic: From Fine Art to Body Modification* (Ann Arbor: University of Michigan Press, 2000); Jeffreys, Sheila, *Beauty and Misogyny: Harmful Cultural Practices in the West* (London: Routledge, 2005); MedicineNet.com., "Body Dysmorphic Disorder," 2005, available at: http://www.medicinenet.com/body_dysmorphic_disorder/article.htm, accessed May 15, 2007; Nathanson, Craig, Delroy L. Paulhus, and Kevin M. Williams, "Personality and Misconduct Correlates of Body Modification and Other Cultural Deviance Markers," *Journal of Research in Personality* 40 (2006): 779–802; Pitts, Victoria L., *In the Flesh: The Cultural Politics of Body Modification* (New York: Palgrave Macmillan, 2003); Sarwer, David B., Thomas Pruzinsky, Thomas F. Cash, Robert M. Goldwyn, John A. Persing, and Linton A. Whitaker, *Psychological Aspects of Reconstructive and Cosmetic Plastic Surgery: Clinical, Empirical, and Ethical Perspectives* (Philadelphia: Lippincott Williams and Wilkins, 2006); Thesander, Marianne, *The Feminine Ideal* (London: Reaktion Books, 1997); University of Pennsylvania Museum (UPM), "Tattooing," available at: http://www.museum.upenn.edu/new/exhibits/online_exhibits/body_modification/bodmodtattoo.shtml, accessed May 18, 2007; University of Pennsylvania Museum (UPM), "Piercing," available at: http://www.museum.upenn.edu/new/exhibits/online_exhibits/body_modification/bodmodpierce.shtml, accessed May 18, 2007.

Julie Nagoshi and Craig Nagoshi

POLITICAL PARTIES

Many people believe that electing more women to political office will work to achieve gender equality and change the policies and issues considered in the national agenda. Others argue that a representative's personal identity is irrelevant, because the electoral concerns of constituents are the dominant concerns.

BACKGROUND

As of 2007, women comprise 16.3 percent of Congress, which ranks the United States in 66th place in terms of women's equality in politics worldwide. At the local level, women comprise 23.5 percent of state legislators. Why are women so dramatically underrepresented in politics when they comprise about 50 percent of the total population? Women's exclusion from equal representation in politics is based on the masculinized status quo of politics. Women have made, and continue to make, slow progress toward political equality, but face unique obstacles to gaining equal representation in elective politics. Scholars have identified a variety of explanations for women's underrepresentation, ranging from cultural norms and stereotypes to institutional barriers keeping women from gaining political equality with men.

HISTORICAL DEVELOPMENTS

After the suffrage movement and the passage in 1920 of the Nineteenth Amendment, granting the women the right to vote, it was expected that women's involvement in elected politics would dramatically increase. While the first woman elected in her own right to the House of Representatives was Janette Rankin, a Republican from Montana (where women gained the right to vote in 1914), in 1916, women did not vote or run for office in large numbers. In fact, women did not vote in nearly equal numbers to men until 1968, and women's entrance into elected office progressed slowly. The first women in Congress were widows and their purpose was to serve out their dead husbands' terms as token leaders rather than as serious members of Congress. Working on behalf of their deceased husbands legitimized their involvement in the traditionally masculine field of politics and also served to de-legitimate their involvement in the political process. From the beginning, elected women representatives were seen not as equals to their male peers but as token representatives of their deceased husbands.

For example, in 1922, Rebecca Felton, a Democrat from Georgia, was appointed by the governor to serve as the first woman in the U.S. Senate. During her time in office, Congress never met and she never had the opportunity to vote. Nellie Taylor Ross, the first woman governor, was elected in 1925 and replaced her deceased husband. In 1932, Hattie Caraway, a Democrat from Arkansas, won election to the U.S. Senate after serving out the rest of her deceased husband's term. It was not until 1948 that Margaret Chase, a Republican from Maine, was elected in her own right as a U.S. senator.

The political climate for women began to change during World War II as women entered the workforce in large numbers to replace men who were serving in the military. This paved the way for the cultural changes of the 1960s, which contributed to more opportunities for women in politics. In 1964, Patsy

Takemoto Mink, a Democrat from Hawaii, became the first woman of color and the first woman of Asian–Pacific Islander descent to serve in the House of Representatives, and in 1968, Shirley Chisholm of New York became the first African American woman to serve in the House of Representatives.

By the 1970s, research on women in politics began to emerge. In 1971, the Center for American Women in Politics (CAWP) at Rutgers University was established; it remains the leader in statistical and empirical research regarding women in politics. In the beginning, researchers could only speculate about the differences women as legislators would make, because of the lack of women politicians. In 1984, Geraldine Ferraro became the first woman to run for vice president on a major party ticket. She ran on the Democratic ticket. In 1989, Ileana Ros-Lehtinen, a Republican from Florida and of Cuban decent, became the first Hispanic woman elected to the House of Representatives.

Research on women in politics exploded after the unprecedented increase in female representatives in the 1992 election, dubbed "the year of the woman." The election was unique in that a record number of women ran for office and won. There were several reasons why 1992 was such a successful year for women candidates. First, the Anita Hill hearings raised awareness about women's lack of representation and involvement in the nation's highest offices. Second, the record number of open seats available during the 1992 election increased the number of women in Congress, as open seats are much easier for new candidates to win. Finally, the campaign environment in general favored women. At this time, Nydia Velasquez became the first Puerto Rican woman to serve in the House of Representatives, and Carol Moseley Braun, an Illinois Democrat, became the first African American woman and the first woman of color to be elected to the U.S. Senate. Because of the dramatic increase in women legislators in 1992, researchers began to document the obstacles to women's political representation, the difference women make in legislative agendas, and the role gender plays in legislative decisions.

In 2001, history was made as Representative Nancy Pelosi (D-CA) was elected by her colleagues as the House Democratic whip, making her the highest-ranking woman in the history of the U.S. Congress. In 2007, Pelosi made history again as she became the first female Speaker of the House of Representatives, achieving the highest-ranking office a woman has ever held in elective U.S. politics.

DEBATES ON WOMEN'S POLITICAL REPRESENTATION

When discussing women in politics, it is important to have a clear understanding of representation in general. Descriptive representation is based on the idea that because a representative is a member of a certain group, he or she will be representative of that group. It is often thought that increasing descriptive representation will lead to better substantive representation, which represents group interests (Pitkin 1967). Alternatively, others argue that the connection between the representative and the interests of the constituents is the most important factor in determining a representative's behavior and not their personal identity markers. For example, women as a group do not necessarily share monolithic, distinct interests and thus one woman can't be counted on to represent the interests of all women.

There is a range of ideological views of women's increased visibility in the traditional political area. In feminism, two dominant theories are used to support women's involvement in politics. These are equality feminism (liberal feminism) and difference feminism (Burrell 2004). Advocating for increased representation of women in politics in order to achieve numerical parity with men is within the boundaries and expectations of liberal feminism. Liberal feminism has a commitment to autonomy and choice and advocates these freedoms for women as well as men. Liberal feminism is often critiqued for not challenging the standards, rules, or structures themselves, but advocating for equal access to the established framework. For example, Ruth Bader Ginsburg spent much of her life's work advocating for women's equal position under the law, but is often critiqued for not acknowledging that the laws and structures themselves uphold the status quo and were created and maintained by men.

By contrast, difference feminism relies on the understanding that women and men are inherently different and that women will bring to politics different styles and approaches that will change the institution to better reflect women's needs and interests. Difference feminism is based on the premise that women's oppression stems from associating the differences between men and women with social constructions, cultural attitudes, ideologies, socialization, and organizational structures. This branch of feminism can be problematic, as advocating for differences between men and women can often work against the overall feminist project of advancing women's stance in society, as it can be used to limit or deny women's equality with men. For example, pregnancy has been used to demonstrate women's unique difference from men and thus demonstrate that women are worthy of special rights in the workplace, but conversely, it can be used to advocate that women's worth is based solely on reproduction and thus provide a justification for limiting women to the home.

DO WOMEN MAKE A DIFFERENCE?

One large area of academic research is the substantive difference women make in politics. In particular, scholars aim to find out if having more women in politics transforms or engenders the political arena, or if their mere participation is enough to create feminist political change. One scholar who has studied the difference women make in Congress is Michelle Swers. Through her research, Swers (2002) has found that gender and other identity markers do make a difference in terms of the policies, issues, and interests addressed in the congressional agenda. In particular, she has found that Democratic and moderate Republican women are more committed to the pursuit of women's interests than are their male colleagues. Female representatives pursue the interests of women, children, and families most strongly at the bill-sponsorship level, demonstrating women's commitment to women's issues. While legislators are limited by their positions within the institution and their concern for the political context, their gender still makes a difference in their commitment to women's issues in public policy.

NANCY PELOSI'S 2007 VICTORY

Nancy Pelosi, the highest-ranking woman in U.S. politics to date, became the first female Speaker of the House of Representatives on January 4, 2007. She represents the Eighth District of California, which includes the San Francisco area, and has done so since 1987. Speaker Pelosi made history previously when she became the first female House Democratic leader. Speaker Pelosi comes from a political background; both her father and brother served as mayors of Baltimore. Prior to her election to Congress in 1987, Speaker Pelosi served in a variety of leadership positions, for example, as chair of the California Democratic Party. She also raised five children with her husband, Paul Pelosi, prior to her Congressional career.

While Democratic women are seen as leaders in feminist and women's legislation, moderate Republican women play an interesting role in supporting women's issues in politics and clearly show the limitations and constraints of their party. For example, moderate Republican women are more able to pursue liberal women's issues when their party is in the minority, because they are expected to bring along their contingent of votes. When the Republican Party is in the majority, however, Republican women generally reduce their support for liberal positions on women's issues and stick to the party line because they risk retaliation by party leaders. Furthermore, liberal women's groups tend to lobby these Republican women in the hope of generating policy changes, and this, again, complicates their stance within their party and makes their balancing act even harder.

In addition to sponsoring women's legislation, women politicians are often used to attract women voters to their party. This can be advantageous for women legislators as it allows them to advance policies for women to some degree. Thus, women become spokespeople or political symbols for their party on certain issues. For example, the Democratic Party highlights its women representatives in order to emphasize and expand its preexisting advantage in terms of female voters and support of women's issues. Conversely, Republicans highlight their women legislators in order the combat the Democratic efforts to paint Republicans as opposed to women's policies.

Overall, research demonstrates that increasing the presence of women in Congress allows for the introduction of more gender-related policy issues. However, in addition to increasing the number of women, activists and supporters of women in politics must continue to pay attention to women's place within the institution, such as their committee membership and their level of seniority, as well as their party status, as in majority or minority status and seniority within the party itself, in order to achieve women's continued goal of parity with men in politics.

BARRIERS TO WOMEN IN POLITICS

Scholars have documented a variety of explanations for women's underrepresentation in politics. The first barrier to women's equal representation is cultural stereotypes and attitudes (Lawless and Fox 2005). Cultural stereotypes are based on gendered expectations about appropriate behavior for men and women. Gender stereotypes associate behaviors and expectations with men and women based on preassigned notions of gender-appropriate behavior. For example, people often say politics is "not a women's place" or is "too dirty" for women, because men are stereotypically seen as better leaders and better able to make difficult decisions on certain issues such as foreign policy, law and order, and the economy. Furthermore, women are stereotypically seen as more responsible for social and moral issues and are viewed as more honest, more trustworthy, and better able to understand ordinary people. These gender stereotypes encourage men and women to assume different gender roles in society and they specifically work against women who upset those gendered norms when they run for political office.

Societal rejection of women and discrimination against them is much less overt now than in the past, but gender expectations and stereotypes still persist and affect women running for office. For example, women candidates, regardless of party, are seen as more liberal than men; they are less likely to think about running for office, they don't consider themselves qualified for public office, and they are less likely to be told to run. Also, concerns about balancing family and work cause women not to run for office. However, conditions have improved for women candidates. While in the 1930s, 60 percent of U.S. citizens rejected the idea that there should be more women in politics, a poll of 1,000 adults taken for *Newsweek* in December 2006 found that 86 percent of respondents said that if their party nominated a woman for president, they would vote for her if she were qualified for the job (Alter 2006).

The second barrier to women in politics is media bias. There is a wide variety of academic research that documents the different treatment of male and female candidates by the media as well as the different candidate communication styles of men and women (Witt, Paget, and Matthews 1994). For example, women candidates receive less issue coverage and are portrayed as less viable than men; and the media focus on women's personal characteristics such as their hair, age, marital status, family, personality, appearance, and clothes while highlighting men's issue positions, voting records, and leadership abilities. This affects women's credibility as candidates, which can then affect a voter's decision to vote for a woman candidate.

The third barrier to women in politics is family demands. Motherhood and politics are often seen as mutually exclusive, and those who challenge this myth often upset gender and cultural stereotypes. The prevailing social attitude is that women with children are less suited than other people for public office. For example, politicians are expected to travel away from their home and keep odd hours, which do not fit in with familial responsibilities; and familial responsibilities do not allow a candidate to fully commit to political responsibilities. In order to compensate for this conflict of interest, women politicians are either childless, have fewer children, delay their entrance into politics because of their children, remain single, or marry a supportive spouse.

A fourth barrier to women in politics is the political institution itself. As has already been mentioned, familial and political responsibilities conflict with each other. Furthermore, issues surrounding money and fundraising have been a huge problem for women in the past (Burrell 1998). For example, women candidates are usually newcomers to the political field and therefore lack knowledge of and access to the fundraising mechanisms necessary to run a successful campaign. One way women have combated this problem is the implementation of women's political action committees (PACs), which have dramatically increased women's fundraising efforts. Now, women such as Patty Murray and Hillary Clinton are top fundraisers for their party. Feminist scholars have also found that women generally do not financially support women who run for office, because of their historic exclusion from higher-paying jobs and their lack of control of familial income.

Another problematic factor for women is the single-member, winner-take-all district (in which scholars have found that women fare less favorably than in proportional representation districts). In addition, certain districts are less likely to elect women because of certain characteristics specific to women-friendly districts. Palmer and Simon (2006) identify these characteristics as urban settings in upper middle class neighborhoods. Woman-friendly districts are defined as districts that, based on geographic and demographic characteristics, are more likely to elect women (Palmer and Simon 2006). Democratic women tend to represent districts that are upscale, diverse, and highly urbanized, while Republican women represent districts that are upscale, less conservative, more urban, and more diverse than those of their white male Democratic counterparts.

The most problematic factor women face is incumbency, as the political system favors those with prior political experience or those who have previously run for office. Incumbents seek reelection more than 75 percent of the time, and are 90 percent more likely than others to win their reelection campaigns. Because women have been excluded from equal participation in politics, incumbents are overwhelmingly male.

Finally, a large barrier to women in politics is the "pipeline" problem. The pipeline refers to careers which traditionally lead to politics, such as law and business, and from which women have been historically excluded. It is generally believed that if women gained access to these careers, they would become involved in politics. Today, encouraging young women to become involved in politics is crucial to increasing the numbers of women in the pipeline to politics.

CONCLUSION

Research has found that when women run, they are just as likely to win as their male colleagues are. Despite this finding, women are still drastically underrepresented in elective office. The debate about women's involvement in politics stems from differing opinions on representation. Women's underrepresentation can be explained by a variety of barriers based on gender issues. Despite the fact that the U.S. is considered a leader in democracy, women's involvement in elective leadership proves otherwise.

See also Politics and Political Ideologies: Leftist Women; Politics and Political Ideologies: Right-Wing Women; Second and Third Wave Feminisms.

Further Reading: Alter, Jonathan, "Is America Ready for Hilary or Obama?" *Newsweek*, December 25, 2006; Burrell, Barbara C., *Campaign Finance: Women's Experience in the Modern Era* (New York: Oxford University Press, 1998); Burrell, Barbara C., *Women and Political Participation: A Reference Handbook* (Santa Barbara, CA: Abc-Clio, 2004); Center for American Women in Politics, *Fact Sheet: Women in the 110th US Congress (2007–2009)* (New Brunswick, NJ: Center for American Women and Politics, Rutgers University, 2007); Douglas, Arnold, *The Logic of Congressional Action* (New Haven, CT: Yale University Press, 1990); Lawless, Jennifer L., and Richard L. Fox, *It Takes a Candidate: Why Women Don't Run for Office* (Cambridge: Cambridge University Press, 2005); McGlen, Nancy E., K. O'Connor, van Assendelft, and W. Gunther-Canada, *Women, Politics, and American Society*, 3rd ed. (New York: Longman, 2002); Palmer, Barbara, and Dennis Simon, *Breaking the Political Glass Ceiling: Women and Congressional Elections* (New York: Routledge, 2006); Pitkin, H., *The Concept of Representation* (Berkeley: University of California Press, 1967); Rosenthal, Cindy S., *Women Transforming Congress*, vol. 4 (Norman: University of Oklahoma Press, 2002); Sanbonmatsu, Kira, *Democrats, Republicans, and the Politics of Women's Place* (Ann Arbor: University of Michigan Press, 2002); Swers, Michele L., *The Difference Women Make: The Policy Impact of Women in Congress* (Chicago: University of Chicago Press, 2002); Thomas, Sue, and Clyde Wilcox, *Women and Elective Office: Past, Present, and Future*, 2nd ed. (Oxford: Oxford University Press, 2005); Witt, Linda, Karen M. Paget, and Glenna Matthews, *Running as a Woman: Gender and Power in American Politics* (New York: Free Press, 1994).

Samantha Casne

POLITICS AND POLITICAL IDEOLOGIES: LEFTIST WOMEN

Leftist theories of women's roles in society and their revolutionary potential have led to a series of questions about whether capitalism or patriarchy is the primary cause of women's oppression; whether leftist political strategies empower or oppress women; and whether a socialist or capitalist economy is better for them overall.

BACKGROUND

Women have participated in leftist movements in various contexts, both within the United States and globally. In the United States, it is important to distinguish between leftist political parties and broader notions of "the Left," which potentially include labor, antiwar, peace, women's, gay and lesbian, environmental, anti-globalization, and other movements for self-proclaimed progressive causes. In the 1960s, the New Left began to take shape and be conceptualized as a left that broke with many of the dogmatisms of earlier leftist party politics. Prior to the 1960s, women played important roles in leftist political parties, most of which adopted some version of Karl Marx's original beliefs, as laid out in his 1848 publication, co-authored with Friedrich Engels, *The Communist Manifesto,* commissioned by the German Communist Party, and Marx's treatise on capitalism, *Das Kapital,* of which the first volume was published by Marx in 1867 and the remaining three volumes were published posthumously. *The Communist Manifesto* and *Das Kapital* provided important critiques of industrial capitalism, including Marx's insights into class formation, whereby the ruling class, or bourgeoisie, owns the means of production (for example, land, labor, capital) whereas the working class, or proletariat, provides labor for a wage and is therefore exploited for its labor. According to Marx, the rise of industrialization in Europe (and later in North America) paved the way for heightened inequalities between social classes. Marx believed that women played particular roles in what he called the capitalist division of labor: As wives without property or inheritance rights (in both British and European law during the nineteenth century), he argued, they were bound by feudalistic relations with their husbands, given the unpaid nature of household labor. In other words, their roles in biological and social reproduction, including childbearing and childrearing, contributed to their oppression as women, regardless of their class location. As laborers in the market economy, proletarian women were also exploited as workers. As they provided labor for a wage, they helped the ruling class accumulate capital, thereby reinforcing and reproducing the system of inequality that they were born into as members of the proletariat. Women of the ruling class were seen as even more oppressed, since they were entirely bound by their housewife roles and were therefore unable to make any profit from their labor. Of course, they benefited from their relationship to men of the ruling class, but some Marxian scholars would argue that this was a form of false consciousness, since ruling-class women had access to this privilege only while they remained married (Lukács 1999; Zaretsky 1976).

In *Das Kapital* and other publications, Marx theorizes about what he sees as the evolutionary stages of the economy. He believed that just as feudalism led to the liberal revolutions in Europe, which formalized the separation of church and state and paved the way for a new kind of citizenship and labor relations, capitalism would (or could) eventually lead to what he termed *communism.* To achieve a truly communist society, it was necessary to go through a temporary stage of state-led socialism, in which the state would direct the economy through state ownership of enterprises and property until it was no longer needed. According to Marx, in a truly communist society, we would no longer need a state to oversee citizenship or the economy; thus, according to his original theory, as of the present century we have not yet witnessed true communism, except perhaps in "primitive" societies that continue to rely upon an exchange of goods rather than on a monetary system that involves the accumulation of capital. Rather, we have seen state-led socialism, many examples of which have utilized authoritarian, rather than democratic, state practices, another important distinguishing factor between Marx's original theory and contemporary forms of socialism. Confusion between Marx's own theory of communism and contemporary uses of the term is compounded by the fact that Western political scientists often use the term *communist state* to refer to any state that has a one-party system, is authoritarian in structure, and is Marxian influenced.

Marx's original ideas have been adapted by later revolutionaries in a variety of ways. Political leaders and/or philosophers as diverse as Rosa Luxemburg, Vladimir Lenin, Leon Trotsky, Mao Zedong, Georg Lukács, Jean-Paul Sartre, Walter Benjamin, Che Guevara, and Louis Althusser all held very different perspectives on how to interpret and translate Marxian thought into practice. While most concur that there is a need for a revolution, in which the proletariat takes over capitalism, thus paving the way for true communism, historical disagreements on how to stage such a revolution, and women's roles in it, have occurred since the mid-nineteenth century. For example, whereas Leninists believe that a vanguard is needed to lead the revolution, a philosophy adopted by most "communist" countries during the cold war period and contemporary Cuba, Trotskyists take a more anarchistic approach and argue against the use of a vanguard on the basis that it leads to state-based authoritarianism, such as that witnessed during Joseph Stalin's years of iron-fisted rule in the USSR.

Female intellectuals and political activists developed their own theories of gender and class oppression by drawing from Marx's original insights, and many of the leftist parties and movements that are studied today continue to build upon Marx's insights, even as they challenge or reframe it. Early leftist female intellectuals included German-born Clara Zetkin and Polish-born Rosa Luxemburg, both of whom were members of leftist political parties in Germany and were actively involved in the struggle for women's rights. On March 8, 1911, Zetkin organized the world's first International Women's Day in Copenhagen, a day of tribute that continues to be celebrated by women's groups around the world.

WOMEN, LABOR MOVEMENTS, AND LEFTIST POLITICAL PARTIES

In the nineteenth and early twentieth centuries, many women became active in labor movements, where some began to learn about Marxian and other leftist philosophies. Early female labor activists included Sarah Bagley, the first president of the Lowell Female Labor Reform Association (LFLRA). Founded in 1844, LFLRA pushed for better pay and working conditions for the "mill girls." Mary Harris Jones, better known as Mother Jones, fought tirelessly for labor rights and helped found the Industrial Workers of the World (IWW) at the beginning of the twentieth century.

Other women prioritized their participation in political parties rather than labor movements. In the United States, major leftist political parties include the Marxist-Leninist Communist Party USA (CPUSA), the Maoist-inspired Revolutionary Workers' Party, and the Trotskyist-influenced Workers World Party and Socialist Action Party. CPUSA has been perhaps the most widely known and influential party in the country; it was particularly so before several splinter parties and newer parties emerged. Although it is difficult to trace how many women have been members of leftist parties in the United States, given these parties' underground nature due to persecution, particularly during the McCarthy era when known Communists were censured, fired, and sometimes imprisoned, many women have been actively involved in leftist parties. Often, these

MOTHER JONES

Mary Harris Jones, a.k.a. Mother Jones (1837–1930), was a well-known labor activist. In 1905, she helped found the anarchist-based Industrial Workers of the World (IWW), whose members were commonly known as Wobblies. She was also active in the United Mine Workers and the Socialist Party of America. She was a union organizer on behalf of women, men, and children and she brought child labor to the attention of national politicians. One district attorney at the time considered her "the most dangerous woman in America," a phrase immortalized in the title of her biography (Gorn 2001). In 1976, *Mother Jones* magazine was founded and named after her; the original editors considered it a news magazine rooted in progressive political values. It currently has the largest readership among progressive publications in the United States. Scholars debate whether Mother Jones was a feminist or not. She dedicated herself largely to labor issues and she was a very strong female role model in a male-dominated political environment, but she did not describe herself as a feminist.

women believe that class struggle should be prioritized over other forms of oppression such as sexism or racism. Others believe in struggling to reform their parties from within, in part by including a women's rights agenda as part of their broader goals. Yet another group of women chose to leave leftist parties precisely because they did not represent or prioritize women's needs or rights; many of these women later joined other social movements that were prominent in the 1960s, including the free speech, antiwar, and women's movements.

ANGELA DAVIS AND THE U.S. LEFT

One example of a legendary activist who worked both within old Left political parties and New Left social movements is Angela Davis. Davis, who became a well-known figure in the media for her association with a 1970 Black Panther effort to free prisoners at the Marin County Hall of Justice, her subsequent status as a fugitive for 18 months, and her capture and imprisonment, was once a member of the Communist Party as well as a supporter of the Black Panthers and a feminist activist. Davis's history serves as an example of the gendered contradictions of leftist party involvement, and reveals some of the reasons for the emergence of the New Left in the United States.

Beginning as a student, Davis became actively involved in leftist intellectual circles, and in college at Brandeis during the late 1950s and early 1960s had the opportunity to study with German-born philosopher Herbert Marcuse of the Frankfurt School, an influential group of scholars dedicated to neo-Marxist thought that was based at the University of Frankfurt. Davis later earned her PhD in philosophy at Humboldt University of Berlin, then in the German Democratic Republic (otherwise known as socialist-led East Germany). Upon her return to the United States, she worked as a philosophy professor at the University of California, Los Angeles (UCLA). In 1969, she was fired from her job at UCLA because of her ties to the Communist Party, a move supported by Governor

Ronald Reagan, only to be rehired several months later, following an outpouring of community support.

Davis worked closely with the CPUSA for many years. In 1980 and 1984, she ran unsuccessfully for vice president on the CPUSA ticket, alongside the CPUSA's five-time presidential candidate, Gus Hall. She later left the party to help found the Committees of Correspondence for Democracy and Socialism, which broke with CPUSA after it supported a 1991 coup attempt in the former Soviet Union, essentially siding with authoritarianism, which Davis rejected in favor of democratic socialism.

As a professor of the history of consciousness at the University of California, Santa Cruz (UCSC), Davis continues to dedicate herself to Marxian analysis, particularly as it relates to struggles against racism and sexism. Her influential 1983 publication, *Women, Race and Class* ([1983] 2001), was one of the first in women's studies scholarship to address the intersectionality of gender, race, and class as they shape women's, and especially women of color's, experiences in a stratified society. She has since published several books and articles on topics including the prison-industrial complex and the prison abolition movement, cultural studies, violence against women, and black feminist thought. Earlier, she had published an autobiographical account of her experience as a target on the FBI's Most Wanted list and her political imprisonment (Davis [1974] 1989).

Davis's participation in the Communist Party, coupled with her membership in the black nationalist Black Panther Party and her general involvement in social justice causes, exemplifies the types of activism that women on the left have been involved in during the twentieth and early twenty-first centuries in the United States. Although Davis believes in democratic socialism, she challenges many of the premises of Marxian thought, particularly where women and racial minorities are left unexamined. Her experience, like that of thousands of other women who have served as members of leftist political parties, exemplifies the tensions that exist in supporting Marxian revolutionary struggle while also believing that racism and sexism are equally oppressive to women. For those who stand outside the Left, all of these perspectives, be they party based or movement based, tend to be viewed as threats to democratic capitalism and are often disputed. Some dismiss these views altogether, due to broader perceptions in U.S. society about the Left in formal politics.

WOMEN AND THE NEW LEFT

In the 1960s, several protest movements emerged that were influenced by leftist thought. At the height of the Vietnam War, many students, workers, and citizens became discontented with the war and demanded an end to it. The civil rights movement was in full sway, with its landmarks including the 1964 Civil Rights Act, which was originally designed to protect African Americans and other U.S. citizens from discrimination on the basis of race (among other things), black power movements came into being, and various identity-based groups drew from Marxian and other progressive ideologies to frame their struggles for social justice. In this context, "the Left" came to be construed as not only emanating from Marxian ideologies and class struggle but also encompass-ing "progressive" struggles that focused on social justice or human rights. The women's movement, in particular, attracted women leftists who were frustrated by their secondary roles as secretaries and coffee makers in the male-based rev-olution, and many of the earliest second wave feminists, including *Ms. Maga-zine* founder Gloria Steinem, were influenced by leftist ideologies. Some women joined the peace, antiwar, free speech, or ethnic nationalist movements and attempted to address sexism from within these movements; others joined the women's movement and developed socialist-feminist theories of social change. Some of the women who participated in non-gender-specific movements, such as the free speech movement or the antiwar protests, acquired leadership skills through their participation and began to think differently about their gender roles, particularly those women who experienced the effects of sexism within the movement or at work, at home, or in their communities. Some of these women then went on to play key roles in social justice, identity-based, and community-based movements. Others remained marginalized due to their gender status within the male-led ranks.

Early second wave socialist-feminist philosophers and activists—those that joined the women's movement—included women who wrote about a wide range of topics: Zillah Eisenstein's 1979 publication, *Capitalist Patriarchy and the Case for Socialist Feminism,* perhaps best captures an overall goal of this group of feminists, namely, to achieve a feminist-oriented socialist society by eradi-cating capitalist and patriarchal inequalities. While the "marriage" of Marxism and feminism resulted in a plethora of creative theories about gender, class, and other forms of social stratification and oppression, some observers viewed the relationship between Marxism and feminism as an "unhappy marriage" at best, as portrayed in Heidi Hartmann's oft-cited 1981 article, "The Unhappy Marriage of Marxism and Feminism: Towards a More Progressive Union." Hartmann ar-gued that the marriage of Marxism and feminism has been like that between husbands and wives in English common law: "Marxism and feminism are one, but in fact, one means Marxism" (Hartmann 1981, 2). Others went on to cri-tique additional oversights in Hartmann's framework and in feminist thought and practice in general, including the general lack of discussion of racism and homophobia within the women's movement (Joseph 1981; Riddiough 1981). Within feminism to this day, many debates continue as to whether a socialist-feminist approach is the most appropriate, both in theory and in practice, in contrast to other types of feminisms such as liberal, cultural, poststructuralist, antiracist, or third wave.

CONCLUSION

Perhaps there will always be an "unhappy marriage" between Marxism and feminism. At the very least, the prevalence of patriarchal-based sexism and capi-talist class exploitation continues to be heavily debated by socialist-feminists, in both the old Left and the new. In addition, new forms of thinking and activism have emerged that draw from these earlier debates and develop new platforms for action. Third wave feminism, such as that advocated by younger generations of feminists, is one example of this new, hybrid political identity that draws from the past but projects a new form of "doing politics" (Baumgardner and Richards 2000). At the level of political participation, few socialist women, let alone socialist-feminists, have been elected into office, with some exceptions at the municipal level. On a general level, while much debate continues about the Left versus the Right in the United States and about women's appropriate roles in politics, at the very least observers might agree that the second wave feminist movement that emerged during the 1960s was heavily influenced by other social movements associated with the New Left in the 1960s. Some of these ideologies have been incorporated into more centrist approaches to politics, in the Democratic Party, for example, while others exert influence outside the realm of formal politics, in emergent struggles concerning immigrant rights, antiracism efforts, homelessness and housing movements, queer and women's movements, and movements for the poor. In addition, Marx's original thought has greatly influenced liberation theologies around the world, leading to new and interesting discussions about the relationship between religion and politics.

From the point of view of scholars of Marxian thought and leftist movements, in U.S. society there continues to be much reluctance to understand and critically analyze Marxism, due in part to longstanding anti-Communist sentiments. Interestingly, this distinguishes the United States from most other Western democracies, which have allowed a broader political spectrum in formal politics. Whether women are better served by leftist political strategies or by reformist or right-wing strategies will continue to be debated as long as there continues to be a stratified social system, be it capitalist, communist, or any other, and as long as people remain divided over political ideology, appropriate forms of governance, and women's roles in the public realm of politics.

See also Leftist Armed Struggle; Political Parties; Second and Third Wave Feminisms; Third World and Women of Color Feminisms.

Further Reading: Aptheker, Bettina, *Intimate Politics: How I Grew Up Red, Fought for Free Speech, and Became A Feminist Rebel* (Emeryville, CA: Seal Press, 2006); Baumgardner, Jennifer, and Amy Richards, *Manifesta: Young Women, Feminism and the Future* (New York: Farrar, Straus and Giroux, 2000); Davis, Angela, *Angela Davis: An Autobiography* (New York: International Publishers, 1989 [1974]); Davis, Angela, *Women, Race and Class* (London: Women's Press, 2001 [1983]); Eisenstein, Zillah, *Capitalist Patriarchy and the Case for Socialist Feminism* (New York: Monthly Review Press, 1979); Gorn, Elliott, *Mother Jones: The Most Dangerous Woman in America* (New York: Hill and Wang, 2001); Hartmann, Heidi, "The Unhappy Marriage of Marxism and Feminism: Towards a More Progressive Union," in *Women and Revolution: A Discussion of the Unhappy Marriage of Marxism and Feminism,* ed. Lydia Sargent, 1–41 (Boston: South End Press, 1981); Hudis, Peter, and Kevin B. Anderson, eds., *The Rosa Luxemburg Reader* (New York: Monthly Review Press, 2004); James, Joy, ed., *The Angela Davis Reader* (Malden, MA: Blackwell, 1998); Joseph, Gloria, "The Incompatible Ménage à Trois: Marxism, Feminism and Racism," in *Women and Revolution: A Discussion of the Unhappy Marriage of Marxism and Feminism,* ed. Lydia Sargent, 91–107 (Boston: South End Press, 1981); Lukacs, Georg, *History and Class Consciousness* (London: Merlin Press, 1999 [1968]); Marx, Karl, *Das*

Kapital (Washington, DC: Regnery, 2000 [1867]); Marx, Karl, and Friedrich Engels, *The Communist Manifesto* (New York: Penguin Classics, 2002 [1848]); Riddiough, Christine, "Socialism, Feminism, and Gay/Lesbian Liberation," in *Women and Revolution: A Discussion of the Unhappy Marriage of Marxism and Feminism,* ed. Lydia Sargent, 73–90 (Boston: South End Press, 1981); Zaretsky, Eli, *Capitalism, the Family and Personal Life* (New York: Harper and Row, 1976).

Amy Lind

POLITICS AND POLITICAL IDEOLOGIES: RIGHT-WING WOMEN

Guided by the dictum that women should "submit to their husbands in every thing," contemporary right-wing women have been critical of and sometimes actively opposed to women's rights initiatives that are viewed as threats to a particular model of marriage and family life that they view as biblically ordained. Feminists and other liberal observers contend that these women are uninformed, in denial, or biased in their approach.

BACKGROUND

Like their male counterparts, right-wing women are part of a broad coalition of active and vocal supporters of religious and political ideologies that are linked with cultural conservatism. A literal reading of Christian scriptures informs their moral and ethical worldview on issues ranging from U.S.-Israel relations and national sovereignty to abortion, euthanasia, and public education. However, it has often been their stances on questions related to gender and sexuality that put right-wing women in the media spotlight.

The labels of "Left" and "Right" have historically been used to identity ideological positions along a political continuum oriented around a moderate center. The terms *liberal* and *conservative* are often associated with the left and right wings of American politics, respectively. So, the "left" wing of contemporary political discourse in the United States is dominated by the Democratic Party, while the "right" wing is dominated by the Republican party. While these tags are perhaps too broad to represent the many types of attitudes and approaches to government that they include, in general, we say that "liberals" tend to talk about the "spirit of the law" in their interpretation of the U.S. Constitution and that "conservatives" refer to the "letter of the law" in theirs.

A relatively recent phenomenon is the use of these terms to describe coalitions of activists (each accused by the other of being extremist or too far from the mainstream). Since the 1960s, the label "New Left" has generally been used to refer to those groups of activists and philosophers whose roots are based in their opposition to McCarthyism and other cold war–era nationalistic measures, and the "New Right" usually describes groups concerned about the influx of countercultural ideals and values—especially those related to gender and sexuality—into mainstream culture. The "New Right" has also been called the "Religious Right" or the "Christian Right," because of its close ties with evangelical and conservative

TIMELINE

1972: Activist Phyllis Schlafly organizes STOP-ERA (later Eagle Forum) in response to concerns that the ERA will degrade women and undermine the structure of the American family.

1973: The Supreme Court issues its decision in the *Roe v. Wade* case, which overturns state laws prohibiting abortion.

1974: *The Total Woman,* an advice book for wives interested in more traditional marriage roles, defeats Woodward and Bernstein's *All the President's Men* to become the *New York Times* Non-fiction Book of the Year. The book will sell over 10 million copies in over a dozen languages before going out of print.

1976: The passage of a human rights ordinance in Miami/Dade County mobilizes right-wing activists in Florida and across the United States.

1977: Anita Bryant publishes *The Anita Bryant Story: The Survival of Our Nation's Families and the Threat of Militant Homosexuality.*

1978: Pastor's wife Beverly LaHaye organizes Concerned Women for America, a profamily, anti-ERA lobbying group in Washington, DC.

1980: Ronald Reagan is sworn in as 40th president, having overwhelmingly defeated Jimmy Carter in an election that turned largely on social issues and religious themes.

1982: The Equal Rights Amendment proposal dies in Congress after 354–24 approval in the U.S. House of Representatives and 84–8 approval in the U.S. Senate. It falls three states short of the 38 (three-quarters) required for ratification.

1983: Feminist author/activist Andrea Dworkin publishes *Right-Wing Women,* one of the first outside analyses of a large and growing cultural group.

1986: Concerned Women for America (CWA) founder Beverly LaHaye testifies in support of Antonin Scalia in congressional hearings on Capitol Hill.

1991: A CWA legal representative testifies in support of Clarence Thomas in congressional hearings on Capitol Hill.

1995: Norma McCorvey ("Jane Roe") becomes involved with antiabortion group Operation Rescue.

1997: Norma McCorvey leaves Operation Rescue to found her own ministry, Roe No More.

2004: Death of Terry Schiavo, a Catholic woman whose parents lost their battle to keep her feeding tubes connected for religious reasons. The court granted her husband's request despite the intervention of Congress.

Catholic churches and its understanding of America as a nation grounded in the Judeo-Christian heritage.

THE NEW RIGHT: ISSUES AND STRATEGIES

Because many of the debates that engage the New Right are related to what are sometimes viewed as women's issues, such as education and the family,

MISSION STATEMENTS

Two contemporary organizations have been especially vocal in advocating for right-wing women's issues at the national level: Concerned Women for America, established by pastor's wife Beverly LaHaye in 1978, and Eagle Forum, the organization that grew from activist Phyllis Schlafly's STOP-ERA movement of the 1970s. The groups' mission statements can be found on their official Web sites:

> *The mission of CWA* [Concerned Women for America] is to protect and promote Biblical values among all citizens—first through prayer, then education, and finally by influencing our society—thereby reversing the decline in moral values in our nation. (http://www.cwfa.org)

> *Eagle Forum's* mission is to enable conservative and pro-family men and women to participate in the process of self-government and public policy making so that America will continue to be a land of individual liberty, respect for family integrity, public and private virtue, and private enterprise. (http://www.eagleforum.org)

right-wing women have played a significant role in grassroots activism and policy and strategy development in politics at local, state, and national levels. Right-wing activists have long understood the importance of state-level elections and their impact on social and cultural initiatives. They have been especially successful in garnering support and building coalitions in the once overlooked area of school board elections, the results of which are related to curriculum choices, sex education, textbook content, the teaching of evolution, and a host of other key issues that motivate a large bloc of voters in many communities.

A popular local issue has been the question of the sex-education curriculum in public schools. This is an issue that often divides conservatives. On the one hand, most conservatives reject attempts by the federal government to force a local entity (for example, a city) to comply with a national policy. In school districts, especially, parents (and other taxpayers) insist on the right to guide decisions that will affect the curriculum their children will follow. At the same time, some right-wing activists have supported the involvement of government at various levels in the establishment of sex-education curricula. Federal and state funds have been used to generate and implement "abstinence only" curricula in health and science classes. Such programs warn about the dangers of premarital sex (from disease to the potential for psychological damage) but prohibit the dissemination of information about protection from pregnancy or sexually transmitted diseases, for fear that such information is too provocative and leads to immoral sexual behaviors.

At the national level, right-wing women have been particularly active in debates related to gay and lesbian rights, the role of women in the family and society, and birth control, abortion, and other right-to-life issues. In 1976, beauty contest winner, popular singer, and sometime television commercial actress Anita Bryant became perhaps the first mobilizing personality in the new

Religious Right—male or female—when she spoke out against a human rights ordinance being debated in her home state of Florida. When she learned from her pastor that the ordinance protected rights for gays and lesbians, Bryant says she felt compelled to take action, having indirectly supported the nomination of the Miami city councilwoman who drafted the ordinance. In her 1977 book, *The Anita Bryant Story: The Survival of Our Nation's Families and the Threat of Militant Homosexuality*, Bryant described her private campaign to convince the councilwoman to reverse her position and the decision to become an activist and a public opponent of what many feared was a "homosexual agenda."

Buoyed by their successes in Miami, Bryant and husband-manager Bob Green went on to found a ministry called Save Our Children (later, Protect America's Children), which aimed to prevent gays and lesbians from "recruiting" children. The organization was neither successful nor long lived, however, and Bryant's career suffered extensive damage in the campaign's aftermath. Sponsors quickly terminated their endorsement contracts with Bryant and promoters canceled shows and projects. Bryant might have survived all this, however, had she not divorced Green in 1980 after 20 years of marriage. Even her most loyal supporters felt betrayed by what they saw as the hypocritical actions of a woman who had spent her public life defending marriage and the Christian family. Despite this sensational rise and fall, Anita Bryant and the Miami crusades are still studied as examples of faith-based grassroots activism at its most effective, and the work they accomplished had a lasting impact that continues to influence Florida adoption law.

In addition to the struggles against gay-rights initiatives, right-wing women have worked on a larger scale to support and defend a nuclear family structure that adheres to Judeo-Christian standards with regard to roles for men and women and parents and children. To this end, they have published hundreds of books of advice for parents and couples. During the 1970s, a handful of right-wing women, including Anita Bryant, published books that advised other women about biblical marriage and femininity. These works based their arguments on scriptural precepts about wives' submission to their husbands and silence in the churches.

Particularly during this period, as more Americans were debating issues raised by women's liberation movements, right-wing women spoke up about the need to maintain the distinct gender roles that were ordained by God in the Garden of Eden and about the need for children to have a full-time mother not only in their early years but through childhood and adolescence as well. Because they believed these ideals were under attack by the feminist movements in general and by the proposed Equal Rights Amendment in particular, many homemakers became politically active for the first time during the 1970s as attorney/activist Phyllis Schlafly launched STOP-ERA, a campaign that eventually reversed the trajectory of the proposed amendment after it had passed easily through both the U.S. House and the Senate. Schlafly and her trained corps of volunteers crossed the country, working one state at a time to ensure that the ERA would not earn the majority (38 states) needed for ratification and amending the U.S. Constitution. STOP-ERA was successful, holding the number of affirmative votes to

35 states, and the proposal died when the final extension expired in 1982. As with the Anita Bryant campaign in Florida, many political analysts have studied the work of Phyllis Schlafly, STOP-ERA, and her current organization, Eagle Forum, as models of large-scale political change effected by coalition building at state and local levels.

ABORTION AND PRO-LIFE POLITICS

While Anita Bryant and Phyllis Schlafly and the movements they led are often associated with a particular time in history, issues related to the right to life—birth control, euthanasia, and especially abortion—link right-wing women across the decades. From the Supreme Court's 1973 *Roe v. Wade* decision to current congressional debates, right-to-life issues have inspired passion and activism and also some internal division among women (and men) of the Religious Right. Subjects of more recent debates have included the ethics of carrying out research on embryonic stem cells (cells taken from an aborted human embryo). Though stem cells have the potential to yield life-saving cures for debilitating or deadly diseases, some conservatives fear an increased desire for stem cells might encourage future abortions, or, worse, the establishment of a pregnancy for the sole purpose of termination of the embryo and the harvesting of stem cells. Stem-cell research proponents respond to this concern by asserting that only existing cells (that is, cells that have already been collected) and the cell lines derived from those cells would be used in research. Most medical ethicists agree that the act of creating an embryo for the purpose of termination would be a violation of medical practice; however, stem-cell research opponents warn that it would be very difficult to prohibit intentional conception and termination while at the same time allowing research on cells acquired in another way.

Some prominent Republicans have acknowledged their support of a woman's rights to safe and legal abortion despite the fact that the Republican Party maintains a right-to-life agenda in its presidential platform. Former first lady Nancy Reagan urged her party to reconsider its stance on stem-cell research, arguing that discoveries in the field might lead to an eventual cure for Alzheimer's disease, the disease her husband, President Ronald Reagan, suffered from for 10 years before his death in 2004. Despite these sometimes vocal minority voices, the Republican Party remains a pro-life party, thanks in large part to the political clout of women of the Religious Right.

Since the *Roe v. Wade* decision, right-wing activists have increasingly turned their focus to the selection and appointment of state and federal judges and especially Supreme Court justices to ensure a long legacy of case law that will continue to limit and maybe even overturn the rights afforded by *Roe v Wade*. One group, Concerned Women for America (CWA), which like Eagle Forum was founded in the 1970s as a response to the ERA campaign, has focused its efforts on lobbying Congress in support of measures that support its mission and agenda. The group's founder and first president, Beverly LaHaye, wife of pastor and popular end-times novelist Tim LaHaye, has a considerable amount of political clout and a broad coalition of allies. Headquartered in Washington, DC, CWA advocates for the nomination and confirmation of conservative justices and sent representatives to testify before Congress on behalf of justices Robert Bork, Clarence Thomas, and Antonin Scalia during their appointment hearings.

In 1995, pro-life activists from Operation Rescue, a group that often uses violent tactics to prevent women's entry into the clinics of abortion providers, announced that Norma McCorvey, the plaintiff in the case of *Roe v. Wade*, had converted to Christianity and become involved with the group's work. Some 20 years after serving as the test case for abortion rights, McCorvey now began accepting public-speaking engagements for pro-life groups, formed a ministry called Roe No More, converted to Roman Catholicism, and publicly expressed disdain for feminist activists and lawyers for their ambition and condescending treatment of her throughout the trial. McCorvey remains full of regret over her decision to participate in *Roe v. Wade*, despite the fact that she did not have the abortion she sought, having won her case too late in her own pregnancy.

Right-wing women continue to work together on issues related to their goal of the eventual reversal of the *Roe v. Wade* decision; the most important component of their work is their commitment to seeing that like-minded judges are appointed to courts at all levels.

OTHER ISSUES

Though so-called women's issues like sexuality, feminism, and abortion have remained at the heart of right-wing women's political agendas, groups like Eagle Forum and Concerned Women for America have, since the 1980s, expanded the scope of their involvement in political affairs at the national level to include issues related to national sovereignty (and a rejection of most United Nations initiatives), the right to bear arms, a free-market economic system, the cultivation of close ties with Israel, and many other areas that link them to the larger ideology of American conservatism.

See also Equal Rights Amendment; Family Values; Political Parties; Right-Wing Women's Movements.

Further Reading: Bryant, Anita, *The Anita Bryant Story: The Survival of our Nation's Families and the Threat of Militant Homosexuality* (Old Tappan, NJ: Revell, 1977); Burkitt, Elinor, *Right Women: A Journey through the Heart of Conservative America* (New York: Scribner, 1998); Burlein, Ann, *Lift High the Cross: Where White Supremacy and the Christian Right Converge* (Durham, NC: Duke University Press, 2002); Critchlow, Donald T., *Phyllis Schlafly and Grassroots Conservatism: One Woman's Crusade* (Princeton, NJ: Princeton University Press, 2005); Dworkin, Andrea, *Right-Wing Women* (New York: Perigee Books, 1983); Griffith, R. Marie, *God's Daughters: Evangelical Women and the Power of Submission* (Berkeley: University of California Press, 1997); Hunter, James Davidson, *Culture Wars: The Struggle to Define America* (New York: Basic Books, 1991); Lienesch, Michael, *Redeeming America: Piety and Politics in the New Christian Right* (Chapel Hill: University of North Carolina Press, 1993); Mason, Carol, *Killing for Life: The Apocalyptic Narrative of Pro-life Politics* (Ithaca, NY: Cornell University Press, 2002);

Morgan, Marabel, *The Total Woman* (Old Tappan, NJ: Revell, 1973); Schlafly, Phyllis, *The Power of the Positive Woman* (New Rochelle, NY: Arlington, 1977).

Jennifer Heller

POLYGAMY

Popular discussion of American polygamy has focused on groups connected to the Fundamentalist Church of Jesus Christ of Latter-Day Saints (FLDS), whose practice of it is seen as sexist, racist, and violent. The polygamists view the practice as a religious calling founded on the idea that plural marriage is commanded by God. These conflicting ways of imagining polygamy tap into the conflict many Americans feel between the right to freedom of religion and personal liberty and sexual values strongly influenced by the idea that marriage involves "one man and one woman."

BACKGROUND

Polygamy, marriage to more than one spouse simultaneously, has historically been practiced in a number of cultures around the world. The most common form of polygamy is polygyny, which occurs when a man takes more than one wife. Polyandry, which occurs when a woman takes more than one husband, occurs primarily in cultures where land is passed in equal shares to male children in a family and where the notion of partible paternity (the theory that more than one father can contribute genetic material to and should participate in the nurturing of a child) is considered possible and desirable.

On January 5, 2007, the CBS crime drama *Numb3rs* aired an episode called "Nine Wives," which portrayed "the fundamentalist leader of a polygamous sect who is on the FBI's most wanted list for committing numerous crimes, including rape and murder" (http://www.cbs.com/primetime/numb3rs/). The show ended with a fiery explosion engineered by the sect leader, who saved himself in a narcissistic display of heartlessness toward his most loyal followers. This television event was clearly motivated by public interest in polygamy resulting from the 2006 placement of fundamentalist Mormon Warren Jeffs on the FBI's Ten Most Wanted list and his subsequent arrest on charges of sexual assault on a minor and conspiracy to commit sexual conduct with a minor. The media spotlight on Jeffs and the polygamous sect he led also contributed to the success of documentaries, docu-dramas, and an HBO dramatic series titled *Big Love*, all dealing with fundamentalist Mormon polygamy in the United States. Though there are in the United States several small groups whose members practice polygamy, much of the popular discussion of polygamy has focused on groups connected to the Fundamentalist Church of Jesus Christ of Latter-Day Saints (FLDS). In general, the media have portrayed that group's practice of polygamy as rooted in sexism, racism, and violence. The polygamists themselves, especially those affiliated with FLDS, view the practice as a religious calling founded in the idea that plural marriage is necessary for "the creation of earthly tabernacles (bodies)

HBO'S *BIG LOVE*

Big Love, the HBO series about a contemporary polygamous family living in the suburbs of Salt Lake City, Utah, focuses on the daily lives of Bill Paxton, his three wives, and their seven children. Paxton and the second of his wives, Nicki, were both raised in Juniper Creek (notice the play on Short Creek, the former name of the best-known polygamist FLDS enclave in the United States), and Nicki is the daughter of Roman Grant, Juniper Creek's ruthless leader. The other two wives in the family are Barb (Bill's first wife) and Margene (Bill's third and youngest wife). The three wives live with their children in adjacent homes that share a backyard, and Bill (who owns two successful home improvement stores) splits his time among them. Much is made of the pressures Bill experiences as a result of managing three households; Barb, Nicki, and Margene vie for Bill's emotional, sexual, and financial resources as they struggle to maintain their own homes and families. As a result, Bill begins a regular regimen of Viagra and seeks support from his friend and fellow polygamist, Don. Reviewers of the show are often careful to mention that the creators of *Big Love,* Mark V. Olsen and Will Scheffer, are a gay couple, the implication being that there is a clear connection between polygamy and gay marriage. The show attempts to establish polygamy as a reasonable choice for contemporary Mormon families at the same time that it highlights the difficulties faced by a family that must remain fairly isolated from judgmental, prying neighbors.

for the countless number of spirits waiting to come to this earth" (Bradley 1996, 3). These conflicting ways of imagining polygamy's purpose tap into the intense conflict many Americans feel between the right to freedom of religion and personal liberty on one hand and sexual values strongly influenced by the idea that marriage involves "one man and one woman" on the other.

MORMON POLYGAMY IN THE UNITED STATES

The Mormon religion is based on four main texts—*The Book of Mormon, The Pearl of Great Price, Doctrine and Covenants,* and the Bible. The text that contains the revelation on polygamy that Joseph Smith, the founder and first leader of the Mormon Church (also known as the Church of Jesus Christ of Latter-Day Saints, or LDS), claimed to have received from God is in *Doctrine and Covenants* (*D and C*). Article 132 of *Doctrine and Covenants* was officially recorded on July 12, 1843, though the Mormon Church did not acknowledge the practice among its members until 1852. Polygamy was practiced by Smith, who had by the time of his death in 1844 "married at least thirty-three women, and probably as many as forty-eight" (Krakauer 2004, 7). Of the 66 parts of this revelation, only parts 59–66 actually set forth the doctrine of plural marriage; most of the revelation refers to the "eternity of marriage" and describes the LDS stand on the nature and purpose of marriage. On the issue of polygamy, though, this section of the *D and C* is clear: if a Mormon man wishes to take more than one wife "he cannot commit adultery, for they belong to him, and they are given unto him; therefore is he justified" (*D and C*). This portion of the *D and C* also makes it clear that women are not commanded to engage in polyandry and that the particular role of women in the church is to "multiply and replenish the earth" (*D and C*).

HISTORICAL PERSPECTIVE ON THE CONTROVERSY

Polygamy created a significant controversy that impeded Utah's initial endeavors to achieve statehood. Mormons, persecuted in the Midwest, had finally settled in the Utah Territory, which was making a second bid for statehood in 1856, after unsuccessfully attempting admission as the state of Deseret in 1850. The Republican Party responded to the 1852 Mormon admission that polygamy was a basic principle of their religion by presenting the following resolution as part of their presidential platform:

> *Resolved:* That the Constitution confers upon Congress sovereign powers over the Territories of the United States for their government; and that in the exercise of this power, it is both the right and the imperative duty of Congress to prohibit in the Territories those twin relics of barbarism—Polygamy, and Slavery. (http://www.ushistory.org/gop/convention_1856.htm)

Partly because of the extraordinary popular success of Harriet Beecher Stowe's *Uncle Tom's Cabin* and a play based on it, slavery was seen by many in the North and West as one of the most pressing human rights issues of the day. By aligning polygamy with slavery, the party was identifying plural marriage as another issue of human rights, equality, and personal liberty, ideas that have become core components of the polygamy controversy in the United States.

The tactic of connecting polygamy to slavery reinforced the way most Americans saw the Mormons and their practice of polygamy in the Utah Territory. President James Buchanan (the Democrat elected in 1856) sent federal troops into the Utah Territory to quell "the Mormon Rebellion," a move that was designed to "dismantle Brigham Young's theocracy, and eradicate polygamy" (Krakauer 2004, 6). In 1862, the Morrill Anti-Bigamy Act, the first piece of antipolygamy legislation in the United States, was passed, and in 1887 the Edmunds-Tucker Act disincorporated the LDS church and the Perpetual Emigration Fund, which provided aid to Mormon converts who wished to settle in Utah. The Edmunds-Tucker Act required the LDS church to forfeit all property in excess of $50,000 and "stipulated that legal wives could testify against their husbands, abolished women's suffrage, instituted a test oath for public service and voting that disqualified any supporter of polygamy, and made judicial and school appointments federal prerogatives" (Bradley 1996, 217). Essentially, polygamy (and Mormonism more generally) had become the focus of such controversy that it was clear to most people that Utah would not be granted statehood until the Mormons renounced polygamy.

In October 1890, Prophet Wilford W. Woodruff delivered to a group of Mormons gathered for the LDS general conference the first manifesto on polygamy, in which he announced that the LDS church would not teach polygamy or plural marriage, "nor permit any person to enter into its practice" (Bradley 1996, 6). In the manifesto (now incorporated into the Mormon *Doctrine and Covenants* as "Official Declaration 1"), which claimed that the charges of polygamy against the LDS church "are false," Woodruff also announced that

> There is nothing in my teachings to the Church or in those of my associates, during the time specified, which can be reasonably construed to inculcate or encourage polygamy; and when any Elder of the Church has used language which appeared to convey any such teaching, he has been promptly reproved. And I now publicly declare that my advice to the Latter-day Saints is to refrain from contracting any marriage forbidden by the law of the land. (*Doctrine and Covenants*, "Official Declaration 1")

The manifesto both renounced the practice of polygamy in the LDS church and denied its existence as part of current Mormon doctrine and practice, by claiming that allegations that current church leaders had "taught, encouraged and urged the continuance of the practice of polygamy" were "false" (*Doctrine and Covenants*, "Official Declaration 1").

Within the LDS church, the manifesto caused deep divisions. LDS members who had been practicing polygamy without official censure were suddenly faced with a dire personal dilemma. Either they must renounce a tenet of LDS doctrine that they believed was central to their spiritual belief system and that defined the nature and parameters of their families, or they would be excommunicated from the church. Feeling disenfranchised, some polygamists chose to leave or were forced out of the mainstream Mormon Church, and most of this group eventually settled on the Utah/Arizona border. The town of Short Creek, Arizona (now Colorado City), is the best-known polygamist FLDS enclave in the United States, mostly because of a series of antipolygamy raids on the town, all of which were covered by the national media. All three of the raids—in 1935, 1944, and 1953—were supported by the mainstream Mormon Church. In fact, the 1944 raid was named the "Boyden Raid," after Mormon U.S. Attorney John S. Boyden, who planned and executed it with Utah State Attorney General Brigham E. Roberts, the grandson of B. H. Roberts, who had been denied a seat in the U.S. Congress because he was a polygamist (Bradley 1996). Characterizing the mainstream Mormon Church as "solidly respectable," *Time* magazine reported on March 20, 1944, that Boyden intended to prosecute the 50 men and women arrested during the raid under the Mann Act, also known as the White Slavery Act. The Mann Act prohibited the transport of females across state lines for "immoral purposes" ("Fundamentalists" 1944). Originally, the Mann Act was adopted to allow the prosecution of Jack Johnson, an African American heavyweight boxer who traveled across state lines with a white woman whom he later married; Johnson was convicted and spent a year in jail.

Arizona Governor Howard Pyle's 1953 raid on Short Creek backfired when the public was shown images of children being separated from their parents during the raid; in the public imagination, the government went beyond protecting women and children and ended up abusing them and infringing on their civil liberties. The 1953 raid on Short Creek may well have been the reason for

Pyle's subsequent failure to secure a second term as governor. The Short Creek debacle of 1953 also contributed to a general hesitancy on the part of government officials to interfere in the lives of FLDS polygamists who had been living there for over 50 years.

THE CURRENT CONTROVERSY

In the first years of the twenty-first century, a number of events refocused attention on polygamy and on FLDS sects, particularly the one based in Colorado City, Arizona, and Hildale, Utah. In June 2002, 14-year-old Elizabeth Smart was kidnapped from her Salt Lake City, Utah, home by Brian David Mitchell and Wanda Ilene Barzee, because Mitchell (who was later found mentally incompetent to stand trial) had received what he believed to be a revelation from God that he should take seven virgin wives, one of whom was Elizabeth. Because this case linked self-proclaimed polygamists Mitchell and Barzee and the Smart family, who were mainstream Mormons, together in the public consciousness, it recalled for some Americans the mainstream Mormon roots of the FLDS practice of polygamy in this country. In September 2002, approximately six months before Smart was recovered, Rulon Jeffs, the beloved leader of the FLDS sect in Colorado City, died, and his son Warren took control of the group.

In 2004, a division of Random House published Jon Krakauer's *Under the Banner of Heaven: A Story of Violent Faith,* which focused on the murders of Brenda Lafferty and her daughter Erica by Ron and Dan Lafferty, who claimed to have received a commandment from God to commit the murders. Probably the most widely read discussion of polygamy available to date, Krakauer's book became a national bestseller and was named a *New York Times* notable book, solidifying an awareness of polygamy in the contemporary national consciousness. Partly because of the publication of Krakauer's book and partly because of Warren Jeffs's notoriety, popular media treatments of polygamy and tales of the FLDS members' polygamous lifestyle have become fairly common in the United States.

CONCLUSION

Controversies about the definition and scope of marriage are both implicitly and explicitly connected to sexual mores in the cultures where they occur, and discussions of those controversies in American popular culture tend to reveal those connections. Because the current discussion of polygamy is coincidentally occurring at precisely the moment at which Americans are considering the issue of same-sex marriage, some writers have drawn connections between the two discussions. Writing for a conservative publication, the *Weekly Standard,* Stanley Kurtz (2003) joined other conservative cultural commentators when he connected the issues of same-sex marriage and polygamy:

> Among the likeliest effects of gay marriage is to take us down a slippery slope to legalized polygamy and "polyamory" (group marriage). Marriage will be transformed into a variety of relationship contracts, linking

two, three, or more individuals (however weakly and temporarily) in every conceivable combination of male and female. A scare scenario? Hardly.

Clearly, Kurtz believes that the legalization of marriages other than those bounded by monogamy and heterosexuality would be dangerous and would finally call into question a number of sacrosanct sexual strictures. The fact that Kurtz is so easily able to make the mere mention of polygamy carry such weight recalls the earlier connection of polygamy with slavery.

Of course, the controversies surrounding polygamy are much more complex than all this indicates. Questions about the rights of women and children to enjoy freedom of thought, association, and expression, as well as sexual autonomy, are among those related to the polygamy controversy. What is more, since many women and male children who have escaped or been expelled from polygamous communities report a culture of physical and sexual abuse of women and children, controversies around polygamy force questions about the line between individuals' rights to practice their religions in their homes and communities and the responsibility of the government to protect citizens from harm.

Women's status in FLDS communities is defined by their relationships to their fathers and husbands. This fact is perhaps central to some of the controversies—historical and contemporary—over polygamy. In most FLDS communities, women are not afforded significant opportunities to choose their husbands, and FLDS women are taught that their access to eternal life is dependent upon the good favor of a husband. Combined with the fact that the doctrine on polygamy requires plural wives to be virgins, these factors create a circumstance in which women and young girls are encouraged, coerced, and sometimes forced, to enter marriages at a very young age and often with much older men. This practice impacts the lives of young boys as well, since boys are sometimes expelled from

---

FLDS AND RACE

Because FLDS groups hold to the fundamental or original tenets of Mormonism, not only their practice of polygamy but also their attitudes toward racial diversity and women's equality are seen by many as wrong headed at best and dangerous at worst. In his role as FLDS prophet, Warren Jeffs made clear the FLDS doctrine on the relationship between his church and African Americans: "The black race is the people through which the devil has always been able to bring evil unto the earth" (Southern Poverty Law Center 2005). This characterization of the FLDS's belief about race is informed by the actions of two of the early leaders of the Mormon Church. Both Joseph Smith and Brigham Young believed that black members of the church could not become members of the priesthood. That practice continued until 1978, when church president Spencer Kimball received a revelation that the church should extend "priesthood and temple blessings to all worthy male members of the Church." Kimball's extension of priesthood and temple privileges to black men is now an official part of the *Doctrine and Covenants* as "Official Declaration 2."

FLDS communities, ostensibly as punishment for showing romantic attention to girls their own age. Julian Borger reported in 2005 in the *Guardian Observer* that Jim Hill of the Utah Attorney General's Office had attributed the expulsion of boys from Colorado City to the "ruthless sexual arithmetic" of the polygamous sect, implying that the intent is to make it easier for older men to marry (and thereby have sexual access to) underage girls (Borger 2005).

Current Massachusetts governor Mitt Romney, a Mormon, included in an address to a 2005 St. Patrick's Day breakfast in Boston, Massachusetts, a joke meant to refer to the complicated historical relationship between the mainstream Mormon Church and the practice of polygamy: "I believe marriage should be between a man and a woman...and a woman...and a woman" (Reilly 2006). Of course, Romney's reference is to discussions about same-sex marriage and to the key role the state of Massachusetts has played in that controversy. As Romney's remarks imply, proponents of polygamy are not likely to align themselves with proponents of same-sex marriage, though the two groups share the desire that the United States begin the process of redefining the legal parameters of marriage.

See also Religion; Religious Fundamentalism.

Further Reading: Borger, Julian, "The Lost Boys, Thrown Out of US Sect so that Older Men Can Marry More Wives," *Guardian Observer* (Manchester, England), June 14, 2005; Bradley, Martha Sonntag, *Kidnapped from That Land: The Government Raids on the Short Creek Polygamists* (Salt Lake City: University of Utah Press, 1996); CBS.com, "Numb3rs," available at: http://www.cbs.com/primetime/numb3rs/, accessed January 28, 2007; *Doctrine and Covenants,* available at: http://www.sacred-texts.com/mor/dc/index. htm, accessed January 10, 2007; *Doctrine and Covenants,* "Article 132," available at: http://www.sacred-texts.com/mor/dc/index.htm, accessed January 10, 2007; Driggs, Ken, "After the Manifesto: Modern Polygamy and Fundamentalist Mormons," *Journal of Church and State* 32, no. 2 (1990): 367–390; "Fundamentalists," *Time,* March 20, 1944, 55; Krakauer, Jon, *Under the Banner of Heaven: A Story of Violent Faith* (New York: Random House, 2004); Kurtz, Stanley, "Beyond Gay Marriage," *Weekly Standard* (Washington, DC), August 4, 2003; available at: http://www.weeklystandard.com/Content/ Public/Articles/000/000/002/938xpsxy.asp, accessed January 20, 2007; Reilly, Adam, "Take My Wives...Please!: Mitt Romney's Clumsy Mormon Schtick," Slate.com, April 26, 2006, available at: http://www.slate.com/id/2140539/, accessed January 28, 2007; Republican Philadelphia, "GOP Convention of 1856 in Philadelphia," USHistory.org, available at: http://www.ushistory.org/gop/convention_1856.htm, accessed January 13, 2007; Solomon, Dorothy Allred, *Predators, Prey, and Other Kinfolk: Growing Up in Polygamy* (New York: Norton, 2006); Southern Poverty Law Center, "In His Own Words," SPLCenter.org., available at: http://www.splcenter.org/intel/intelreport/article.jsp?sid= 342, accessed January 10, 2007.

Michelle Gibson

POPULATION POLICY

Debates on women and population policy revolve around issues pertaining to the controversial notion of overpopulation and its causes, to women's political rights concerning their reproductive choices, to the reasons why specific groups of women are (or are not) considered worthy of motherhood, and to the question of who should be allowed to control others' ability to have children or not.

BACKGROUND

Behind population policy, there are often assumptions about a population "problem" that needs to be managed. This problem is often framed in terms of overpopulation, but underpopulation and declining population can also be considered problems in certain contexts. Those who believe that overpopulation or population growth causes poverty and hunger, and other ills such as political instability, are often called Malthusians. Many see economist Thomas Robert Malthus's writings on population about 200 years ago as the starting point of the population debates that continue until today. Malthus believed that the earth has limited resources and that these resources are in danger of being stressed to the limit by too many people (Meadows 1993). He warned that the world's food supply would not be able to keep up with the rapid population growth, and he advised against helping poor people, as giving aid to the poor, he argued, would only allow them to procreate more and worsen the population problem.

Today, Malthusians still believe that population growth is out of control and that if we simply reduce the number of people, we will have more resources and less poverty. On a small scale, this way of thinking seems to make sense: for example, if we think of two families with similar resources and incomes, one with two children and one with eight children, it seems easy to argue that the family with the higher population would be poorer because of the larger number of mouths to feed. Indeed, partly because of its apparently simple logic, this view of poverty being caused by an overpopulation crisis has become so ingrained as to be considered conventional wisdom, and it has certainly impacted population policy over the years (Hartmann 1987).

However, others argue that the population explosion is a myth and that the causes of poverty are not as simple as Malthusians make them out to be. Rather than simply concluding that more people equals more poverty and fewer resources, scholars take into account a number of factors that play into the complex

---

DID YOU KNOW?

On average, one U.S. citizen consumed as much energy as the following, in the indicated years:

2001 2.1 Germans
2002 12.1 Colombians
2003 28.9 Indians
2004 127 Haitians
2005 395 Ethiopians

Source: Sierra Club, http://www.sc.org/population/consumption/.

issue of population, such as culture, gender roles, education level, access to and information about birth control, eugenics and racism, different conceptions of what makes a "normal" family and what constitute "normal" standards of living, and so on. How population policy is crafted is dependent upon how these types of factors and attitudes are taken into account (or not taken into account) and also upon what are presumed to be the causes of population growth and shifts.

LOOKING AT THE "BOOM" AND ITS CAUSES

Some scholars have examined whether or not there has even been a population boom or threat, as well as examining the causes behind population growth. During the span of the twentieth century, there was indeed a remarkable increase in population. According to a recent report from the United Nations Population Division, the world's population increased from 1.65 billion in 1900 to 6 billion in 1999. Although this is the largest population the world has experienced, it does not necessarily have to be considered an out-of-control threat. Indeed, instead of such a growth causing a scarcity of food as Malthus had predicted, much of the boom is said to be caused by advances in food production, as well as advances in health and medicine (Hartmann 1987). Economist Dennis Avery reports that just in the years between the 1960s and 1990s, we have more than doubled the world's food supply (Simon 1995). In addition, initial rapid growth has now stabilized, and some countries are actually experiencing a decline in population.

It is interesting to note that in contrast to the view held by some Westerners that population growth is caused by people in the third world "overbreeding," much of the world's population growth can be attributed to Western advancements. However, because three-quarters of the world population live in the third world (Hartmann 1987) and because of the poverty we see in many parts of the world, critics argue that it is easy to forget about the surplus of food the world actually has and instead blame the poor for having too many children. From this perspective, the population issue cannot be understood unless people consider the underlying structural causes of poverty as they relate to social

---

DID YOU KNOW?

- Even though the world's food production has increased at a far greater rate than world population growth, about 830 million people in the third world continue to go hungry (Millen, Irwin, and Kim 2000).
- In the world, there are about 200 billionaires and more than 3 million millionaires, but there are also 100 million homeless people (Durning 1992).
- If the 225 richest people in the world gave even 4 percent of their wealth away in aid to the poor, it would be enough "to achieve and maintain access to basic education, basic health care, reproductive health care, adequate food, safe water, and adequate sanitation for all people living on the planet" (Millen, Irwin, and Kim 2000).

reproduction. The underlying structural causes of poverty include the ways food, wealth, and resources are distributed; inequalities in levels of education, healthcare, and social services throughout the world; and related attitudes about race, class, and gender as they shape how people think about survival, development, and poverty.

DEBATES ON POPULATION POLICY AND POVERTY

As mentioned above, there have been advancements in food production since Malthus's era, and the evidence of food surplus helps negate his concerns about a population "problem." Thus, many scholars have moved away from the stance that population growth causes poverty. Instead, they argue that an unequal distribution of resources is a main cause of poverty, and that population growth is in fact a symptom of poverty. Poor families throughout the world often deliberately have multiple children because they do not view children as just mouths to feed. Rather, multiple children may mean more hands to help tend the farm or to work in other ways to bring in more income for the family. More children also help ensure that the parents will be taken care of in their old age (Hartmann 1987). While many people in the United States have the luxury of Social Security and can afford retirement or nursing homes, not everyone in the world (and not even everyone in the United States) has such safety nets, and many people depend on their own children to look after them later in life.

People living in poverty may also have more children because of high infant mortality rates. Again, because not everyone has equal access to proper nutrition and adequate healthcare, many women face the reality that some of their children will die: "Each year in the Third World more than 10 million children die before reaching their first birthday. The average infant mortality rate is more than 90 deaths per 1,000 live births, compared to 20 in the industrialized countries.... The poor are thus caught in a death trap: They have to keep producing children in order that some will survive" (Hartmann 1987).

Not only are there unequal levels of wealth and resources throughout the world, but there are also unequal levels of consumption and energy use between the first and third worlds. While the mainstream notion is often that the poor masses of the developing world are draining our energy resources and harming the environment, "Analysts...point out that the developed world's consumption and capital are often more responsible for resource depletion in the poorer countries than are the growing populations of those countries" (Sagoff 1994). While the developing world makes up 75 percent of the world's population, the developed countries still manage to "account for 75 percent of world energy use and consume 85 percent of all forest products and 72 percent of steel production" (Sagoff 1994). Thus, many social scientists are pushed to rethink the "over-" population problem as a problem of "over-" consumption by a small segment of the world's population; many do not agree that harsh population control policies should be imposed on those living in the third world because of the reality that the first world often has both greater wealth and greater power to consume energy and resources.

DEBATES ON POPULATION POLICY AND EUGENICS

Many scholars argue that eugenicist and racist attitudes have been evident historically throughout population debates and have been a driving force behind many harmful and oppressive population policies. A eugenicist belief is a belief that there are lesser peoples who should be eliminated or at least decreased and contained, and a belief that there are better races or classes of people who should be preserved and whose race should remain "pure" or "uncontaminated" by the undesirable "others." Well-known extreme examples of eugenics include the genocide in Rwanda and the Nazis' extermination of Jews during the Holocaust. With regard to population policy and the control of fertility, there are eugenicist, racist, and classist attitudes about who should be permitted to reproduce and who should not. The inaccurate assumptions that many in the West or developed world have about birth rates in developing countries, for instance, may be due in part to a lack of examination of the unequal distribution of resources. However, the idea that third world people are somehow hypersexualized or not intelligent enough to use proper birth control also has racist connotations.

Historically, eugenicist policies have been implemented in the United States as well as elsewhere. In the late nineteenth century, some states began imposing restrictive population policies on a range of people considered undesirable, such as criminals, alcoholics, and the "feeble-minded." The states passed laws to restrict marriage among certain targeted populations, in order to prevent the propagation of children who might share the same characteristics as their parents (Jalsevac 2004). In the early years of the twentieth century, laws enforcing the sterilization of those somehow deemed unfit were also passed in most states, and by 1968, 65,000 U.S. citizens had been forced to undergo sterilization (Chase 1975).

Margaret Sanger is often considered one of the pioneers of the eugenicist movement in the United States. Although she helped found Planned Parenthood, which today helps to provide for the reproductive health of many women, she has been criticized for racist remarks and for her ties to eugenics groups (Hartmann 1987; Jalsevac 2004). Scholars such as Betsy Hartmann (1987) argue that Sanger's ideas about population control and birth control were fraught with ideas about who is suitable to have children and to make intelligent decisions about reproductive choice, and who needs to be controlled. In a 1930s article, Sanger's plan to spread eugenics included a call for aspiring parents to apply for a parenthood permit, as well as the suggestion that "feeble-minded persons, habitual congenital criminals, those afflicted with inheritable diseases, and others found biologically unfit should be sterilized in cases of doubt and should be isolated so as to prevent the perpetuation of their afflictions by breeding" (cited in Jalsevac 2004, 36).

High incidences of sterilization and other forms of unsafe or long-term birth control continue for certain segments of the population. Feminist scholar Andrea Smith (2002) notes that Native American women and women of color in general are seen as "polluting," and Smith cites numerous studies from the 1970s showing that Native American women (and sometimes men) were systematically sterilized, usually without their consent. Despite the desire of many poor or third world women to have large families, because of concerns about having enough children to work and support the family, these women do indeed want reproductive choice and access to safe and effective means of birth control, just as women of privilege do. Hartmann (1987) describes women she met in Bangladesh who particularly wanted birth control options that would allow them to space their pregnancies. However, the Bangladeshi women seemed to be experiencing one of two extremes: In some areas there was simply no access to birth control, and in other areas, women were persuaded and coerced, with little medical screening or counseling, to undergo irreversible sterilization or to try methods, like Depo-Provera or IUDs, that resulted in negative side effects. These "other" women were viewed and continue to be viewed as inferior and undeserving of the right to reproduce, and undeserving of the right to choose and have access to safe and effective means of birth control.

Whether we talk about an official, sanctioned international family planning policy or about the unofficial habit of a U.S. doctor to recommend sterilization for young, poor U.S. women deemed "welfare queens," population policy takes many forms and varies depending on its intended target. Supporters of top-down types of population policies believe that far-reaching birth control programs will curb poverty and will enable women in third world countries to have fewer children. In contrast, critics contend that women themselves should be able to make their own reproductive decisions and that population policies are often disproportionately implemented and/or encouraged in specific targeted communities, often in discriminatory ways.

DEBATES ON POPULATION POLICY AND REPRODUCTIVE FREEDOM

Additional debates concern how population policies serve either to empower women or to limit women's reproductive rights. Feminist scholars and social scientists have noted the complicated ways in which population policy and reproductive rights are interrelated. Scholar Betsy Hartmann argues, for instance, that although excessive sterilizations without consent are not good for women, antichoice groups that have supported putting an end to these sterilizations do not necessarily have women's best interests at heart:

> The population control and antiabortion philosophies...are both antichoice. Population control advocates imposed contraception and sterilization on women; the so-called Right to Life movement denies women the basic right of access to abortion and birth control. Neither takes the interests and rights of the individual woman as their starting point. Both approaches attempt to control women, instead of letting women control their bodies themselves. (1987, xii)

Indeed, population policies are often crafted in a disinterested manner, removed from the women and families they will influence. Feminists have pushed to shift the focus and reframe the "problem" of population as a problem of women's lack of reproductive freedoms.

LA OPERACIÓN IN PUERTO RICO

Rather than understanding Puerto Rico's economic problems in the 1920s and 1930s as a result of the United States' conquest of the island and its resources, U.S. officials declared that overpopulation was the main problem (Mass 1977). For example, with the help of exploitative trade policies, U.S. sugar interests moved in and disrupted the economy, uprooting thousands from their land and leaving 70 percent of the people landless by 1925 (Hartmann 1987). Instead of seeing this change in the distribution of wealth and land as a cause of poverty and social unrest, authorities identified overpopulation as the problem. With funding from the United States, the Puerto Rican government and agencies like the International Planned Parenthood Federation promoted *l'operación*, the sterilization of women, as the remedy. Other contraceptive methods were deemed too complicated for poor Puerto Rican women, and although many women wanted birth control of some kind, many did not understand that sterilization was permanent. By 1968, "one third of women of childbearing age had been sterilized on the island, the highest percentage anywhere in the world at that time" (Hartmann 1987).

Although much of the current debate concerning reproductive freedom, at least in the U.S. context, centers on access to birth control and the right to terminate an unwanted pregnancy, another basic reproductive right that is not necessarily discussed as much is the right of women to *have* children. Because the right and choice to have children are highly contextual and dependent on women's different circumstances, many feminists have argued for a broader definition of reproductive rights. For example, some argue that corporations that dump toxic chemicals infringe on the reproductive right of a woman to raise a child in a clean and healthy neighborhood. Anannya Bhattacharjee writes about how poor women and women of color are criminalized and are robbed of their right to be mothers because they are incarcerated at an excessive rate (2002). These concerns can be seen as a sort of population control, and are just as much violations of reproductive freedoms as are enforced sterilizations.

CONCLUSION

In general, women, rather than men, bear the greater burden of reproduction concerns. Although, biologically, women may have to go through pregnancy and bear children, from a social constructivist view it is not inherently necessary for women to be primarily or solely responsible for birth control, nor to be the sole targets of population policies (Hartmann 1987). Women generally have less political and economic power than men, have less access to formal education, are less able to get jobs outside of the home and are paid less if they do have jobs, and are more likely to be victims of rape or abuse during their lifetimes (Hartmann 1987). Despite these forms of structural inequalities, poor women in particular are often blamed for their reproductive decisions or practices. Thus, women are often put in a lose-lose situation because they can be blamed for having too many babies and punished for it through population policies like unnecessary sterilizations, while they are simultaneously told that their only value is as mothers and caregivers. While supporters of population policies believe that they are helping societies develop or modernize by lowering birth rates, critics of these policies tend to emphasize women's subjective experiences of motherhood and reproduction, and to acknowledge women's "rights" in controlling their reproductive lives as against the "rights" of governments to determine birthing patterns in a given country or community.

See also Birth Control; Birthing Practices; Gender and International Development; Medicine and Medicalization: Views on Women's Bodies.

Further Reading: Balkin, Karen F., *Population: Opposing Viewpoints* (Detroit: Greenhaven Press, 2005); Bhattacharjee, Anannya, "Private Fists and Public Force: Race, Gender, and Surveillance," in *Policing the National Body,* ed. Jael Silliman and Anannya Bhattacharjee (Cambridge, MA: South End Press, 2002); Chase, Allen, *The Legacy of Malthus* (New York: Alfred A. Knopf, 1975); Durning, Alan Thein, *How Much Is Enough? The Consumer Society and the Fate of the Earth* (New York: W. W. Norton, 1992); Franks, Angela, *Margaret Sanger's Eugenic Legacy: A Control of Female Fertility* (Jefferson, NC: McFarland, 2005); Hartmann, Betsy, *Reproductive Rights and Wrongs* (New York: Harper and Row, 1987); Jalsevac, Paul, *The Inherent Racism of Population Control,* 2004, LifeSiteNews.com, a division of Interim Publishing, available at: http://www.lifesite.net/waronfamily/Population_Control/Inherentracism.pdf; Mass, Bonnie, "Puerto Rico: A Case Study of Population Control," *Latin American Perspectives* 4, no. 4 (Autumn 1977): 66–81; Mazur, Laurie Ann, ed., *Beyond the Numbers* (Washington, DC: Island Press, 1994); Meadows, Donella H., "Seeing the Population Issue Whole," *Economist,* June 1993; Millen, Joyce V., Alec Irwin, and Jim Yong Kim, "Introduction: What Is Growing? Who Is Dying?" in *Dying for Growth,* ed. Jim Young and Joyce V. Millen, 2–10 (Monroe, ME: Common Courage Press, 2000); Population Council, available at: http://www.popcouncil.org/index.html; Sagoff, Mark, "Population, Nature, and the Environment," in *Beyond the Numbers,* ed. Laurie Ann Mazur, 33–39 (Washington, DC: Island Press, 1994); Sierra Club, available at: http://www.sc.org/population/consumption/; Simon, Julian, ed., *The State of Humanity* (Malden, MA: Blackwell, 199); Smith, Andrea, "Better Dead than Pregnant: The Colonization of Native Women's Reproductive Health," in *Policing the National Body,* ed. Jael Silliman and Anannya Bhattacharjee (Cambridge, MA: South End Press, 2002); United Nations Population Division, available at: http://www.un.org/esa/population/unpop.htm.

Heidi Pitzer

PORNOGRAPHY

Pornography has been opposed on the grounds of indecency, obscenity, its purported harmful effects on viewers, and its role in the objectification of women. Anti-pornography advocates, including neoconservatives and feminists alike, who argue that harmful images should not be protected under free speech laws, have fought to ban pornography through censorship. Sex-positive feminists and pro-pornography advocates typically defend free speech and argue that not all pornography is bad and that censorship will not end violence against women.

BACKGROUND

While various forms of visual erotica have been around for centuries in cultures around the world, in modern Western society pornography has become a highly commercialized phenomenon. In the late twentieth century and the early twenty-first century, the meaning of pornography, including the question of what distinguishes art from pornography, has been a subject of heated debate. What does it mean to call something pornography? Does pornography have a positive or negative effect on women's (and men's) lives? These are some of the central questions asked by both supporters and critics of the modern pornography industry.

Many scholars agree that the 1980s were the decade when pornography debates exploded into national discussion. Three major groups have been involved in the debates around pornography: (1) pro-censorship, anti-pornography neoconservative groups; (2) pro-censorship, anti-pornography feminist groups; and (3) anti-censorship feminist groups. Interestingly, although feminists and right-wing neoconservatives rarely agree on issues, in the case of pornography some groups of feminists have sided with right-wing neoconservatives (many of whom are men) in their fight to ban pornography and promote its censorship wherever possible. This has prompted other groups of women's rights advocates to take a different stance on pornography by focusing on freedom of speech and the labor rights of women who work in the pornography industry rather than focusing on its censorship. Additionally, some groups argue that violent and/or sexual visual images do not have an adverse affect on people's socialization; therefore, they point out, pornography is no different from other forms of erotica that are often viewed as socially acceptable forms of art. Finally, critics of anti-pornography crusaders point out that often these individuals target groups they perceive as deviant, such as African Americans and/or gays and lesbians, adding fodder to an already complicated debate about the effects of pornography as a visual medium on people's consciousness.

HISTORY OF PORNOGRAPHY LEGISLATION AND POLICY

In 1986, the Meese Commission, officially known as the Attorney General's Commission on Pornography, published a controversial report claiming a causal link between pornography and violence, with little scientific evidence to back up this claim (Hefner 1987, 25). Despite its widely recognized lack of scientific evidence, this report has provided a strong justification for subsequent federal policies concerning pornography and violence against women. For example, following the Meese Commission's report, the 1992 Pornography Victims' Protection Act and the 1994 Violence against Women Act were passed, both contributing to criminalizing the production, distribution, and consumption of pornography.

Following the Meese Commission's report, right-wing neoconservative Senator Jesse Helms led a censorship crusade that targeted specific artists. In particular, Helms led a crusade against the artist Robert Mapplethorpe and the portion

DID YOU KNOW?

The 1986 Meese Commission Report on Pornography argues that while free speech is protected, anything that causes harm can be censored. Although the commission gathered information with the purpose of showing that pornography causes violence, some have pointed out that the commission's own evidence did not support that claim (Hefner 1987, 25). The Meese Commission used the term *pornography* with all its negative connotations to describe everything from magazines like *Playboy* to anything that depicts sexuality. Critics charge that the members of the commission exaggerated their report by evaluating only the most violent images and by imbuing their argument with biases about homosexuality, cross-racial desire, and other forms of sexuality that they viewed as deviant. Ironically, this report and subsequent legislation, including the 1994 Violence against Women Act and President George W. Bush's legislation on sex trafficking, were designed in the name of women's rights, yet arguably through a neoconservative lens.

of his art that depicted homoeroticism and sadomasochism. Robert Mapplethorpe's photography included many types of subjects, including still lifes, portraits, human nudes, and studio depictions of sadomasochism (a small percentage of his work). Robert Mapplethorpe's exhibit, *The Perfect Moment,* provoked a national campaign for the censorship of his explicitly gay-themed and sado-masochist-themed photographs.

Following Helms's attack on Mapplethorpe's exhibit, *The Perfect Moment,* a gallery director in Washington, DC, refused to display Mapplethorpe's exhibit on the grounds that it would only provide more material that Jesse Helms would exploit in his attacks on lesbian- and gay-themed work. The exhibit moved to the Contemporary Arts Center in Cincinnati, where curator Dennis Barrie faced criminal charges for exhibiting "obscene" material. (The charges were later dismissed.) In 1989, the director of the National Endowment for the Arts (NEA) withdrew funding from Mapplethorpe's exhibit, and in 1990 the NEA withdrew funding from four other artists, three of whom produced work on lesbian and gay identities and sexualities while the fourth produced work opposing violence against women (Duggan and Hunter 2006, 24–25).

In that same year, the rap group 2 Live Crew was prosecuted in Florida for the "obscene" lyrics in their album *As Nasty as They Wanna Be,* while white comedian Andrew Dice Clay peddled racism and misogyny on nationwide television and Madonna performed sexually explicit acts during live performances. Certainly 2 Live Crew's lyrics, which refer to black women as "cunts," bitches," and "hos" and advocate violent sex and even rape, are misogynist and deserve strong criticism, but is prosecution under obscenity laws the correct response (Crenshaw 1993)?

In 1991, Congress limited National Endowment for the Arts funding to art that passes a test of "decency," further institutionalizing the view that certain forms of art that are erotic in nature (especially gay and lesbian art and art that challenges heterosexual, white, middle-class norms) are potentially "indecent" and must be further assessed before being funded by the government. Between 1992 and 2000, during the years of the Clinton administration, less emphasis was placed on pornography and indecency in art. However, in 2005, under the leadership of George W. Bush (2000–2008), Attorney General Alberto Gonzalez resurrected the Meese Commission report and associated legislation in order to create the Justice Department Task Force on Obscenity and renew the prosecution of lesbian and gay, racial, and other controversially themed art (Duggan and Hunter 2006, 28).

ANTI-PORNOGRAPHY DEBATES

Those who oppose the production and consumption of pornography, including many neoconservative groups, tend to view pornography as obscene. Their notion of obscenity or indecency is often based on religious or cultural arguments about socially acceptable forms of art in modern society. They apply their definition of pornography to material that is self-defined as such, including magazines such as *Hustler* and *Playboy,* and to some sexually themed art, such as that of Robert Mapplethorpe.

Right-Wing Conservatives

Prominent neoconservative crusaders in the anti-pornography movement include Senator Jesse Helms, Reverend Jerry Falwell, and the right-wing women's Eagle Forum founder, Phyllis Schlafly. As early as 1977, in her crusade against feminism, Phyllis Schlafly fought to ban the Boston Women's Health Book Collective self-help manual for women, *Our Bodies, Ourselves,* on the basis of pornography. The manual, which is now in its eighth edition and has been translated into at least 19 languages, focuses primarily on women's health (BWHBC 2007). The American Library Association lists culturally transformative literary classics such as *The Color Purple* by Alice Walker, *Of Mice and Men* by John Steinbeck, *The Catcher in the Rye* by J. D. Salinger, and *The Handmaid's Tale* by Margaret Atwood among the top 100 challenged books of the twentieth century.

Many anti-pornography activists claim that because pornography is obscene and therefore not art, it is not subject to protection under the U.S. Constitution's guarantee of free speech. Some also argue that pornography causes violence against women through individual men copying practices they see in pornography, although research on this subject is highly divided. Particularly in cases of serial sexual murder like that of Ted Bundy, individual men have admitted to imitating pornography and named it as the cause of their sexualized violence (Cameron and Frazer 1994, 242–47). The "copycat" and "addiction" models can lead to excusing the perpetrators' sexualized violence by saying that they copied the violence of pornography and that they became addicted to it following the addiction models used for drugs and alcohol (Cameron and Frazer 1994, 248–53). According to this addiction model, the perpetrators start with less violent pornography to obtain their "fix" but then need more and more violent images, until watching the most violent pornography no longer satisfies them and they must commit the violent acts themselves (Cameron and Frazer 1994, 243–44).

These causal models of pornography ignore the following facts: (1) that most pornography is not violent (Hefner 1987); (2) that most incidents of sexualized violence are not copies of pornography (Cameron and Frazer 1994, 243); and (3) that the models pathologize the perpetrator of the violence as the victim of an illness who is therefore not responsible for the violence. What is most troubling is the way that causal models deny individual agency by ignoring the fact that the vast majority of consumers of pornography do not commit sexualized violence. What is more credible than a linear, causal model that leads from the consumption of any and all pornography to the consumption of violence is an analysis that focuses on the subset of pornography that *is* violent, and here, as feminists have argued, rape and other forms of sexualized violence are first and foremost violence, not sex.

Feminists

Anti-pornography feminists, historically led by Catharine MacKinnon and Andrea Dworkin, protest pornography on the basis that it causes violence against women. Legal scholar Catharine MacKinnon names pornography as the cause of violent acts against women and the overall subordination of women in society. She views pornography as one symptom of the patriarchal mistreatment of women. In contrast to neoconservatives who have sought to ban pornography on the basis of obscenity laws that imply criminal penalties under the law, MacKinnon was among the first to argue that pornography is a violation of women's civil rights and that women harmed by pornography should be allowed to press charges in civil courts (MacKinnon 1987). She and other pro-censorship feminists advocate restricting the production, sale, and consumption of pornography due to their belief that ending or reducing pornography would end or reduce violence against women and the subordination of women. Andrea Dworkin, a writer and radical feminist activist who died in 2005, worked with MacKinnon to ban pornography through local ordinances and federal legislation. This led to the unlikely alliance of feminists and right-wing neoconservatives in the crusade to ban pornography.

MacKinnon's and Dworkin's perspectives on pornography were the product of the broader radical feminist movement that emerged in the late 1960s and continued through the 1970s. The 1970s were the decade of lesbian feminism, which was dominated by white women and included consideration of violence against women and responses that named sexism as the central cause of inequality, and called men and patriarchy the sources of violence against women (Lorber 2007). Anti-pornography, pro-censorship groups, of which Women against Pornography is the most famous, were formed during the 1970s in response to the theory that pornography, with its violent and sexualized images of women, caused violence against women through individual men copying scenes from pornography and through the creation of a misogynist society. They also denounced the production of pornography as exploitative of the women

ANNIE SPRINKLE, SEX-POSITIVE FEMINIST

A former prostitute, stripper, and porn star, Annie Sprinkle left the traditional porn industry to become a sex-positive performance artist and educator. She received her PhD in human sexuality studies and has produced several performance tours and sex-positive videos including *The Sluts and Goddesses Video Workshop—Or How to Be a Sex Goddess in 101 Easy Steps*. She has also published a memoir, *Post-Porn Modernist: My 25 Years as a Media Whore* (San Francisco: Cleis Press, 1998).

who worked in the industry. It was not uncommon to read about local feminist groups committing acts of civil disobedience by entering stores that sold pornography and tearing up pornographic magazines in front of store owners and clients. Many feminists were willing to go to jail to defend their cause. In northern California, members of the Preying Mantis Brigade, an underground revolutionary feminist group, emphasized this type of civil disobedience as a reflection of their belief that violent representations led to violent crimes against women, including rape, sexual harassment, and sexual abuse. Some even trained themselves in arms as a way to protect women against what they perceived as an abusive, patriarchal society.

Anti-pornography feminists hypothesized that outlawing pornography would reduce its production and consumption, which would in turn reduce violence against women and the objectification and exploitation of women as well as all others involved in the pornography industry. In 1983, MacKinnon and Dworkin worked with neoconservative legislators and activists to write the first anti-porn law for the City of Minneapolis, which was twice passed by the City Council and twice vetoed by the mayor. In 1984, the City of Indianapolis successfully passed the first anti-pornography legislation based on MacKinnon and Dworkin's civil rights framework, legislation that was later ruled unconstitutional by the Supreme Court. To date, this case is considered legally significant in debates on free speech versus pornography.

ANTI-CENSORSHIP DEBATES

Anti-censorship feminists, while they agree that pornography may include degrading and dehumanizing pictures of women, do not believe that all pornography is exploitative or that restricting pornography would reduce the incidence of violence against women. They argue instead that censorship, the main vehicle of attempts to suppress pornography, differentially suppresses free speech and is ineffective in reducing the production, sale, and consumption of pornography.

Anti-censorship feminist groups were formed in the 1980s in response to the attack on freedom of expression. The Feminist Anti-Censorship Taskforce began and grew to four chapters in 1984. Anti-censorship and pro–freedom of speech advocates generally do not argue that there is nothing wrong with pornography and the way it represents women (see, for example, Cameron and

Frazer 1994). Rather, they argue against censorship because it is a violation of the right to free speech, which in the United States is protected by the First Amendment to the Constitution. Concerned by Dworkin and MacKinnon's alliance with right-wing neoconservatives, many groups of feminists began to oppose the feminist anti-pornography stance on the basis that it was problematic or elitist, leading to what many scholars now refer to as the "sex wars" of the 1980s (Duggan and Hunter 2006). Anti-censorship feminists have pointed out that not all pornography is violent, and that often neoconservatives have selectively targeted forms of art that they view as controversial because of their own racism or homophobia, rather than because of objective societal standards on decency in art. They also point out that even in the mainstream media, there are many violent representations of sex and of men and women that may cause as much harm to viewers as pornography. That is, if pornography causes violence against women by devaluing and degrading them, one must critique all the other types of images that devalue and degrade women. Finally, they argue that banning pornography will not alleviate the problems it allegedly causes: It will not eliminate the demand for pornography, nor will it eliminate the supply of a product that is so cheap and easy to produce. Some also point out that completely removing pornography from circulation will have a detrimental effect on the livelihoods of people who act and are photographed in pornography, which is now a multi-billion-dollar industry.

DOES PORNOGRAPHY CAUSE HARM?

Central to the debates on pornography is the idea that sexual images may cause harm to viewers. The question has been raised, then, as to whether pornography causes harm, and if so, what can be done to reduce or eliminate it. This, of course, also depends upon how one defines pornography, further complicating any policy or legal discussion. Some observers point out that one must differentiate between the different types of harm that pornography may cause: harm to those who make porn, harm to individuals who view it, and harm to society. Debates also continue on whether the harmful effects of pornography, however defined, should be criminalized or addressed through education, and how censorship boards can most appropriately distinguish between harmful and nonharmful images, in mainstream popular culture (for example, television, film, radio) as well as in the pornography industry itself.

CONCLUSION

Is pornography a reflection of violence in society or a cause of it? This question continues to perplex both supporters of free speech and supporters of censorship, feminists and neoconservatives alike. On an interpersonal level, most men do not perpetrate violence against women, although clear gendered cultural patterns exist that illustrate a disproportionate amount of violence against women, including rape, sexual harassment, and sexual abuse, MacKinnon herself being one of the most widely cited feminists writing on this topic. On a societal level, pornography may arguably normalize violence against women and dehumanize women in ways that make violence more likely, but mainstream images also objectify, dehumanize, and sexualize women. As the mainstream media are so ubiquitous, what is the ultimate merit of focusing on a small subset of largely avoidable images to the exclusion of all the other ways in which women are exploited, visually and physically? Just as criminalizing pornography would not stop its production, eliminating pornography would not necessarily end violence against women. At the very least, more research needs to be conducted to assess the relationship between violent images and violent acts. And importantly, what we now know as pornography has long existed in both Western and non-Western societies, a historical fact that many current crusaders tend to forget.

See also Crime and Criminalization; Media Images of Women: Music; Media Images of Women: Television and Film; Sex Trafficking; Sex Work.

Further Reading: Boston Women's Health Book Collective (BWHBC), 2007, available at: http://www.ourbodiesourselves.org/, accessed May 26, 2007 (this Web site explains the history of the collective and its publication, *Our Bodies, Ourselves*); Cameron, Deborah, and Elizabeth Frazer, "On the Question of Pornography and Sexual Violence: Moving beyond Cause and Effect," in *Feminisms and Pornography*, ed. Drucilla Cornell, 240–253 (Oxford: Oxford University Press, 1994 [2000]); Cornell, Drucilla, *Feminism and Pornography* (New York: Oxford University Press, 2000); Crenshaw, Kimberle, "The 2 Live Crew Controversy," in *Feminism and Pornography*, ed. Drucilla Cornell, 218–239 (Oxford: Oxford University Press, 1993 [2000]); Delacoste, Frances, and Priscilla Alexander, eds., *Sex Work: Writings by Women in the Sex Industry* (London: Virago, 1988); Duggan Lisa, and Nan D. Hunter, *Sex Wars: Sexual Dissent and Political Culture*, 10th anniversary edition (New York: Routledge, 2006); Feminists against Censorship, available at: http://www.fiawol.demon.co.uk/FAC/. Feminist anti-censorship organization; Feminists for Free Expression, available at: http://ffeusa.org; Gibson, Pamela Church, *More Dirty Looks: Gender, Pornography and Power*, 2nd ed. (London: British Film Institute, 2004); Hefner, Christie, "The Meese Commission: Sex, Violence and Censorship," *The Humanist* 47, no. 1 (January/February 1987): 25–29, 46; Lorber, Judith, *Gender Inequality: Feminist Theories and Politics*, 3rd ed. (New York: Oxford University Press, 2007); MacKinnon, Catharine A., *Feminism Unmodified* (Cambridge, MA: Harvard University Press, 1987); MacKinnon, Catharine A., and Andrea Dworkin, eds., *In Harm's Way: The Pornography Civil Rights Hearings* (Cambridge, MA: Harvard University Press, 1997); Mercer, Kobena, "Just Looking for Trouble: Robert Mapplethorpe and Fantasies of Race," in *Feminism and Pornography*, ed. Drucilla Cornell, 460–476 (Oxford: Oxford University Press, 2000); National Coalition for the Protection of Children and Families, formerly National Coalition against Pornography, available at: http://www.nationalco alition.org/; Segal, Lynne, and Mary McIntosh, eds., *Sex Exposed: Sexuality and the Pornography Debate* (New Brunswick, NJ: Rutgers University Press, 1993).

Chana Wolfson

POSTFEMINISM

Postfeminism is a term as complex and imbued with multiple paradoxes as its predecessor, *modern feminism*. There is vocal and vigorous debate about whether the term *postfeminism* represents a profeminist position, signifying the next stage of feminist evolution, or an antifeminist position, claiming that feminism is "dead," no longer necessary, or problematic.

BACKGROUND

Postfeminism is not a concept with a unified meaning for those who might be considered stakeholders in the ongoing social discussion, debate, and research on women's status in the social world. Given the conflicting definitions of the term being circulated and the multiplicity of interests and constituents, it is useful to begin with a brief examination of its genesis.

The term *postfeminism* is generally believed to be an artifact of late-twentieth-century rhetoric. It is asserted (usually in the mass media) that postfeminism is a term of the 1980s, some placing its inauguration in 1982, with the publication of Susan Bolotin's article, "Voices from the Post-Feminist Generation," in the *New York Times Magazine.* In this article, Bolotin describes the phenomenon of 20-year-old women who have benefited from second wave feminism and endorsed feminist goals but rejected the label of "feminist." This piece is only one of many pronouncements of the death, demise, end, or rejection of feminism to appear in mass media outlets from the early 1980s onward. Taken together they represent a concerted assertion of the collapse of feminism and feminist goals (Brooks 1997; Faludi 1991; Gamble 2000; Hawkesworth 2004). Some have placed the use of the term *postfeminism* as beginning with Susan Faludi's 1991 *New York Times* bestseller, *Backlash: The Undeclared War against American Women,* and through her analysis of the development of the social momentum against the gains made by second wave feminism in the United States.

This genealogy contrasts with that of Phoca and Wright (1999), who argue that postfeminism initially developed in France during the late 1960s as an extension of the deconstructionist movement in French feminist theory. For these scholars, the genesis of the term is not an ending but rather a new beginning. It signals an intellectual movement against the assumptions and categories established in the first and second wave feminist movements. Thus the foundational concepts of these movements are not simply challenged but destabilized and rejected, so as to advance feminist theory and reposition it in the face of reasserted institutional patriarchal authority (Andermahr, Lovel, and Wolkowitz 1997; Murray 1997). Despite these arguments for the mid- to late-twentieth-century development of the term, there is persuasive evidence that it was in use much earlier. According to some scholars, postfeminism was in use near the end of first wave feminism in the early twentieth century. Cott (1987) points out that at that time, "some progressive women were referring to their position as 'post-feminist'" (13). This use of the term was not a repudiation of feminism or feminist goals but a statement about the next stage of engagement. Faludi argues that the postfeminism that emerged in the 1980s and early 1990s is the result of a concerted conservative effort to roll back the gains of second wave feminism and reimpose traditional gender hierarchies. The competing understandings of the origin(s) of postfeminism are important, as they serve to influence the themes that can be glimpsed in its use and meaning within the currents of the mainstream media and academic discourses pertaining to shifting power relations.

THEMES AND CONTROVERSIES

Five fairly distinct motifs and themes are typically revealed in the various meanings given to the term *postfeminism.*

Profeminism and the Antifoundational Movement

The first usage of the term is as a theoretical outgrowth of the antifoundational movement. The postfeminism that grew out of the deconstructive analysis of French feminists led to a new set of self-reflective queries about the subject of feminism; these queries grew out of the antifoundational movements of the 1960s and 1970s (Brooks 1997). The past few decades have seen the emergence of a number of antifoundational "posts," in particular, postmodernism, poststructuralism, postfeminism, and posthumanism. Each of these has its roots in the deconstructive techniques of Jacques Derrida and each has become influential within academia and academic feminism. All of these "posts" serve to challenge, albeit in different ways, the fundamental canons of social theory, social structures, the concept of society itself, and the human subject, along with claims to truth made by classical social theories. The stance here is not one that rejects or repudiates feminism because its work is concluded, but one that significantly seeks to deconstruct the notion of gender and heterosexuality while building on its initial stages of development. From within this perspective, this is the necessary next step, and only by calling into use and borrowing the deconstructionist tools to deconstruct concepts of power, social categories, and gender is there a way forward for gender equality.

However, this deconstructive focus is one that has engendered some significant criticisms as being not at all useful or practical for dealing with oppression. This focus has been seen as an abandonment of the "real-life problems and discourses of most women" (Murray 1997, 44). For some scholars, the deconstructive techniques of postmodernism, and thus postfeminism, leave little space for addressing the more critical questions: What sort of social world do we desire? How can we improve the overall lives of women if we can make no claims about what should be done? Young (1997) even argues against theory altogether, by stating that

> feminists do not need and should not want theory in this sense. Instead, we should take a more pragmatic orientation to our intellectual discourse. . . . I mean categorizing, explaining, developing accounts and arguments that are tied to specific practical and political problems. (Young 1997, 16–17)

From this pragmatic perspective, it is of little use to ask for a deconstruction of the feminine as a category of subordination if it leaves little room for an active engagement with women's status and oppression.

The Backlash against Second Wave Feminism

A second common usage of the term *postfeminism* is as a social rejection of feminism. This usage has been popularized by the media and by social critics, especially on the political and religious right, in what has been described (see Faludi 1991; Henry 2004; Marx Ferree and Hess 1995) as a "backlash" against second wave feminism. In this analysis, postfeminist rhetoric seeks to place all feminisms in an antipleasure, antimasculinity, antifemininity, and antifamily framework. Observers who claim that we live in a postfeminist society often believe that feminism has destabilized the family, gender social relations, the economy, religion, and the very fabric of society. Thus, the corrective action is to restore women to the home and men as "heads of families," as the only cure for the excesses of feminism. The relegation of the period of the 1980s and early 1990s to postfeminism is key to the backlash against feminism and is therefore seen by profeminists as a conscious strategy deployed by antifeminists to further their political cause. As Henry (2004) points out, "the notion that the 1980s can be dismissed as a post-feminist decade is, in great part, a fiction that has helped to propagate conservatives' views of feminism" (21). In other words, as profeminists have pointed out, this view of postfeminism has served to persuade women, in a Madison Avenue–like manner, that feminism is dangerous, unnecessary, and passé.

Postfeminism as the Next Stage of Feminism

A third way of looking at the term *postfeminism* focuses primarily on the historical continuity and development of feminism as a form of social thought and action. In this analysis, postfeminism is the next developmental stage for feminism. It has become the inheritor of the gains of first and second wave feminism and thus it is really a sort of linearly anchored feminism that continues the work of previous feminisms. In this view, postfeminist thought also includes new voices that are addressing new concerns, particularly in a feminist context. In this scenario, postfeminism is sometimes conflated with third wave feminism, since both have provided important critiques of second wave feminist political practices. However, most would agree that postfeminism and third wave feminism are distinct theoretical strands of feminism, each with its own proponents. One of third wave feminism's strongest voices, Rebecca Walker, stated in a 1992 interview in *Ms Magazine* that "she wasn't post-feminist, she was the Third Wave" (Walker 1992, 41). In the foreword to the anthology *The Fire This Time: Young Activists and the New Feminism,* Walker states, "we want to be linked with our foremothers . . . but we also want to make space for young women to create their own, different brand of revolt, and so we chose the name Third Wave" (1995, xvii). This statement points to one of the areas of tension between postfeminism and third wave feminism: The generational relationship between mothers and daughters became the focus of feminist debate within a moment of social transition. A key component of third wave feminism is the continued importance of feminism in politics, economy, culture, and education, as these areas involve more than mere social institutions that required the corrective remedy of inclusion to dismantle patriarchy. As Labaton and Martin (2004) argue, "the feminism of younger activists goes beyond the rhetoric of inclusion. The significant important lesson we have learned from the second wave's faux pas is that a feminist movement cannot succeed if it does not challenge power structures of wealth and race" (xxix). However, some would argue that the claim by some third wave feminists that they seek to create a feminism that is outside the second wave ignores the fact that historically the third wave has emerged from and developed after the second wave. Furthermore, the notion that third wave feminism is outside second wave feminism, rather than a continuation of it, can be seen as emblematic of the rejection of earlier (that is, second wave) feminists by the current "twenty something" feminists who tend to identify with the third wave. The ongoing definitional efforts of third wave feminists point to the continued ontological evolution of feminism. It is worth noting with that while the *Routledge Critical Dictionary of Feminism and Post-feminism* includes "postfeminism" in its title, the editors of the dictionary argue for a superior functional quality for the term *third wave feminism* over *postfeminism*. This advantage is, according to the authors, that third wave feminism "stands on the shoulders of other, earlier, feminist movements" (Gamble 2000, 54). Thus the implication is clear: third wave feminism allows the ready acceptance of ongoing feminist efforts because it builds on a foundation laid by earlier feminists. In sum, while some equate postfeminism with third wave feminism, there are at least as many voices claiming that they are entirely different concepts.

Postfeminism as Personal Empowerment

A fourth meaning given to the term *postfeminism* is that of a type of personal empowerment that rejects the so-called Victorian effects of prior feminisms.

WOMEN'S ACTIVISM IN A POSTFEMINIST ERA

It is ironic that in an era when *postfeminism* often means that feminism is dead and that feminists have moved on from collective social action, on Sunday, April 25, 2004, more than a million people converged on the mall in Washington, DC, for the largest march on Washington in U.S. history. Named the March for Women's Lives, it was the latest and largest in a series of women's marches that date from 1989. The March for Women's Lives was organized by seven national women's rights groups to support woman's access to legal abortion and birth control. In addition, a diverse range of supporting organizations with varied constituencies and interests also participated, including the National Latina Institute for Reproductive Health, the Black Women's Health Imperative, the American Civil Liberties Union, the National Association for the Advancement of Colored People, the Feminist Majority, Planned Parenthood, and representatives from 57 other countries. The issues raised included economic rights, women's reproductive health issues, and global family planning. Although the march focused on reproductive rights, it was also a political rally around a variety of social justice issues such as AIDS, equal pay, and healthcare access.

Denfeld (1995) maintains that embracing feminism means the development of "a moral and spiritual crusade that would take us back to a time worse than our mother's day—back to the nineteenth-century values of sexual morality, spiritual purity, and political helplessness...current feminism would create the very same morally pure yet helplessly martyred role that women suffered from a century ago" (46–47). According to this view, second wave feminism was antisex and is as sexually repressive as Victorian ideologies (Denfeld 1995). In this analysis, postfeminism is a pro-pleasure or sex-positive perspective (typically heterosexual) that argues that since second wave feminism was "antisex," it follows that postfeminism is sexually liberated, feminine, and fun. An example of this is the assertion of Camille Paglia, one of the postfeminist pundits of the early 1990s: "The reform wing of feminism to which I belong burst into public view in the early 1990s, but it actually has a long lineage. The most radical pro-sex of us began our struggles with the *puritanism* and *groupthink* of feminist leaders from the moment the women's movement revived in the late 1960s" (Paglia 1997). In addition to Paglia's work, there emerged other, equally visible, antifeminist postfeminist voices. The early 1990s postfeminist movement publications, such as René Denfeld's *The New Victorians* (1995), Katie Roiphe's *The Morning After* (1994), and Christina Hoff Sommers's *Who Stole Feminism?* (1995), catapulted the so-called crisis of feminism into the public's eye. In different ways, each of these authors serves up a cautionary tale with feminism as the villain. All of these works enjoyed considerable mainstream media attention and fueled the media's claims of a crisis and of the "death" of feminism.

An important aspect to the rise of these works is that each author claims a type of feminism for herself that gives her a credibility that the other critics of feminism lack. Further, these authors employ a "common sense" stance with regard to gender relations that emphasizes what they describe as the extreme nature of feminism, which, they claim forced women to view themselves as victims.

Feminism as No Longer Necessary

Finally, there are those who maintain that the "post" really refers to the obsolescence of second wave feminism as a necessary tool for destabilizing patriarchy and/or addressing gender inequities. From this perspective, the work of feminism has been accomplished, since we now have gender equality. Dow (1996) points out that "media accounts [of feminism] often assume that opportunity for women has exploded, thus confirming the belief that feminism has triumphed, at least in the public sphere" (87). Thus, in this view, if women aren't successful in the public sphere it is the result of individual choices and a personal lack of resourcefulness. Critics of the obsolescence argument (see Faludi, 1991; Marx Ferree and Hess 1995) maintain that women have been seduced, primarily by the media, into believing that gender inequality is passé or unnecessary. Central to the message that feminism is largely irrelevant is the notion that women have achieved all that is achievable. The critics of what might be termed a type of postfeminist false consciousness argument ask us to consider who has been left out of this achievement. From this perspective, then, it is clear that working-class and poor women, lesbians, transgendered women, women of color, and disabled women (to name only a few) comprise a category of "other women" for whom the feminist ideals have yet to materialize.

Often the argument that feminism is irrelevant is linked with the notion that feminism is responsible for the multiple problems besetting U.S. women today as they enter the public sphere while maintaining their private realms, often with little help or formal support. In this interpretation of feminism, it is argued that the contemporary pressures of having to work and manage family life are the result of the "successes" of second wave feminism, which is blamed for having seduced women into "having it all" but at a cost. The increasing demands of work and family have placed women in a no-win situation that forces them into the competing demands of work and home. Proponents of this notion argue that women who choose home and family, such as "stay at home" moms, are viewed as "victims" by feminists.

CONCLUSION

It is clear that among the varied voices claiming a postfeminist stance there are distinct and at times oppositional themes that are part of the larger circulating tropes of gender, sex, and feminism at the beginning of the twenty-first century. These themes are imperfect yet provide the building blocks for a basic working understanding of the concepts under contention in postfeminism. It is both ironic and significant that the term *postfeminism* implies that there is some level of ideological agreement about the term *feminism*. Further, it implies that this agreement serves as the foundation for some sort of ontological stability within feminist enterprises. This implied stability belies the fact that the term *feminism* has never existed as a specific concept. There has never been *a feminism* but rather *multiple feminisms* that share a common core concern—that of women's status in the world. And while the multiple feminisms that have developed share a core concept, that of gender as a central social force or set of social relations, the tensions between them provide a useful tool for exploration and for developing new understandings. The disparate feminisms will likely never agree on the exact shape and structure of this social force and its impact on the lives of women. Some might maintain that the lack of unity is a weakness that leaves feminism powerless to affect social and economic change. However, this position is shortsighted, because the value of feminist discourses lies in the very debates and dialogues that occur within all areas of feminism, including postfeminism.

See also Family Values; Politics and Political Ideologies: Right-Wing Women; Postmodernist and Poststructuralist Feminisms; Second and Third Wave Feminisms.

Further Reading: Andermahr, Sonya, Terry Lovel, and Carol Wolkowitz, eds., *A Glossary of Feminist Theory* (London: Arnold, 1997); Bolotin, Susan, "Voices from the Post-Feminist Generation," *New York Times Magazine,* October 17, 1982 (Sunday late city final edition), sec. 6, p. 29, col. 1; Brooks, Ann, *Postfeminisms: Feminism, Cultural Theory, and Cultural*

Forms (New York: Routledge, 1997); Cott, Nancy, *The Grounding of Modern Feminism* (New Haven, CT: Yale University Press, 1987); Denfeld, Rene, *The New Victorians: A Young Woman's Challenge to the Old Feminist Order* (New York: Warner Books, 1995); Derrida, Jacques, *Of Grammatology*, trans. Gayatri Chakravorty Spivak (Baltimore: Johns Hopkins University Press, 1995); Dow, Bonnie, *Prime Time Feminism: Television, Media Culture, and the Women's Movement since 1970* (Philadelphia: University of Pennsylvania Press, 1996); Faludi, Susan, *Backlash: The Undeclared War against American Women* (New York: Crown Publishers, 1991); Gamble, Sarah, ed., *The Routledge Critical Dictionary of Feminism and Postfeminism* (New York: Routledge, 2000); Hawkesworth, Mary E., "The Semiotics of Premature Burial: Feminism in a Postfeminist Age," *Signs* 29, no. 4 (2004): 961–986; Henry, Astrid, *Not My Mother's Sister: Generational Conflict and Third-Wave Feminism* (Bloomington: Indiana University Press, 2004); Hoff-Sommers, Christine, *Who Stole Feminism? How Women Have Betrayed Women* (New York: Simon and Schuster, 1995); Labaton, Vivien, and Dawn Lundy Martin, *The Fire This Time: Young Activists and the New Feminism* (New York: Anchor Books, 2004); Marx Ferree, Myra, and Beth B. Hess, *Controversy and Coalition: The New Feminist Movement across Four Decades of Change* (New York: Routledge, 1995); Modleski, Tania, *Feminism without Women: Culture and Criticism in a Postfeminist Age* (New York: Routledge, 1991); Murray, Georgina, "Agonize, Don't Organize: A Critique of Postfeminism," *Current Sociology* 45, no. 2 (1997): 37–47; Paglia, Camille, "Feminists Must Begin to Fulfill Their Noble, Animating Ideal," Colloquy, *Chronicle of Higher Education,* July 25, 1997, available at: http://chronicle.com/colloquy/97/feminism/46b00401.htm, accessed March 29, 2007; Phoca, Sophia, and Rebecca Wright, *Introducing Postfeminism* (New York: Totem Books, 1999); Roiphe, Katie, *The Morning After: Sex, Fear and Feminism* (Boston: Back Bay Books, 1994); Walker, Rebecca, "Becoming Third Wave," *Ms* (January/February 1992): 39–41; Walker, Rebecca, "Introduction," *The Fire This Time: Young Activists and the New Feminism,* ed. Vivien Labaton and Dawn Lundry Martin, xvii (New York: Anchor Books, 2004); Young, Iris Marion, *Intersecting Voices: Dilemmas of Gender, Political Philosophy, and Policy* (Princeton, NJ: Princeton University Press, 1997).

Elizabeth Jenner

POSTMODERNIST AND POSTSTRUCTURALIST FEMINISMS

Postmodernist and poststructuralist theories, both of which challenge earlier philosophical traditions, have been central to questions about identity, representation, and politics in the contemporary era. Feminist debates concerning postmodernism and poststructuralism involve disputes as to whether universalistic thinking is appropriate or not, the nature of the self in Western society, and whether gender and sexual differences function as oppressive or as liberatory.

BACKGROUND: WHAT ARE POSTMODERNISM AND POSTSTRUCTURALISM?

Postmodernism is often used as an overarching term that describes a general break with conventional and dominant ways of thinking (poststructuralism and some strands of feminism are frequently classified as tenets of postmodern thinking). Although there are many theoretical perspectives that fall under postmodernism and poststructuralism, these two terms mainly designate the collapse of wholeness or totality in Western philosophical concepts, notions of the self, and modes of representation. The "post" in postmodernism and post-structuralism indicates that these theories come after and in response to earlier (broadly conceived as from the early twentieth century through the middle of the century) ideas about what constitutes "modern" identity and society. In being prefaced with "post," both terms would seem to delineate historically specific periods of critical theory; however, as terms, postmodernism and post-structuralism are not so much about naming time periods as they are about rethinking and expanding upon previous theories and cultural practices. These terms generally refer to particular arenas of critical thought that emerged in the post–World War II era. Both terms are used to question hierarchical models, power structures, and the integrity of authority, although they tend to maintain different emphases.

Postmodernism, as a critical term, is often used to theorize cultural production, that is, literary and artistic practices, and what these practices reflect about how society operates. The term has been used to describe textual and cultural methods that respond to a wide range of turn-of-the century and early-twentieth-century avant-garde practices known as modernism; modernism is generally characterized in terms of unconventional methods of representation (such as Picasso's scrambling of facial features in his paintings of women). While modernist practices accent individual style, authorship, and originality, these styles have become classic rather than retaining the radical effect they had at the time of their creation. Postmodernism tends to blur the boundaries between high art and popular culture, often attacking the elitism that modernist styles are thought to represent. For example, art made of found objects and art that depicts banal items are categorically postmodern. Like modernist styles, postmodern styles are historically contingent in becoming standard art practice; thus postmodernism often characterizes aesthetics that parody older styles and art that calls attention to artistic processes themselves (Jameson 1991). In critiquing general ideas about individual creativity and about what constitutes reputable art, postmodernism, then, parallels feminism's critique of "masterpieces" as mostly being work by men. Because it indicates socially and politically relevant theoretical thinking that problematizes dominant thinking as such, postmodernism should not be thought of as merely designating artistic styles. Therefore, what Jean-François Lyotard (1984) calls a rejecting of "grand narratives," or denying the universals behind much philosophical thinking, points to feminist views of questioning the idea of "man" as the universal marker for humanity; in other words, what becomes universally "human" is that which operates through a specifically male-dominated framework. Generally speaking, second wave feminism shares with postmodernism a critique of master narratives, in this case, examining how men are viewed as the unmarked, natural norm in society whereas women are viewed as "others" (de Beauvoir [1952] 1989).

Poststructuralism, on the other hand, is a field of inquiry concerned with the relationship between language and culture. Important poststructuralist thinkers include French philosopher Jacques Derrida (1978), whose theories

FRENCH FEMINISMS

Psychoanalytic theory is a key methodology used and critiqued within debates between feminism and poststructuralism. Psychoanalytic constructions of the female body—as hysterical, as multiple, and as "lack" (of a penis)—directly link to the ways in which feminist psychoanalytic theorists destabilize language and writing as male forms of signification. By using fluid, poetic, and unconventional syntactical styles, these feminist theorists tackle the patriarchal underpinnings of psychoanalytic understandings about "femaleness" in demonstrating their critiques at the level of their theoretical texts' structures. Luce Irigaray's *This Sex Which Is Not One* (1985) and Hélène Cixous's essay "The Laugh of the Medusa" (1976) are frequently referenced examples of this theoretical writing. Also known as "French feminism," or *l'écriture feminine* (feminine writing), these theories have been criticized for attempting to radically destabilize putatively masculine expressions through styles of writing thought to reflect a biologically centered notion of female difference.

highlight language's inability to fully signify stable meanings, as well as French historian and philosopher Michel Foucault (1973), whose work emphasizes the link between language, as a power structure, and the regulation of universal ways of thinking. While the earlier school of structuralism posited that meaning is culturally independent, poststructuralists view meaning as inseparable from culture and ultimately unstable. Thus, poststructuralists tend to emphasize the instability inherent in how meanings are generated by the structure of language. The linguistic sign, in structuralism, is composed of the signifier (the word) and the signified (the concept of the word). By breaking down how meaning is constructed via this linguistic structure, structuralism shows that the link between a word and its concept is random (de Saussure [1916] 2000). For instance, the same concept may be expressed by several different words depending on the language used to communicate that concept. Going beyond the arbitrary relationship between a word and its concept, poststructuralism instead shows that signifiers infinitely point to other signifiers (Lacan 1977), that concepts themselves are linguistic formations. Put differently, there is nothing stable about the concept of a word because words' definitions are simply other words. Thus, because the human subject conceives, understands, and communicates itself through language, the idea of an individual or unified sense of self cannot exist, since it cannot exist outside of language.

FEMINIST CRITIQUES OF POSTMODERNISM AND POSTSTRUCTURALISM

Feminist scholars have been heavily divided on the significance of poststructuralist and postmodernist thought for feminist scholarship and activism. Some feminist scholars have been suspicious about postmodernism's gaining theoretical ground at the height of the women's movement in the 1960s and 1970s. For these feminists, the skepticism revolves around the notion that postmodernist

MICHEL FOUCAULT AND FEMINISM

French-born Michel Foucault, often considered an important philosopher in the structuralist and/or postmodern traditions, has been highly influential among feminist theorists, although tensions have always existed between Foucault's male-based analysis and the gendered visions of feminist scholars. Foucault's genealogical method involved tracing the historical development of institutions or fields as wide ranging as the medical profession, the criminal justice system, psychology and sexology, and academia. Significantly, Foucault emphasized the relationship between power, knowledge, and discourse through his historical examinations of these institutions, causing many to consider him a philosopher of discourse, and his work continues to be highly influential in contemporary discourse analysis. His insight shook the foundations of modernist thought as he addressed the making of subjectivities as produced and exercised through relations of power, which he viewed as occurring not only within powerful institutions such as the state or the military, as earlier liberal and Marxian scholars posited, but also through people's everyday interactions, expressions of identity, and most intimate feelings. Because of his emphasis on subjectivity, biopolitics, and power, which he viewed as something we all possess and exercise even if we are also oppressed, therefore making the exercise of power contradictory at best, his work has influenced many strands of feminism. This is perhaps ironic, since Foucault himself never theorized gender identity or gender inequalities in Western society and some even consider him misogynist in his thinking. Because of this, feminist scholars have debated the significance of his work for their own understandings of power, as reflected in publications such as Caroline Ramazanoglu's 1993 edited volume, *Up against Foucault: Explorations of Some Tensions between Foucault and Feminism.*

Foucault did, however, write three volumes on the history of sexuality, which earned him great admiration among contemporary queer studies scholars and activists, who have largely viewed his work as pivotal for their own thought and activism (Foucault [1978] 1990; Halperin 1995). In addition, AIDS activists have been greatly influenced by his work on sexuality, and radical groups such as the AIDS Coalition to Unleash Power (ACT-UP), which was particularly strong in the 1980s in the United States, utilized Foucault's genealogical method in their fight for governmental and societal acknowledgment of the HIV/AIDS pandemic and the rights of people living with HIV/AIDS. A dedicated scholar turned AIDS and gay rights activist in the 1980s, sadly, Foucault himself died of AIDS complications in 1984.

---

theory may be "male" theory: the argument being that just when feminists begin to have some voice of political authority, the very notion of "authority" begins to be questioned (Nicholson 1990). In general, though, the debates that have surrounded feminism and theories of postmodernism and poststructuralism are less about necessarily working with or against these theories and more about reconceptualizing and negotiating with them. Rather than either strictly reifying or rigidly opposing postmodernism, many scholars, coming from both feminist and nonfeminist perspectives, have questioned postmodernism as itself counterintuitively becoming a "grand narrative" like the one it theoretically seeks to oppose. In exposing the patriarchal sources of the way power socially functions, feminism is similar to postmodernism's critique of dominant power structures, but it also retains some of postmodernism's contradictions. Feminism, too, shares the problem of being perceived as a "grand narrative": while feminism resists and reveals formulations of sexism that function to marginalize women, it may do so under a universal definition of feminism. For instance, feminism was largely critiqued as "white" and "middle-class" by theorists and activists who looked at feminism as falling into other traps of dominant thinking in trying to represent all women.

FEMINIST POSTSTRUCTURALIST/POSTMODERNIST SCHOLARS

In contrast to those discussed above, many feminists have embraced and utilized poststructuralist and postmodernist thinking in their own theoretical production. Judith Butler (1990) is one of the best-known examples of a feminist poststructuralist scholar. As a philosopher, Butler questions the biological ground of feminism by asking what women actually share in politically mobilizing under the signifier "woman." For Butler, the problem lies with claiming that there is a stable idea of "woman" and, therefore, of feminism's aims. Radicalizing previous feminist views that gender is constructed while biological sex is fixed, Butler argues that the sexed body's meanings are constructed and mediated by (heterosexist ideas about) gender. What ensues is a clash between theory and politics: how to have a definition of feminism without a concrete idea about what "woman" signifies and how differences in race, class, and sexuality may modify issues around social inequalities and political identifications.

FEMINIST DEBATES ON THE POLITICS OF POSTMODERNISM

Several feminist viewpoints on the uncertainty about the "real world" significance of postmodern feminism developed, alongside reservations about connecting women's oppressions with set ways of identifying with being female-bodied in society. For many feminist scholars, then, the question becomes how to position oneself both politically and theoretically: in other words, how to adhere to feminist principles of doing away with dominant thinking that has the effect of subordinating women while simultaneously not having a fixed idea about who feminist subjects are and what a feminist issue should encompass. Yet for a number of theorists, postmodern feminism is a viable feminism of multiplicity: recognizing differences among women without claiming that the political needs around these differences will be universal (Fraser and Nicholson 1990). In short, theorizing feminism alongside postmodernism and poststructuralism means understanding that there is not just one way of "doing" feminism, that feminist political projects may diverge, meet, and be in conflict in their various aims.

CONCLUSION

The intersections, conflicts, and affinities between feminism and postmodern/poststructuralist theories have been and continue to be central for questions about the political implications of feminist critical theory. While postmodern feminist perspectives have been regarded as more elusive about the political stakes of doing away with collective notions about women and feminist issues, these perspectives have also been integrated into political critiques of dominant universals and patriarchal notions about the individual self. Ultimately, the seeking out of middle grounds within these perspectives will continue, potentially creating ways of articulating feminisms that both embrace diversity and simultaneously reinforce political commonalities.

See also Postfeminism; Second and Third Wave Feminism; Third World and Women of Color Feminisms.

Further Reading: Alcoff, Linda, "Cultural Feminism versus Post-Structuralism: The Identity Crisis in Feminist Theory," in *The Second Wave: A Reader in Feminist Theory*, ed. Linda Nicholson (New York: Routledge, 1997); Butler, Judith, *Gender Trouble: Feminism and the Subversion of Identity* (New York: Routledge, 1990); Cixous, Hélène, "The Laugh of Medusa," *Signs* 1 (1976): 875–893; de Beauvoir, Simone, *The Second Sex*, trans. H. M. Parshley (New York: Vintage, 1989 [1952]); Derrida, Jacques, "Structure, Sign, and Play in the Discourse of the Human Sciences," in *Writing and Difference*, trans. Alan Bass (Chicago: University of Chicago Press, 1978); de Saussure, Ferdinand, *Course in General Linguistics*, trans. Roy Harris (Chicago: Open Court, 2000 [1916]); Foucault, Michel, *The Order of Things: An Archaeology of the Human Sciences* (New York: Vintage, 1973); Foucault, Michel, *The History of Sexuality, An Introduction*, vol. 1 (New York: Random House, 1990 [1978]); Fraser, Nancy, and Linda J. Nicholson, "Social Criticism without Philosophy: An Encounter between Feminism and Postmodernism," in *Feminism/Postmodernism*, ed. Linda J. Nicholson (New York: Routledge, 1990); Halberstam, Judith, *Female Masculinity* (Durham, NC: Duke University Press, 1998); Halperin, David, *Saint Foucault: Towards a Gay Hagiography* (New York: Oxford University Press, 1995); Irigaray, Luce, *This Sex Which Is Not One* (Ithaca, NY: Cornell University Press, 1985); Jameson, Fredric, *Postmodernism, or, The Cultural Logic of Late Capitalism* (Durham, NC: Duke University Press, 1991); Lacan, Jacques, "The Agency of the Letter in the Unconscious or Reason since Freud," in *Écrits: A Selection*, trans. Alan Sheridan (New York: W. W. Norton, 1977); Lurie, Susan, *Unsettled Subjects: Restoring Feminist Politics to Poststructuralist Critique* (Durham, NC: Duke University Press, 1997); Lyotard, Jean-François, *The Postmodern Condition: A Report on Knowledge*, trans. Geoff Bennington and Brian Massumi (Minneapolis: University of Minnesota Press, 1984); Nicholson, Linda J., ed., *Feminism/Postmodernism* (New York: Routledge, 1990); Owens, Craig, "The Discourse of Others: Feminists and Postmodernism," in *Beyond Recognition: Representation, Power, and Culture*, ed. Scott Bryson, Barbara Kruger, Lynne Tillman, and Jane Weinstock (Berkeley: University of California Press, 1992); Ramazanoglu, Caroline, ed., *Up Against Foucault: Explanations of Some Tension between Foucoult and Feminism* (New York: Routledge, 1993); Riley, Denise, *"Am I That Name?": Feminism and the Category of "Women" in History* (Minneapolis: University of Minnesota Press, 1988).

Yetta Howard

Q

QUEER

Queer is most often used as the reclamation of a previously hurtful term for lesbian, gay, bisexual, and transgender (LGBT) people. Since it retains the mark of stigmatization, *queer* is employed controversially even among insiders in order to designate a political stance against assimilation. Activists and theorists use the idea of queerness to criticize the gay and lesbian rights movement's adherence to conventional and conservative gender and sexual roles.

BACKGROUND

A word with the baggage of perversity, *queer* is often reappropriated by activists in the twenty-first-century United States as an emblem of pride and as a marker of difference from traditional sex, gender, and sexual norms. While clearly there is a range of views on the meaning of homosexuality and gender and on the status of individuals who do not fit within prescribed gender and/or sexual roles in U.S. society, nowhere has the debate on queerness been more intense than among gay, lesbian, transgender, and queer activists and scholars themselves. On the one hand, gay and lesbian activists have fought for their inclusion in U.S. policy and law and for their equality with heterosexuals. On the other hand, queer activists have challenged the gay and lesbian rights movement and created their own, which calls into question the underlying theoretical premise of identity in Western society, thereby calling into question the very meanings of *gay* and *lesbian* as well as *heterosexual*. In doing so, they have referred to gay and lesbian rights-based political models as reformist and assimilationist rather than radical or transformative. While clearly the dominant heterosexual society continues to hold biases toward these groups, and while some people with homophobic attitudes continue to use the term *queer* in a derogatory fashion, the more explosive debate has concerned whether or not activists and scholars themselves should reappropriate such a historically derogatory term as a way to advance their own liberatory cause. Queer activists often claim that gay and lesbian activists are reproducing the very analytical biases that heterosexist society has created to define them as "deviant" in the first place; gay and lesbian activists often claim that queers are too radical and that the term *queer* is derogatory, harmful, and not useful for advancing a civil rights political agenda.

HISTORICAL USAGE OF THE TERM

Historically, the notion of queerness has held a variety of connotations. *Queer* is generally attributed to the sixteenth-century German word *quer,* meaning "at an oblique angle" or "out of alignment." Some scholars have also associated the word with sixteenth-century slang for counterfeit money (Fisher 1999, 1). They contend that "shoving the queer" has colloquially implied trying to use counterfeit money. Queerness continues to imply illegitimacy, oddness, or a poor comparison to an original, when used by outsiders in a derogatory fashion.

In the early twentieth century in the United States, the notion of queerness was not necessarily tied to the sexual. Rather, it was sometimes used as a way to designate all kinds of human activity and identity that were apart from what was considered "normal":

> Girls are so queer you never know what they mean. They say No when they mean Yes, and drive a man out of his wits for the fun of it.
>
> *Louisa May Alcott*

Historically, this usage as a synonym for "deviant" or "abnormal" has carried negative connotations, usually implying that an object or person is odd, peculiar, unacceptable, curious, or bizarre:

> Any child knows that history can only be a reduced representation of reality, but it must be a true one, not distorted by queer lenses.
>
> *Samuel E. Morison*

> If I read a book that impresses me, I have to take myself firmly by the hand, before I mix with other people; otherwise they would think my mind rather queer.
>
> *Anne Frank*

In these quotes, *queer* signifies "odd," "abnormal," or "distorted." Even in current use, *queerness* might signify a range of outsider experiences not limited to the sexual alone, and can allude to crossing the borders of acceptability or normalcy.

By the early twentieth century, however, *queer* also took on meanings of sexual "oddness." Effeminate gay men first bore the brunt of disdain as queers for transgressing gender ideals but with the added onus that they transgressed sexual boundaries as well. This meaning is widely attributed first to gay poet W. H. Auden, who first deployed the word in 1932 as an epithet against and synonym for homosexuality, implying that gay sexuality made someone illegitimate *(Oxford English Dictionary,* 2nd ed. *[OED])*. However, the *Oxford English Dictionary* also cites a U.S. Department of Labor report labeling sexual transgression as queer as early as 1922. "A young man, easily ascertainable to be unusually fine in other characteristics, is probably queer in sex tendency," the report claimed (Children's Bureau, U.S. Dept. of Labor, 8, in *OED*). This description suggests that gay sexual transgression was associated with gender transgression, and that one could be surmised from the other: in other words, that effeminacy in men meant that they would likely choose other men as sexual partners. In this definition, queer sexuality and gender roles go hand in hand, contrary to recent usage of the term.

The first modern reclamation of the word *queer* came in 1969, when countercultural writer Paul Goodman penned his well-known essay "The Politics of Being Queer." In the essay, Goodman contended that rigidly straight sexual attractions were as pathological as rigidly gay ones. He argued that his own relationships with young boys were neither, as public opinion contended, exploitative nor pathological. Same-sex sexuality, according to Goodman, was often a healthy precursor to friendship and to a successful student/teacher relationship, even across the adult/child divide. While Goodman's ideas were not all taken up by the emerging lesbian and gay civil rights movement, galvanized in the 1960s, his reclamation of the word *queer* and the assertion that queerness was not pathological were instrumental in laying the groundwork for activist reclamation of the term.

Currently, those who self-identify as queer do so as a way to reclaim and challenge its historically derogatory usage. Individuals use this term as a way to describe their gender and/or sexual identities as outside the norm and importantly, to reclaim that which is viewed as abnormal by mainstream society. Intellectuals, artists, and activists also use the term to explain their approach, or methodology, to analyzing popular culture. For example, filmmaker Prathibha Parmar describes her queer artistic vision as one stemming from a "politics of difference." Parmar says:

> We are not interested in defining ourselves in relation to someone or something else, nor are we simply articulating cultural and sexual differences. We are creating a sense of ourselves and our place within different and sometimes contradictory communities, not simply in relation to...not as a corrective to...in and for ourselves. Precisely because of our lived experiences of racism and homophobia, we locate ourselves not within any one community but in the spaces between those different communities. (Parmar 1993, 5)

Parmar tells us that queerness falls in the spaces between identities rather than encompassing any whole identity in and of itself. This definition gels with the word's etymology.

In spite of the different meanings historically given to *queerness,* the term *queer* is often employed in current parlance as a synonym for LGBT sexual relationships, since they necessarily break apart the idea that erotic attachments can only form across the sex and gender divide. Recent U.S. television programs like *Queer as Folk* and *Queer Eye for the Straight Guy* help to popularize the terms as interchangeable. However, many non-LGBT people also consider themselves queer, as noted in a recent autobiographical piece, "I Am A Queer Heterosexual" (Kelly 2003). Typically these individuals are critical of normative gender and sexual categories within the range of heterosexual experience, and therefore choose to consider themselves queer or claim to have a queer perspective.

QUEER STUDIES: RETHINKING SEX, GENDER, AND SEXUALITY

In many ways, contemporary political notions of queerness emerged in intellectual settings. Michel Foucault's groundbreaking research on the history of sexuality in Western society paved the way for more recent scholars to address and rethink heteronormativity, the view that heterosexuality is the norm and homosexuality is abnormal, in Western thought. This led to changes in university curricula concerning courses on gay and lesbian topics. By the 1990s, in many universities, queer theory began to be taught in various disciplines, and scholars attempted to avoid a dichotomous divide such as that of heterosexuality/ homosexuality or male/female. At the same time, gay and lesbian studies programs were becoming institutionalized. Today, universities have adopted a variety of approaches to addressing gender and sexuality studies in light of this new scholarship: some universities describe them as "Gay and Lesbian Studies" or "Gay, Lesbian, Bisexual and Transgender Studies"; others use "Queer Studies," while yet others use "Sexuality Studies." Many of these debates on queerness and their relationship to institutional and political change remain unresolved.

Scholars of queer studies take issue with the way in which biological sex has become inextricably tied to people's gender roles and sexual identities. For example, women's biological sex is often assumed to be tied to traditionally defined feminine gender characteristics such as passivity, emotionality, or compassion. Likewise, men are assumed to carry traits such as strength, stoicism, and violence. Queer studies scholars argue that these social roles and expectations are mapped onto people's bodies in a way that is not natural but rather socially constructed. They also point out that in a culturally normative relationship (one that fills the expectations of the dominant norms in a given society), the biological sex and social roles of two romantic or erotic partners are seen as necessarily opposed. In this scenario, masculine males sexually pursue feminine females. Men exclusively pay for dates, open doors for their romantic partners, and make the first moves. They value delicacy, demureness, and prettiness in their partners, who take a more submissive role, accepting advances or gifts but never initiating relationships or erotic encounters. An example of the dominance of this model is the Western, Christian wedding ritual: a woman, dressed in white to symbolize sexual innocence, is escorted to her partner on her father's arm; the partner stands watching the procession, including his bride, as she moves toward him.

Her father "gives her away" to her new husband, and rice is thrown to remind the couple of the duty to produce and raise children within the union. Flowers, also symbols of fertility, are likewise abundant.

A queer outlook questions the comfortable truth of an unbroken sex/gender/sexual grouping, pointing to the range and diversity of human experience instead. It is because of this stance that queers consider themselves anti-essentialist, or against the idea that our identities are innate. Queer activists point to changes across nations and time periods in our notions of sex, gender, and sexuality, in order to break down the popular biological assumption. They argue that very few human relationships actually follow the narrowly defined normative gender and sexual roles prescribed for people and they seek to challenge binary constructions of gender such as strong versus weak, producer versus reproducer, protector versus protected, and he versus she. They seek to celebrate the instability and fluidity of gender, sex, and sexuality, ultimately dismantling a system that normalizes men, masculinity, and heterosexuality while relegating women, femininity, and queer identification to a position of otherness. Queers question the traditional nuclear family as a fiction entrenched in power norms rather than in any material reality. With 25–40 percent of U.S. children born to "single" moms and other nontraditional heterosexual households, and an increasingly significant percentage to gays and lesbians, only a fragment of families reflect the ideal of the traditional nuclear family, they say. Further, queers call attention to the ways in which our individual identities, in addition to our romantic relationships, do not mirror the absolutist social rules.

Not only may our own identities not be congruent with one another, say queers, but they may change across our lifetimes. For example, we can alter our biological sex by medically changing our genitalia or by taking hormones. Our gender may change as we shift roles from pursuer to pursued in a new romantic relationship, or take up a new hobby that is not ordained as appropriate in the existing gender order, like car mechanics or baking. Our sexuality is also unstable, changing when people "come out," when the object of our attraction changes sex, or when we discover that the person who catches our eye is a different sex than we first supposed.

Often, queer theorists point out that sexuality is a function of representation: it is constructed in the culture through representations (Case 1991). Queer theory assumes that representations exist prior to identities, that they define identities rather than vice versa. In other words, people compose their sexualities by working within and against the existing representations that the culture provides to us. This notion differs from that of mainstream gay and lesbian activists whose brand of sexual accommodation posits that sexuality is constructed in the womb, not by the culture. As such, they argue, sexuality is unchangeable and therefore lesbians and gays "can't help" their orientation and therefore should not endure discrimination. And even those gay and lesbian activists who view sexuality as socially constructed have fallen into the trap of using existing dichotomous representations of "gay" versus "straight" to further their cause, a problem according to queer theorists and activists who believe that the dichotomy itself is the problem in the first place.

Some have pointed out that the notion of "queer" is vague and difficult to pin down. Eve Kosofsky Sedgwick, often considered one of the founders of contemporary queer theory, contends that the difficulty in pinning down "queerness" is part of the essence of queerness itself, which she describes as "the open mesh of possibilities, gaps, overlaps, dissonances, and resonances, lapses and excesses of meaning when the constituent elements of anyone's gender, of anyone's sexuality aren't made or can't be made to signify monolithically" (1990, 8). Though the word *queers* is sometimes used as an umbrella term for sexual "others," queers are not united by any common behavior or identity but merely by their opposition to normalizing identities (Seidman 1993, 16). In short, queer activists attempt to define queerness lightly, excluding as few people and practices as possible, and instead they define queerness as any identity or practice that flies in the face of conventional, heteronormative, and patriarchal relationships. A queer point of view questions why continual and often repressive adherence to social role playing makes some relationships legitimate and in fact, natural, while those that do not measure up suffer stigmatization.

QUEER POLITICS VERSUS GAY AND LESBIAN POLITICS

People who identify in nonnormative terms in relation to their gender and/or sexual identities strongly disagree on the usage of the term *queer* and on the deployment of a queer political approach. This debate pits the gay and lesbian movement, often perceived as liberal and assimilationist by queer activists, against the queer movement, often perceived as too radical or agitative by gay and lesbian activists. In the wake of the 1969 Stonewall Riots at a New York City bar, gay liberation activists began to take up traditional activist campaigns as a way to influence local and national political processes. The historical struggle for gay and lesbian rights has been largely based on a civil rights model, in which gays and lesbians have sought to eliminate their second-class-citizen status through struggles for legal equality with heterosexuals. Especially since the 1980s, gay and lesbian activists have fought for legal recognition on a variety of grounds: antidiscrimination legislation (for example, with regard to hate crimes, and to protection in employment, housing, and healthcare), custody of children, inheritance rights, the right to serve in the military, marriage rights, and the appeal against antisodomy laws are only a few of the legal issues that they have addressed. For example, the 2003 U.S. Supreme Court's overruling of antisodomy laws, commonly known as *Lawrence v. Texas,* challenged the way in which U.S. courts traditionally viewed the state's role in people's private lives and helped pave the way for future legal victories for gays and lesbians. Over the years, various national and regional marches and protests have been organized, including the well-known marches on Washington. The 1987 March on Washington, for example, heralded the first public display of the AIDS quilt, in homage to lives lost from the disease.

The AIDS pandemic fueled high levels of activism by gay men and lesbians. Although HIV/AIDS first became public in the early 1980s, it was not until the late 1980s that the federal government mentioned the word, let alone addressed

MICHELANGELO SIGNORILE'S GOSSIP WATCH COLUMN IN *OUTWEEK*

Michelangelo Signorile, a controversial gay journalist, is considered an "outing" pioneer by many in the queer generation. In his "Gossip Watch" column in *Outweek*, a national gay news magazine that began circulation in 1989, Signorile regularly outed celebrities and public figures such as Malcolm Forbes, the publisher of *Forbes* magazine, Sonny and Cher's daughter, Chastity Bono, movie actor Richard Chamberlain, and several politicians who supported homophobic legislation. *Outweek* publisher Gabriel Rotello viewed outing as an "equalizer" of homosexuality and heterosexuality. Some supporters of outing have even offered monetary rewards for the outing of individuals from specific institutions such as the Catholic Church or the U.S. Supreme Court. Critics contend that outing violates the privacy of people's personal lives and have largely framed their opposition in terms of the right to privacy. Interestingly, Signorile himself is often considered to be a conservative despite his belief in outing.

the crisis, in public. Given that initially it was largely perceived as a "gay disease," and given the large numbers of gay men dying during that period, many gay men and lesbians felt alienated by the mainstream political strategies of seeking change from within the system, which they felt had caused thousands of deaths. Faced with a neoconservative political climate in the United States, these activists began centering their efforts on the urgency of the AIDS crisis and on what they viewed as the horrific underbelly of violence against lesbians and gays. They rallied around the term *queer* in order to highlight the ostracism felt by those whose most basic human rights needs were being ignored. So influential was the swelling of anti-assimilationist activism that the *Advocate,* the largest circulating gay news magazine, called 1990 "the year of the queer" (Thompson 1994, 357).

Unlike earlier gay social movements, which emphasized fitting into mainstream society, 1980s and 1990s queer organizations did not encourage their members to dress conservatively or to behave obsequiously, but instead urged them to demand acceptance on their own terms. Queer agendas were AIDS centered and more broadly addressed the needs of LGBT people. Members of the movement started organizations with names like Queer Nation, ACT-UP (AIDS Coalition to Unleash Power), Lesbian Avengers, Stonewall Now!, WHAM! (Women's Health Action and Mobilization), OutRage, Subversive Street Queers, Gran Fury, and a proliferation of queer organizations acting for global progressive causes such as Queers United in Support of Political Prisoners. In fact, the queer agenda spurred human rights organization Amnesty International to begin lobbying on behalf of jailed gay and HIV-positive prisoners, and queers were also active in antiwar protests during the U.S. Gulf War in January 1991. So wide did they cast their activist net, in fact, that many questioned whether or not the queer umbrella undermined its own goals by focusing on too many issues and being too inclusive (Jagose 1997).

QUEER THEORIST JUDITH BUTLER

Judith Butler's research has been highly influential in the field of queer studies. Her 1990 publication, *Gender Trouble: Feminism and the Subversion of Identity,* was among the first to systematically attempt to destabilize gender, sex, and sexuality. Drawing from poststructuralist thought, including the work of Jacques Derrida, Jacques Lacan, Monique Wittig, and Michel Foucault, in *Gender Trouble* Butler argues that the coherence of gender and sexual identities results from their stylized repetitive acts over time. These stylized acts result in the appearance of an ontological "core" gender. Viewing gender as essential, natural, and unchangeable also contributes to reinforcing the notion that sex and sexuality themselves are natural categories. Over 100,000 copies of *Gender Trouble* were sold immediately following its publication, and it is now considered a classic text in feminist and queer theory. Fans have published scholarly books about Butler's work and even an intellectual fanzine, *Judy!*

Queer Nation, founded by ACT-UP members, sought to bring direct-action activist tactics to the issue of violence against gays and lesbians. The organization was founded in 1990 and employed controversial strategies in the fight for visibility, including "outing" prominent gay and lesbian political leaders, publicly exposing their sexuality, and targeting those who had voted against gay civil rights legislation. The strategy of outing created one of the biggest divisions among activists during this time period. Posters began appearing in New York, outing politicians, actors, and business leaders as "absolutely queer"; individuals were then forced to make public statements about their identities. This provoked a national debate on the tactic and on the sexualities of figures that most heterosexuals had heretofore taken for granted. The debates led to public controversy: should gay and lesbian lives be confined to bedrooms or declared in public spaces? Since the 2003 overruling of *Bowers v. Hardwick* (by *Lawrence v. Texas,* which overturned the antisodomy laws), gay bedrooms could hardly be considered private. But queer activists persevered, calling attention to the erroneous divide between public and private. Governors bent on signing discriminatory legislation were outed, children of conservatives were outed, and military spokespersons were outed.

Whereas gay and lesbian activists can be credited with developing political strategies that influenced state legislatures and the federal government through traditional political mechanisms such as lobbying, polling, voter mobilization, and political campaigning, queer activists can be credited with broadening the scope of the political platform. Specifically, queer activists adopted an intersectional approach to understanding oppression: They often fought against racism, sexism, and class exploitation alongside the struggle against heteronormativity and gender normativity in the law. Racism, biphobia, and global imperialism were typically seen as queer problems, as evidenced by queer protests against gay and lesbian groups that failed to include these issues under their rubric of acceptance. For example, queers protested a Lambda Legal Defense Fund fundraiser that featured the play *Miss Saigon,* because of its stereotypically racist depictions of Asian women. Others protested the First Gulf War in the Middle East on the grounds that monies spent on securing Kuwait's independence and guaranteeing U.S. dependence on foreign oil could have funded research and development for 109 new AIDS drugs. Queers first defined the sense that interlocking oppressions, whether they involved race, class, transgender representation, or capitalism, were all related to the plight of lesbian and gay people.

Queer Nation also took up the negative portrayal of lesbians and bisexual characters in the media: they protested what they considered the problematic depiction of a bisexual, ice-pick-wielding murderer in 1992's *Basic Instinct,* arguing that negative representations were not mere fiction, but that they influenced the ways in which straights thought about real-life gays and the ways in which gays thought about themselves. The group delayed filming by blowing whistles on the set and by wielding signs asking nearby motorists to honk their horns "if they support U.S. troops" as a noise-making tactic (Fox and Rosenthal 1991). The group also penned controversial slogans like "We're here, we're queer. Get used to it!," "Fags and dykes bash back," and "2, 4, 6, 8, How do you know your kids are straight?" The Lesbian Avengers, like Queer Nation, emerged out of local ACT-UP chapters and utilized direct-action tactics like street theater and fire eating in order to convey their pro-lesbian and pro-activism message. "Be the bomb you throw," the Avengers told young women.

All of these instrumental groups believed that they must demand acceptance rather than asking for tolerance or acceptance based on heterosexual norms. Mall kiss-ins and the distribution of safe-sex materials to high school students cemented Queer Nation's reputation for actions counter to the moderate tactic of accommodation. Further, the groups cemented queer organizing methods as decentralized, without permanent leadership, but instead as grassroots democratic organizations in which all members might participate in planning protests. The feminist impulse toward decentralization, in which each member's voice can be heard, coupled with the immediacy of their goals in the face of an ever-escalating AIDS death rate, meant that the organizations were often caught between contradictory desires, wanting to make each member's voice meaningful and yet also needing to actualize their events quickly and efficiently. This contradiction made it difficult for queer groups to realize their goals, and many disbanded in the early 1990s, including Queer Nation, whose San Francisco chapter folded in December 1991 over issues of religion, race, and gender.

Apart from the need to see AIDS and LGBT discrimination as a direct and pressing risk, the wave of queer activism in the late 1980s derived from a generational shift in LGBT politics, with teenage and 20-something activists at the fore in the queer movement and their elders entrenched in more mainstream LGBT groups. Queer youth were less likely to see their interests represented by the vanguard of the mainstream movement and to look elsewhere for representation. Economic challenges added to the alienation of young LGBT people from mainstream organizations. The methodology of direct action was useful for these disenfranchised members of the LGBT community who had little opportunity to air their views through traditional LGBT channels. The use of the term *queer* highlighted their difference within the LGBT movement as well as their disenfranchisement. They embraced militancy and rage uncompromisingly as tools in the fight for belonging *as different* within the greater heteronormative as well as LGBT cultures.

During the height of the queer activist movement, queer organizing spread to music and the arts as well as to direct-action protesting. An aesthetic and a celebration of otherness bubbled in popular music; queer groups such as homocult (later queercore) rose out of the punk rock scene at the same time as independently produced advertisement-free magazines (called zines) proliferated, giving voice to marginalized minorities within the movement and creating a forum that was democratic and inclusive in principle. Riot grrl offered the same visibility, community, and safe space within music to women, many of whom became involved with radical antiessentialist organizing and zine publishing. The Radical Cheerleaders' anarcho-protest cum performance tactics dominated pride marches as chapters cropped up in the mid-1990s, spreading both feminist and queer-positive messages.

AGAINST THE NOTION OF QUEERNESS

Critics of queerness often argue that the term is vague, harmful and/or problematic when used to deploy a concrete political agenda. Gay and lesbian rights activists who base their struggles on a civil rights model continue to believe that legal reform is necessary, important, and central to the overall goals of the movement, despite the queer critiques. If it were not for organizing on the basis of gay and lesbian identity, they argue, homosexuals would not have gained historical and political visibility. So despite using the terms of the oppressor, as queer activists might contend, calling oneself "gay" or "lesbian" can be empowering and can serve to mobilize large communities of people to effect social change.

Furthermore, given that the origins of the contemporary political usage of *queer* are in poststructuralist intellectual traditions, some also consider queer studies to be inaccessible to the majority of people, who have not been trained in this academic tradition. Within academia, queer studies has been most influential in the humanities and arts; hence the emphasis on cultural studies, which tends to focus on popular culture more than on issues of political economy and social stratification. Critics argue that this approach, as an academic enterprise that focuses on popular culture and representations, therefore forgets the real conditions of oppression in people's lives (Jagose 1997).

An additional critique of the notion of queerness concerns the fact that it too can become a hegemonic identity marker just like any other label. For example, some gays, lesbians, bisexuals, and transgendered people from communities of color claim that the term *queer* is often associated with whiteness, thereby limiting its political salience and potential in communities already at odds with a racially stratified society (although this is also disputed within ethnic/racial communities). And in contexts where the term *queer* is still used derogatorily, often in conjunction with violence against gays and lesbians, there is great hesitancy about, and sometimes outright rejection of, the use of this term as a way to describe a liberatory project.

Finally, the new gay Right has emphatically dismissed some of the primary strategies and ideas put forth by queer scholars and activists. While many scholars have pointed out that gay and lesbian politics (and, later, queer politics) emerged primarily from progressive social movements in the 1960s, conservative gay public intellectuals such as Andrew Sullivan and Bruce Bawer have promoted an entirely different kind of political agenda since the 1980s. Bruce Bawer, author of *Beyond Queer: Challenging Gay Left Orthodoxy* (1996), argues that fighting for gays' inclusion in the military and for same-sex marriage are based on inherently conservative ideas about family and serving one's country, values that reflect the traditional values of most Americans. Bawer opposes queer activism because he disagrees with its general emphasis on critiquing free market capitalism and the principles of liberalism. Like other gay conservatives, Bawer wishes to delink the struggle for homosexual acceptance from what he views as sexual and gender deviance. Marshall Kirk and Hunter Madsen (1989) make a similar argument when they argue that activists must "counteract the association of homosexuality with political radicalism, gender-bending and sexual excess" (see Robinson 2005, 11). Gays and queers must change, they argue, because "they are making a bad impression on heterosexuals" (Robinson 2005, 10)

CONCLUSION

Despite the controversies surrounding the historical usage of the term *queer,* it appears that notions of queerness are here to stay. Queer studies is now an important area of scholarship in university curricula and the "queer wars" continue to rage among political activists of various ideological and party affiliations in the United States (Robinson 2005). While the broader issue of heterosexist bias continues to affect the way gay people are perceived by mainstream heterosexual society, for example, being deemed deviant, abnormal, or queer, activists who wish to address heterosexism and homophobia are deeply divided as to whether or not notions of queerness, in its many definitions, are necessary or useful for effecting political change. The new gay Right, in particular, is decidedly opposed to all definitions of queerness as they have been presented by progressive gay, lesbian, and queer activists and scholars. Given the general political, cultural, and ideological context within which queerness is understood and negotiated, these debates will surely continue in the future.

See also Bisexuality; Family Values; Heterosexism and Homophobia; Nature versus Nurture; Sex versus Gender; Sexual Identity and Orientation; Transgender and Transsexual Identities.

Further Reading: Bawer, Bruce, *Beyond Queer: Challenging Gay Left Orthodoxy* (New York: Free Press, 1996); Brandt, Eric, ed., *Dangerous Liaisons: Blacks, Gays, and the Struggle for Equality* (New York: The New Press, 1999); Butler, Judith, *Gender Trouble* (New York: Routledge, 1990); Case, Sue-Ellen, "Tracking the Vampire," *Differences: A Journal of Feminist Cultural Studies* 3, no. 2 (1991): 3; Fisher, Will, "Queer Money," *English Literary*

History 66, no. 1 (1999): 1–23; Fox, David, and Donna Rosenthal, "Gays Bashing 'Basic Instinct,'" *Los Angeles Times,* April 29, 1991; Goodman, Paul, *Nature Heals: The Psychological Essays of Paul Goodman* (Goldsboro, ME: Gestalt Journal Press, 1969); Jagose, Annamarie, *Queer Theory: An Introduction* (New York: New York University Press, 1997); Kelly, Sharon, "I Am a Queer Heterosexual," in *Sexual Lives,* ed. Robert Heasley and Betsy Crane, 400–403 (New York: McGraw Hill, 2003); Parmar, Pratibha, "That Moment of Emergence," in *Queer Looks: Perspectives on Lesbian and Gay Film and Video,* ed. Martha Gever, John Greyson, and Prathiba Parmar, 3–11 (New York: Routledge, 1993); Phelan, Shane, *Sexual Strangers: Gays, Lesbians, and Dilemmas of Citizenship* (Philadelphia: Temple University Press, 2001); "Queer," *Oxford English Dictionary,* 2nd ed. (Oxford: Clarendon, 1989); Robinson, Paul, *Queer Wars: The New Gay Right and Its Critics* (Chicago: University of Chicago Press, 2005); Schneer, David, and Caryn Aviv, eds., *American Queer: Now and Then* (New York: Paradigm, 2006); Sedgwick, Eve Kosofsky, *Epistemology of the Closet* (Berkeley: University of California Press, 1990); Seidman, Steven, "Identity and Politics in a 'Postmodern' Gay Culture: Some Historical and Conceptual Notes," in *Fear of a Queer Planet,* ed. Michael Warner, 105–142 (Minneapolis: University of Minnesota Press, 1993); Sonnie, Amy, *Revolutionary Voices: A Multicultural Queer Youth Anthology* (Los Angeles: Alyson Books, 2000); Sullivan, Andrew, *Virtually Normal: An Argument against Homosexuality* (New York: Vintage Books, 1996); Sycamore, Matt Bernstein, ed., *That's Revolting! Queer Strategies for Resisting Assimilation* (New York: Soft Skull Press, 2004); Sullivan, Nikki, *A Critical Introduction to Queer Theory* (New York: New York University Press, 2003); Thompson, Mark, ed., *The Long Road to Freedom: The Advocate History of the Gay and Lesbian Movement* (New York: St. Martin's Press, 1994); Warner, Michael, *The Trouble with Normal: Sex, Politics, and the Ethics of Queer Life* (Cambridge, MA: Harvard University Press, 1999); Wilchins, Riki, *Queer Theory, Gender Theory: An Instant Primer* (Los Angeles: Alyson Books, 2004).

Jessica Share

RACE AND RACISM: SOCIAL STRATIFICATION IN THE UNITED STATES

Increasingly, scholars have addressed the intersection of gender, race, and class, although they often disagree as to which influences social stratification more. Controversy surrounding the causes of social stratification in U.S. society stems from longstanding views on racial, gender, and class categories and from disagreements over the sources of poverty and inequality in marginalized communities.

BACKGROUND

In every society, social stratification exists. Some skills that are needed in society require more talent and training than others. For example, becoming a doctor requires years of education and training while becoming a store clerk does not. Therefore, when people make sacrifices to develop their talents they are usually rewarded (Tumin 2001). Social class distinctions are especially seen within the United States, a country characterized by a wide range of immigrant groups and classes: as Fischer et al. state, "Americans have created the extent and type of inequality we have, and Americans maintain it" (2001, 73). Some argue that class is the least understood of these forms of stratification: "Americans believe that they live in a classless society, that class is a matter of achievement, and that, in theory, anyone can make it to the top" (West and Fenstermaker 2002, 539). Many observers would argue, however, that in the United States, social class is not usually based solely on merit. Other factors, including race and gender, factor into a person's social class, and debates on why some groups are less successful than others, economically speaking, stem from the divergent views on what these factors contribute to social stratification.

Recently, scholar and popular author Barbara Ehrenreich has written about her investigations of social class. In *Nickeled and Dimed* (2001), a book that has also been turned into a play, Ehrenreich went undercover to live a working-class life. She found jobs as a maid, a waitress, and a Wal-Mart clerk, and discovered that her salary could not cover her expenses or keep her standard of living above the federal poverty line. In her next book, *Bait and Switch* (2005), she went through the process of looking for a middle-class job, where she encountered many obstacles related to industrial downsizing. She described the financial, mental, and emotional stresses that come with taking on both of these class identities. Ehrenreich shows how social class can impact women's lives. Whether it concerns wages, employment, education, health, childcare, or retirement, socioeconomic class is a material aspect of women's daily existence.

Yet, there is usually contention as to what impacts social stratification more, including the questions of why some racial groups end up poorer than others and how gender or race play into this process. Many feminists believe that being a woman results in lower pay and being left out of decision-making arenas; beginning in the 1960s, this was one of the central tenets of liberal feminist thought. However, the same is true regarding race. When people must contend with both racism and classism, the question of which is more salient arises. Which impacts social stratification more? Many feminist scholars focus on gender. However, other scholars, such as womanists, multiracial feminists and third world feminists also discuss the huge impact of race and ethnicity on social stratification, including poverty.

The question of what affects social stratification the most is of considerable importance, as the answer greatly influences political and policy responses to poverty. Some believe that people can work themselves out of poverty. In the United States, it is often assumed that people are able to succeed and achieve the American dream simply through hard work. Yet some observers such as Michael Zweig explain that luck has much to do with financial success (Zweig 2000). Major catastrophes, such as illness, death, or natural disaster, also greatly impact how people fare economically.

SOCIAL STRATIFICATION IN THE WORKPLACE

When women are in the workplace they come up against the assumption that they would rather spend more time with their children than in moving up the corporate ladder (Wood 2005). This belief disadvantages both men and women. Women are seen as not taking their jobs as seriously as men. Employers think either that women have a husband who is supporting the family or that women will need to put their families first at the expense of their jobs. Men are expected to concentrate on their jobs at the expense of their families (Wood 2005). However, many men want to focus on their families instead of their careers. When women prioritize their families in the workplace, it is known as being on the "mommy track." There has been increasing discussion regarding the "daddy track" for men.

CLARENCE THOMAS HEARINGS

During Clarence Thomas's 1991 confirmation hearings, Anita Hill, Thomas's former aide, stepped forward and stated that Thomas had sexually harassed her. This led to strong reactions by American viewers, whose perspectives were often shaded by their own gendered and racialized experiences. Although both of the individuals involved were African American, many white women supported Hill, whereas many black men supported Thomas and viewed the hearing as another example of white racism, given the fact that Thomas would be the first African American Supreme Court justice to be appointed in U.S. history. Black women were often divided in their opinions. Some, for example, believed that Hill should have stayed silent in order to support her race; others supported her and believed that she was standing up for women's rights. Ultimately, Thomas was sworn in as a Supreme Court justice and Anita Hill lost her case, making this case a failure for sexual harassment advocates and underscoring the long history of racial and gender tensions in U.S. society.

Many men are opting to follow the "daddy track" and are using many of the employment policies that were originally designed for women. Achieving a work-life balance, taking paternity leave after the birth of a child, and using flex time have allowed men to take a more active part in their families' lives (Wilcox 1989). Many of these policies have arguably helped men as much as women (Brady 2004).

However, these policies have social class implications. Many of the people who describe using these policies are middle-class employees. Thus, employees who depend on hourly wages do not see the benefits of many of these policies. Also, maternity or paternity leave is not guaranteed through the Family and Medical Leave Act of 1993 for every workplace, nor does the act mandate employers to pay their employees while they are taking time off.

People who depend on hourly wages must either go without pay or forgo the opportunity to spend time with their families. Rarely are flex time or parental leaves an option for lower-middle-class or working-class families. Technological devices such as cell phones, e-mail, or fax machines will not help those in areas such as construction, housecleaning, waiting at tables, or other blue-collar jobs. Furthermore, employees in blue-collar jobs are more likely to be racial minorities, which puts them at a disadvantage due to the racial bias or discrimination that they are likely to face.

THE PAY GAP

Pay inequity, or the difference in pay among people in society, furthers the social class divide regarding race and gender. According to the U.S. Census Bureau, women make approximately $.76 for every $1.00 a man makes. This is the same amount black men earn compared to white men. Wage inequality is even more severe when both race and gender are factored into the equation: women members of minority groups are among the lowest-paid workers. The National Committee of Pay Equity states that in the year 2000, black women earned

64 percent of the income of white men. During that same year, Hispanic women earned 54 percent of the median income of white men. At the same time, women with bachelor's degrees made only $1,545 more than white males who had completed high school (National Committee on Pay Equity 2004–2006). This data point toward inequality based not only on gender but also on race, which explains, in structural terms, why so many women members of minority groups live in poverty.

Some dispute this research by saying it makes unfair comparisons. They argue that the numbers assume that every factor is completely equal. That is, in the research, everyone is assumed to be the same age, with the same education, and with the same work experience. These critics argue that comparing a young college graduate to an older educated person with more experience is unfair in analyzing pay. Furthermore, the research does not take into account the fact that women tend to go into fields that pay less, such as liberal arts or nursing (Keller 2000). This further illustrates the devaluation of women in regard to pay.

Some argue that gender and race impact the type of labor that people participate in. For example, women tend to be responsible for domestic work in their homes and they also work in the domestic labor market much more frequently than men. Some women work as maids or nannies or in other jobs outside the home while they must come home to take care of their own families. Some argue that this leaves women at a disadvantage. Others emphasize the racial implications of this experience over the gender dimensions. Historically, for example, African American women participated in hourly paid work, especially in domestic labor such as housekeeping and working as nannies. However, now, as African American women have acquired access to other job arenas, many Latinas are filling these low-paying, insecure types of domestic labor (Hondagneu-Sotelo 2001).

SOCIAL STRATIFICATION, HIGHER EDUCATION, AND UPWARD MOBILITY

Many people believe they can improve their social class status. However, social mobility is difficult to achieve. Leonhardt (2005) and Egan (2005) both studied the experiences of white men without a college education. According to their research, even though these men were able to achieve middle-class status, they felt as though they were in a precarious situation. Losing their current jobs would create the difficult situation of trying to find a new one without having a college education. With no college degree to fall back on, they could potentially find their middle-class social status threatened. Without a college degree, however, some of these men obtained management jobs in their industries. Yet rarely can an uneducated woman or a member of a racial/ethnic minority group achieve the same level of success, as these and other studies indicate.

One way in which many people try to change their social status is by obtaining a higher education. A college degree should allow doors to be opened for people of various socioeconomic classes. However, obtaining a college degree is difficult, especially for women of minority groups. Many students struggle with racial, gendered, and class issues that arise within higher education.

Social stratification occurs at the college level, where structural inequalities based on gender, race, and class become clearly apparent. The scholars bell hooks (2000) and Kathleen Wong (2004) explore the ways in which their social class intersected with their race and gender while attending college. They describe feelings of isolation and uncertainty; the need to navigate various identities based upon their gender, race, and class; and the difficulty of obtaining support from family and friends who did not understand what they were going through. Sometimes families may feel threatened by the new status of their relative (Engen 2004) or believe that their relative is a "traitor" (Bell et al. 2000). These reactions within the community can affect the success of a student. Students may not understand the college system and may not know how to find social support; at the same time, many colleges may not know how to provide such support (Alessio 2006). Also, the low numbers of minority students on many college campuses can aggravate the problems. Despite all this, the arguments regarding higher education rarely include discussion of the importance of social and community support.

SOCIAL STRATIFICATION AND AFFIRMATIVE ACTION

Affirmative action policies, which are designed to give historically disadvantaged minority groups an equal opportunity to participate in employment and higher education, have been highly controversial in terms of their impact on social stratification and upward mobility. Some argue that affirmative action allows companies and colleges to mirror societal social variations: because society is diverse in race and gender, colleges and the workplace should be diverse as well. Race, in particular, is what has been viewed as the most important issue in terms of implementing affirmative action policies. Due to historical discrimination, including the institutionalized discrimination of slavery and segregation, many argue that affirmative action is necessary. However, some argue that it puts white men at a disadvantage because it favors less-qualified people in gaining access to competitive jobs and schools (Steele 1994). It has also been argued that many minority groups other than African Americans, such as women, people from other racial and ethnic minority groups, and people with disabilities, have benefited more from affirmative action than African Americans, whose civil rights struggle in the 1960s largely paved the way for the successful legislation of this policy (Edmond 1995). Since the 1990s, such policies have been under attack, especially in regard to higher education. And even with affirmative action policies in place, there continues to be stratification among social classes and within power structures.

In addition, little has been done to address forms of social stratification that affirmative action alone cannot address. The micro-inequities that occur within organizations, where, for example, employees of racial minority backgrounds or women are treated as inferior to white male employees or treated differently from them, are difficult to address at the legal level, unless systematic discrimination has occurred and a group of employees can file a class-action lawsuit. Even though there are laws specifying that state companies must recruit or hire people of certain racial or gendered groups, there are no laws that say such people must have their say or be allowed to participate in the social aspects of the organization (Steele 1994).

In the most recent challenge to affirmative action policies, the U.S. Supreme Court ruled in *Gratz v. Bollinger* that in its undergraduate admissions process the University of Michigan could not give points to applicants for being part of a particular racial group, making it more difficult for minority students to be accepted. At the same time, in *Grutter v. Bollinger,* a parallel case that the court also reviewed, the court determined that race could be a factor in considering applicants to the University of Michigan's law school, as long as applicants did not receive an explicit benefit from being in a particular minority group. Being part of a minority group can be an influence on decisions, but explicit benefits, like the point system used in Michigan undergraduate applications, were deemed illegal.

This has led many higher education institutions to try to increase diversity without using racial or ethnic classifications. Many universities and colleges have now eliminated scholarships and programs that were geared toward African American and/or Hispanic applicants, or have changed the requirements so that they are more inclusive. Institutions have tried to increase diversity by identifying students not by race but by socioeconomic class. Recruiting and programming geared toward students from disadvantaged backgrounds is one way in which colleges and universities are attempting to increase diversity without using race or ethnicity as a factor (Schmidt 2006).

The implications of these decisions are twofold. First, the new emphasis on socioeconomic class over race validates the view that socioeconomic class can impact students' achievement. This type of policy works to help students whose social class puts them at a disadvantage, regardless of their racial background. In addition, this type of policy differentiates levels of need. Students who are in a particular racial or ethnic category may belong to a privileged social class (for example, middle-class African American, Hispanic, American Indian, Asian); they are therefore not necessarily those most in need, despite their racial disadvantage in a stratified society.

CONCLUSION

In examining gender, race, and class, it is difficult to determine which of these impacts social stratification the most. Women experience inequality in pay, higher education, and many other aspects of their lives. However, middle- and upper-class white women have access to privileges that provide them with access to opportunities that many racial minorities and poor communities cannot access. Racial minorities contend with some of the same issues: they, too, experience inequality in pay, in higher education, and in their daily lives. While scholars disagree on which factor is most likely to affect one's access to opportunities or promise of upward mobility, some scholars simply argue that all of these factors matter. For example, feminist scholars such as Patricia Hill Collins (2000)and Maxine Baca Zinn and Bonnie Thornton Dill (1996) discuss the multiple oppressions that occur, particularly as they affect black and other minority women. Whereas Hill Collins argues for a specifically black feminist approach to understanding these multiple forms of oppression, Zinn and Dill argue for a multiracial approach; in both cases, these scholars are pointing us in the direction of an intersectional approach to understanding how gender, race, and class interact with each and in combination lead to what we understand as social stratification in U.S. society.

See also Affirmative Action; Race and Racism: Whiteness and White Supremacy; Third World and Women of Color Feminisms.

Further Reading: Alessio, Carolyn, "When College Advising Must Cross Cultural Gaps," *Chronicle of Higher Education* 52, no. 44 (2006): B18–B20; Baca Zinn, Maxine, and Bonnie Thornton Dill, "Theorizing Difference from Multiracial Feminism," *Feminist Studies* 22, no. 2 (1996): 321–332; Bell, Katrina E., Mark P. Orbe, Darlene K. Drummond, and Sakile Kai Camara, "Accepting the Challenge of Centralizing without Essentializing: Black Feminist Thought and African American Women's Communicative Experiences," *Women's Studies in Communication* 23, no. 10 (2000): 41–62; Brady, Diane, "Hopping aboard the Daddy Track," *Business Week*, November 8, 2004, 100–101; Edmond Jr., Alfred, "25 Years of Affirmative Action," *Black Enterprise* 25, no. 7 (February, 1995): 156–157; Egan, Timothy, "No Degree, and No Way Back to the Middle," *New York Times*, May 24, 2005, A14; Ehrenreich, Barbara, *Bait and Switch: The Futile Pursuit of the American Dream* (New York: Metropolitan Books, 2005); Ehrenreich, Barbara, *Nickel and Dimed: On (Not) Getting By in America* (New York: Henry Holt, 2001); Engen, David, "Invisible Identities: Notes on Class and Race," in *Our Voice: Essays in Culture, Ethnicity, and Communication,* ed. A. Gonzalez, Marsha Houston, and Victoria Chen, 250–255 (Los Angeles: Roxbury Publishing, 2004); Fischer, Claude S., Michael Hout, Martin Sanchez Jankowski, Samuel R. Lucas, Ann Swidler, and Kim Voss, "Inequality By Design," in *Social Stratification: Class, Race, and Gender in Sociological Perspective,* ed. David B. Grusley (Boulder, CO: Westview Press, 2001); Hill Collins, Patricia, *Black Feminist Thought: Knowledge, Consciousness, and the Politics of Empowerment,* 2nd ed. (New York: Routledge, 2000); Hondagneu-Sotelo, Pierrette, *Doméstica: Immigrant Workers Cleaning and Caring in the Shadows of Affluence* (Berkeley: University of California Press, 2001); hooks, bell, *Where We Stand: Class Matters* (London: Routledge, 2000); Keller, Larry, "Women and Men: Payday," 2000, available at: www.cnn.com; Leonhardt, David, "The College Dropout Boom," *New York Times,* May 24, 2005, A14; Moreno, Pamela Barta, "The History of Affirmative Action Law and Its Relation to College Admission," *Journal of College Admission* 179 (2003): 14–21; National Committee on Pay Equity, "Women of Color in the Workplace," 2004–2006, available at: www.payequity.org/info-race.html; New York Times correspondents, *Class Matters* (New York: Henry Holt, 2005); Schmidt, Peter, "From 'Minority' to 'diversity': The Transformation of Formerly Race-Exclusive Programs May Be Leaving Some Students Out in the Cold," *Chronicle of Higher Education* 52, no. 22 (2006): A24–A30; Steele, Shelby, "A Negative Vote on Affirmative Action," in *Debating Affirmative Action,* ed. Nicolaus Mills, 37–47 (New York: Dell, 1994); Tumin, Melvin, "The Dysfunctions of Stratification," in *Social Stratification: Class, Race, and Gender in Sociological Perspective,* ed. David B. Grusky, 65–73 (Boulder, CO: Westview Press, 2001); West, Candance, and Sarah Fenstermaker, "Accountability in Action: The Accomplishment of Gender, Race and Class in a Meeting of the University of California Board of Regents," *Discourse and Society* 13, no. 2 (2002): 537–563; Wilcox, John, "In Practice," *Journal of Training and Development* (September

1989): 12–14; Wong (Lau), Kathleen, "Working through Identity: Understanding Class in the Context of Race," in *Our Voice: Essays in Culture, Ethnicity, and Communication,* ed. A. Gonzalez, Marsha Houston, and Victoria Chen, 256–263 (Los Angeles: Roxbury, 2004); Wood, Julia, *Gender Lives: Communication, Gender, and Culture,* 6th ed. (Belmont, CA: Thomson Wadsworth, 2005); Zweig, Michael, *Working Class Majority* (Ithaca, NY: Industrial and Labor Relations, 2000).

LaKresha Graham

RACE AND RACISM: WHITENESS AND WHITE SUPREMACY

Whiteness and white supremacy are both founded on the concept of a racial hierarchy in which people are privileged and oppressed according to the color of their skin. This logic is also based on hidden systems of sexism and gender oppression, with different results for men and women.

BACKGROUND

The controversy over whiteness challenges the normative status of white men and women in today's society, calling attention to the power and privileges that accompany such positioning. Perspectives vary on how whiteness and white supremacy are made manifest and on appropriate methods of response. In the last two decades there has been a proliferation of scholarship on the concept of whiteness, or how and why the position of the white heterosexual male is viewed as superior to that of other groups in society, including white women, men and women of racial and ethnic minority groups, and/or gays and lesbians. Whiteness works with patriarchy in setting up a hierarchy that privileges certain people while oppressing others. While gender has been used to oppress women since the time of ancient Greece, race has arguably been used in this way only since the 1600s. Interdisciplinary studies of whiteness, largely aligned with feminist perspectives, have attempted to explain the origins of whiteness; how it works in everyday life; and the connections and gaps between whiteness, white people, and white culture. Additionally, this work tries to understand the ways in which the concept of whiteness is founded on white supremacy and sexism, and the fact that even analyzing whiteness can still result in support for a white supremacist and patriarchal view of the world. Some people argue that whiteness is entirely oppressive and discriminatory so we should get rid of it, and race, altogether. Others claim that some, perhaps most, of whiteness is problematic, but that parts of it are not necessarily so. Consequently, they assert that whiteness can be fixed. Is whiteness completely oppressive? How is whiteness different for men and for women? What can be done about whiteness? Can we resist it without re-creating it? There is a far more foundational question for many people (particularly, but not only, people who are white): does whiteness really exist? These questions, and the concept of whiteness itself, are complex and controversial because they are intertwined with issues of race and racism, privilege and guilt, culture and everyday life. White women are faced with a set of contradictions pertaining to their inferior gender status and superior racial status; women of color are faced with the double burden of racism and sexism.

WHAT IS WHITENESS?

Whiteness often escapes definition, or at the very least resists it. Whiteness can be seen as an abstract concept that orders our world. It exists broadly in and through social institutions like education and the legal system. It is also involved with the way people, both white and nonwhite, relate to each other. At the same time, whiteness has material or concrete consequences such as how much a person earns or where she or he can purchase a home. In both senses, abstract and material, whiteness is historically located and gender specific. This means that over time, the meaning of whiteness changes, as does the way it is enacted. In the 1950s, being a white man helped you get a job, whereas being a white woman meant you shouldn't have to work. Today, being a white woman will help you to get a job, though not the same salary as a white man. There are some key characteristics of whiteness that can be used to describe it, including normativity, power, and privilege, as well as how whiteness is linked to the ideas of white supremacy and patriarchy.

At its core, whiteness is seen as the unquestioned norm or the status quo, instead of simply one of many different options. Usually taken for granted, it remains invisible. People, specifically white people, are taught not to question the fact that they are privileged by the way society works. These norms have developed over time based on the behavior and cultural traditions of white men who have historically been in social positions of power. Essentially, the way white folks do things becomes the "normal" way to do them, the commonsense way, the status quo. Society continues to work around and with these norms without questioning who is advantaged by this framework and who is disadvantaged. For example, in popular culture, and even in everyday conversation, race is often used when describing other people. Charlie Wheeler from *Friends* would likely be described as "the black woman that Joey and Ross both dated." But white is not seen as raced; it is seen as the normative. So white people are not marked as racially white people; they are simply people. Mike Hannigan would be described as "the guy Phoebe married on *Friends*." He is not constructed as a *raced* person; he is merely a "normal" person. It happens all the time and there are many different consequences of this type of practice. First, through language, Charlie is connected to black women. When she speaks, she is seen as speaking from a specific standpoint, from the viewpoint of a black woman, and thus she speaks for black women. Second, Mike is not linked to any particular group (either raced or gendered), so he is not seen as speaking for any group of people in particular. Instead he is just a normal guy speaking for and to all people. When you are framed as just human (as white men are) you get to speak for all of humanity. When you are framed as gendered or raced (as women and nonwhite people are), you are only allowed to speak for your race and/or gender. Third, because the nonmarked person is constructed as normal, racially marked people are, by default, constructed as different and abnormal. The hierarchy of power between normal and abnormal functions as a subtle form of racism. So not only is whiteness based on the historically overt racism of white supremacy, but it continues to covertly locate white people in positions of power based on their unmarked race. This positioning also comes with unearned privileges that are given and available to white people based solely on the color of their skin (see sidebar, "Peggy McIntosh's *White Privilege and Male Privilege*"). White privilege works to unfairly benefit some, because the entitlements are not universally available, and consequently confers dominance upon white folks (McIntosh 1995). For white women, this is complicated, as they are both privileged by their race and oppressed by their gender. Unlike extreme examples of white supremacy such as the Ku Klux Klan, Aryan Nation, and other hate groups that are often

---

PEGGY MCINTOSH'S *WHITE PRIVILEGE AND MALE PRIVILEGE*

One of the foundational readings on whiteness is feminist scholar Peggy McIntosh's (1995) *White Privilege and Male Privilege*. McIntosh describes white privilege as "an invisible weightless knapsack of special provisions, assurances, tools, maps, guides, codebooks, passports, visas, clothes, compass, emergency gear and blank checks" (77). She goes on to articulate 46 specific effects of this privilege, including the following (the original numbers are given):

3. If I should need to move, I can be pretty sure of renting or purchasing housing in an area which I can afford and in which I would want to live.
5. I can go shopping alone most of the time, fairly well assured that I will not be followed or harassed by store detectives.
7. When I am told about our national heritage or about "civilization," I am shown that people of my color made it what it is.
12. I can go into a book shop and count on finding the writing of my race represented, into a supermarket and find the staple foods that fit with my cultural traditions, into a hairdresser's shop and find someone who can deal with my hair.
13. Whether I use checks, credit cards, or cash, I can count on my skin color not to work against the appearance that I am financially reliable.
18. I can swear, or dress in secondhand clothes, or not answer letters, without having people attribute these choices to the bad morals, the poverty, or the illiteracy of my race.
25. If a traffic cop pulls me over or if the IRS audits my tax return, I can be sure that I haven't been singled out because of my race.
30. If I declare there is a racial issue at hand, or there isn't a racial issue at hand, my race will lend me more credibility for either position than a person of color will have.
35. I can take a job with an affirmative action employer without having my co-workers on the job suspect that I got it because of my race.
41. I can be sure that if I need legal or medical help, my race will not work against me.
46. I can choose blemish cover or bandages in "flesh" color and have them more or less match my skin.

WOMEN IN WHITE SUPREMACIST GROUPS

There is a wide variety of beliefs concerning women within white supremacist groups. While they are largely encouraged to participate in white supremacist movements, there is much debate over what form that participation should take. Based on traditional notions of gender, some argue that white women's great contribution is found in the domestic realm—church, home, and children. Others argue that white women should be involved in violent action and political office in order to further the cause. In most cases, white women find themselves playing traditional roles in the movement; often they are used to recruit others and they typically lack the authority of their white male counterparts in the groups.

---

condemned even by white people, everyday practices of whiteness often go unnoticed due to their appearing normal and natural rather than deviant, hierarchical, power-laden, or racist (Dyer 1997).

DOES WHITENESS REALLY EXIST?

To claim that whiteness exists is also to claim that race still matters. In the current political climate, drawing such attention to race is often controversial. On one side, the notion of racial colorblindness, or not seeing anyone's race, is valued. This position argues that we have reached a state of racial equality and that drawing any attention to skin color is problematic. For white people, the only acceptable option is not to have anything to say about race, otherwise one risks being labeled racist just by having something to say. The other side argues that despite recent advances, racism still exists. While overt and extreme racism is no longer socially accepted, there are myriad ways in which people of color are still marginalized. From this perspective, denying the visibility of race covers up the subtle ways in which race still functions in society. Racial equality can be achieved only by continuing to discuss issues of race, including the white race and whiteness and the complicated relationships between race and gender.

THE PROBLEMS OF STUDYING WHITENESS AND WOMEN

It should be noted that whiteness as a legitimate area of study did not gain widespread currency until white women and men started looking at themselves. This was despite the fact that racially marginalized scholars and lay people had for centuries made white people and whiteness objects of inquiry (Roediger 1998; hooks 1992). Feminist scholars, in particular, laid some of the groundwork for examining how whiteness affects the lives of white and nonwhite women in U.S. society (Frankenberg 1993; Winddance Twine 1997). Ruth Frankenberg's research on white women and racism identified how white women of various socioeconomic backgrounds come to identify themselves as "race-less," a reality that is not possible for women who are not white. France Winddance Twine's research on "brown skinned white girls" demonstrates how African American girls growing up in primarily white suburbs identify as "white" in terms of their identification with mainstream U.S. (white) culture. This type of scholarship shows us that whiteness is an ideological construct with powerful material effects for all racial and ethnic groups in society.

While there is a political need to analyze and critique whiteness, this project does not come without certain problems. One danger is using whiteness scholarship to justify focusing on only white people and their achievements, events, and so on, when most of the educational curriculum in the West already does that. A second risk is that of permitting white victimhood, the sentiment of "it's so hard to be white these days," along with calls of reverse racism. White guilt is a third problem associated with talking about whiteness; in this case, the focus is taken away from the oppression caused by systemic whiteness and shifted onto the extremely penitent white person effectively paralyzed by guilt over his or her own unconscious contributions to a racist system (Dyer 1997).

ABOLISHING WHITENESS

One position in the debate on whiteness, held by the "new abolitionists" and articulated through the journal *Race Traitor,* advocates for the abolition of the white race. New abolitionists are quick to explain that this does not mean destroying people with white skin; instead it is the destruction of race as a meaningful concept. They argue that because race has been socially constructed over time, it can also be undone. They claim that there is nothing positive about whiteness and that it is wholly oppressive. Based on this premise, *Race Traitor* has adopted the motto "treason to whiteness is loyalty to humanity" (Ignatiev and Garvey 1996, 10).

New abolitionists visualize the white race as a club that inducts its members at birth without their consent. These white people go through life reaping the benefits of whiteness without reflecting on its racist costs or its support of white supremacy. The club is perpetuated primarily through the assumption that those who look white are loyal to the system that provides them with unearned privileges. Social institutions dole out these advantages to people who look white, to induce their continued consent. Simultaneously, people who do not look white are assumed to be enemies of the structure and are routinely and systematically punished by these social institutions. To disband the club and destroy whiteness, the central assumption of loyalty/enmity based on skin color must be undermined. This can be accomplished by white people becoming traitors to their race. Race traitors are white people who publicly display their disloyalty to whiteness. This includes rejecting the notion that they are white, drawing attention to unearned privileges, and working to subvert institutions that reproduce race. Race traitors are not limited to socially acceptable means of protest, as these norms are often meant to reproduce whiteness (Ignatiev and Garvey 1996).

A number of scholars, including Dreama Moon and Lisa Flores, have critiqued the new abolitionist's position for perpetuating whiteness despite the professed goal of destroying it, arguing that the line of thinking is problematic in a number of ways. First, the discussion trivializes the contributions of racially marginalized people in history. The emphasis is placed on the white person who becomes a race traitor and identifies with the racially marginalized groups rather than on the accomplishments of those groups. This continues to position white folks as the agents of change, and thus in a dominant position, since only they possess the power to perpetuate whiteness or to destroy it and enable social progress. Second, against whiteness, which is portrayed as monolithically evil, blackness is uncritically lauded and valorized. Framing black culture as the exotic "other" oversimplifies the discussion, presenting a white/black binary and erasing other racially marginalized cultures and people. Third, the race traitor move is itself an exertion of white privilege. Only white people who systematically avoid being racially marked can renounce a racial identity, claiming not to be white. And despite this rejection, they do not dislodge the power that accompanies being white.

As Alcoff (1998) points out, some feminist scholars argue that a focus on racist oppression distracts from oppression based on sexism, which has a longer history. They claim that discussions of whiteness and race divide women so that they will not focus their efforts on fighting patriarchy. Other feminist scholars advocate for an intersectional approach. They claim that racism and patriarchy do not work in isolation; or, to put it another way, white women are always already both white and women. You cannot simply reject a single part of your identity because it exists in the intersection of gender, race, socioeconomic status, sexual orientation, age, religion, and other social identity categories. Whiteness is inherently tied in complex and fluid ways to patriarchy, heteronormativity, and other forms of oppression. From this perspective, any approach to changing whiteness must be both coalitional and intersectional (focused on multiple axes of identity) (Alcoff 1998; Moon and Flores 2000).

TRANSFORMING WHITENESS

Another position in the debate on whiteness is that rather than trying to abolish it, scholars and activists should work to further understand it. This perspective sees whiteness as a system that has been used for domination but is not entirely oppressive. Therefore research should work to articulate how whiteness functions and develop methods of resistance and transformation. A related objective, from this viewpoint, is to differentiate between whiteness (as predominantly and systemically oppressive) and white culture or a white cultural identity (based upon the lived experiences of white folks).

This perspective argues that whiteness is constantly made and remade through language. As an oppressive system, it retains its power through what is said and, significantly, what is left unsaid. Scholars have worked to identify and make visible the rhetorical strategies that are used to further whiteness. For example, one study discovered how white people talk about being white in ways that make white seem only natural or equate being white with a national identity (Nakayama and Krizek 1995). Carrie Crenshaw (1997) demonstrated how silence is used to maintain whiteness as the invisible norm and how Senator Carole Moseley Braun's racially marginalized, female bodily presence in the U.S. Senate functioned as a powerful (and successful) counterargument.

Lorraine Kenny (2000) has explored the cultural norms of white middle-class girls in order to discover what might be called white female culture or a feminine white cultural identity. This position argues that part of the cost of whiteness's invisibility is a lack of understanding of the cultures of white folks. When whiteness and masculinity are rejected as the universal norm, the cultural practices of white men and women are not seen as normal or natural but rather culturally specific. This view does not claim there is a singular white culture but rather many cultures that are predominantly racially white and also intersected with other identity categories, such as gender, regional, and socioeconomic statuses (see also Frankenberg 1993).

These approaches believe that with further understanding of whiteness, people can call attention to how whiteness functions, preventing it from continuing to be the invisible norm in society. At the same time, there are parts of whiteness, tied to the lived experiences of white folks, that do not confer dominance upon them. As pointed out with regard to white women, part of the experience of being white, for them, is still an experience of being oppressed as women (whereas for white men, being recipients of gendered oppression is not part of white culture). Part of transforming whiteness includes separating what is oppressive from parts of the white experience that are neutral or positive.

CONCLUSION

Through these discussions we can see that whiteness is gendered as masculine. The normative strategies of whiteness and white privilege run parallel to patriarchy and male privilege. Responses to whiteness view it as something to be dealt with independently, relying on the masculine value of autonomous individuality. Segrest (2002) further explains that whiteness has harmed the souls of white folks with its masculine violence and repression of emotion. The interwoven nature of whiteness and masculinity works to privilege white men, while providing grounds on which to feminize racially marginalized men. Racially marginalized women are further excluded from dominant subject positions while in certain respects white femininity is paradoxical.

As the numerical majority of white people continues to decline, the controversy over whiteness will likely intensify. Identifying the diversity of racial and gendered positions and acknowledging differences within these categories will become increasingly important as we work toward equitable representation in the workplace and educational systems (for example, through affirmative action programs), as well as within the realms of the media, law, and medicine. Feminist and LGBTQ social movements continue to grapple with the way invisible whiteness and white privilege undermine goals of equality. Intersectional analyses continue to highlight the ways in which power and privilege work across identity categories, including gender, race, and class. In this context, identifying whiteness, and working to either abolish or transform it, challenges its normative status and contributes to a crisis of identity for white folks. For white women in particular, this forces a realization of the way their whiteness works to oppress others, contradicting feminist values of community and collaboration. Questions remain about the possibility of reconfiguring whiteness or rescuing a nonoppressive white cultural identity. On the other hand, supporting a policy of racial colorblindness maintains the hierarchy of white patriarchal supremacy.

See also Affirmative Action; Race and Racism: Social Stratification in the United States; Third World and Women of Color Feminisms.

Further Reading: Alcoff, Linda Martin, "What Should White People Do?" *Hypatia* 13, no. 3 (1998): 6–26; Crenshaw, Carrie, "Resisting Whiteness' Rhetorical Silence," *Western Journal of Communication* 61, no. 3 (1997): 253–278; Dyer, Richard, *White* (London: Routledge, 1997); Ferber, Abby L., *White Man Falling: Race, Gender and White Supremacy* (Lanham, MD: Rowman and Littlefield, 1998); Frankenberg, Ruth, *White Women, Race Matters: The Social Construction of Whiteness* (Minneapolis: University of Minnesota Press, 1993); Hill, Mike, ed., *Whiteness: A Critical Reader* (New York: New York University Press, 1997); hooks, bell, *Black Looks: Race and Representation* (Boston: South End Press, 1992); Ignatiev, Noel, and John Garvey, "Abolish the White Race," in *Race Traitor*, ed. Noel Ignatiev and John Garvey, 9–14 (New York: Routledge, 1996); Kenny, Lorraine D., *Daughters of Suburbia: Growing Up White, Middle Class and Female* (New Brunswick, NJ: Rutgers University Press, 2000); Kincheloe, Joe L., Shirley R. Steinberg, Nelson M. Rodriguez, and Ronald E. Chennault, eds., *White Reign: Deploying Whiteness in America* (New York: St. Martin's Press, 1998); McIntosh, Peggy, "White Privilege and Male Privilege: A Personal Account of Coming to See Correspondences through Work in Women's Studies," in *Race, Class, and Gender: An Anthology*, ed. M. L. Andersen and P. H. Collins, 76–87 (Belmont, CA: Wadsworth, 1995); Moon, Dreama, and Lisa A. Flores, "Antiracism and the Abolition of Whiteness: Rhetorical Strategies of Domination among 'Race Traitors,'" *Communication Studies* 51, no. 2 (2000): 97–115; Nakayama, Thomas K., and Robert L. Krizek, "Whiteness: A Strategic Rhetoric," *Quarterly Journal of Speech* 81 (1995): 291–309; Nakayama, Thomas K., and Judith N. Martin, eds., *Whiteness: The Communication of Social Identity* (Thousand Oaks, CA: Sage, 1999); Roediger, David R., ed., *Black on White: Black Writers on What It Means to Be White* (New York: Schocken Books, 1998); Segrest, Mab, "Of Souls and White Folks," in *Born to Belonging: Writings on Spirit and Justice*, ed. Mab Segrest, 157–175 (New Brunswick, NJ: Rutgers University Press, 2002); Winndance Twine, France, "Brown Skinned White Girls: Class, Culture, and the Construction of White Identity in Suburban Communities," in *Displacing Whiteness: Essays in Social and Cultural Criticism*, ed. Ruth Frankenberg, 214–243 (Durham, NC: Duke University Press, 1997).

Jason Zingsheim

RELIGION

Women's roles in religion and gender ideologies regarding religion have undergone major changes in the twentieth century. On one hand, critiques of the patriarchal bias within most institutionalized religions have led to women's extended participation and leadership rights in various religious institutions as well as to the search for new forms of religious expression. On the other hand, some religious groups resist these reforms and continue to enforce a conservative gender ideology.

BACKGROUND

The major religious institutions in the world—Christianity, Judaism, Buddhism, Islam, and Hinduism—have all historically been dominated by men. Men have generally held leadership positions in these religions while women have usually occupied roles that were only of a supportive nature and peripheral. Still, while women historically had fewer laity and no leadership rights in these religious institutions, they were crucial in the development and establishment of these institutions.

Broadly speaking, men dominate in traditions that rely on written and theological interpretation, such as the classical Judeo-Christian tradition. These traditions emphasize scripture and cultivate a professional priesthood. Since women, until the middle of the twentieth century, had little or no access to education and advanced literary training relative to men, they were excluded from the beginning from the decision-making process of the religious traditions. In the religious traditions that are transmitted primarily orally and that emphasize roles guided by divine inspiration (that is, where a person believes him/herself to be qualified to communicate a sacred revelation) rather than by authority (that is, where a priest is authorized by religious doctrine), women tend to have leadership functions. In shamanic traditions, for example, women have held shamanic positions equally with men. In radical Christian and quasi-Christian movements, such as those of the Quakers and the Pentecostals, women have held many preaching positions. Women founders of religions are usually found in more recently established religions, in sects, cults, and new religious movements, while all of the founders of the main world religions were men (King 1989).

The story of women and religion in the United States includes continuity and transformation at the same time. In the last 30 years, as a result of the first and second waves of feminism and broader social changes with regard to habits and cultural norms, gendered religion has increasingly been criticized. There are more and more challenges to the patriarchal bias of religion in contemporary Western society. What was once taken for granted as ultimate truth is now questioned primarily by feminists. Pertinent questions are the following: Why have women generally been excluded from higher religious leadership and laity positions? Where does the seemingly inherent male bias in institutionalized religion come from? And can institutionalized religion, as it is currently practiced in the United States, still give meaning to women today? While, on one hand, within mainline Protestant denominations women gained full leadership and laity rights by the end of the twentieth century, they continue to encounter more or less subtle forms of resistance and discrimination. On the other hand, as a reaction to the changing cultural norms and habits, fundamentalist and evangelistic religions have been enforcing a conservative gender ideology that strictly separates the roles of women and men. Finally, women-centered religious groups with a specific female spirituality hope to offer women a holistic alternative to the mainline religious traditions.

WOMEN'S CRITIQUE OF GENDERED EXPERIENCE WITHIN TRADITIONAL RELIGION

Religion and religious ideologies have been regarded as major avenues for the social control of women. The justification of the exclusion of women from positions of church leadership and from ordination to the priesthood or full-time religious office is primarily based on theological teaching. At the same time, scholars have argued for an expanded role for women, based on certain biblical passages that emphasize a more egalitarian core of the religious tradition. Feminist scholars concluded that most of the unequal treatment of women in religion is not part and parcel of the teachings of Christianity but an attempt by male clerics to ensure that any equality among women and men will not come to fruition (*Encyclopedia of Religion and Society* 1998). At the core of feminist theology is the belief in the full equality of women and men in church and society. Feminist theology argues that Christianity and Judaism are essentially patriarchal and that they have contributed to the oppression of women. Therefore, according to these feminist scholars, change is needed.

A feminist critique of religion began in the nineteenth century and reemerged in the last decades of the twentieth century as similar ideas were taken up by feminist thinkers: they include the power of religion in safeguarding gender inequalities, issues of female ordination based on new scriptural interpretations, the authority of the Bible, and the idea of an ancient matriarchate.

At the core of their critique are three issues: the patriarchal and sexist bias within religion, the androcentric (male-centered) language within religious scripture, and the female religious experience. With regard to these themes, one can differentiate between two different approaches to a feminist critique: the approaches of the reformers and the revolutionaries (Lindley 1996).

Reformists: Reinterpreting Religious Scripture

The goal of the reformist feminist thinkers is to create change from within their various religious traditions. While they critique patriarchy and point out that its power should never be underestimated, feminist theologians like Rosemary Radfort Ruether, Elizabeth Schuessler Fiorenza, and Phyllis Trible argue that there are resources and themes within the religious tradition and its scripture that support equality and liberation for women. According to them it is the task of the feminist historian today to recapture this theme and to make it available for women who are on a spiritual journey.

Via the methods of retrieval, reinterpretation, and reconstruction of scripture and tradition, feminists are arguing for change today. Scholars have taken a closer look at the Gospel of Luke, for example, a gospel showing that women played an important role as disciples, apostles, and aides in the early Christian ritual meal, as well as at examples in Jesus' teachings (King 1989).

The "language question" remains a big part of the debate. It questions the validity of much of the "male" God language and looks for changes in language, to achieve "neutral language" or the addition of female images to male ones. It assumes that language about God is symbolic or metaphorical. As such, many passages in the Old Testament have been interpreted to express maternal aspects and activities of God. In addition, feminist researchers have pointed to the feminine aspects of the figure of the Holy Spirit, which is part of the Trinity. Sally McFague has suggested an altogether different model of God. It consists of three parts, which have a more holistic and relational approach to God, and includes an ecological awareness: God as Mother (or Father, in a parental sense), God as Lover, and God as Friend (Lindley 1996).

Moreover, reformists stress the role of human experience in theology, particularly women's experience, which has largely been ignored. However, their views of the nature of men and women differ. While some argue that men's and women's nature is essentially the same and that they are thus equal, others argue that there are some basic differences and that patriarchal structures have simply devalued the different nature of women.

Another important leitmotif within reformist feminist theology is the "wisdom tradition." This implies a concept of divine wisdom, as illustrated by the feminine term "Sophia," which first appears as a female personification of God in Hebrew scripture and which is then carried forth into other Christian texts, such as the New Testament. The image of Sophia provides a way for contemporary feminist theologians to argue against the normative maleness of Jesus as savior. It presents a way to critique gendered God language (King 1989).

Significant, influential reformist women thinkers of the nineteenth century included Frances Wright (1795–1852), Ernestine Rose (1810–1892), Margaret Fuller (1810–1855), Elizabeth Cady Stanton (1815–1902), and Matilda Joslyn Gage (1826–1898). All of these writers argued that women's rights are rooted in a view of men and women as persons first and that their equality is based on this. They were all critical of the male leadership of the church and supported the view that priesthood was the main reason why women had few or no rights compared to men. Their goal was to educate women to think for themselves, rather than buying into what the church led them to believe. This meant a more critical interpretation of the Bible. While Fuller and Stanton disqualified only parts of the Bible and still saw validity and usefulness, even for women, in parts of Christianity, Gage and Wright were more radical in their approach in that they supported a total rejection of the Bible (Lindley 1996).

The sociological work *Defecting in Place: Women Claiming Responsibility for Their Own Spiritual Lives,* by Therese Winter, Adair Lummis, and Allison Strokes (1994), is an example of the impact of feminist theology on religion. The authors argue that many women who are involved with the church challenge the institution from within by working with women's spirituality groups.

Revolutionaries: The Creation of a Feminist Spirituality outside the Dominant Cultural Tradition

In contrast to the reformist approach to a feminist critique of religion, revolutionary feminists regard Christianity and Judaism as irrevocably sexist. While the reformist feminist approach is focused on religious reconstruction, the revolutionary approach is interested in the creation of new religious movements, which seek religious experience outside traditional religion. These new religious groups are relatively small and more research needs to be done on them.

The most prominent theme among feminists is the "Religion of the Goddess." This concept is used as an alternative to Christianity and Judaism, based on the anthropological theories of an ancient matriarchy, to which some of the nineteenth-century feminists had also referred. The concept of the goddess varies among groups (King 1989). However, the various forms of goddess religion all share common themes. They reject the patriarchal god-image and replace it by the mother-goddess symbol. They support religious communities and rituals run by women or entirely composed of women, and they all have a strong connection to nature. Moreover, rather than emphasizing a divine transcendence and an otherworldly afterlife, they stress the immanence of the divine in all humans and in all of nature. Finally, personal experience plays a crucial role in their theology and spirituality, and their religious life is lived in a multitude of ways. Rituals involve enacting ancient myths from a feminist point of view, revering nature, sacralizing women's bodies, and mourning the abuse of women in patriarchal society. The goal of the rituals/ceremonies is to share experiences and to increase self-confidence and bonding. The woman's spirituality movement is characterized by both retraditionalization and religious innovation. It is a synergy of both old and new. In contrast to traditional religion, the theology of the goddess religion emphasizes symbols rather than rational explanations.

The most prominent tradition within the goddess religion and the major producer of its goddess theology is the feminist witchcraft movement, also sometimes referred to as neopaganism. Research shows that for women the symbol of the witch is empowering, even though feminists and nonfeminists alike have challenged this notion. The Dianic Coven, also known as Feminist Witchcraft and Feminist Wicca, is a radical form of this religious belief system and belongs to the "women-only tradition." Since the 1990s there has been a growing interest in paganism and goddess religions in America. In 1990, there were as many as 100,000 witches, mostly women, in the United States.

Feminist matriarchy groups provide another direction within feminist spirituality. Characteristic of the matriarchy are the values of peace, harmony, and female ascendancy. The members of matriarchy groups believe in the primacy of matriarchal society. They are devoted to the cult of the goddess and propose a woman-centered worldview. They also connect spirituality and politics as a way to create a new social order. Matilda Joslyn Gage's *Woman, Church and State: A Historical Account of the Status of Woman through the Christian Ages: With Reminiscences of the Matriarchate* (first published in 1893) and Merlin Stone's *When God Was a Woman* (1978) are classic texts on the topic. Critics of matriarchy concepts argue that the exclusive focus on the female is not that different from the exclusive focus on the male—how can one bring about social transformation if the same dualisms are being perpetuated? Matriarchy groups are also criticized for their lack of historical, empirical evidence. Because of this lack, it is not possible to link images of female goddesses to the actual roles and positions of women in society, that is, to draw parallels between statues, symbols, and sacred images, the cult of female deities, and actual women's life in society. Moreover, within feminism there are many contradictory arguments with regard to matriarchy and the goddess movements (King 1987).

The model of the androgyny leads to another important debate among revolutionary feminists. This model entails the symbolic integration of male and female aspects with regard to the concept of "ultimate reality." However, while the idea of the androgyny seeks to overcome the male-female dualism, it remains dualistic in that it continues to facilitate an opposition of male and female.

Feminists continue to search for a symbol that goes beyond patriarchal, matriarchal, and androgynous models, a symbol that transcends these oppositions and addresses a unitary expression of the religious. Some argue that this integral concept of God can actually be found in the classical theologies of many religions as well as in the discussion about transcendence and the immanence of the divine.

SUPPORTERS OF GENDERED EXPERIENCE WITHIN RELIGION

Traditional Judeo-Christian Religion

While feminist critiques led to reforms within the mainline Judeo-Christian tradition, some Christian denominations continue to support the argument that women's traditional roles in the church are acceptable and should not be drastically changed. Among these groups are the Roman Catholic Church (even though the Second Vatican Council announced significant changes in female religious leadership), the Lutheran Church—Missouri Synod, and the various Eastern Orthodox churches. They, for example, never endorsed the views on female ordination that most mainline denominations within the Judeo-Christian tradition accepted. The reasons for adhering to a more conservative congregational polity vary. Some religious groups are trying to keep their ethnic identity and are attempting to shield their members from too much Americanization. Others justify the continued exclusion of women from leadership positions by using a theological interpretation of religious scripture that denies female ordination. Still others simply want to keep in line with their tradition.

Rather than referring to the law against female ordination as an aspect of female inferiority, these groups emphasize a "complementary" understanding of

---

WOMEN'S LEADERSHIP IN THE CATHOLIC CHURCH

The Second Vatican Council took place in 1962–1965. It significantly empowered women within the Roman Catholic Church, who could now act as eucharistic ministers, as chancellors of dioceses, and as lectors. However, up to the present, women in Roman Catholicism are not allowed to be ordained as priests. The Vatican adheres to its traditional argument that women cannot function as natural symbols of Christ because of their gender.

In the early 1980s, the woman-church movement emerged from a coalition of Catholic feminist organizations in order to keep the issue of ordination going.

male and female humanity. This means that, according to their religious understanding, gender-specific roles at home and in the church are beneficial for both men and women.

Fundamentalists, Evangelicals, and New Religious Movements: Reactions to Social Change

The Episcopal Church's decision to ordain women in 1976 has led fundamentalist groups to enforce conservative gender ideologies (Baber 1987). In addition, there was a backlash within Holiness and Pentecostal groups, which had formerly begun to endorse female leadership rights but were now reverting to conservative views on women and ministry. These groups' resistance to reforms is based on a more general resistance of these groups to social change, changing moral habits, changing popular culture, and the increase in women working outside the home. These developments were regarded as negative and as a threat to the ordered worldview of fundamentalist groups. They were interpreted as a possible threat to the male-dominated structure of the church and were thus not likely to be welcomed by conservative male clergy. Fundamentalists and evangelicals used theological assumptions to justify the continued gender inequality within their groups. The "modern" woman, for example, according to religious fundamentalists, symbolizes a rebellion against biblical authority and the traditional social order. The tumultuous years of the 1960s and 1970s reinforced the rise of conservative religious groups (Lindley 1996).

But what is it that causes modern Western women to be attracted to conservative religious groups? From a sociological point of view, the appeal of fundamentalist and evangelistic religions to women lies in a theology that advocates a certain, structured universe, which is not affected by the uncertainties of life in modern society. Studies of women's roles in new religious movements (NRMs) link women's interest in these movements to the challenge of social change as illustrated by gender confusion, family breakdown, and moral ambiguity in contemporary North American society. A study of seven groups, the International Society for Krishna Consciousness, the Unification Church, the Rajneesh Movement, the Institute of Applied Metaphysics, the Messianic Community, the Raelian Movement, and the Institute for the Development of the Harmonious Human Being, supports the argument that most women are voluntarily seeking involvement in these NRMs because they are attracted by the groups' theology of love. This reinforces their identity as women, while at the same time taking away the burden of being "worker-wife-mother-housekeeper" and giving a spiritual meaning to their relationships (Palmer 1994). Some of these groups emphasize the traditional role of a woman as procreator and housewife; others free women from this expectation by denouncing pregnancy altogether and allowing their members to remain "youthful" in all regards. These NRMs offer the space and setting in which each ideal can be lived without restrictions imposed by mainstream society.

What all seven groups have in common is that they challenge preconceived notions of sexuality and family and address the issues of instability and insecurity that come with the decline of the traditional family. These diverse NRMs provide women with specific models of womanhood. They offer solutions to the increasing fragility of the marriage bond, the declining parent-child bond, and the increase in female breadwinners by providing an environment that supports the desired, fulfilling relationship and family life without taking anything away from a woman's identity. At the same time, a close examination of these NRMs shows that these groups can serve as areas of experimentation for women to explore unconventional forms of relationships and sexuality. The author of the study of seven NRM groups argues that the rules and rituals in these groups help women define their feminine identity and helps prepare them to cope with the challenges of "normal" society (Palmer 1994).

WOMEN'S ROLES WITHIN MAINLINE PROTESTANT CHRISTIANITY

Gendered Religious Experience as a Breeding Ground for Female Rights

The twentieth century witnessed many crucial changes with regard to women's religious leadership and laity rights in most mainline denominations within the Judeo-Christian tradition, the most important being the right of female ordination in the Protestant churches and Reform Judaism. It is important to note that these changes did not occur suddenly but were the result of the work of women in the nineteenth century who increasingly questioned the patriarchal bias within religion and demanded more, if not equal, religious rights for women.

Women's roles here were twofold: on one hand, they played a crucial part in the spread of Christianity. On the other hand, while most mainline churches have historically regarded women as subordinate to men, it was precisely women's work within the churches that provided a space from which they could challenge these sexist structures and work for more female rights in the church and in society.

Women played a big part in the revival of Christianity during the Second Great Awakening (roughly from the end of the eighteenth century through the first three decades of the nineteenth century) because they outnumbered men as converts and church members. They were interested in joining the church because it helped them shape their lives and female identities apart from the domestic sphere (Lindley 1996). Gendered religious experience, thus, fostered the rise of female rights. The church community gave women a space where they could thrive outside their prescribed domestic realm. At the same time, as converts they could spread their religious belief at home, where the role of mother now gained a whole new significance in that it served a greater, missionary cause.

Women's work in the churches took place primarily within the context of women's church groups. Here they focused on foreign and home missions, on Bible study and spiritual development, and on practical support for individual churches, for example, cooking for church suppers, funerals, and weddings, cleaning the church, and taking part in maintenance activities. Also during these years, a number of religious associations that provided specific areas of organization for women emerged. These areas included maternal associations, the Sunday school movement, and charitable organizations. A general belief in the significance of women's work as religious guardians of the home also led to increased women's education. This in turn fostered the establishment of various female reform movements that proved to be pivotal in promoting women's rights.

The female-based religious groups were of crucial importance to women in that they were a source of meaning, a source of activity, and a source of female fellowship at a time when women's lives were usually restricted to the domestic sphere. Moreover, female religious reform groups and benevolent activities made women's voices heard in a more public sphere (Lindley 1996).

Religious suffrage for southern Methodist women was achieved in 1920, marking a special year in the history of women's religious rights. Still, religious suffrage and other laity rights varied greatly within denominations, and it was not until the second half of the twentieth century that laity rights became widespread. Even then, until they were given the right to formal ordination, women's status remained limited.

ORDINATION OF WOMEN

Historical Development

Female ordination is one of the most important recent developments within religious institutions in the United States. While a few Protestant denominations ordained women in the late nineteenth and early twentieth centuries, it was not until the 1970s that female ordination became widespread. The vote of the General Convention of the Episcopal Church to allow women to be ordained as priests in 1976 sealed the official right for women to enter leadership positions within liberal Protestant Christianity.

Several factors led to the rapid expansion of female clergy. Formal theological education was opened to women after World War II, and this led to the erosion of the cultural assumption that a woman's place was in the home. While traditionally women were excluded from advanced learning and teaching in most religions, after the war, theology courses became more available to the laity and thus to women. In addition to preparing them for careers in the church, theological education gave women a better understanding of their religious tradition and thus fostered a critical view of it. The move toward women's rights in the twentieth century was generally accepted within mainline Protestant denominations—thus, female religious leadership was not seen as a very drastic change and was fairly easily accepted. Society in general took to these reforms with relative ease because of the ongoing overall process of social and cultural change. Male opposition to female ordination eventually surrendered to the reforms put forward by Protestants; "white men" in mainstream Protestantism still constituted the "cultural establishment" and thus did not need to fear loss of power any time soon (Lindley 1996).

Furthermore, conservative and mainstream Protestants differed in their view of the nature of sin: for evangelicals, sin meant rebellion and disobedience, while mainstream Protestants had a less literal understanding of sin, one that was more influenced by liberation theology—to them, sin was linked to injustice, dehumanization, and oppression, as well as to a lack of self-acceptance or self-realization. In the former case sin is linked to a paradigm of hierarchy, while in the latter case it is linked to a paradigm of partnership and equality. This latter understanding of the meaning of sin reflected the general value change that that had already begun to take place in the 1960s in society in general (Lindley 1996).

The first denominations to ordain women were the Methodist, Baptist, Free Baptist, Congregational, Universalist, and Unitarian churches. While by 1921 approximately 3,000 women had positions as ministers in the United States, by 1998 women constituted approximately 15 percent of all clergy in most mainline denominations (Lehman 2002). In 1995, female religious leadership reached another high point, when women reached the highest levels of some major Christian denominations: the Lutheran Church elected two women bishops, and the Episcopal Church four women bishops; among the Methodists, eight women had been elected as bishops and 80 as district superintendents (Lindley 1996). By the end of the twentieth century, American women could be ordained as ministers and priests in most mainline Protestant denominations, and as rabbis in three of the four major Jewish groups. In evangelical and fundamental groups, 7 percent of all clergy members were female.

Arguments in Favor of Female Ordination

Supporters of the ordination of women refer to biblical passages that point at the inherently egalitarian core of the Christian tradition. Among these is the passage in Genesis declaring both male and female as being created in the name of God, as well as the numerous examples of women as prophetesses and witnesses to the resurrection of Jesus Christ and at Pentecost. Others argue that women's successes within the church and as religious missionaries, as well as the qualities of "womanhood," qualify them for ordination (Lindley 1996).

Arguments against Female Ordination

The exclusion of women from ordination was historically based on theological arguments that were also in line with current conventions and cultural

ANTOINETTE BROWN: FIRST ORDAINED WOMAN IN THE CHRISTIAN RELIGION

Antoinette Brown, born May 20, 1825, was the first woman to be ordained to the ministry in the history of Christianity. She was ordained on September 15, 1853, at the First Congregational Church in Butler, New York. Antoinette was a revolutionary in her time, but due to pressures from conservatives she had to resign after only a few years of work. Antoinette stuck to her vocation and, 10 years later, in 1863, she was ordained again, as a Unitarian minister.

assumptions about men and women. A common justification of the law against ordination of women is the Creation and Fall narrative in Genesis, which is interpreted as proof of woman's lower status, as well as her guilt in the Fall of man. Protesters against female ordination refer to biblical passages showing the social hierarchy of husband and wife. Others argue that women are unable to function as natural symbols of Christ simply because, visually, they can never be a symbol of Jesus Christ (Baber 1987).

However, according to some studies, theological issues alone do not account for the resistance to female clergy (Lehman 2002). Men have been found to hold conservative views of the role of women in society beyond religion. The belief in certain female and male characteristics that attest to inherent differences between men and women and therefore make women unfit to act as leaders is a popular justification for opposition to female ordination. Women are regarded, for example, as receptive, patient, nurturing, and intuitive, while men are supposed to be initiative-taking, rational, and detached, and they supposedly transcend the natural order (Baber 1987). In line with this reasoning is the argument of the incompatibility of motherhood and ministry. It states that the nature of womanhood provides an inevitable conflict between the role of women as mothers and guardians of the home and their duties as ministers.

Women's Continued Struggle in Religious Leadership Positions

Female ordination, however, did not automatically mean that women were actually accepted as ministers by their peers and fellow clergy members. Studies have shown that women continue to be disadvantaged as ministers: the timing of pregnancy and pregnancy leave and problems with regard to the geographic mobility of married women are but a few of the reasons why the path to women's ordination is prolonged. Then, once ordination has occurred, placement issues appear. Frequently, women are overrepresented in junior positions and seem to be ignored in the selection process. In addition, once a woman has been ordained as a minister, she often faces continued resistance from her male colleagues. Recent research has shown that some male clergy members feel threatened by ordained women. In order to prevent the "feminization" of the ministry, they try to limit women's involvement as leaders in the church. This then causes a backlash regarding females' religious rights in some churches (Lehman 2002). The continued sexist behavior is most likely linked to the sexist cultural stereotypes of men and women that are still present in mainstream society.

Women's Experience within Asian Spirituality

Since the 1950s, the United States has witnessed a steady interest in Asian forms of religiosity and spirituality, influenced mainly by Hinduism and Buddhism. The interest in these religions has been explained, for example, as a reaction to an increasingly materialistic society that values status and money above everything else. Interestingly enough, while these religions are community oriented in their original nature, American women and men converts hope to find through them a way toward individual self-fulfillment, which is often accompanied by detachment from broader social bonds. And while most seekers of Asian spirituality are disenchanted with the money-oriented emphasis of American society, the average white member of religious groups of Asian origin tends to be quite prosperous and unusually well educated (Lindley 1996). Groups like Transcendental Meditation and the International Society for Krishna Consciousness (ISKCON), which were first introduced to the United States in the 1960s, as well as Siddha Yoga, introduced in the 1970s, offer individual paths to enlightenment through a specific theology that, among other things, emphasizes the practices of meditation and yoga. While most religious leaders in these groups are men, most members are women. Still, there are a few women leaders and women gurus in Siddha Yoga, and it has been argued that women are attracted to these religious groups because they generally espouse a theology that implies the acceptance of women in roles other than those within the domestic sphere (Lindley 1996).

In addition, research on popular yoga groups in the West has shown that it is primarily women who partake in this exercise. There are indicators that yoga, when practiced with an emphasis on its spiritual and philosophical framework, helps women cope with the challenges of an increasingly fast-paced daily life in modern, Western society (Henrichsen-Schrembs 2007).

CONCLUSION

Feminist research, theory, and practice show that women have been challenging the patriarchal bias of traditional Western religion in the United States in many different ways. However, even though, at the beginning of the twenty-first century, female religious leadership and laity rights, equal on paper to those of men, have been established within liberal Protestant Christianity and Reform Judaism, women continue to be faced with latent and subtle sexism in the church or synagogue and beyond. Despite women's official recognition in the ministry, a gendered division of labor still exists in many churches. Whether the presence of women in the ministry will eventually lead to a truly egalitarian church, or whether women will experience a reactionary backlash, remains uncertain. Nevertheless, because women have entered positions of power in churches, the female perspective on religion is now taken into account in order to develop new, more appropriate statements of belief.

Moreover, other avenues of religious expression are being explored: The women's spirituality movement, in its various forms, hopes to give meaning to those who are disenchanted with the patriarchal structures of the Christian tradition. At the same time, some Christian denominations adhere to their traditional view of women, and as a reaction to the drastic reforms of the twentieth century, fundamentalist religious groups and NRMs purposely enforce a conservative gender ideology.

Whatever direction women will take, they might find answers in a new reading of the traditional religious scripture or in alternative forms of religiosity.

See also Gender Socialization; Polygamy; Religious Fundamentalism.

Further Reading: Adler, Margot, *Drawing Down the Moon: Witches, Goddess Worshippers, and Other Pagans in America Today* (New York: Penguin Books, 1979); Baber, Harriet E., "The Ordination of Women, Natural Symbols, and What Even God Cannot Do," in *Women in the World's Religions, Past and Present,* ed. Ursula King (New York: Paragon House, 1987); Chaves, Mark, *Ordaining Women: Culture and Conflict in Religious Organizations* (Cambridge, MA: Harvard University Press, 1997); Daly, Mary, *The Church and the Second Sex* (Boston: Beacon Press, 1985 [1968]); Fiorenza, Elizabeth Schuessler, *But She Said: Feminist Practices of Biblical Interpretation* (Boston: Beacon Press, 1992); Gage, Matlida Jocelyn, *Women, Church, and State: A Historical Account of the Status of Women through the Christian Ages, with Reminiscences of the Matriarchate* (New York: The Truths Seeker Company, 1893); Griffith, Elizabeth, *In Her Own Right: The Life of Elizabeth Cady Stanton* (New York: Oxford University Press, 1984); Henrichsen-Schrembs, Sabine, "Modern Life Courses: Yoga and the Search for Meaning in German Society," 2007, PhD dissertation in progress; King, Ursula, "Goddesses, Witches, Androgyny and Beyond? Feminism and the Transformation of Religious Consciousness," in *Women in the World's Religions, Past and Present,* ed. Ursula King (New York: Paragon House, 1987); King, Ursula, *Women and Spirituality: Voices of Protest and Promise* (London: Macmillan Education, 1989); Lehman, Edward C. Jr., "Women's Path into Ministry: Six Major Studies," *Pulpit and Pew Research Reports* 1 (2002): 2–38; Lindley, Susan Hill, *"You have Stept out of your Place." A History of Women and Religion in America* (Louisville, KY: Westminster John Knox Press, 1996); Palmer, Susan Jean, *Moon Sisters, Krishna Mothers, Rajneesh Lovers: Women's Roles in New Religions* (Syracuse, NY: Syracuse University Press, 1994); Plaskow, Judith, and Carol P. Christ, *Weaving the Visions: New Patterns in Feminist Spirituality* (New York: HarperCollins, 1989); Ruether, Rosemary Radford, *Sexism and God-Talk: Towards a Feminist Theology* (Boston: Beacon Press, 1983); Stone, Merlin, *When God Was a Woman* (San Diego: Harvest Books, 1978); Swatos, William H. Jr., *Encyclopedia of Religion and Society* (Walnut Creek, CA: Altamira Press, 1998); Winter, Miriam Therese, Adair Lummis, and Alison Strobes, *Defecting in Place: Women Claiming Responsibility for Their Own Spiritual Lives* (Nashville, TN: Crossroad Publishing Co., 1994).

Sabine Henrichsen-Schrembs

RELIGIOUS FUNDAMENTALISM

Historically, women have been drawn to fundamentalist religious traditions despite feminist criticism. Often we think of feminist Christians and feminist Muslims as an oxymoron. This entry summarizes the debate over gender and fundamentalism by explaining the feminist critique of fundamentalism as well as presenting reasons why women are attracted to fundamentalism.

BACKGROUND

The topic of women and fundamentalism is controversial because of debates related to patriarchy, the church, leadership roles, and gender roles. Women continue to have a strong involvement in fundamentalist strains of Judaism, Christianity, and Islam although all of these religions are seen as patriarchal. In general, research suggests that women are often drawn to fundamentalist traditions because of clear gender norms, support for the traditional family, friendship networks, and a safe sense of community. In addition, research on fundamentalist Jewish, Christian, and Muslim communities suggests that women in these communities find their roles empowering and not oppressive. Though outsiders view these communities as oppressive, women tend to find ways of negotiating power within fundamentalist congregations.

Feminist criticisms of women in fundamentalism have focused on issues and questions related to patriarchy. Feminists raise questions such as the following: How can women be attracted to religious traditions in which they cannot be leaders of congregations? How can women choose to be submissive to men? Why would women want to be in traditional marriages?

THEORETICAL UNDERSTANDING OF FUNDAMENTALISM

What exactly do we mean when we use the word *fundamentalism* in regard to religion and gender? There are many definitions of fundamentalism. This essay focuses on a sociological understanding. Steve Bruce traces the origins of the term *fundamentalism* to 1920s America. The term was first used to describe "the consciously anti-modernist wing of Protestantism" (Bruce 2000, 10). Bruce differentiates between individual fundamentalism and communal fundamentalism (2000). He sees Islamic fundamentalism as having more of a communal form and Protestant fundamentalism as having an individualist form. There are four key characteristics of world fundamentalism: scripture is considered divine revelation (the Bible and the Quran); followers believe that at some time in history an ideal version of the religion existed; fundamentalisms are threatened by change so they are radical revisions of the past; and they often appeal to a marginalized group (Bruce 2000, 14). Religious fundamentalism in Protestantism and Islam is very concerned with norms surrounding gender, sexuality, and family. Therefore, changes in women's roles are problematic to basic fundamentalist ideology (Bruce 2000, 32). The family and gender norms help organize social life in fundamentalist traditions. Therefore, clear and rigid gender norms are strongly reinforced.

Ammerman (1987) also finds that fundamentalist ideology is created in opposition to modernity and that this fundamentalist ideology is only able to thrive with support from a strong community. A focus on community is seen in the research on Jewish, Muslim, and Christian fundamentalisms. A strong community is required to reinforce the norms of the fundamentalist groups.

Pasquinelli's (1998) research examines Protestant and Islamic fundamentalism with an emphasis on their relationship to modernity and tradition. Like Bruce, she claims that fundamentalism is characterized by its reference to a text that is believed to contain revelations and infallible truths. She argues that despite a prevalent ideology of antimodernism, fundamentalist movements do not negate modernity. Instead, they use modern technologies to come to terms with modernity by fighting against the notion that modernity has only one path forward.

DID YOU KNOW?

- That there is a tradition of modesty in Judaism, Islam, and Christianity? In Orthodox Judaism, women today still cover their hair, often with wigs or short scarves. In Islam, women often cover their hair wearing a scarf *(hijab)* or a full *nikab* (which covers the hair and face, leaving only the eyes exposed). Until the 1950s, many Christian women covered their hair in church. Today the Amish and Mennonite sects continue to observe modesty norms.
- That Muslim woman can get divorced? Many people see Islam as the most patriarchal religion because of its strict gender norms. However, Islamic law does allow women to initiate divorce in some countries.
- That strong friendship networks are one of the most significant gains that women in fundamentalist congregations cite? Women in fundamentalist congregations often enjoy very strong friendships that are reinforced by shared values and belief systems.

Riesebrodt's research correlates fundamentalism with literalism. His research examines fundamentalism in Iran (Shia Islamic) and the United States (Protestant). His research reiterates the idea that Christian and Muslim fundamentalism reinforce traditional patriarchy. Fundamentalism aims to maintain patriarchy through its interpretation of scripture, societal norms, and community (1993, 178).

In the end, a theoretical understanding of fundamentalism is complicated; as Appleby (1994) points out, it is difficult to define fundamentalism in general as it applies to all religious traditions. However, there are some key themes that seem to appear in the sociological research on fundamentalism. Fundamentalism tends to flourish in times of crisis and conflict. Fundamentalism grows in modernity. Sociologists of religion claim that fundamentalism is a social construction. It is not a true return to a pristine version of Christianity or Islam. A pristine or perfect version of religion never existed. Sociologists of gender and religion see the apparent return to an earlier or more traditional version of religion as a reaction to the contemporary social climate. As gender roles become more fluid, fundamentalists choose to reinforce conservative and traditional gender norms as a form of control.

APPEAL OF FUNDAMENTALISM TO WOMEN

Though Western feminists continue to regard fundamentalism as oppressive and patriarchal, women continue to join fundamentalist traditions. Women are attracted to fundamentalist strains of Christianity, Judaism, and Islam. The fundamentalist traditions offer women a strong sense of community, access to peer networks, and clear gender roles.

An interesting aspect of the recent research on women and fundamentalism is that fundamentalism appeals to women in both the West and the East. Franks chooses to use the term *revivalism* rather than *fundamentalism* when referring to conservative religious traditions. Her research examines the appeal of revivalism to women. She specifically focuses on issues related to the empowerment that Christian and Muslim women find through fundamentalism or revivalism. Her analysis finds that women attain spiritual, intellectual, emotional, practical, and material gains through a revivalist, traditional religion (2001, 170). Franks defines the practical gains as those things that make life easier, such as a clear family structure. Another example she gives of practical gains is the *hijab*, or scarf-like garment used by observant Muslim women to cover their hair, because, she contends, it allows women to move around more freely than Western clothing (2001, 177).

Another type of gain that fundamentalist women acquire is what Franks terms material gain. This is related to financial gain that women receive either through marriage within the community or as financial help from the religious community in terms of housing. "Intellectual" gain is seen in becoming more educated or knowledgeable about one's traditions. Spiritual and emotional gains come in both individual and communal forms. Spiritual gains often come in the form of feeling a closer connection to God. Emotional gains are often in the form of emotional support from family and friends in the religious community. Franks is able to make a strong argument that women are attracted to fundamentalist strains of Christianity and Islam because they feel empowered by the "gains" they make.

There are also several similarities in the themes found in the research on women in the West and women in the Middle East. Gerami's research finds that fundamentalism in Iran, Egypt, and the United States increases women's group solidarity and feminist consciousness. Women gain support networks while at the same time they become more conscious of their identities. This research shows that participation in these networks enables women to reexamine their relationship to power in the family and in society and increase their group solidarity and feminist consciousness. Gerami ultimately argues that "Current fundamentalist movements within Islam and Western Christianity promote reconstruction of rigid sex roles" (1996, 3). She also asserts that "Despite their call for a return to original scripture, religious fundamentalists do not seek replication of the early years of a religion; rather, they reformulate their religious ideology to formulate a political agenda" (1996, 19).

Gerami finds that a substantial concern about morality and sexuality causes Protestant and Muslim fundamentalists to focus on women and the family. Strict gender norms are therefore a significant focus of fundamentalism. Ultimately, Gerami cites the losses and gains that fundamentalism provides for women. She highlights the following as losses: essentializing women as mothers, "constructing family as a tool of political manipulation and conformity," "constructing female symbolism as a vehicle of boundary maintenance," demonizing female sexuality, and reinforcing the ideal of women as submissive (1996, 155). Gerami also highlights several gains, which include encouraging Muslim women who are from the middle and working class to mobilize, encouraging women to read and interpret scripture, creating a grassroots movement, and reaffirming "motherhood as a legitimate feminist agenda" (1996, 156).

Finally, Gerami's research affirms that Islamic feminists like some Christian feminists oppose gender equality and espouse "gender complementarity." They believe that man's role is to be a provider, and women's role is to be a caretaker. For them, this is the foundation of their feminist goals. Therefore Muslim and Christian women who are involved in fundamentalist strains of these traditions do not necessarily see feminism and religion as in opposition. They believe that a women's role is different from a man's role, not a lesser role.

Christianity

Brasher finds that fundamentalist Christianity is empowering to women because it creates two gendered congregations. One congregation is led by women while the other is led by men. Thus, women have power within the female congregation (1998, 4). Women-only activities such as women-led Bible study play a special part in empowerment. Empowerment comes in the forms of female networks, material and spiritual resources, and political coalitions (Brasher 1998).

Judaism

Judaism like Christianity is a scripture-based tradition. Orthodox, Conservative, and Reform Judaism exist in the United States. Recent research in the United States suggests that women continue to be attracted to Orthodox Judaism because of the ethno-religious identity it offers. However, more specifically, this ethno-religious community offers clear gender norms, reinforces traditional families, and provides a strong sense of community for women (Davidman 1991). Davidman puts this succinctly when she writes: "Joining a religion community in which women are placed squarely in the home is thus one way of avoiding the tensions and difficulties that face the women who challenge the system by attempting to have both successful careers and families" (1991, 195).

Islam

Since September 11, 2001, Islam has become synonymous with fundamentalism, the *hijab* continues to be a symbol of oppression, and women's rights in Muslim countries continue to be an area of controversy. However, Muslim women continue to challenge our understandings of women and religion. Read and Bartkowski's recent research (2000) on the veil and Muslim women suggests that women choose to wear the veil. Muslim women in the United States choose to wear the veil because they believe it is a modest way to dress, it is prescribed in the Quran, it gives them respect within the Muslim community, and it is often empowering.

In addition, Muslim women in the United States continue to be active participants in religious communities. The Islamic Society of North America elected a female president in its 2006 election.

However, though it can be argued that there is a central role for Muslim women in society, fundamentalism remains a common strain of Islam. Literalist interpretations as well as revivalist groups comprise an Islamic fundamentalism that continues to attract women. Muslim women continue to be attracted to fundamentalism for many of the same reasons that Protestant and Jewish women are. They find fundamentalist Islam a stricter and more orthodox version of Islam. Fundamentalist Islam may not emphasize "choice" for women; however, it does reward women for their traditional gender roles. For example, fundamentalist Muslim women have the right not to work. Therefore, any money a married Muslim woman earns is her own.

SUPPORT OF WOMEN IN FUNDAMENTALISM

Brink and Mencher find that the impact of fundamentalism on some women has been beneficial and has led to greater economic power and autonomy. In other areas, women must maneuver within the constraints of fundamentalism to gain power and autonomy.

Most fundamentalist groups are concerned with control of female sexuality. "Thus, they draw strict boundaries between good and proper behavior for their women and deride the so-called free western or secular women"(Brink and Mencher 1996, 3). Nonfundamentalist women are viewed as confused and overburdened.

Fundamentalist women know their roles within the family and the community. They are aware of women's place. However, nonfundamentalist women become torn over careers and families. This often results in women feeling they have to do it all. Fundamentalist women, however, know that their roles surround being primary caregivers as wives and mothers.

CRITICISM OF WOMEN IN FUNDAMENTALISM

Feminists are critical of religious fundamentalism because they see it as oppressive. Clear examples of this can be seen in the scholarly responses to Islamic polygamy (Hawley 1994). Hawley and other scholars of Islam point to the practice in some Muslim societies of allowing men to have more than one wife (up to four). This practice is based on the sharia (Islamic law). The sharia allows Muslim men to take up to four wives as long as they provide for them equally in financial and emotional ways. This practice is often viewed as patriarchal and oppressive to women, both within Muslim societies and among outsiders.

Other common areas of criticism include leadership. Within Islam, fundamentalist Protestantism, and Orthodox Judaism, women can not become imams, ministers, or rabbis. In addition, women generally cannot lead the prayers of mixed congregations in Islam.

Another area of criticism is the laws pertaining to divorce and family. Women in Christian fundamentalist traditions are not permitted to divorce. Women in Islam are permitted to divorce, but in most Islamic countries men must initiate the process and therefore it can be very difficult for a woman to be granted a legal divorce. In addition, in fundamentalist communities, women are strongly discouraged from gaining a divorce because divorced women are often viewed as deviants.

Fundamentalist traditions also strongly reinforce women's roles of childbearing and childrearing in the family. In many fundamentalist traditions including those of Christianity, Judaism, and Islam, it is a woman's primary duty to have children and be a homemaker. The reason why some feminists are critical of this is that there is often no choice in the matter.

CURRENT RESPONSES

Current responses to women in fundamentalism are mixed. Historically, Western feminists were critical of all fundamentalisms and found them harmful to women. However, in the present period of cultural relativism, scholars including feminists realize that fundamentalism can function as a sacred canopy for some women, especially in non-Western cultures (Gerami 1996).

In particular, research on Muslim and Christian fundamentalism has found that women see fundamentalism in the United States, Egypt, and Iran as empowering, as it allows them to develop strong community ties as well as a "feminist consciousness" (Gerami 1996). Muslim fundamentalists in particular use the intellectual gains they find in fundamentalism to empower their strategies for social activism.

CONCLUSION

Women in the Abrahamic traditions of Christianity, Islam, and Judaism will continue to be attracted to fundamentalist sects. These fundamentalist ideologies offer women community, friendship, and often a sense of empowerment. Women within these fundamentalist traditions do not see religion as anti-woman. They see these traditions as giving women a special place in their religious communities, a role that is viewed as complementary to men's roles in society.

Feminist criticism will continue to point to the patriarchy and the disempowerment of women to which fundamentalism can lead. Feminists argue that within patriarchal structures, women are oppressed and limited in their opportunities. However, as feminist studies reexamine the women-led groups within fundamentalist groups, perhaps these conclusions may also be challenged.

See also Polygamy; Religion.

Further Reading: Appleby, Scott, *Religious Fundamentalism and Global Conflict* (New York: Foreign Policy Association, 1994); Ammerman, Nancy, *Bible Believers: Fundamentalists in the Modern World* (New Brunswick, NJ: Rutgers University Press, 1987); Brasher, Brenda, *Godly Women: Fundamentalism and Female Power* (New Brunswick, NJ: Rutgers University Press, 1998); Brink, Judy, and Mencher, Judy, *Mixed Blessings: Gender and Religious Fundamentalism Cross Culturally* (New York: Routledge, 1996); Bruce, Steve, *Fundamentalism* (London: Polity Press, 2000); Cochran, Pamela D. H., *Evangelical Feminism: A History* (New York: New York University Press, 2005); Davidman, Lynn, *Tradition in a Rootless World: Women Turn to Orthodox Judaism* (Berkeley: University of California Press, 1991); Franks, Myfanwy, *Women and Revivalism in the West: Choosing "Fundamentalism" in a Liberal Democracy* (London: Palgrave Macmillan, 2001); Gallagher, S. K., "Where Are the Anti-Feminist Evangelicals?" *Gender and Society* 18

(2004): 451–472; Gerami, Shahin, *Women and Fundamentalism* (New York: Garland, 1996); Griffith, R. Marie, *God's Daughters: Evangelical Women and the Power of Submission* (Berkeley: University of California Press, 1997); Hawley, John Stratton, ed., *Fundamentalism and Gender* (New York: Oxford University Press, 1994); Mahmood, Saba, *Politics of Piety: The Islamic Revival and the Feminist Subject* (Princeton, NJ: Princeton University Press, 2005); Manning, Christel, *God Gave Us the Right: Conservative Catholic Evangelical Protestant and Orthodox Jewish Women Grapple with Feminism* (New Brunswick, NJ: Rutgers University Press, 1999); Moallem, Minoo, *Between Warrior Brother and Veiled Sister: Islamic Fundamentalism and the Politics of Patriarchy in Iran* (Berkeley: University of California Press, 2005); Pasquinelli, Carla, "Fundamentalisms," *Constellations* 5, no. 1 (1998): 10–17; Read, Jen'nan Ghazal, and John P. Bartkowski, "To Veil or Not to Veil? A Case Study of Identity Negotiation among Muslim Women Living in Austin, Texas," *Gender and Society* 4 (2000): 395–417; Riesebrodt, Martin, *Pious Passion: The Emergence of Modern Fundamentalism in the United States and Iran* (Berkeley: University of California Press, 1993).

Farha Ternikar

RIGHT-WING WOMEN'S MOVEMENTS

Right-wing women have made significant contributions to conservative political movements around the world, yet they are often viewed by their opponents and even by some men in conservative movements as pawns or of negligible importance. Opposing views of the desired nature of society and women's roles within it, competing definitions of family, sexuality, and women's social status, and differing cultural, religious, political, economic, and ideological beliefs contribute to the participation of women in right-wing political movements.

BACKGROUND

In the early twentieth century, Afrikaner women in South Africa helped construct the Afrikaner national identity through their social and educational programs for poor whites, programs that simultaneously emphasized race and religion (the Afrikaans Dutch Reformed Church) and oppressed the majority African population. In the 1990s, Hindu nationalist spokeswoman Sadvi Rithambara provoked Hindu nationalist men to anti-Muslim violence through speech-performances that traveled via cassette recordings into the homes, courtyards, and streets of India. Islamist women in Turkey have demanded the right to wear the veil in institutions such as schools and Parliament. Their actions simultaneously challenged the secular state established by Kemal Ataturk in the early twentieth century and sparked mass protests when the government rejected their requests and sanctioned those women who donned the veil in public institutions. Anti-Communist women in Chile built up a movement against the socialist government of President Salvador Allende, applauded the military coup that overthrew him on September 11, 1973, and supported the 17-year military dictatorship that ensued. Why did these women do what they did? Why are they considered right wing?

THE ANTI-ALLENDE WOMEN'S MOVEMENT IN CHILE

On December 1, 1971, more than 5,000 women marched through the streets of Santiago, Chile, beating pots and pans to protest the Popular Unity government of Salvador Allende. During the next two years, they organized a movement of women against Allende. This movement successfully convinced the majority of Chilean women that the socialist government was responsible for the problems they experienced: lack of food and supplies and high levels of insecurity. The variety of anti-Popular Unity activities these women engaged in—ranging from the distribution of leaflets and the circulation of petitions to demonstrations and demands that the military overthrow the government—undermined the government and fostered an atmosphere that favored the military coup of September 11, 1973. Although it was elite women who began the movement against Allende, they built a cross-class movement of women that opposed the Popular Unity government. In the March 1973 parliamentary elections, the last elections held before the September coup, 60 percent of women voted against Allende and for the opposition. The key factors that facilitated the multiclass organization of women were the fact that many women felt that the policies of the Allende government were responsible for the economic shortages that plagued Chile, the spread of social chaos and street-level violence, and the fear and insecurity that these problems produced. Because they associated womanhood with motherhood, many women believed that their inability to feed their families signified their personal failure as mothers. These women taunted the members of the armed forces, calling them weaklings because they did not intervene in Chilean politics. Once the military overthrew Allende, many of these women celebrated and, like women in Nazi Germany, ignored the imprisonment, torture, and murder that thousands of their fellow citizens suffered under the repressive regimes these women supported.

To answer these questions, I begin with a brief discussion about what it means to be right wing. The definition of the Right is not fixed; it changes depending on the historical context and the spectrum of other political forces involved. Nor is the Right a monolithic force; it ranges along a continuum from extreme to moderate. Thus, in the 1930s and 1940s, both the Nazi Party of Germany (extreme) and the Conservative Party of Britain (moderate) were on the right. Nevertheless, they fought each other during World War II. During the second half of the twentieth century, the Right in the United States and around the world was strongly nationalistic and anti-Communist, upheld capitalism, supported racial hierarchies and a conservative social agenda, viewed militarism positively, and opposed feminism and gay and lesbian rights.

Right-wing women accept, sponsor, and actively promote many of these political ideas. They maintain essentialist ideas about what it means to be a woman or a man. They reject the notion that femininity and masculinity are socially constructed. Instead they believe that the biological differences between women and men define the roles, identities, personalities, and vocation of each sex. Far from viewing these set conceptions about women and men as limiting or oppressive, they accept them as just and as necessary to the smooth functioning of society. Thus, being female means being a wife and a mother. Heterosexuality is the desired norm and homosexuality is an abhorrent aberration, a sin, or both. The heterosexual family constitutes the ideal realization of a woman's destiny; it is within this institution that she is fulfilled, spiritually, sexually, emotionally, and mentally. Because feminism challenges the belief that a person's sexual organs define that person's personality, identity, and function, most right-wing women reject it as an alien and dangerous philosophy.

Two other factors are key to understanding right-wing women. First, fear plays a powerful role in defining their political beliefs and personal identity. Fear is a potent emotion, and the ability to produce and manipulate it offers those in positions of power—or those hoping to obtain positions of power—enormous advantages. Many right-wing women respond to the personal and political fear they experience by calling for authoritarian measures and repressive governments. For example, women in Chile who feared the socialist government of Salvador Allende called for his overthrow and supported the installation of a military dictatorship. In a similar fashion, following the 9/11 terrorist attacks in the United States a large number of women (and men) in this country supported military attacks against Afghanistan and Iraq, the erosion of civil liberties, and the use of torture. A second element that defines many right-wing women's attitudes is their construction of the enemy "Other," which for conservative Chilean women was the Communist and for many in the United States since 9/11 has been the terrorist, the Arab, or the Muslim. The element of fear and the construction of the enemy "Other" are powerful forces that coalesce to shape many right-wing women's worldview and guide their political decisions and actions.

RIGHT-WING WOMEN AND FASCISM

In the 1920s and 1930s, extreme right-wing forces came to power in Europe and gained support in the United States. Although popular images equate the Nazi Party in Germany or the U.S.-based Ku Klux Klan (KKK) with men, in fact women were active in both movements. Conservative women contributed to these fascist movements and to the Right in general because they successfully interpreted many women's grievances and longings and skillfully formulated a political agenda that reflected their realities, demands, and goals. Right-wing women's ability to incorporate women into these projects enhanced (and enhance) the capacity of right-wing parties or movements to implement their agendas and achieve their objectives.

Despite the fact that many Nazi Party leaders were openly misogynist (they viewed women fundamentally as breeders and considered them, at best, as second-class citizens), hundreds of thousands of German women joined the party, propagated its ideas, and carried out its program. They supported German nationalism, opposed the conditions of the Versailles Treaty that followed the German surrender at the end of World War I, considered Jews as vermin who were responsible for most of the nation's misfortunes, hated Communists, and rejected the liberated women of the 1920s because they challenged other women's ideas about femininity. They marched, attended rallies, campaigned, and voted for the Nazi Party prior to its seizure of power in 1933. Women continued to support the party once it assumed national control, despite their exclusion from any real positions of power. They joined sewing circles where they studied *Mein Kampf,* or the Nazi-run Women's Bureau; provided a secure and serene home that belied the reality of Nazi brutality and (ideally) restored the soul and encouraged the fighting spirit of the German man; produced and raised children for the Third Reich; carried out charity work in their communities, in the service of the Nazi state; and turned a blind eye to the atrocities that their government carried out against other human beings. Their acquiescence and support contributed to the functioning of the Nazi state and, ironically, to their own treatment as inferior beings.

In the 1920s, close to half a million white women joined the U.S.-based Ku Klux Klan (out of a total membership of two or three million), at a time when the KKK was anti-Catholic, anti-Jewish, and xenophobic, and preached white and male supremacy. Many women joined the Klan (and were confined to all-women's sections within it) because they believed that membership would serve to guarantee their rights as white Protestant women. These women believed that the radical Right offered them security and respect, as well as offering the vision of a racist society that ensured them a secure place within it. Klan women were very effective in conducting the organization's campaigns. They joined Klan marches, making them simultaneously family affairs and angry displays of racial hatred; prepared the picnic lunches that people ate as they watched black people being lynched; organized boycotts of stores owned by Jews or Catholics; voted for KKK or Klan-endorsed candidates in elections; and organized other white Protestant women to share their beliefs and join in their actions.

RIGHT-WING WOMEN AND ANTI-COMMUNISM

In 1945, World War II ended and the cold war began. Many women joined the anti-Communist crusade, both in the United States and around the world. Fighting Communism in the United States was linked to the family, which was defined as the basic unit of society and one of the most important defenses against Communist penetration of the country. Thus, many women in the United States believed that by performing their critical functions in the family they were at the same time contributing to the domestic fight against the Communist "other." As wives, they offered their husbands a secure, warm, and welcoming environment, a satisfying sexual relationship (to prevent him from straying and undermining the family), and confirmation of his role as breadwinner and head of the family. As mothers they maintained the unity and strength of their family, provided a nurturing and moral environment, and educated their children in patriotic and anti-Communist values.

Conservative Greek women also participated in the anti-Communist fight. After World War II, a civil war between the right-wing government, backed by the United States, and the Democratic Army, led by the Communist Party, took place. Right-wing women contributed to the government's victory by mounting a highly successful national and international campaign against Communists.

Claiming that Communists were abducting Greek children and sending them to Eastern bloc nations, these women, led by Queen Fredericka, the "mother of the nation," set up "childtowns" throughout Greece to house the children they had "saved from the Communists." Portraying themselves as mothers whose only concern was the preservation of the family, and by extension the nation, these women took their case to the United Nations and convinced that body that it must recognize their efforts to save the children and their nation by sponsoring the repatriation of the children. Their appeals served a dual purpose: to undercut support for the leftist forces and to vindicate the women's right to speak for the nation, not as politicians but as mothers.

Right-wing women marched in cities throughout Brazil in the name of motherhood and against Communism in 1964. Claiming that the elected government of João Goulart supported Communism and threatened democracy and religious freedom, they mobilized against his government, calling their protests the "March of the Family with Liberty for God." They supported Goulart's ouster by the military and, after his overthrow in April 1964, held marches to thank the armed forces for their (antidemocratic) actions.

RIGHT-WING WOMEN AND ANTI-FEMINISM

Many women welcomed the (re)emergence of the feminist movement in the United States, Europe, and globally in the 1960s, 1970s, and 1980s and the changes it proposed and, in some cases, achieved; right-wing women did not. The feminist movement questioned many of the patriarchal values and practices that conservative women esteemed and relied on, and therefore it represented a threat that they mobilized to oppose. Feminists became the new "other," the source of fear and the target of right-wing women's oppositional campaigns. Conservative women organized to defend the "naturalness" of gender, the notion of separate gender spheres, the conflation of womanhood with motherhood, the heteronormative family, and heterosexual sexuality as the only legitimate form of sexuality.

In the United States, conservative women joined together to oppose reproductive rights for women and the passage of the Equal Rights Amendment (ERA). Phyllis Schlafly (see sidebar, "Phyllis Schlafly") and the Eagle Forum convinced a large number of women that if the ERA passed they would lose the rights they had as women, along with the privileges they enjoyed as "ladies."

Antifeminism extended beyond the United States. In France in the 1990s, women in the right-wing National Front Party claimed they were liberating women from feminism, which, they claimed, worsened women's position by dissolving the heteropatriarchal family. Islamist women's repudiation of feminism is complex and reflects both their own position as (former) colonial subjects and their position as women who accept defined gender roles. Many Islamist women's opposition to feminism parallels their rejection of the West and their identification with Islam. (Islamism is a quintessentially political ideology and movement, dedicated to bringing about an Islamic regime that will rule by sharia [Islamic law] and thereby Islamizing the entire society. It is distinguished from

PHYLLIS SCHLAFLY

If any one person can be credited with the defeat of the Equal Rights Amendment (ERA) in 1982, it is Phyllis Schlafly. Her success was due to the fact that she skillfully marshaled public opinion against the ERA and built an activist movement to oppose it. Schlafly spearheaded the national campaign against the passage of the ERA and devised much of the negative publicity about it. However, Schlafly's contributions to the conservative cause began much earlier and stemmed from her profoundly anti-Communist beliefs. In 1945 she worked as a researcher at the American Enterprise Association, now the conservative think tank called the American Enterprise Institute. She published *A Choice Not an Echo* (1964) to promote Barry Goldwater's 1964 presidential campaign and anti-Communism; although he lost the election, her book sold three million copies. She embodies the bridge between anti-Communism and anti-feminism. Angered by the rise of the women's liberation movement, she founded the Eagle Forum in 1975 to oppose it.

Schlafly is highly educated; she earned an undergraduate degree from Radcliffe and a law degree from Washington University. A tireless political activist and a prodigious writer, she has given dozens, sometimes hundreds, of speeches a year; written several books and numerous pamphlets; published a weekly column appearing in 100 newspapers; and edited the *Phyllis Schlafly Report*. A wife (now widow) and mother of six children, she advocates domesticity as women's natural calling in life, ignoring her own active political life. A firm believer in sex-based differences between men and women, Schlafly castigates the "women's liberationists" for denying the true nature of women and claims they are imprisoned by their own negative view of men, society, and themselves.

Schlafly's message fell on receptive ears. She convinced a large number of women, and men, that instead of women gaining rights, the ERA would cause women to lose the privileges they enjoyed. At a time when the draft and the Vietnam War were still fresh in people's minds, she scared women by telling them that the ERA would lead to the drafting of 18-year-old girls. Anti-ERA propaganda also horrified women by stating they would have to share public bathrooms with unknown (and presumably dirty and dangerous) men. These fear tactics worked, and in 1982 the states needed to ratify the ERA fell short by three; as a result, the ERA failed to pass, largely due to the efforts of Schlafly and the Eagle Forum.

---

mainstream Islam, which eschews political ambitions.) Islamist women equate feminism with Western imperialism and a decadent, immoral, and ultimately insecure lifestyle.

One reflection of this approach has been seen in Turkey. In Turkey, conservative women lead the new veiling movement, which is the struggle to ensure Islamist women's right to wear the veil. These women reject the secular Turkish state that Mustafa Kemal Ataturk established in the 1920s and argue for their right to appear veiled in public and in Parliament. Instead of viewing the veil as a sign of oppression, these women see it as an affirmation of the golden age of the Islamic (Ottoman) Empire and a rejection of Western and secular norms of conduct. Donning the veil, according to these women, is a source of empowerment, since it allows them to be intelligent, brave, chaste, productive, and virtuous women and to lead their lives through complete submission to Islam.

RIGHT-WING WOMEN AND TRANSNATIONAL CONNECTIONS

Right-wing women from different nations have worked with each other, united by shared ideologies. During the cold war, anti-Communism inspired women to share ideas and resources. Today antifeminism plays much the same role, as was evidenced in the 1995 Women's Conference in Beijing. Conservative women who opposed the use of the word *gender,* fearing that it would open the door to the legalization of abortion and gay and lesbian rights, joined with the Vatican and Islamic fundamentalists to fight for a conservative social agenda for women.

One earlier example of transnational connections between anti-Communist women occurred following the military overthrow of João Goulart in Brazil in 1964. Leaders of the women's groups that had organized the anti-Goulart marches traveled to the United States in November 1964, invited by the U.S. State Department, to share the lessons of their success with women in this country. They traveled around the United States and spoke to women at Wellesley College, to the League for Women Voters, and to the 32nd National Convention of Catholic Women, telling them how they had built such a large and successful anti-Communist women's movement. Chilean women who opposed socialist Salvador Allende traveled to Brazil to speak with these Brazilian women about their work and to attend the 1967 conference the Brazilian women sponsored for anti-Communist women throughout the region.

CONCLUSION

Right-wing women have made and continue to make significant contributions to the causes they support. Far from being pawns of male leaders, they join the Right because they share its beliefs and want to advance its program. During much of the twentieth century, they opposed Communism, which they associated with the loss of religious and political freedoms. Today, with the demise of socialist governments, right-wing women oppose feminism and are active in antiabortion and anti–gay rights movements. They uphold ideas about women and men's fixed roles in society and oppose the questioning of gender roles that feminism presents. Frequently motivated by fear, they construct the enemy "other," against which they call on masculine institutions, the military or the state, to defend them.

See also Nationalism; Political Parties; Politics and Political Ideologies: Right-Wing Women; Second and Third Wave Feminisms.

Further Reading: Bacchetta, Paola, and Margaret Power, *Right-Wing Women around the World: From Conservatives to Extreme* (New York: Routledge, 2002); Blee, Kathleen M., *Women of the Klan: Racism and Gender in the 1920s* (Berkeley: University of California Press, 1991); Critchlow, Donald T., *Phyllis Schlafly and Grassroots Conservatism: A Woman's Guide* (Princeton, NJ: Princeton University Press, 2005); De Grazia, Victoria,

How Fascism Ruled Women, Italy, 1922–1945 (Berkeley: University of California Press, 1992); Franco, Jean, "The Gender Wars," *North American Congress on Latin America (NACLA)* 29, no. 4 (1996): 6–9; Koonz, Claudia, *Mothers in the Fatherland: Women, the Family and Nazi Politics* (New York: St. Martin's Press, 1987); May, Elaine Tyler, *Homeward Bound: American Families in the Cold War Era* (New York: Basic Books, 1999); Power, Margaret, *Right-Wing Women in Chile: Feminine Power and the Struggle against Allende, 1964–1973* (University Park: Pennsylvania State University Press, 2002); Schlafly, Phyllis, *A Choice Not an Echo* (Alton, IL: Pere Marquette Press, 1964).

Margaret Power

SADOMASOCHISM, DOMINATION, AND SUBMISSION

In sadomasochism, traditional gender roles are often inverted or challenged through role playing. Debates concerning sadomasochism revolve around conceptions of gender socialization and sexuality, issues of power, and controversy concerning the fine line between sexual consent and sexual force or abuse.

BACKGROUND

Sadism refers to one's arousal being caused by dominating, humiliating, or inflicting pain on one's partner(s), while *masochism refers* to one's arousal caused by being submissive, controlled, or humiliated, or by receiving pain during sexual activity. In 1886, Krafft-Ebbing was the first person to define the terms *sadism* and *masochism,* in his book *Psychopathia Sexualis.* This book was intended to be a forensic reference work for doctors and judges that outlined and labeled specific perversions or sexual deviancies. The word *sadism* is believed to be derived from the name of a nineteenth-century Frenchman, the Marquis de Sade, whose books *Justine* and *120 Days of Sodom* caused a public outcry due to their depiction of torture and pain. The word *masochism* is believed to be derived from the name of Leopold von Sacher-Masoch, who is infamous for portraying a beautiful woman dressed in furs with a whip as a symbol of strength in his book *Venus in Furs.* Sigmund Freud also had theories about sadomasochism. He believed that sadists were trapped in the anal stage of development and were attempting to control the parent figure. Freud believed that sadomasochism may be linked with childhood parental punishment and adult fantasies about punishment. Today, some people identify with the sadomasochist or S and M movement as consenting adults. In contemporary sadomasochism, the idea is that as long as the behavior is chosen, is consensual, and doesn't undermine autonomy, that is, freedom and choice, then the act is not considered to be a threat (Sanchez, Kiefer, and Ybarra 2006). This sexual act is considered to be role play and can be stopped at any time by certain cues given by the partner that signal the dominating partner to either ease up on the act or stop the act completely.

MEN'S AND WOMEN'S EXPRESSIONS OF SEXUALITY

In heterosexual relationships in U.S. society, most men are socialized to express their sexuality by expressing desire, engaging frequently in sex, and trying new sexual activities. Men are shown to be highly aroused by both sexual fantasies and sexual behaviors. Women, on the other hand, are taught to play the more passive, submissive role in sexuality. Women who are sexually submissive display characteristics that show they are fearful of being sexually assertive, are unwilling to ask for what they desire, and/or believe that sexual satisfaction is tied to the man's arousal and orgasm but not their own (Tevlin and Leiblum 1983). Women are reluctant to express their sexual desires and are told to refrain from sex and to be hesitant about new sexual activities (Warshaw 1998). Women who are sexually assertive and dominant question these traditional sexual roles.

WOMEN AND MASOCHISM

Scholars debate why women might choose to engage in S and M. Recent research shows that many heterosexual women are unlikely to engage in masochistic activities due to their past experiences with rape and/or child abuse (Leitenberg and Henning 1995). A woman's smaller size and lack of physical strength may keep her from a sexual encounter that she may find to be risky. Women may also not be as aroused, because of the similarities they experience to past rape or child abuse. They may become conditioned to associate sexual submission with negative sexual arousal. Submission may then be correlated with unpleasant memories or flashbacks of past rape or abuse, thus making women uncomfortable when they feel they are not in control. On the other hand, some women have been conditioned to experience sexual arousal through sexual abuse. When they grow older, many women then correlate their sexual desires with the need for the man to be in control of the sexual activities.

WOMEN AND SADISM

Women who engage in sadistic, dominant activities are thought to be transgressing expected gender roles and men's expected use of power. The sadistic woman is considered the dominant one and the man is expected to play the passive role. According to some scholars, in extreme cases, some women use sadomasochism as a way to turn the tables on someone, such as a person who has abused them (Warren 2000). This power helps women to feel that they are controllers instead of victims.

Women's sexuality can spill over to other parts of their relationships where they may want control and/or power. This can be a concern for men, who like to assume the role of the dominant partner. This may also be of concern to women, since some researchers point out that the more successful a woman is, the less likely it is she will find a husband (Hewlett 2002).

CONCLUSION

If women play the passive role, are they letting society dictate that role? If women play the dominant role, are they transgressing traditional gender roles? For many heterosexual women, the argument for assuming a more aggressive gender role will continue. For many men, the argument for assuming a passive sexual role will also continue. Defining and recreating these sexual roles and deciding when painful sexual interplay constitutes force, abuse, or loving consent between partners will clearly be debated and questioned throughout the years to come.

See also Female Sexuality and Dysfunction; Femininities and Masculinities.

Further Reading: Chancer, Lynn, *Sadomasochism in Everyday Life: The Dynamics of Power and Powerlessness* (New Brunswick, NJ: Rutgers University Press, 1992); Donnelly, Denise, and James Fraser, "Gender Differences in Sado-Masochistic Arousal among College Students," *Sex Roles* 39 (1998): 391–407; Franks, Violet, and Esther D. Rothblum, eds., *The Stereotyping of Women: Its Effects on Mental Health* (New York: Springer, 1983); Garton, Stephen, *Histories of Sexuality: Antiquity to Sexual Revolution* (New York: Routledge, 2004); Hewlett, Sylvia, *Creating a Life: Professional Women and the Quest for Children* (New York: Miramax Books, 2002); Leitenberg, Harold, and Kris Henning, "Sexual Fantasy," *Psychological Bulletin* 117 (2002): 469–496; Sanchez, Diana T., Amy K. Kiefer, and Oscar Ybarra, "Sexual Submissiveness in Women: Costs for Sexual Autonomy and Arousal," *Society for Personality and Social Psychology* 32 (2006): 512–524; Tevlin, Helen, and Sandra Leiblum, "Sex Role Stereotypes and Female Sexual Dysfunction," in *The Stereotyping of Women: Its Effects on Mental Health,* ed. Violet Frankes and Esther D. Rosenblum (New York: Springer, 1983); Warren, John, *The Loving Dominant* (Emeryville, CA: Greenery Press, 2000); Warshaw, Robin, *I Never Called It Rape* (New York: Harper and Row, 1998).

Julie Nagoshi

SAME-SEX MARRIAGE

Same-sex marriage is a major civil rights issue that has been heavily debated on legal, political, moral, and religious grounds. Opposing views of personal rights, competing definitions of marriage and its purpose, and differing moral and religious beliefs on sexuality and gender are the driving forces behind this debate.

BACKGROUND

Same-sex marriage is one of the most hotly contested political issues in the twenty-first century. Quite possibly, no other social issue today has been more passionately debated in churches, courtrooms, state houses, and living rooms across the nation. Since the mid-1980s, same-sex marriage has been debated as part of a broader legal discussion about the right to privacy among consenting adults. Opponents have drawn from a combination of legal and moral claims to argue that same-sex couples have no legitimate right to privacy. Supporters argue that same-sex couples deserve equal access to the institution of marriage under the law. The federal government continues to weigh in on the topic, although most legal experts support the idea that it is a states' rights concern. Schools, popular culture, health and religious institutions, families, and communities have all played important roles in shaping cultural perceptions about same-sex marriage and about homosexuality and sexual identity more generally. Gay celebrities such as Rosie O'Donnell, Melissa Etheridge, and Elton John have announced their weddings to the press, setting an important public precedent for other same-sex couples. While there is a great deal of disagreement among gay rights activists about the merits of marriage privileges for lesbians, gays, and bisexuals (LGB), many claim same-sex marriage as one of their primary goals. Opponents claim that marriage has been and should continue to be a sacred commitment exclusively between a man and a woman. The administrations of William J. Clinton (1992–2000) and George W. Bush (2000–present) have publicly supported legislation opposing same-sex marriage, and conservative religious sectors continue to oppose it and to oppose homosexuality more generally. Why the controversy? Why so much dissent within and among groups about the importance of securing or prohibiting same-sex marriage rights? Differing moral and religious beliefs about sexuality and gender, as well as divergent perspectives on the role of the state in regulating people's private lives, contribute to the controversy. While some claim that allowing same-sex marriage would contribute to the erosion of family values in the Unites States, proponents argue that same-sex marriage would help to establish equality under the law for gays and lesbians. Broadly speaking, public opinions about same-sex marriage and about the institution of marriage in general underscore broader debates on citizenship, religion, and what it means to be a "proper" American (Brandzel 2005).

LESBIAN ACTIVISTS DEL MARTIN AND PHYLLIS LYON MARRY IN SAN FRANCISCO

On February 12, 2004, Del Martin, 84, and Phyllis Lyon, 81, became the first legally married same-sex couple in U.S. history when, on his 12th day in office, Mayor Gavin Newsom of San Francisco, California, instructed the county clerk to allow same-sex marriages. Mayor Newsom interpreted the ban on same-sex marriages as being discriminatory and in violation of the equal protection clause in the California State Constitution. Martin and Lyon's legally sanctioned marriage was short-lived, as on August 12, 2004, the California State Supreme Court declared that Mayor Newsom did not have the legal authority to change the state marriage laws. Del Martin and Phyllis Lyon had been intimate partners for over 50 years, and they founded the first national lesbian rights organization, Daughters of Bilitis, in 1955.

WHAT IS MARRIAGE?

Marriage rights include a range of laws and policies and involve legal as well as moral and religious dimensions. A civil marriage is typically a ritualized ceremony of commitment between two people to share a life together that is legally sanctioned by the state. The marriage license, issued by local government authorities, becomes a binding contract providing access to numerous government protections and benefits that ensure financial and social security for couples and their children if they choose to create a larger family unit. Marriage is considered a core institution in the United States and is often considered important for social well-being and stability. Over 1,000 federal laws and benefits are tied to marriage (Cahill 2004). Marriage is also considered a core institution in religious communities, and religious institutions are very often the places where civil marriages are performed, in conjunction with religious ceremonies based on church traditions. This intersection of church and state creates a contested terrain where conflicts arise on how marriage is defined, who has the right to define it, and ultimately who has the right to marry.

SUPPORTERS OF SAME-SEX MARRIAGE

Many liberal ideologies view the right to marry as a basic civil right that is denied to same-sex couples based on discrimination against lesbian, gay, bisexual, and transgender individuals as a class of citizens. This view holds that marriage is a secular institution that should not be denied to any citizen who wishes to claim this right. The argument continues that the denial of the right to marry interferes with an individual's right to life, liberty, and the pursuit of happiness and violates a person's right to equal protection under the law. The 1967 Supreme Court decision in *Loving et ux. v. Virginia* (U.S. Supreme Court, 388 U.S. 1, June 12, 1967), which found the laws banning interracial marriage to be unconstitutional, is often used in comparison to the banning of same-sex marriage today. Justine Warren wrote in the majority decision that "marriage is one of the basic civil rights of men [*sic*]" and that the freedom to marry is "one of the vital personal rights essential to the orderly pursuit of happiness by free men [*sic*]."

While many gay rights activists support same-sex marriage, some believe that legalizing same-sex marriage would not in itself bring equality to gays and lesbians because it does not challenge the exclusionary nature of the institution of marriage or the state's role in regulating sexuality. For example, some scholars argue that marriage creates "selective legitimacy" as it necessarily privileges some couples over others and so, by definition, is discriminatory (Warner 1999). Others argue that there are other more important issues to address than same-sex marriage: hate crimes and antigay violence, job discrimination, social and economic policies that privilege heterosexual over gay families, and lack of access to healthcare are just some of the issues that create additional daily inequalities and hardships for lesbian, gay, and bisexual people according to this view (Warner 1999).

DEFENDERS OF TRADITIONAL MARRIAGE

More conservative ideologies view marriage as a fundamental institution protected by the state to support a union between a man and a woman. In this view, marriage is seen as an institution that furthers procreation, protects the rearing of children, ensures the caretaking of families based on traditional gender roles, and creates financial security for the stability of society (Sullivan 2004). Marriage is viewed in some religious traditions as an institution based in religious principles and ceremonies that do not support the right of same-sex couples to marry. Not all religious communities ban same-sex marriage, and heated debates have taken place within and among religious communities about their views and institutional policies on same-sex marriage. There is a lack of consensus on this issue. Currently, some large churches that support same-sex marriage include the United Church of Christ, the Unitarian Universalist Association, the Episcopal Church, and the Evangelical Lutheran Church. The United Church of Christ has over a million members and is considered as the first major U.S. Christian denomination to support same-sex marriage (Glassman 2005). The case for denying same-sex marriage is often based in religious beliefs that view homosexuality as morally wrong and against biblical teachings. The Christian Coalition, one of the most powerful conservative lobbying organizations in the nation, has developed an explicit political agenda to counter the same-sex marriage movement. According to conservative Christians, allowing same-sex marriage is an attack on traditional Christian notions of "family values" and on the institution of marriage, an institution they perceive as already unstable due to high divorce rates, single-parent families, and pregnancy without marriage (Sullivan 2004).

STATE AND FEDERAL RESPONSES

Federal and state governments have played important roles in shaping the debate over same-sex marriage. It became a topic of significant national debate in 1993 when the Supreme Court of Hawaii in *Baehr v. Miike* (formerly known as *Baehr v. Lewin*) ruled that the denial of marriage licenses to same-sex couples was sex discrimination. This ruling fueled national fears that same-sex couples would marry in Hawaii and then return to their home states and expect their marriages to be recognized. In reality, states had the legal right to deny these marriages. The underlying debate was primarily a moral one about who should have the civil right to marry. Religious institutions wanted to maintain the power to decide this question for themselves and for society at large, and politicians began to see this as a possible wedge issue between conservatives and liberals to be exploited for political gain. As it turned out, same-sex marriages were never allowed in Hawaii because of a state constitutional amendment, passed after the ruling, that defined marriage as a union between a man and a woman. The ruling, however, set the stage for the national dialogue that continues until today.

Because of the Hawaii ruling and other cases that were making their way through state court systems, a few states began to pass legislation that defined marriage as a union between a man and a woman. This type of legislation, known as "defense of marriage" legislation, continues to be pushed as a way to prevent same-sex marriage legislation from being passed. While the federal government had historically taken the position that marriage law was a states' rights issue, it decided to enter the dialogue. In 1996, the U.S. Congress passed the Defense of Marriage Act (DOMA), which President William J. Clinton (1992–2000) signed into law. DOMA defined marriage, for federal purposes, as a union between one man and one woman. It also allowed states not to recognize the marriage laws of other states that grant same-sex marriage. As same-sex marriage proponents pointed out, this second clause was not necessary, as states already had this right. At the time the federal Defense of Marriage Act was passed, no states allowed same-sex marriages. Nonetheless, following its enactment, a flood of states began passing their own state-level defense of marriage bills. Currently, 41 states have such laws. This appears to be a strong reaction to a hypothetical situation, but the passage of the Defense of Marriage Act represented the social sentiment that homosexuality is an illness, deviant and/or sinful, and that gay people do not deserve the right to marry. In addition, to further reinforce the legal protection of this sentiment, numerous states went on to amend their constitutions to define marriage as a union between one man and one woman. To date, 19 states have amended their constitutions (National Conference on State Legislatures 2006). Many states also have strong citizen movements organized to oppose these legislative initiatives.

SAME-SEX MARRIAGE AND CIVIL UNIONS

Thus far, two types of legal partnership frameworks have been proposed for same-sex couples: marriage and civil unions. Same-sex couples currently are denied the right to legally marry in every state except Massachusetts, although in some states they are allowed to form civil unions. The Massachusetts law came into effect in 2003, following the legal case brought by seven couples who were refused marriage licenses by city or town clerks and challenged the state law. In November 2003, *Goodridge v. Mass. Department of Public Health* (440 Mass. 309, 798 NE2d 941, November 18, 2003) was ruled on by the Massachusetts Supreme Court. The court ruled that the ban on same-sex marriage violated the state's constitution by denying due process and equal protection under the law to same-sex couples. The court argued that civil marriage is a government-created secular institution from which all citizens have a right to benefit, and that central to the state's legal definition of personal freedom and security is the assumption that the laws of the state will apply equally to all citizens. Based upon this ruling, the state legislature initially passed a "separate but equal" civil union law that conferred state rights and benefits on same-sex couples. Later, the Massachusetts Supreme Court ruled that a "separate but equal" civil union created second-class citizenship and that it was not constitutionally acceptable. Rather, the court argued, only civil marriage would meet the standard set by the court. On May 17, 2004, Massachusetts became the first and only state (thus far) to grant same-sex couples the right to marry. Obtaining the right to marry in Massachusetts was a historic moment for lesbian, gay, and bisexual (LGB) people and their supporters. For the first time ever, same-sex couples had equal legal status with heterosexual couples and this was seen as a civil rights victory by supporters of same-sex marriage rights.

However, the backlash from the Massachusetts decision is significant and continues today. Many same-sex marriage opponents fear that a case may someday be heard by the U.S. Supreme Court that will universally overturn the ban on same-sex marriage. As a result of this decision, President George W. Bush and other conservative politicians are calling for an amendment to the U.S. Constitution to further define marriage as a union between one man and one woman. In January 2005, the U.S. Senate Judiciary Committee passed a resolution to amend the federal Constitution. In the spring 2006, First Lady Laura Bush indicated in public statements that she does not believe a constitutional amendment defining marriage between a man and a woman should be used as a campaign strategy in the mid-year election cycle, illuminating how significant a wedge issue same-sex marriage is between conservative and liberal politicians and their supporters. At the same time, the majority leader of the Senate, Republican Bill Frist, called for a debate of the full Senate on the constitutional amendment resolution. He claims that an amendment to the U.S. Constitution is important in order to stop the attack on marriage by "activist judges" who are overturning defense of marriage laws in states. Although such a resolution has not yet progressed through Congress at the time of writing, President Bush and other conservative politicians and religious sectors continue to support it.

Opposition to same-sex marriage also continues at the state level, where there has been a significant push to amend state constitutions to define marriage as a union between a man and a woman. In some cases, these amendments also void domestic partnership laws. Currently, 19 states have successfully amended their constitutions: a victory for opponents of same-sex marriage who fear that the institution of marriage will deteriorate if marriage rights are extended to gay and lesbian couples. Proponents of same-sex marriage point out that the "defense of marriage" laws have had unintended consequences for same-sex as well as heterosexual couples. For example, in the state of Ohio, the constitutional amendment effectively banned same-sex marriage and all domestic partnership arrangements in the state. This more encompassing attack made void, among other things, domestic violence laws that protected intimate partners in

SAME-SEX MARRIAGE VERSUS CIVIL UNIONS

May 17, 2004, marked a historic day in the expansion of civil rights for same-sex couples when the first legally sanctioned marriages were performed in the state of Massachusetts. The Massachusetts State Supreme Court ruled in November 2003 that the laws prohibiting same-sex couples from marrying violated the state constitution. Seven couples had sued for the right to marry. Massachusetts is the only state that currently allows same-sex couples to marry. State Supreme Court decisions in Vermont and Connecticut require same-sex couples to have access to the same benefits that married couples are given. Those states created a "separate but equal" status called a civil union.

nonmarital relationships and domestic partner laws and policies for heterosexual couples. Seven additional states currently have amendments to ban same-sex marriage on their ballots.

CONCLUSION

The debate over same-sex marriage will likely continue into the foreseeable future. It is difficult to determine what the outcome will be in the legal and public policy arenas. To date, most state and federal legislation continues to ban same-sex couples from marrying. Only one state has granted the right to marry and perhaps one or two more will grant this right in the near future. While numerous municipalities (over 60) have set up domestic partnership registries that offer recognition to same-sex and opposite-sex partners, states play the leading role in making major public policy decisions in this area. At the same time, federal politicians opposing same-sex marriage continue to push for more significant federal action. namely, amending the U.S. Constitution. While Americans have increasingly shown more support for same-sex marriage in general population surveys, the votes still show a very divided public on the issue. However, the majority of Americans do not feel that the U.S. Constitution should be amended to ban same-sex marriage. And so the debate continues.

See also Lesbian, Gay, Bisexual, Transgender, and Queer Movements; Queer; Sexual Identity and Orientation; Sexual Orientation and the Law.

Further Reading: Boswell, John, *Christianity, Social Tolerance, and Homosexuality* (Chicago: University of Chicago Press, 1980); Brandzel, Amy, "Queering Citizenship? Same-Sex Marriage and the State," *GLQ: A Journal of Lesbian and Gay Studies* 11, no. 2 (2005): 171–204; Cahill, Sean, *Same-Sex Marriage in the United States: Focus on the Facts* (New York: Rowman and Littlefield, 2004); Chambers, D., "What If? The Legal Consequences of Marriage and the Legal Needs of Lesbian and Gay Male Couples," in *Queer Families, Queer Politics: Challenging Culture and the State,* ed. Mary Bernstein and Renate Reimann, 306–337 (New York: Columbia University Press, 2001); Chauncey, G., *Why Marriage? The History Shaping Today's Debate over Gay Equality* (Basic Books, 2004); de Sève, Jim, *Tying the Knot* (Outcast Films, 82 min., 2005); Epstein, Steven, "Gay and Lesbian Movements in the United States: Dilemmas of Identity, Diversity, and Political Strategy," in *The Global Emergence of Gay and Lesbian Politics: National Imprints of a Worldwide Movement,* ed. Barry D. Adam, Jan Willem Duyvendak, and André Krouwel, 30–90 (Philadelphia: Temple University Press, 1999); Eskridge, William, *The Case for Same-Sex Marriage: From Sexual Liberty to Civilized Commitment* (New York: Free Press, 1996); Gerstmann, Evan, *Same-Sex Marriage and the Constitution* (Cambridge, MA: Cambridge University Press, 2004); Glassman, Anthony, "United Church of Christ Endorses Marriage Equality," *Gay People's Chronicle* (Cleveland, Ohio), July 8, 2005; Goldberg-Hiller, Jonathan, *The Limits to Union: Same-Sex Marriage and the Politics of Civil Rights* (Ann Arbor: University of Michigan Press, 2002); National Conference on State Legislatures, "Same-Sex Marriage Policy Information," 2006, available at: http://www.ncsl.org/programs/cyf/samesex.htm; Sullivan, Andrew, *Same-Sex Marriage: Pro and Con* (New York: Knopf Publishing Group, 2004); United Church of Christ Coalition for Lesbian, Gay, Bisexual and Transgender Concerns, 2006, available at: www.ucccoalition.org; Warner, Michael, *The Trouble with Normal: Sex, Politics, and the Ethics* of *Queer Life* (Cambridge, MA: Harvard University Press, 1999); Wolfson, Evan, *Why Marriage Matters: America, Equality, and Gay People's Right to Marry* (New York: Simon and Schuster, 2004).

Stephanie Brzuzy

SECOND AND THIRD WAVE FEMINISMS

The twentieth century saw the emergence of three "waves" of the feminist movement in the United States; while the first wave focused on the goal of suffrage for women, the second and third waves have focused on a wider range of issues, including women's rights to sexual self-determination and gender expression, freedom from violence, access to institutions, pay equity, feminist cultural projects, and women's health issues. Participants in the second and third waves often disagree about the origins of women's oppression and the strategies feminists should use to address gender and sexual inequality.

WHAT IS FEMINISM?

What is feminism? Both formal and popular definitions, as well as positive and negative definitions, have circulated across the three waves of the women's movement. Early-twentieth-century activist Rebecca West quipped, "I only know that people call me a feminist whenever I express sentiments that differentiate me from a doormat" (1913). Second wave feminists Cheris Kramerae and Paula Treichler circulated a definition of feminism as "the radical notion that women are human beings" in their 1997 *Feminist Dictionary*. A detractor, the evangelical minister Pat Robertson, at the 1992 Republican National Convention, opined that "the feminist agenda is not about equal rights for women. It is about a socialist, anti-family political movement that encourages women to leave their husbands, kill their children, practice witchcraft, destroy capitalism, and become lesbians" (Robertson 1992). While one classic second wave description of feminism defines it as "a movement to achieve the social, political, and economic equality of women with men," one pair of third wave writers refers to feminists as including "each and every politically and socially conscious woman or man who works for equality within or outside the movement, writes about feminism, or calls her- or himself a feminist" (Baumgardner and Richards 2000). These writers also elaborate on the definition of feminism by drawing attention to the fact that there is no singular "women's experience" but that gender is shaped by its intersections with systems of race, sexuality class, ability, nationality, and other forms of social hierarchy: "because 'women' is an all encompassing term that includes middle-class white women, rich black lesbians, and working-class straight Asian women, an organic intertwining with movements for racial and economic equality, as well as gay rights, is inherent to the feminist mandate. Some sort of allegiance between women and men is also an important component of equality. After all, equality is a balance between the male and female with the intention of liberating the individual" (Baumgardner and Richards 2000).

SECOND WAVE FEMINISM

The second wave of the women's movement in the United States emerged in the context of what sociologists call a "cycle of protest." As a result of a complex combination of demographics, politics, and economics, a number of movements for social change in the United States emerged from the late 1950s to the beginning of the 1970s (Rupp and Taylor 1990). These movements included the civil rights movement, the anti–Vietnam war movement, the free love movement, the gay liberation movement, and the women's movement, also known as the women's liberation movement or feminist movement. Many early women's liberation activists learned movement politics, theory, and strategy in other movements, including the civil rights movement; their experiences in these movements, however, also helped them to develop a critical consciousness about the status of women in society and even in these radical movements, in which many felt relegated to secondary status because of their sex (Evans 1980). Increasingly frustrated by their own sense of oppression within so-called progressive movements for social change, radical women activists began to organize around issues of concern to women.

Second wave feminists often deployed the motto "the personal is political" to draw attention to the power imbalances between men and women in interpersonal relationships, the domestic sphere, and the workplace (Morgan 1970). From a feminist perspective, "politics" had been previously limited to considerations of events in the public sphere, mostly a male domain, while power imbalances at home were seen as private, domestic problems. Second wave feminists used a methodology called consciousness raising to help make clearer the systematic oppression of women. By creating consciousness-raising groups, spaces in which women gathered to share their personal experiences, second wave feminists began to make apparent the systematic nature of dynamics previously considered personal and idiosyncratic: domestic violence, sexual exploitation, dissatisfaction within marriage, sexual harassment, workplace inequalities, and sexual assault all became more visible as women shared their stories and came to understand that these experiences were (a) not unique or individual and (b) served systematically to limit women's mobility, autonomy, equality, and power (Richardson 1987).

LIBERAL VERSUS RADICAL FEMINISM

Second wave feminists devised a wide array of strategies for addressing the concerns of the movement. The second wave may be conceptually divided into two branches or streams: the liberal and the radical. While the media and anti-feminists often bandied about the phrase "militant radical feminist" to discredit women's movement activists, even radical feminists were rarely militant, in the conventional sense of the word—though this description of them indicates the anxiety their presence caused to nonfeminists. Radical feminism sought directly to address root causes of the oppression of women, often working to design alternatives to existing systems. Liberal feminists, on the other hand, worked within existing institutional systems, operating under the assumption that the institutions themselves were not irredeemable, simply exclusive of women; within that framework, the goal was not to replace or transform existing institutions but to give women equal access to them or to address women's needs within them.

The example of violence against women provides an interesting opportunity to illustrate the difference between liberal and radical feminist approaches. Although feminists from both liberal and radical perspectives analyzed violence against women as a systematic form of men's social control of women, their activism around sexual and domestic violence took different directions. Liberal feminists worked to reform laws so that domestic and sexual violence became seen as crimes punishable by law; they also worked to establish battered women's shelters and rape crisis centers that provided support, respite, and intervention for women who had been sexually assaulted or otherwise violently victimized by men. While radical feminists appreciated the value and impact of these efforts, they also criticized them as insufficient. From a radical feminist perspective, the liberal approaches did little to prevent men's violence against women or to eradicate it from society; instead, they seemed to treat men's violence as a given and merely offer support to women unfortunate enough to experience it, after they had been violated.

Radical feminists took the position that violence against women must end and explored ways to pursue that vision. Women in the feminist self-defense movement, for example, learned and then taught other women how to defend themselves against attack, thereby preventing or reducing their vulnerability. They advocated for and developed educational programming designed to teach young people how to resolve conflicts nonviolently, as well as programming designed for men around ending the "rape behaviors" frequently taught to boys as part of their sexual socialization. Whereas liberal feminism addressed the problem in the context of existing institutions, radical feminism advocated the prevention of sexual assault and domestic violence as the most powerful response to the inculcation of fear in women through the use or threat of physical force.

Because of their commitment to creating feminist alternatives to existing institutions, radical feminists of the second wave founded a wide range of programs, services, and cultural institutions dedicated to supporting women and women's work. For example, in response to the exclusion of women writers by mainstream publishing houses, second wave feminists founded women's presses and women's bookstores, a move that pressured mainstream presses and bookstores to carry women's books, once they recognized their profitability. Second wave feminists started recording companies, auto mechanics' shops, community centers, and "women's lands"—large parcels of land owned, occupied, and maintained by women. Second wave feminists founded *Ms. Magazine,* which has now served as an extremely powerful voice in the women's movement for four decades.

Liberal feminists concurrently worked to make established institutions—in education, government, the law, religion—recognize women as full, equal participants. They accomplished legal reform in the areas of educational access, athletics, employment, and family law, as well as in religious institutions, which have increasingly recognized women in leadership roles and have revised their liturgies and religious laws to make them more feminist friendly.

Closely related to both the liberal and the radical branches of the women's movement was the emergence of women's studies as an academic discipline. Feminists developed a thorough critique of the ways in which Western scholarship ignored women's interests, women's perspectives, women's scholarship, women's writing, and women's research. In addressing this problem, women scholars within traditional disciplines began the processes of drawing attention to the ways in which women and women's work had been ignored, erased, or exploited by male academics, and to ways of making that work visible. More radically, scholars began to institutionalize a new "interdiscipline" devoted explicitly to the multidimensional analysis of women. By working both within established disciplines and in the new field of women's studies, feminist scholars changed the shape of knowledge and knowledge production, as well as the representation of women in higher education, in a few brief decades.

DIFFERENCE FEMINISM VERSUS SAMENESS FEMINISM

In addition to conceptualizing second wave feminism along the liberal-radical continuum, it is possible to understand second wave feminism along another axis—that of "difference feminism" versus "sameness feminism." Much second wave activism centered on achieving the same rights for women as those enjoyed by men—hence, "sameness." People who use a sameness perspective argue that all citizens in a democratic society should have access to the same resources, opportunities, and rights, regardless of sex, gender, sexual identity, race, class, ability, or other forms of difference.

"Difference" feminists argued that to advocate that women be treated the same as men was (a) to set the movement's sights too low; (b) to allow men's interests to set the terms of women's achievements; and (c) to ignore real differences between men and women that reflect both biology and socialization. From this perspective, women are best served by the recognition of uniquely female needs they may have, and by activism focused on meeting those needs. For example, in the area of childbirth, difference feminists argue that women should be given extended maternity leave after the birth of a child, no matter what benefits are available to men. The intersection of these two perspectives has resulted in some interesting policy changes—for example, recognizing that women have the need for job protection and leave time after giving birth (difference) has resulted in gender-neutral policies that also allow men leave time after the birth of a child (sameness).

FEMINISM AND SEXUALITY

Lesbianism figured prominently in the discourses generated by and about the second wave women's movement. Playing on deeply entrenched homophobia in U.S. society, people hoping to discredit the women's movement frequently referred to feminist activists as "militant dykes." This stereotype, designed to provoke anxiety, has persisted to the present, as the Reverend Pat Robertson's Republican National Convention invective illustrates.

"Lesbian baiting" created a challenge for second wave feminists: on one hand, to acknowledge that many women did discover an erotic connection with other women in the movement would add fuel to this particular fire designed to discredit the movement; on the other hand, if the movement itself denied women's right to form social and sexual relationships with other women, it ran the risk of hypocrisy as well as the risk of creating divisions between lesbians and heterosexual women within the movement. While feminist scholars developed a well-considered critique of compulsory heterosexuality, feminist activists continued to experience difficult choices about when to make lesbian issues prominent and when to de-emphasize them.

Lesbians, of course, played a critical role in the second wave. Although the phrase "women-loving-women" has been challenged as a description of lesbianism by subsequent generations, lesbians of the second wave used this conceptualization of themselves to support the emergence of a wide range of thinking about feminist ethics and practices. The women's movement empowered many women to "come out" as lesbians; it also challenged lesbians who had been out during the 1950s to reconceptualize lesbian gender. As the women's movement critiqued traditional male-female roles in heterosexual relationships, it also examined how the dynamics of heteropatriarchy shaped butch-femme roles among lesbians, roles that were common in many lesbian communities at the time. Younger lesbian activists rejected butch-femme roles in large part, preferring to adopt a model of androgyny that combined elements of conventional masculinity and femininity (a model that would be revisited by the third wave of feminist activists). Among lesbians of the second wave there were also "political lesbians." Although many political lesbians were women whose primary sexual attraction was to men, their political conviction that giving attention, support, and "energy" to men was contrary to the goal of ending male dominance inspired them to create primary relationships with women instead of with men.

SECOND WAVE FEMINISM AND RACE

Issues of race and class figured significantly in the feminist theorizing of the second wave. Many of the earliest activists in the second wave women's movement had earned their activist credentials in the civil rights movement, and therefore had a connection to issues of concern for women of color (Evans 1980). Theorizing by women of color themselves made clear their unique position—marginalized as people of color in the women's movement, and as women in the civil rights and black power movements (Davis 1983). From this unique speaking position, feminist theorists of color in the second wave were able to deepen the women's movement's analysis of inequality. For example, such theorizing made clear that while white women were oppressed by white men, they also often benefited from white privilege and had a history of actively engaging in the exploitation and oppression of people of color. Women of color who theorized

SECOND WAVE FEMINIST STRATEGIES: VIOLENCE AGAINST WOMEN

A central concern of second wave feminism was the issue of violence as a systematic means to control women. Through consciousness-raising groups, women shared their experiences of male violence and began to articulate a collective understanding of domestic violence as a *means* of social control: through the use of force or threats of force, men in relationships with women pressure them to live in fear. Because of women's economic dependence on men, women's choices for leaving battering relationships are often limited. When women try to address this issue through increasing their educational achievement, employment status, and income, or by leaving the relationship, they are prevented from doing so by male partners' use of violence.

Looking closely at battering relationships, psychologist Lenore Walker was able to identity the three stages of violence relationships and to argue that such relationships follow a predictable cycle: tension-building, battering, contrition. Following an acute battering incident, batterers show remorse and promise never to be violent again, in an effort to convince their victimized partners to stay. When the partner agrees to stay, a new tension-building phase begins, lasting until it culminates in another acute battering incident. In addition to the structural constraints of economic inequality, the intermittently positive interactions between the batterer and victim, as well as common beliefs about women's obligations to husbands, children, and the domestic sphere, discourage women from leaving battering relationships.

---

from a lesbian speaking position further enriched feminist thinking by examining the complexities of sexuality between women across the lines of social difference and challenging lesbian feminists to develop a critical race consciousness as a means to ending male dominance, infused as it is in this society with race privilege and heterosexism (Lorde 1984).

THIRD WAVE FEMINISM

Although many historical developments lead to the emergence of a movement, some stand as signal events. For the women's liberation movement of the 1970s, one of those was the 1968 Miss America beauty pageant, at which women staged a protest centered on a ritual bra burning. For the third wave, such a moment came on the floor of the U.S. Senate in 1991, when Oklahoma law professor Anita Hill came forward with allegations of sexual harassment against Supreme Court nominee Clarence Thomas, for whom she had worked years earlier. Hill recounted, in detailed, sworn, televised testimony, in front of a riveted audience of millions of U.S. citizens, the graphic details of Thomas's alleged sexual misconduct toward her. Thomas denied her allegations and called the proceedings a "high tech lynching." When the Senate confirmed Thomas as a Supreme Court Justice despite Hill's testimony, a generation of women came to political consciousness. Despite the advances women had made in the 1970s and 1980s, it was clear that sexual harassment was still regarded by the men in power in the U.S. political machinery as irrelevant.

The Hill-Thomas controversy challenged the complacency of a generation of young women who had been raised in the most feminist environment in the nation's history, and who had assumed, based on their socialization, that women and men were equal. The hearings created a national conversation on sexual harassment, and inspired many women to document and report the unwanted sexual experiences they endured in their workplaces. Equal Employment Opportunity Commission filings of sexual harassment cases more than doubled, from 6,127 in 1991 to 15,342 in 1996, while financial awards to victims increased from $7.7 million to $27.8 million (Center for History and New Media 1996).

Attention to and action on sexual harassment in the workplace, however, also inspired third wave interest in electoral politics:

> Another repercussion of the Hill-Thomas controversy was the increased involvement of women in politics. The media heralded the 1992 election year as the "Year of the Woman" when a record number of women ran for public office and won. In the U.S. Senate, eleven women ran and five won seats—including one incumbent candidate. In the House of Representatives, twenty-four women won new seats. Many commentators saw this increase as a direct reaction to the Thomas nomination. His appointment dismayed many women, who felt that Anita Hill's allegations were not taken seriously by a Senate that was 98% male. (Center for History and New Media 1996)

The abeyance period between the heyday of the second wave of the women's movement and the third wave of feminist activism in the United States was shorter than that between the first and second waves (Rupp and Taylor 1990). As a result, many activists who participated in late second wave activities have been active in the cultural and intellectual work of the third wave. Many third wave women are also daughters of second wave feminists, and have been raised in environments infused with feminist consciousness as it was articulated by the second wave. Indeed, Rebecca Walker, who popularized the phrase "the third wave" is the daughter of black feminist writer Alice Walker.

Third wave feminism continues to articulate concerns about many of the issues significant to second wave women: violence against women, reproductive freedom, and sexual self-determination figure prominently in the writings of third wave women. In addition, women of the third wave have worked to further expand definitions of gender and practices around the presentation of the gendered self. Often embracing a radical indeterminacy relative to both gender and sexuality, many third generation women prefer to define themselves as bisexual rather than as heterosexual or gay. to preserve a sense of sexual possibility. Many third wave thinkers embrace the possibility of expressing gender in ways that transcend conventional notions of masculinity and femininity, as well as the second wave's notion of androgyny, and accept the possibility of combining new forms of gender expression with sexuality to create innovative social categories referencing both gender and sexuality.

Third wave feminist perspectives reflect a social milieu in which sex and gender have become even more complex since the emergence of second wave feminist theory and women's studies. Throughout the 1990s (Kessler 1998), academics and activists drew attention, for example, to the situation of intersexed children, whose bodies incorporate features of both biological masculinity and biological femininity. Academics and activists have both challenged the long-standing practice of the medical profession of surgically reconstructing such children as biological males or biological females shortly after birth; as a result, more intersexed children are being allowed to follow their natural developmental pathways until they are old enough to decide whether to live as men, women, or intersexed people. Third wave feminists acknowledge the diversity of sexes possible among human beings.

Mirroring the recognition of additional categories on a sexual continuum is the third wave understanding of gender as exceeding a simple masculine/feminine binary. Among third wave feminists there are increasing numbers of transgendered people, people whose gender presentation incorporates elements of both masculinity and femininity, or whose gender presentation differs from people's expectations of their biological sex. While second wave feminists critiqued rigid gender roles and often adopted various forms of androgyny, they were often critical of and hostile to male-to-female transsexuals, whom they criticized as reinforcing stereotypes of sex and gender by adopting hyperfeminine forms of gender presentation or continuing to use male privilege following their surgical transitions. Third wave feminists have embraced the possibility of people crossing over the gender divide, as well as the prospect of people living out or "performing" gender in ways that are ambiguous within this cultural context.

Third wave feminists further recognize ambiguity and indeterminacy in the area of sexuality. While claiming bisexual identity was anathema to many second wave feminists, who regarded it as reflecting a woman's inability to commit to loving other women fully, bisexual identity has become institutionalized over the course of the 1990s, making it a common and commonly accepted identity marker for women of the third wave, who often express the opinion that bisexuality is a more flexible and inclusive way of describing sexuality and is therefore more consistent with the feminist goal of sexual egalitarianism.

Second wave feminist scholars used the activist tool of consciousness raising and the academic resources of social science research to articulate a feminist speaking position and capture the systematic oppression and exploitation of women in workplaces, education, government, politics, the academy, and domestic life. A powerful tool in drawing attention to inequalities between men and women, scholarship that directly and simply addresses "women's situation" also sometimes neglects the complexities of difference among women. Third wave feminist scholarship, in the recently emerged disciplines of queer studies, post colonial studies, and so forth, emphasizes these very differences. In a challenge to both nonfeminist and feminist scholars who are prone to talking about "women" as a category, third wave feminists are deeply interested in the ways in which the differences among members of any particular category complicate conceptualizations of their locations in society. Like their second generation feminist forebears who were concerned with "gender, race, and class," third wave feminists have explored these forms of difference while also asking questions about diversity within the categories of sex, gender, race, and sexual identity themselves.

While nonfeminist and feminist scholars of previous generations have spoken generally about black women, for example, third wave scholars have criticized generalizations that do not reflect both the biological indeterminacy of race and the multiracial histories of most women who are considered black. Using this epistemological approach, third wave feminist scholarship expands the nuances of understanding regarding the language of social categories. At the same time, such understandings create challenges in the process of devising antiracist, antisexist strategies for social change; if it is impossible to identify a common experience or unified speaking position, it also becomes less possible to advocate for social change that will benefit the members of a particular group.

Despite having these differences with second wave feminists, third wave women have continued to carry on work in areas addressed by previous generations of activists. In the area of sexual violence, third wave women have continued to organize feminist "Take Back the Night" marches, and have extended community awareness of violence against women by enthusiastically staging Eve Ensler's (2002) edgy *Vagina Monologues* in fundraising events to support violence prevention/intervention initiatives across the country. Third wave women have also continued the struggle to secure women's employment access and pay equity, women's rights to sexual self-determination, including the right to abortion and contraception, and women's educational success.

Many third wave women were raised by feminist parents and educated by feminist teachers in environments that gave girls the message that they could be or do anything they wanted to be or do, unlike second wave feminists who were raised with a clear awareness of the limitations girls and women faced in employment, education, sports, politics, and culture. As a result, many third wave feminists come to consciousness as feminists comparing the ideal that "girls are as good as boys" with the real practices they encounter in the wider world, in which women are still underrepresented in politics, underpaid in the employment sector, objectified in popular culture, and harmed by sexual assault and domestic violence. Because of

THIRD WAVE FEMINIST PERSPECTIVES ON SEXUALITY AND POWER

Issues of sexuality and violence against women continue to be important concerns for third wave women activists and scholars. Leora Tanenbaum's 2007 book, *Slut! Growing Up Female with a Bad Reputation,* documents in painstaking detail the ways in which a "sexual double standard" for men's and women's sexuality still prevails in the United States, especially among adolescents. Tanenbaum shares stories of young women whose lives have been made intensely painful by rumor, gossip, and innuendo that describes them as sexually active or available—independent of their actual sexual behavior. Girls and women who abstain from sex with men may be labeled "sluts" in retaliation, as may women who date boys another woman is interested in. Women who are sexually active may also be labeled "sluts," or may be coerced into unwanted sexual behavior by men who threaten so to label them. Men, by comparison, do not often suffer from sexual stigmatization because of either their actual or their reputed sexual behavior.

the institutionalization of feminist ideals, if not the institutionalization of feminist practices, nearly 70 percent of respondents in popular polls "agree with" feminist statements such as "women should be paid the same as men for doing the same work," although substantially fewer actually call themselves feminists. For third generation women, politicization often occurs when the now taken-for-granted ideals of feminism fail to correspond with their lived realities. In that breach, the work of activist third wave feminist women (and men) begins.

See also Affirmative Action; Equal Rights Amendment; Postmodernist and Post-structuralist Feminisms; Third World and Women of Color Feminisms.

Further Reading: Baumgardner, Jennifer, and Amy Richards, *Manifesta: Young Women, Feminism, and the Future* (New York: Farrar Straus, Giroux, 2000); Butler, Judith, *Gender Trouble* (New York: Routledge, 1999); Center for History and New Media, "An Outline of the Anita Hill and Clarence Thomas Controversy," 1996, available at: http://chnm. gmu.edu/courses/122/hill/hillframe.htm; Davis, Angela, *Women, Race and Class* (New York: Vintage, 1983); Ensler, Eve, *The Vagina Monologues* (New York: Virago, 2002); Evans, Sara, *Personal Politics: The Roots of Liberation in the Civil Rights Movement and the New Left* (New York: Vintage, 1980); Findlen, Barbara, ed., *Listen Up: Voices from the Next Feminist Generation*, 2nd ed. (New York: Seal Press, 2001); Gamble, Sarah, ed., *The Routledge Critical Dictionary of Feminism and Postfeminism* (New York: Routledge, 2000); Hernández, Daisy, and Bushra Rehman, eds., *Colonize This! Young Women of Color on Today's Feminism* (New York: Seal Press, 2002); Heywood, Leslie, and Jennifer Drake, eds., *Third Wave Agenda: Being Feminist, Doing Feminism* (Minneapolis: University of Minnesota Press, 1997); hooks, bell, *Feminist Theory: From Margin to Center,* 2nd ed. (Boston: South End Press, 2000); Kessler, Suzanne, *Lessons From the Intersexed* (New Brunswick, NJ: Rutgers University Press, 1989); Kramerae, Cheris, and Paula Treichler, *The Feminist Dictionary* (Champaign: University of Illinois Press, 1997); Lorde, Audre, *Sister/Outsider* (Boston: Crossing Press, 1984); Morgan, Robin, *Sisterhood Is Powerful* (New York: Vintage, 1970); Muscio, Inga, and Betty Dodson, *Cunt: A Declaration of Independence,* updated 2nd ed. (New York: Seal Press, 2002); Richardson, Laurel, *The Dynamics of Sex and Gender: A Sociological Perspective* (New York: HarperCollins, 1987); Robertson, Pat, "1992 Republican Convention Speech," available at: http://www. patrobertson.com/Speeches/1992gopconvention.asp; Rupp, Leila J., and Verta A. Taylor, *Survival in the Doldrums: The American Women's Rights Movement, 1945 to the 1960s* (Columbus: The Ohio State University Press, 1990); Tanenbaum, Leora, *Slut! Growing Up Female with a Bad Reputation* (New York: Harper, 2007); Taylor, Verta, Nancy Whittier, and Leila J. Rupp, *Feminist Frontiers* (New York: McGraw-Hill, 2006); Walker, Lenora, *The Battered Woman* (New York: Harper and Row, 1979); West, Rebecca, "Mr. Chesterton in Hysterics," *The Clarion* (Manchester, England, November 14, 1913).

Amber Ault

SELF-INJURY AND BODY IMAGE

Self-injury tends to be associated with young women and girls, whereas injuring others is associated with young men and boys. Both behaviors may be understood as forms of gendered violence, directed outward for men and boys and inward for women and girls. While boys learn to act *through* their bodies with physical violence, girls learn to act *on* their bodies with self-inflicted violence.

BACKGROUND

Adolescence and young adulthood are rife with both physiological transformations (for example, puberty) and social transitions (for example, changing schools, shifting orientation from family to peers) that young people often experience as distressful. However, there is evidence suggesting that the ways people respond to this distress are gendered. Specifically, girls and women are more likely to direct their distress inward, taking it out on themselves, while boys and men are more likely to direct their distress outward, taking it out on others. This can be seen in the higher rates of other-directed violence among boys and young men and higher rates of eating disorders and self-injury among young women.

Of these responses to distress, self-injury has only recently received attention from the media and scientific communities, increasing public attention and debate about the topic. First and foremost, these debates center on the definition of self-injury. Currently, most researchers view self-injury as some type of deliberate harm to one's own body without conscious suicidal intent. However, definitions of the behavior vary greatly in terms of social acceptability, severity, and frequency. For example, some researchers include such behaviors as interfering with wound healing (that is, picking at scabs) and nail biting in their definition, while others specify much more severe and stigmatized behaviors such as self-castration and bone breaking. Additionally, some researchers focus on repetitive self-injurious behaviors, such as head banging or self-hitting, particularly among people who are differently abled. Finally, researchers even disagree about what to call the behavior. While "self-injury" is probably the most common term used, other terms include cutting, deliberate self-harm, self-abuse, self-injurious behavior (SIB), self-mutilation, and suicidal or parasuicidal behavior.

In addition to disagreement about how to define self-injury, there is also disagreement about who engages in self-injury and how common it is. Estimates of the prevalence of self-injury vary from less than 1 percent to 4 percent in the general population, and from 15 to 35 percent among adolescent and college-aged samples (Briere and Gil 1998; Favazza 1996; Gratz 2003; Laye-Gindhu and Schonert-Reichl 2005; Whitlock, Powers, and Eckenrode 2006). These differences are mostly due to the fact that there are no nationally representative data on self-injury, so most samples are small or highly specific (for example, students sampled in a university class). Also, while most research has focused on self-injury among white women in the United States, there is a growing body of research on self-injury among other racial groups and in other countries, particularly among Asian women (see Bhardwaj 2001, and Marshall and Yazdani 1991, on self-harm among Asian women; Kinyanda et al., 2005, on self-harm in Uganda). Additionally, there is some research suggesting that self-injury is more prevalent among gay, lesbian, and bisexual people (Adler and Adler 2005; Alexander and Clare 2004, Whitlock, Powers, and Eckenrode 2006) as well as among prison populations. One of the few consistencies across most studies is that self-injury typically begins during adolescence or young adulthood and tends to persist for an average of 10 to 15 years, though it may continue for decades

TALKING ABOUT IT: SELF-INJURY ONLINE

A 2006 study by Whitlock, Powers, and Eckenrode identified over 400 online message boards dedicated to the topic of self-injury, with girls and women between the ages of 12 and 20 visiting the boards more than men. The study found that these message boards provide a relatively anonymous forum for self-injurers to share personal stories and problems, voice opinions and ideas, and give and receive support—all of which may be particularly helpful for adolescents and young adults who may have no one else to confide in. However, the study also found that some message boards may encourage self-injury when, for example, they provide instructions for new self-injury techniques or promote self-injury as a pleasurable, painless behavior.

(Favazza 1996; Muehlenkamp 2005). However, there is some research indicating that self-injury may be likely in some elderly populations, due in part to higher rates of depression and isolation (Dennis et al. 2005).

For the most part, media depictions of self-injury paint it as a uniquely adolescent and female problem, as evidenced by movies such as *Thirteen* and *Girl, Interrupted,* as well as talk shows such as *Oprah* featuring only female guests who self-injure (Brickman 2004). Yet, because there are no nationally representative data on the prevalence of self-injury, it is unclear to what extent women really *are* likely to self-injure, or if it is a media myth. While a few clinical and community studies have shown that self-injury is as common among men as it is among women (Briere and Gil 1998; Gratz 2003), other studies show that self-injury is less common among men and may be carried out differently among men as well. For example, a study of 2,875 students at Cornell and Princeton found that 17 percent had self-injured at some point in their lives, and females were about 1.5 times as likely as males to be repeat self-injurers (Whitlock, Powers, and Eckenrode 2006). Additionally, females were more than twice as likely as males to scratch or cut themselves, while males were almost three times as likely as females to punch an object. This difference in the method of injuring reflects a bigger pattern: women and girls may be more likely to act on their bodies, for example, by cutting or scratching themselves with an object, while men and boys may be more likely to act through their bodies, whether by punching some*one* else or by punching some*thing* else.

SELF-INJURY AS GENDERED VIOLENCE

Whether inflicted through punching an object or punching, cutting, scratching, or burning oneself, self-injury can be seen as a form of violence toward oneself and one's body. For instance, James Gilligan (2004) defines violence as

> the infliction of physical injury on a human being by a human being, whether oneself or another, especially when the injury is lethal, but also when it is life-threatening, mutilating, or disabling; and whether it is

caused by deliberate, conscious intention or by careless disregard and unconcern for the safety of oneself or others. (6)

This somewhat broad definition of violence differs from more traditional definitions because, although it is limited to physical injury, it includes the act of injuring oneself. Self-injury, according to this definition, is a form of violence, whether or not the self-injurer interprets it as such. Self-injury meets all of Gilligan's qualifications: it involves the infliction of physical injury on a human being by a human being (oneself), it is mutilating and sometimes life threatening, and it is done by "deliberate, conscious intention." Viewing self-injury as a form of violence allows us to compare it to the other-directed or "outward" forms of violence more common among men.

James Messerschmidt's study of adolescent boys' violence toward others in *Nine Lives* (2000) is a particularly useful reference. In this book, Messerschmidt considers the social settings—such as family, school, neighborhood, and even one's own body—that influence and are influenced by violence. He also takes an explicitly gendered approach to violence, arguing that social settings also influence and are influenced by gender. In other words, one's family, one's school, and even the larger society (for example, the media) influence how we define masculinity and femininity, and how we behave according to these definitions. From this perspective, gender is not just about one's biological "male" or "female" status, but instead it is something that we "do" in everyday social interactions, including how we walk and talk, dress, sit, and eat, and even how we do violence.

In *Nine Lives,* Messerschmidt argues that boys are not violent by nature, but they are more likely to become violent if they have been in social settings that define sexually and/or physically fighting back as *the* appropriate expression of masculinity or *the* best way to "be a man." For instance, John, a young man who experienced severe sexual abuse at the hands of his father, learned that "dominating someone sexually" was "what a male just did" (37). On the other side of the coin, Sam came from a nonviolent home but was abused by peers at school because of his body size and shape (short and overweight). Lacking the physical resources to fight back, he instead made up for the masculinity threats at school by sexually assaulting the young girls he babysat. As these cases illustrate, the masculinity "lessons" do not come from just one source but can grow out of any one or more of a variety of settings—family, school, neighborhood, or even one's own body.

Within this framework, self-injury can be seen a form of violence that stems from a variety of social sources. Furthermore, self-injury may be as gendered as other forms of violence. While lessons in masculinity taught the boys in Messerschmidt's study to inflict violence on others, lessons in femininity lead some women (and fewer men) to inflict violence on themselves. Girls and women learn from various social settings—the media, family, school, peers—that they are "inferior" and some women and girls take this out on themselves and their bodies (Brown 2003). This self-inflicted violence is manifested in the various body projects women and girls engage in, from restrictive dieting to starving oneself, and from piercing to cutting (Jacobs Brumberg 1997). Whereas boys

SELF-INJURY AWARENESS, PREVENTION, AND TREATMENT

- Awareness of self-injury is increasing, as evidenced by the movement for a Self Injury Awareness Day, set for March 1 of every year, on which people may promote awareness by wearing an orange ribbon.
- As awareness increases, prevention becomes easier. First and foremost, self-injurers may be best served by being listened to and encouraged rather than stigmatized or ignored. Building allies in communities and schools, raising awareness, and promoting a sense of power among young people—particularly young women—are all essential steps toward prevention.
- Treatment for self-injury is available in many places, in many forms. The SAFE (Self Abuse Finally Ends) program supports a national hotline: 1–800-DONTCUT. There are also many therapists, counselors, and other mental health professionals who specialize in treating self-injury. Visit http://www.selfinjury.com for more information.

learn to act *through* their bodies with physical violence, girls learn to act *on* their bodies with self-inflicted violence.

CONTROL, BODY IMAGE, AND SOCIETAL MESSAGES

Why are girls and women more likely to act *on* their bodies? Some argue that control is at the center of the picture. Like many self-injurers, some of the boys in Messerschmidt's study had been physically, sexually, and/or emotionally abused at home or at school, resulting in a sense of helplessness and lack of control. In turn, they sought and gained a sense of control by physically and sexually assaulting others, often people whom they viewed as weaker (for example, girls and younger boys). But girls and women sometimes view themselves as weaker or inferior as well, and so instead of trying to control those who are more powerful (that is, men), they try to gain control of girls, including themselves. Lyn Mikel Brown (2003), for example, argues that fighting between girls exists in part because of girls' struggle for power, voice, and legitimacy. The limited power to which girls have access often stems from "qualities they either have little control over, don't earn, or openly disdain," such as their bodies and appearance, and so they take their frustration out on each other and themselves (32).

Furthermore, when this search for control is combined with poor body image and self-esteem, it often results in self-harming practices such as extreme dieting and exercise, disordered eating, and self-injury. From a young age, women and girls are bombarded with images of unrealistically thin and beautiful women in the media. Often these images are so airbrushed and digitally altered that even the models themselves do not measure up. These images, along with other social influences, set a standard of femininity that is thin and beautiful, sexy but sweet, yet relatively passive and powerless. One of the few "appropriate" sources of power regularly advertised to girls and women is sexiness through their bodies and appearance. As a result, girls and women sometimes go to great lengths to fit the sexy media image. As this image is virtually unattainable, their efforts become self-destructive rather than self-enhancing. Adolescent women and girls may be particularly susceptible to this, given the powerlessness they often feel amid the myriad physical, hormonal, and social changes they have to contend with. While it is difficult, if not impossible, to argue that media images and societal messages directly cause girls and women to engage in self-harming behaviors, they certainly do not help girls and women gain the sense of control and independence they may be seeking.

CONCLUSION

Although self-injury has only recently received mass media attention, it is not a new problem. People have been self-injuring in cultural and religious rituals, and likely in private as well, for centuries (see Favazza 1996). While the definitions and explanations of self-injury and the responses to it have varied greatly, the practice itself has not changed dramatically: people inflicting violence on themselves without necessarily intending to die. Like violence toward others, violence toward the self results, at least in part, from social surroundings. If boys' and men's violence toward others stems from settings that define fighting back and controlling others as appropriate and valued expressions of masculinity, then perhaps girls' and women 's violence toward themselves results from social settings that define fighting back and controlling others as inappropriate. Instead, girls and women are encouraged to control themselves, to be pretty, nice, and quiet, and this results in either turning aggression down—like young girls who learn to lower their voices when fighting—or turning it toward themselves (Brown 2000). Until these messages change, girls and women will continue to find ways to "take it all out" on themselves, with boys and men sometimes taking it out on them too.

See also Barbie and the Feminine Ideal of Beauty; Beauty Industry; Plastic Surgery, Tattooing, and Piercing.

Further Reading: Adler, Patricia A., and Peter Adler, "Self-Injurers as Loners: The Social Organization of Solitary Deviance," *Deviant Behavior* 26 (2005): 345–378; Alexander, Natasha, and Linda Clare. 2004. "You Still Feel Different: The Experience and Meaning of Women's Self-injury in the Context of a Lesbian or Bisexual Identity," *Journal of Community & Applied Social Psychology* 14: 70–84; Bhardwaj, A. 2001. "Growing up Young, Asian and Female in Britain: A Report on Self-harm and Suicide," *Feminist Review* 68(1): 52–67; Bordo, Susan, *Unbearable Weight: Feminism, Western Culture, and the Body* (Berkeley: University of California Press, 2004); Brickman, Barbara J., "'Delicate' Cutters: Gendered Self-Mutilation and Attractive Flesh in Medical Discourse," *Body and Society* 10, no. 4 (2004): 87–111; Briere, John, and Eliana Gil. 1998. "Self-mutilation in Clinical and General Population Samples: Prevalence, Correlates, and Functions," *American Journal of Orthopsychiatry* 68(4): 609–620; Brown, Lyn Mikel, *Girlfighting: Betrayal and Rejection among Girls* (New York: New York University Press, 2003); Brumberg, Joan Jacobs, *The Body Project: An Intimate History of American Girls* (New York: Random House, 1997); Dennis, Michael, Penny Wakefield, Caroline Molloy, Harry Andrews, and Trevor Friedman. 2005. "Self-harm in Older People with Depression: Comparison of Social Factors, Life Events and Symptoms," *British Journal* of *Psychiatry* 186: 538–539; Favazza, Armando R., *Bodies under Siege: Self-Mutilation and Body Modification in Culture and Psychiatry* (Baltimore: John Hopkins University Press, 1996); Gilligan, James, "How to Think about Violence," in *Violence and Gender: An Interdisciplinary Reader,* ed. P. R. Gilbert and K. K. Eby, 3–8 (Upper Saddle River, NJ: Prentice Hall, 2004); Gratz, Kim L., "Risk Factors for and Functions of Deliberate Self-Harm: An Empirical and Conceptual Review," *Clinical Psychology: Science and Practice* 10, no. 2 (2003): 192–205; Groves, Abigail, "Blood on the Walls: Self-Mutilation in Prisons," *Australian and New Zealand Journal of Criminology* 37 (2004): 49–65; Hodgson, Sarah, "Cutting through the Silence: A Sociological Construction of Self-Injury," *Sociological Inquiry* 74, no. 2 (2004): 162–179; LifeSIGNS Self Injury Awareness Booklet, Version 2, 2005, available at: http://www.selfharm.org/publications/sia/index. html; Kinyanda, Eugene, Heidi Hjelmeland, and Seggane Musisi. 2005. "Psychological Factors in Deliberate Self-harm as Seen in an Urban African Population in Uganda: A Case-control Study," *Suicide and Life-Threatening Behavior* 35(4): 468–477; Laye-Gindhu, Aviva and Kimberly A. Schonert-Reichl. 2005. "Nonsuicidal Self-harm among Community Adolescents: Understanding the 'Whats' and 'Whys' of Self-harm," *Journal of Youth and Adolescence* 34(5): 447–457; Marshall, Harriette, and Anjum Yazdani. 1999. "Locating Culture in Accounting for Self-harm amongst Asian Young Women," *Journal of Community & Applied Social Psychology* 9: 413–433; Messerschmidt, James W., *Nine Lives: Adolescent Masculinities, the Body, and Violence* (Boulder, CO: Westview Press, 2000); Milia, Diana, *Self-Mutilation and Art Therapy: Violent Creation* (London: Jessica Kingsley Publishing, 2000); Miller, Dusty, *Women Who Hurt Themselves* (New York: BasicBooks/HarperCollins, 1994); Muehlenkamp, Jennifer J., "Self-Injurious Behavior as a Separate Clinical Syndrome," *American Journal of Orthopsychiatry* 75, no. 2 (2005): 324–333; Paul, Thomas, Kirsten Schroeter, Bernhard Dahme, and Detlev O. Nutzinger, "Self-Injurious Behavior in Women with Eating Disorders," *American Journal of Psychiatry* 59, no. 1 (2002): 408–411; SAFE Alternatives: Self Abuse Finally Ends, 2005, available at: http://www.selfinjury.com; Strong, Marilee, *A Bright Red Scream: Self-Mutilation and the Language of Pain* (New York: Penguin, 1998); White Kress, Victoria. E., "Self-Injurious Behaviors: Assessment and Diagnosis," *Journal of Counseling and Development* 81, no. 4 (2003): 490–497; Whitlock, J. L., J. E. Eckenrode, and D. Silverman, "The Epidemiology of Self-Injurious Behavior in a College Population," *Pediatrics* 117 (2006): 1939–1949; Whitlock, Janis L., Jane L. Powers, and John Eckenrode, "The Virtual Cutting Edge: The Internet and Adolescent Self-Injury," *Developmental Psychology* 42 (2006): 407–417.

Margaret Leaf

SEX REASSIGNMENT SURGERY

Debates on sex reassignment surgery concern an individual's right to determine his or her self-identity; societal views on gender as a binary versus a continuum; and medical, cultural, and religious views on surgically modifying one's body.

BACKGROUND

Sex reassignment surgery (SRS) is controversial in raising broader issues about socially ascribed male and female gender identities and invoking strong reactions with regard to what is "best" for the person considering this type of surgery.

People who identify as transsexual may be either pretransition/operative; transitioning, that is, in the process of hormonal and surgical sex reassignment; or posttransition/operative (Bornstein 1994). While some transsexuals want to live as the "opposite gender," others care little about fitting into one of the two normative gender categories, "male" or "female." Some transsexuals may want to have the surgery done, but cannot do so due to costs, medical barriers, or religious reasons. Some people identify as transgender rather than as transsexual, as a way to invoke a different gender identity altogether, one that does not fall into either the male or the female category. "Transgender" often refers to the concept of breaking and/or transcending the boundaries of gender identity and roles as they are traditionally defined (Green 2004). Many transgender individuals have little or no intention of having genital surgery (Bornstein 1994), although transgender views on SRS vary greatly depending upon personal self-definition and beliefs.

HISTORY OF SEX REASSIGNMENT SURGERY

Lili Elbe was the first person to have sex reassignment surgery, in a series of five operations carried out over two years (1930–1931). Sadly, she died in 1931 due to surgery complications. In 1952, Christine Jorgensen made headline news due to her sex change, which included the first use of hormone therapy. Many other, less well-known individuals also opted for surgery, which became more commonly practiced beginning in the late 1960s, as medical technologies improved.

Though many may want access to the hormones and surgery, there are many obstacles to this process. There are very few surgeons willing to perform SRS. Certain steps must be followed before SRS is permitted. Most jurisdictions and medical boards require a minimum duration of psychological evaluation, hormone replacement therapy (HRT), and living full-time as a member of the "target gender," that is, what some doctors refer to as the real life experience (RLE) or real life test (RLT; see HBIGDA 2001).

Opponents of SRS argue that getting SRS and HRT is not in the best interest of the individual. These surgeries and treatments can cost tens of thousands of dollars, and insurance companies will usually not pay for them. There are also many risks associated with the surgery. Though medicine has advanced, many people are left permanently scarred and/or without physical sensation, and there are people who still die due to complications (Stryker and Whittle 2006).

MATCHING IDENTITY TO A NEW BODY

Many transgender and transsexual individuals are searching for a physical embodiment that conforms to their personal sense of self. Many transsexuals are not comfortable identifying as simply "male" or "female" before or after the surgery, and neither are they aspiring to meet the stereotypical ideals of being a male or female in their postoperative life. Yet having sex reassignment surgery helps facilitate being perceived by others as a man or woman, thereby allowing individuals to better fit into society (Green 2004). In general, society requires people to fit into the male or female gender box throughout their daily functioning, with regard to, for example, their driver's licenses, work histories, birth certificates, school transcripts, and parents' wills, and what public restroom to use (Green 2004). The problem of needing to conform to society's binary gender arrangements often becomes a secondary motivation for transsexuals to have the surgery.

Scholars and activists debate what rights transsexuals and transgenders should have regarding SRS. Leslie Feinberg (1996) argues that it is the right of the individual to be able to modify the body through surgery. Feinberg points out that women already get HRT for menopause and fertility assistance, and many have cosmetic surgery done, including breast implants, breast reductions, face lifts, or belly tucks. In contrast to cosmetic surgery, SRS patients must be diagnosed as having gender identity disorder and must undergo extensive evaluations. To get around these institutional barriers, some transsexuals buy hormones on the street, get prescriptions from underground doctors, or travel to other countries for the surgery, placing them at further health risk (Feinberg 1996).

TRANSGENDERISM AND FEMINISM

The presence of transsexuals brings into consideration the category "woman," and some feminists reject the idea that male-to-female transsexuals can ever be "real women" (Stryker and Whittle 2006). Gender politics are based upon male-female categories, even when practiced by feminists and gay rights advocates, thus remaining problematic. Many feminists, for example, insist on the idea that feminism is about embodied women, that is, those born female, and their struggle to acquire the same social privileges as men, that is, those born male. This viewpoint reinforces the gender binary in both gender roles and the physical basis of gender. Many transsexual individuals look at gender roles and gender identity as being more fluid and on a continuum, while others still see their transition as a way to conform to society's binary gender role ideals (Bornstein 1994).

CONCLUSION

The debate on whether or not a trans individual should have the right to surgery will continue for years to come. Yet recent researchers argue that the need to change one's gender is based on a false premise to begin with, since gender is experienced on a continuum rather than as a mere binary. The question remains, should gender be redefined as fluid and/or continuous, or does society need to maintain the binary system? This debate will continue as long as transgenders and transsexuals redefine these roles from both a biological and a social perspective, and as long as sex reassignment surgery is seen as more problematic than socially accepted forms of body modification such as plastic surgery.

See also Gender Identity Disorder; Transgender and Transsexual Identities.

Further Reading: Bornstein, Kate, *Gender Outlaw: On Men, Women, and the Rest of Us* (New York: Vintage Books, 1994); Feinberg, Leslie, *Transgender Warriors* (Boston, MA: Beacon Press, 1996); Green, Jamison, *Becoming a Visible Man* (Nashville, TN: Vanderbilt University Press, 2004); Harry Benjamin International Gender Dysphoria Association (HBIGDA), "Standards of Care for Gender Identity Disorders," 6th ed., 2001, available at: http://www.wpath.org/Documents2/socv6.pdf, accessed April 30, 2007; Meyerowitz, Joanne, *How Sex Changed: A History of Transsexuality in the United States* (Cambridge,

MA: Harvard University Press, 2002); Rubin, Henry, *Self-Made Men: Identity and Embodiment among Transsexual Men* (Nashville, TN: Vanderbilt University Press, 2003); Stryker, Susan, and Stephen Whittle, eds., *The Transgender Studies Reader* (New York: Routledge, 2006).

Julie Nagoshi

SEX TRAFFICKING

While most people agree that sex trafficking is a problem that merits legal or policy intervention, debates continue as to how to frame the problem, who the primary victims are, and how to legally combat human trafficking within and across national borders.

BACKGROUND

Broadly speaking, sex trafficking can be understood as the often forced, deceptive, or coerced recruitment, transport, holding, purchasing, and selling of persons for commercial sexual exploitation. While the U.S. State Department reports that approximately 14,000 to 17,000 people are trafficked into the United States annually, though not all for purposes of sexual exploitation, other reports put the number closer to 45,000 to 50,000 a year (Lederer 2005; World Conference against Racism 2001). Around the world, roughly 600,000 to 800,000 people are trafficked annually (Lederer 2005). While trafficking flows change over time, the majority of the women trafficked to the United States into the sex industry originate from either Latin American or Southeast Asian countries.

While sex trafficking is often thought of as a recent phenomenon, laws concerning the trafficking of women and children in the United States date back

---

BORN INTO BROTHELS

Many U.S. audiences were introduced to the idea of sex trafficking through the 2004 Academy Award–winning documentary *Born to Brothels*. This film, directed by Zana Briski and Ross Kauffman, presents a view of the lives of children who grow up in the Sonagchi red-light district of Calcutta, India. The film follows several children as they learn how to use cameras and begin to capture their own perspectives of Sonagchi on film. Many acclaim the documentary as a step in helping these children have a better life as well as for bringing important attention to the experiences of individuals living and working in Sonagchi. Many, however, criticize the film for the stereotypical way it represents the children, their mothers, and the red-light district in general, as well as for a narrative progression that depicts yet again white Western women saving brown children. Take a look at this film if you haven't already, and consider the way the film represents sex work and the mothers and children as agents, as well as trafficking policy and activist work.

---

to the early twentieth century. The 1910 Mann Act, the so called White-Slave Traffic Act, prohibited "white slavery" and the transport of women across state lines for the purpose of prostitution or immorality. This meant that any immigrant woman, either living in the United States or seeking entrance to the United States, who was suspected of prostitution could be deported, regardless of how long she had been in the United States. This law was part of the federal immigration legislation that was designed to exclude "immoral" immigrants from entry into the United States (Moloney 2006).

At an international level, concern about sex trafficking was first addressed by the United Nations in 1949, when it introduced the Convention for the Suppression of the Traffic in Persons and of the Exploitation of the Prostitution of Others. This convention, which was ratified by 49 nations, urged states to "punish any person who procures, entices or leads away another person for purposes of prostitution, even with the consent of that person; exploits the prostitution of another person, even with the consent of that person; or keeps or supports a brothel" (United Nations n.d.). In the 1980s, following the emergence of women's rights activism around the world, activists began to make connections between sex trafficking and violence against women. Gretchen Soderlund explains that this happened in two ways: "in a broad-based campaign to introduce women's sexual and reproductive rights into traditional human rights doctrine and in media attention to the plight of sex trafficking victims" (2005, 69). This then led to an international push to recognize gendered and sexual violence as human rights violations.

POLITICAL AND POLICY RESPONSES TO SEX TRAFFICKING

In 2000, the U.S. government became a major actor in the debate concerning sex trafficking. Surprisingly, this was not initiated by the feminist and human rights actors of the 1990s; rather, the legislation was initiated by new antitrafficking actors including former U.S. senator Linda Smith of Shared Hope International, Gary Haugen of the International Justice Mission (IJM), and Dr. Kevin Bales of Free the Slaves (Soderlund 2005). The first proposed bill, the 2000 Trafficking Victims Protection Act (TVPA), was designed to target sexual trafficking as well as some forms of forced labor. This bill proposed a concept of "sexual slavery" that did not distinguish between forced and voluntary prostitution. A second bill, sponsored by Senator Paul Wellstone, aimed at prosecuting those who perpetrated all forms of forced labor—not solely trafficking for sexual purposes, and did not include voluntary prostitution as part of its definition of trafficking. Many key actors, including sex worker rights groups and President Clinton, supported this bill; however, abolitionist feminist groups such as Protection Project and faith-based groups such as IJM lobbied strongly against it, "threatening to publicly label the Clinton Administration 'pro-prostitution' should the bill be signed into law" (Soderlund 2005, 73). Under this pressure, the TVPA was signed into law.

The Victims of Trafficking and Violence Prevention Act (VTVP) also went into effect in 2000, creating the Office to Monitor and Combat Trafficking in

Persons. The VTVP established safeguards so that targets of trafficking are not prosecuted. Under this law, however, perpetrators of sex trafficking are tried as rapists. Furthermore, the act designated funds to support the rehabilitation of targets, including provisions for shelters, as well as educational programs and allotments for small business grants.

Those heralding these legislative moves considered both of them a step toward vanquishing forms of sexual slavery prevalent throughout the world, as these moves set up ways to prosecute traffickers, protect trafficked persons, and prohibit the overall trafficking system (Chuang 2006). Opponents of this approach stress that the legal approach may respond to trafficking but it does not combat the causes of trafficking. Moreover, opponents call for an understanding of the current legislation as part and parcel of the current national desire to "secure borders" and curtail women's sexual and reproductive freedom. Additionally, the criminalization of trafficking, alongside border security legislation, often fails to consider the difference between smuggling and trafficking of persons; Chuang explains that trafficked persons—those protected under the antitrafficking legislation—are often caught in the middle when picked up in border areas, and sometimes incarcerated or deported (2006).

CONCLUSION

The current national and international debate over sex trafficking involves two major components. First there is a discussion of whether sex trafficking should be taken up as a feminist and human rights issue, and if so, how best to do that without infringing on sex workers' rights and freedom. Second, we see a debate about how best to respond to sex trafficking. Currently the legal model's mantra—prosecute traffickers, protect trafficked persons, and prevent trafficking—is predominant. Supporters of this model say that the goal is to stop sex trafficking and the best way to do that is through the law. Opponents of this model note that prosecution does not solve the systemic problems that propel sex trafficking to occur.

See also Child Sexual Abuse; Gender and Globalization: Trends and Debates; Human Rights: International Laws and Policies.

Further Reading: Beeks, Karen D., *Trafficking and the Global Sex Industry* (Lanham, MD: Lexington Books, 2006); Chuang, Janie, "Beyond a Snapshot: Preventing Human Trafficking in the Global Economy," *Indiana Journal of Global Legal Studies* 13, no. 1 (2006): 137–163; Daywalka Foundation, 2006, available at: http://www.daywalka.org/; Farr, Kathryn, *Sex Trafficking: The Global Market in Women and Children* (New York: Worth Publishers, 2004); Free the Slaves, 2006, available at: http://www.freetheslaves.net/; Guinn, David E., and Steglich, Elissa, *In Modern Bondage: Sex Trafficking in the Americas* (Ardsley, NY: Transnational Publishers, 2003); International Justice Mission, 2005, available at: http://www.ijm.org/NETCOMMUNITY/Page.aspx?&pid=178&srcid=178; Kempadoo, Kamala, Jyoti Sanghera, and Bandana Pattanaik, *Trafficking and Prostitution Reconsidered: New Perspectives on Migration, Sex Work and Human Rights* (Boulder, CO: Paradigm Publishers, 2005); Lederer, Laura J., "Trafficking in Persons: A Global Challenge," Washington, DC, U.S. State Department, 2005, available at: http://www.

state.gov/g/tip/rls/rm/2005/56027.htm; Moloney, Deirdre M., "Women, Sexual Morality and Economic Dependency in Early U.S. Deportation Policy," *Journal of Women's History* 18, no. 2 (2006): 95–122; Shared Hope International, 2006, available at: http://www.sharedhope.org/; Soderlund, Gretchen, "Running from the Rescuers: New U.S. Crusades against Sex Trafficking and the Rhetoric of Abolition," *NWSA Journal* 17, no. 3 (2005): 64–87; United Nations, Convention for the Suppression of the Traffic in Persons and of the Exploitation of the Prostitution of Others, n.d., available at: http://untreaty.un.org/English/TreatyEvent2003/Treaty_8.htm; World Conference against Racism, *The Race Dimensions of Trafficking in Persons—Especially Women and Children*, 2001, available at: http://www.un.org/WCAR/e-kit/issues.htm.

Sara McKinnon

SEX VERSUS GENDER

Whether differences between women and men are rooted in biology or in socialization constitutes the central "sex versus gender" debate. This issue has been central to social struggles over civil rights for women, issues of educational and employment access for women, and issues of domestic power within heterosexual households.

BACKGROUND

Even in the twenty-first century, women in Western societies do not enjoy full civil rights or social and economic equality with men. Women earn less money, own less property, do more housework, and suffer more relationship violence than do men. Men far outnumber women in positions of power: as elected officials, Supreme Court appointees, corporate CEOs, and university presidents. Women are disproportionately represented in low-wage jobs without health and retirement benefits and in the ranks of the poor.

The United States still has no equal rights amendment in its Constitution: although one that read "equality of rights under the law shall not be denied or abridged by the United States or any state on account of sex" was proposed in 1923, it was never ratified, because the required number of states did not approve it by 1982 (Eisler and Hixon 1986).

This pattern of systematic inequality has long been a source of contention; the first wave of the women's rights movement in the United States sought the right for women to vote and eventually succeeded in gaining it, with the idea that an electorate inclusive of women would shape a government responsive to the full inclusion of women (Evans 1997), an idea long since disproved. The second wave of the women's rights movement sought to further women's equality in the United States by advocating a series of legal reforms ending discrimination in employment, guaranteeing educational access (including access to athletic programs) to girls and women, promoting the criminalization of sexual assault and domestic violence, and increasing women's access to no-fault divorce (Morgan 1970) Across the discourses on women's equality in the twentieth century, ongoing attention has been paid to this question: are differences between men and women a function of sex or of gender? This question has been treated as significant in conversations on women's equality; the status of this question is similar to the status occupied by questions in discourses around slavery about whether African Americans were fully human. Such questions clearly serve as a distraction from giving direct attention to the simple, broader issue that some social groups are oppressed by others. In all such instances, groups with the power to control social systems adopt arguments that center on biological essentialism, while subordinated groups adopt positions centered on social constructionism.

BIOLOGICAL VERSUS SOCIAL CONSTRUCTIONIST EXPLANATIONS OF GENDER DIFFERENCE

Biological essentialism is a philosophical stance that explains differences among human groups in terms of purported biological differences among them. In the case of the sex versus gender debate, biological essentialists emphasize biological differences between human males and females as a way of explaining the different social statuses occupied by each sex. Social constructionism, on the other hand, is a philosophical stance that explains differences between groups in terms of social factors that create groups and maintain differences between them. In the sex versus gender debate, social constructionists emphasize the ways in which societies shape the behaviors of boys and men and girls and women in order to create appearances of differences between these groups and to subsequently use these differences to justify giving greater privileges to men than to women. In the conversation on sex versus gender, biological essentialists focus on sex while social constructionists focus on gender as a way of explaining both differences and inequalities between women and men.

WHAT IS SEX?

As a concept, *sex* refers to biological differences between males and females in any given species. In our species, Homo sapiens, all of us carry one X chromosome inherited from our mothers; our genetic sex is determined by our biological father's contribution to our genetic makeup: an additional X chromosome promotes development as an XX/female individual; a Y chromosome promotes development as an XY/male individual. In some instances, individuals will carry a complement of more than two sex chromosomes, with varying implications for development. Moving from the level of genotype to the level of phenotype, that is, to how genes are expressed, sexual characteristics are often sorted into "primary" and "secondary" categories. Organs of reproduction are defined as primary sexual characteristics and other patterns of biological difference between males and females are defined as secondary sexual characteristics. Primary sexual characteristics in biological females consist of the ovaries, uterus, and vagina, while secondary sexual characteristics include breast and hip development and facial contours; primary sexual characteristics in males include the penis and testes, while secondary characteristics include the development of prominent Adam's apples and more extensive facial hair growth, although this varies by genetic population. Our species is generally conceptualized as sexually dimorphic, that is, as consisting of two neatly and clearly defined sexes, one male and one female, with each making different and necessary contributions to sexual reproduction. Such definitions offer a clear introduction to the concept of sex, but may create the impression that human males and females are more different than alike, that there is little variation within each sex, and that human beings are never "sexed" in ways that combine genetic, hormonal, or structural features of both sexes.

Recent scholarship has challenged all of these notions. A consideration of secondary sexual characteristics provides an important example. European-derived Western understandings of the secondary sexual characteristics of human males and females, for instance, focus on differences in height and weight, facial and body hair, breast development, and voice quality as points of differentiation. Cross-cultural comparisons demonstrate that these differences do not always hold between men and women, and that members of one sex from different genetic populations across the world exhibit many differences from one another. Some male populations, for example, have little or no facial hair, while others are hirsute; women in some populations have an average height several inches taller than men in other populations; and ultimately, there exists more variation among members of each sex in the species than between the two sexes (Fausto-Sterling 2000).

The existence of a clear, distinguishing line between biological maleness and femaleness has also been challenged in recent years by both scholarship and activism around intersexuality. Suzanne Kessler's (1998) research on children born with sexual anomalies has been used to support the idea that significant numbers of children are born with a constellation of sexual traits that does not neatly conform exclusively to the criteria for maleness or the criteria for femaleness, and that, indeed, such children often have features of both sexes. This development raises interesting questions about the distinctiveness of maleness and femaleness, as well as about how our genetic and phenotypic sexual biology expresses itself in culture and society.

WHAT IS GENDER?

Gender refers to those traits and behaviors in human beings that are socially associated with masculinity and femininity. While *male* and *female* are biological terms, *boy* and *girl* and *man* and *woman* are gender terms that refer to a person's social status. When we encounter a person, we are usually aware of our sense of the person's gender; unless we meet the person when he or she isn't clothed, we can't truly know his or her sex. Unlike other species, which, as far as we know, are "sexed" but not "gendered," humans have devised myriad ways to express their masculinity and femininity. These include clothing styles, color codes, hair lengths and styles, ways of sitting, walking, running, and horseback riding, variations in material objects coded as boys' or girls' things, modification of the body, language use, and variations on ways of practicing social customs.

Feminist theorists have used the concept of gender to highlight the fact that many of the differences between men and women that have been presumed to reflect essential biological differences are actually socially produced. For example, U.S. society expects women to shave their legs to create the impression that

WOMEN ATHLETES: THE WEAKER SEX?

The belief that women should not compete in athletic events, and that they should especially avoid endurance events, was common throughout the twentieth century in the West. This belief is an effect of gender, not of biological sex, as recent evidence makes clear. Although women were not permitted to compete in an Olympic marathon until 1984, they have quickly become some of that sport's most ardent and competitive enthusiasts. T. J. Murphy (2006), reporting in *Triathlete Magazine*, notes that in 1976, of the 1,175 athletes entered in the Marine Corps Marathon in Washington, DC, only 40 were women; in 2006, the same race had a field composed of 30,000 runners, 47 percent of whom were women. In the 2006 Boston Marathon, a race that requires athletes to meet a qualifying time in order to participate, women outnumbered men in the 18–39 age group. In the triathlon, in which athletes swim, bike, and run various challenging distances, men still outnumber women, but the picture is changing rapidly: at the national youth triathlon competitions in 2006, girls outnumbered boys. Murphy predicts that by 2010, women will constitute at least 40 percent of the adult field in one of the world's most challenging sports.

---

women and men are biologically distinguishable with regard to body hair. On a more psychological level, feminists argue, boys and girls are socialized differently, leading men and women to emphasize different emotional, intellectual, and personality traits, although the potential for all of these characteristics is not sex linked but fundamentally human. Members of one sex who engage in the behaviors typically associated with the other are, in Western societies, often stigmatized or punished in order to pressure them into gender conformity (Butler 1990). For feminist theory, the concept of gender provided a means to distinguish between the social and the biological, to see how gender is systematically produced and tied to dynamics of power, and to question the cultural assumption of the "natural" basis of inequalities between men and women.

Feminist scholars have documented the extensive, pervasive, and ideological quality of gender socialization. Following on from decades of feminist women's theorizing of gender, Robert Connell (1995) proposed the concept of "hegemonic masculinity" to make explicit the relationship between the social expectations for masculinity and the links between masculinity and social power. Judith Butler (1990), challenging earlier models of gender as so deeply inculcated during socialization as to be unconscious, posited the concept of "gender performance," suggesting that even in societies in which normative concepts of masculinity and femininity are deeply entrenched and fiercely enforced, individuals exercise agency in their presentation of gendered selves.

In the world beyond social theory, the emergence of visible transgendered populations in the West has held dual significance for social understandings of gender. On one hand, the existence of people who choose to present a gender contrary to their sex points out the socially constructed nature of gender and its wide variability; on the other, a discourse arguing that transgendered people are members of one sex born into bodies of the other deploys an updated biological determinism to suggest that there is, after all, something essential about gender, and that one is "born" one gender or the other, even if one may be in the "wrong" body.

SEX VERSUS GENDER IN EXPLAINING SOCIAL INEQUALITY

Although sexual differentiation is a far more complex a process than it would usually appear to the casual observer, human societies universally use sex as a primary principle of social organization. No matter the genes, reproductive organs, or facial hair of the people described as women or as men, in any particular society, people in those categories are socialized to fill distinctive roles. Most societies organize work, economies, familial roles, religious roles, education, and knowledge production along the lines of sex (de Beauvoir [1949] 1952). It is important to note that while differences between groups do not by necessity reflect inequalities, most contemporary societies exhibit patterns of social differentiation in the status of men and women along the lines of power, privilege, and access to goods, services, and resources that can be described as socially stratified, that is, as fundamentally unequal.

In the sex versus gender debate, neither side contests the fact that men and women have different levels of access, privilege, control, or power in society; instead, they focus on sex or gender as a means of explaining these inequalities. For biological essentialists, women's biology both explains and justifies women's treatment as social inferiors. Sometimes it is argued by biological essentialists that men and women play different gender roles but that these are not necessarily unequal or hierarchical in nature; they are simply reflections of men's and women's naturally prescribed gender roles in the societal division of labor. For social constructionists, gender as a social system explains how men and women come to accept inequalities between them, as well as how those differences are enacted at an individual level.

Feminist scholars have often conceptualized the social stratification of men and women as being rooted in patriarchy, a system of social organization in

---

SIMONE DE BEAUVOIR

Simone de Beauvoir (1908–1986), French philosopher, social critic, and writer, made a significant impact on the world with her 1949 book *La Deuxième Sexe* (translated as *The Second Sex*, 1952), which claimed that dominant groups always position subordinated groups as "the Other." She argued that men systematically position women as "other" in Western society and similarly, racially dominant groups position members of nondominant groups as different and deviant. De Beauvoir provides a critique of classic Western philosophy and argues that men of European origin describe themselves and their qualities as normal, natural, and right, making women the "Other" by describing the ways in which they are different as deviant, wrong, or inferior. De Beauvoir's most famous line, "One is not born, but rather becomes, a woman," laid the foundation for contemporary women's studies in both the United States and Europe. As a self-defined bisexual, de Beauvoir's relationships with men and women no doubt gave her an intimate view of both men's and women's experiences in society.

---

which males are dominant and control the society's resources through a variety of mechanisms ensuring that men will continue to inherit and accumulate power while women will continue to be excluded from access to power. Patriarchy assumes the right of men to control women's sexuality and fertility, and this assumption is reflected in religious, social, and legal standards (Richardson 1988). For example, in extremely patriarchal societies, women have little or no self-determination about when, whom, or how they will marry; girls' sexuality is seen as a resource belonging to their fathers, and violations of a girl's sexual integrity are seen as violations of the father's property that make it impossible to marry the girl to other men, so that the girl represents less exchange value. While patriarchal ideologies justify male dominance as rooted in biological determinism and the natural order of things, feminist scholars have challenged the claim that male dominance is universal. Challenges have come both from specific locations contesting specific claims, for example, the claim that women are constitutionally incapable of doing physically demanding labor (Fonow 2003), and from historians of patriarchy itself. Gerda Lerner's (1987) carefully researched *Creation of Patriarchy,* for example, makes the very strong argument that patriarchy is a historical phenomenon designed to consolidate male power and privilege through the exploitation of women's labor; Lerner argues that because patriarchy is neither universal nor biologically determined, it can be displaced by more egalitarian forms of social organization in which women and men share access to resources, power, and privilege.

Sexual essentialists, in contrast, argue that women are physically weaker than men, less aggressive than men, more emotionally variable than men, and more nurturing than men, and that, as a result, they should be restricted from positions of political leadership, military combat, and a wide range of occupations (Richardson 1988). Feminist scholars have dismissed both of these claims by arguing that they reflect the biases of the group with the most accumulated privilege. For example, scholars note that all wars have been initiated and executed by men, in an example of men's extreme emotionality, and that the privileging of aggression reflects men's tendency toward it, instead of any inherent value in aggression.

CONCLUSION

In both popular culture and academic research, the debate over the best explanation for differences between men and women and their unequal statuses in society continues. Biological determinists seek to explain academic differences between boys and girls by looking at structures in their brains; social scientists seek to explain academic differences between boys and girls by looking at the structures in their societies, in their socialization, in their treatment by teachers, in the kinds of role models available to them, and in the kinds of punishments and rewards they receive for excelling in particular areas of study.

In some areas of life, the collapse of the conceptual distinctions between sex and gender have become increasingly common as political debates over women's roles in society have become intensified. In the everyday world, the words *sex* and *gender* are commonly used interchangeably, resulting in their widespread misuse. For example, official documents often now ask patients, students, and applicants to identify themselves by gender instead of by sex. Inquiring about both a person's sex and a person's gender might provide healthcare providers and educational institutions with useful information. Knowing that a person uses a masculine name and presents himself as a man although he is biologically female could be helpful to a healthcare provider in delivering care to the patient or helpful to a college in making residence hall assignments. Asking only for gender, however, as is commonly the practice, seems simply to elide the differences between sex and gender, collapsing the two and giving the impression that sex and gender are interchangeable, that sex is gender. Obviously, this move reproduces earlier models that naturalize social differences between men and women, undermining the power of distinguishing between those aspects of men's and women's lives that are not natural but indeed rooted in long-held beliefs and biases about gender identity.

Alternative ways of conceptualizing the sex versus gender debate shed light on the limitations of its terms. For example, unlike U.S. feminists, leading scholars in French feminist theory have embraced the notion that women are different from men, and have seen the U.S. feminist goal of achieving equality with men as setting the bar too low, advocating instead a whole range of rights and reforms that take into account women's unique needs (see Cixous 1994). In some areas of interdisciplinary research on how social interaction and biology mutually shape each other, scholars are beginning to suggest that our genes, our hormones, and our features are shaped by our interactions with other people, and that our behavior is, in turn, shaped by our biology (Goleman 2006). Expanded into the sex versus gender debate, such insights hold the suggestive possibility that sex and gender are *both* systems of social organization, and that the interaction between them may explain the human sense of masculinity and femininity, as well as the behaviors that keep inequalities between women and men in place.

See also Femininities and Masculinities; Gender Socialization; Nature versus Nurture.

Further Reading: Butler, Judith, *Gender Trouble: Feminism and the Subversion of Identity* (New York: Routledge, 1990); Cixous, Helene, *The Helene Cixous Reader* (London: Routledge, 1994); Connell, Robert W., *Masculinities: Knowledge, Power, and Social Change* (Berkeley: University of California Press, 1995); de Beauvoir, Simone, *The Second Sex* (New York: Vintage 1952; orig. pub. in French, 1949); Eisler, Riane, and Allie C. Hixon, *The ERA Facts and Action Guide* (Washington, DC: National Women's Conference Center, 1986); Evans, Sara M., *Born for Liberty* (New York: Simon and Schuster, 1997); Fausto-Sterling, Anne, "The Five Sexes, Revisited," *Sciences* 40 (July/August 2000): 18–23; Fonow, Mary Margaret, *Women of Steel* (Minneapolis: University of Minnesota Press, 2003); Goleman, Daniel, *Social Intelligence* (New York: Bantam, 2006); Kessler, Suzanne, *Lessons from the Intersexed* (New Brunswick, NJ: Rutgers University Press, 1998); Lerner, Gerda, *The Creation of Patriarchy* (Oxford: Oxford University Press, 1987); Morgan, Robin, *Sisterhood Is Powerful: An Anthology of Writings from the Women's Liberation Movement* (New York: Random House, 1970); Murphy, T. J., "Women on the Rise," *Triathlete Magazine*, no. 272 (Encinitas, CA: Triathlon Group North America, LLC, 2006); Richardson, Laurel, *Dynamics of Sex and Gender* (New York: HarperCollins, 1988).

Amber Ault

SEX WORK

Discussions about sex work inspire a range of reactions and opinions, including those related to morals, rights, law, and gender inequalities. Many of these arguments can be distilled into a specific controversy that revolves around the competing assertions either that sex work empowers women or that it victimizes them. It is important to explore the intricacies of this empowerment/victimization debate to arrive at a full understanding of the issue of sex work.

BACKGROUND

The controversies about sex work are as old as the profession itself. It is difficult to discuss sex work, which ranges from prostitution to stripping, without invoking a combination of arguments related to law, rights and freedoms, morality, and gender. Although some types of sex work are legal and others are not, there are times in the public arena when its condemnation or support seems a matter of greater preoccupation than its legality. Conservative religious groups have denounced strip clubs on the basis of morality, residents have protested the existence of such establishments in their neighborhoods, but bachelor parties are rarely considered complete without the requisite visit to the local "gentleman's" club. Even celebrities are involved: in 1995, movie star Hugh Grant was famously arrested in Hollywood for soliciting the prostitute Divine Brown.

Debates about sex work also cue wider-ranging, deeply rooted cultural conflicts about gender, sex, and inequality. Since most sex workers are women, sex work is of feminist concern. Yet feminist thought is fractured on the issue. One perspective, endorsed by Andrea Dworkin and Catherine MacKinnon, suggests that "the very meaning of sex is male domination. Prostitution and pornography only reveal this message more clearly" (Chapkis 1997, 17). In contrast, there are those who see sex work as potentially liberating for women. Some, like sexual libertarian Camille Paglia, view women's capitalization on their sexuality as women's greatest source of power. These two extremes funnel into camps—one believing that sex work victimizes women, and the other asserting that it empowers women. Taking this controversy to its extremes, however, ignores the complexity of the argument and the nature and nuances of power. Feminist sex radicals, for instance, assert that "sex is a terrain of struggle, not a fixed field of gender and power positions" (Chapkis 1997, 26). One way to challenge the victimization/empowerment dualism is to consider how the day-to-day lives and experiences of sex workers are located within broader understandings of gender issues in our society. Such an analysis might reveal contradictions and negotiations that inform debates about this social issue.

WHAT IS SEX WORK?

Sex work is "a generic term for commercial sexual services, performances, or products given in exchange for material compensation [money]" (Weitzer 2000, 3), and includes prostitution and exotic dancing (stripping), as well as peep shows, telephone sex, and pornography. Social attitudes toward the women

LOCAL COMMUNITIES RESPOND TO STRIP CLUBS

Law and religion collide across the nation as various conservative groups agitate to restrict the existence of strip clubs in certain areas of towns, arguing that the establishments are immoral, and that they increase crime and lower property values. Opponents of such restrictions believe this violates the First Amendment's protection of free speech. Legislation like Proposition 401 in Scottsdale, Arizona, is placed on local ballots in an attempt to garner votes to shut down strip clubs. Proposition 401 aimed to outlaw lap dances and other types of touching at two Scottsdale-area cabarets. It failed in September 2006, with 23 of Scottsdale's 87 precincts voting against the proposed legislation.

workers are generally harsher than those toward the male customers, and this is reflected in institutions like the criminal justice system. Until the 1960s, the Model Penal Code stated that prostitution was a misdemeanor, punishable by incarceration, while being a "john" was simply a violation, warranting only a fine. Many state laws continue to punish patrons less severely than prostitutes (Weitzer 2000). Further, 90 percent of prostitution arrests are arrests of the female worker rather than the male customer (Monto 2000).

Unlike prostitution, which is illegal in all but two states, exotic dancing is legal across the United States. Beginning as burlesque entertainment, exotic dancing has evolved into a highly sexualized performance (either nude or topless) that involves a stage show and can include "table dances," "lap dances," or "private dances." Management often expects dancers to "work the floor" when they are not performing on stage. This involves approaching customers and soliciting an individual dance. At some clubs, these dances occur at the customer's table and last for the length of one song. During table dances, the dancer performs for the customer, and the two are in very close proximity. Customers and dancers are more likely to have body contact during table dances, although officially there are strict rules about the type of contact allowed. Some strip clubs tacitly allow lap dancing, which involves the dancer straddling the customer and grinding against the customer's genital area. Officially, lap dances are illegal in many states. Indeed, the lap dance is "situated in a legal gray area in the United States between prostitution, which is illegal, and performance, which is protected" (Chapkis 2000, 184). Enforcement of these rules varies wildly from establishment to establishment; customers may try to take advantage of dancers by groping or fondling them, or dancers will engage in sexual activities to make more money.

THE CONTROVERSY

Victimization

The position that sex work victimizes women begins with the idea that it reduces women to sex objects. One definition of sexual objectification goes as follows: "A person is sexually objectified when her sexual parts or sexual functions are separated out from the rest of her personality and reduced to the status of mere instruments or else regarded as if they were capable of representing her" (Bartky 1990, 26). In general, modern feminist thought suggests that the sexual objectification of women is a large component of female identity as well as a tool for the oppression of women (Bartky 1990; Bordo 1993; Chapkis 1986; Griffin 1981; Martin 1992):

> The disciplinary project of femininity is a "setup": it requires such radical and extensive measures of bodily transformation that virtually every woman who gives herself to it is destined in some degree to fail. Thus, a measure of shame is added to a woman's sense that the body she inhabits is deficient.... In spite of unrelenting pressure to "make the most of what they have," women are ridiculed and dismissed for the triviality of their interest in such "trivial" things as clothes and make-up. (Bartky 1990, 72)

In other words, although the ideal is largely unattainable, the sexually objectified view of female bodies garners women more attention than any other aspect of their identities. At the same time, this sexually objectified view of women is not particularly respected and can be used to justify treating women badly (Bartky 1990; Chapkis 1986). (It is easier to devalue people when they are seen only, for instance, as "tits and ass"). The present author's research, based on in-depth interviews with exotic dancers, reveals the ways in which work in the sex industry compounds these conflicts for the women involved (Wesely 2002, 2003). One interviewee, Sheila, noted that dancing "reinforced everything from my childhood, that sex was all important—and once I started dancing, I was a piece of meat, that's all they want. It just reinforced what I thought. Day after day after day." Julie, another study participant, stated, "It didn't have anything to do with my brain, or stimulating my mind, or passion. It all had to do with, yeah, you want to feel my 36–26–36, you just want to touch my tits." Being degraded—feeling "like a piece of meat"—corresponded to the women's objectification in the strip club.

Not only does sex work focus on the sexually objectified image of women, but it revolves around the exchange value of this objectified body: how much is it worth in cold hard cash? Those who suggest that sex work victimizes women point to this as an inherently unequal transaction, since the trade makes it difficult for sex workers to avoid reducing their own bodies to their weight in dollars. Valerie noted, "All you're doing all day long is asking someone, 'Am I worth five dollars to you?'" Similarly, Sheila stated,

> You're peddling yourself.... You have to go to these different guys, you think they're the scum of the earth anyway, but these people, they have your livelihood in their hands.... There's always the fact of who's really in control. They're in control, because they have the money.

Sheila also experienced strong reactions when she was not paid at all:

> They weren't paying me, and I was there, and that's my body, and they're wanting to just take it without doing what they're supposed to do. 'Cause

they're paying for your body, no matter how they say it, they're paying for your body. Five bucks a song, five bucks a song. Buy the song. But you're ruining my mind. And my soul. So when they were sitting there thinking they didn't have to give me the money, I felt violated. And I felt very angry. Rage.

Money worries can compel sex workers to take jobs they would otherwise avoid, jobs that make them feel vulnerable and degraded. Marie, a stripper, worked at a private bachelor party to make extra money:

> There was a prostitute that was supposed to come after I left to take care of the bachelor. I guess the prostitute took all the money and went out of the picture. Then I was there and they were looking at me like, how are you going to take care of it? I did let them ejaculate on my breasts.... And that was the worst thing I ever did. I went home and showered, and scrubbed and cried. I sat on the floor of the shower and cried. I felt like I was raped. I felt so disgusting when I walked out of that house. I cried all the way home.

Marie felt violated in the extreme, reduced to a sexualized body that she compromised for money. Feeling repeatedly reduced, degraded, or violated has psychological (as well as physical) consequences for sex workers. They may struggle to cope and begin to feel numb, disconnected, or dissociated from their bodies. As Marie stated:

> When I was in [the dancing industry], I had no clue how much pain I was in. Things that I was doing because I knew that that was the only way I was going to get something out of somebody. Lower myself. To get a dollar out of them. There was a situation where I gave a blow job to a manager at the club. After work, had a couple beers, doing the job all night long. And you feel like you can't say no. "I'm going to turn on the music, why don't you dance for us?" It's like, what can you say? I've been doing it all night long, you've seen me do it all night long, so what does it matter? You start to get to the point, well, what *does* matter? You've given yourself up to so many situations, it really doesn't matter anymore.

The seeming indifference and numbness Marie described is dangerous, because it makes her more vulnerable to further exploitation, violation, and violence.

Those who argue that sex work victimizes women point to the elevated levels of violence against them. In fact, the homicide rate for prostitutes is one of the highest for any occupation in the United States, and sex workers are inconsistently and unreliably protected from violence. This is illustrated by Marie:

> He'd try to show off in front of his guy friends and bite you on the rear end. All the friends would go, wooo! The bouncer would say, don't do that. If you got bit in a grocery store, the guy would get prosecuted for

that, and go to jail. You do it in a topless bar and it's OK. It's ridiculous. Just because you're in the atmosphere you have permission. It's like when we get bit on the rear, they don't give you counseling for that. But if a police officer came to a case where you got bit, they would give you a card: here, you can call this counselor, this is a form of victimization or whatever. And you would go to get counseling. But dancing, all these things would happen to you and you don't get one ounce of counseling. You're just getting victimized left and right. And they don't treat it as victimization, they treat it as, oh, it comes with the territory. They don't tell you that when you're getting hired! They don't tell you, oh, you can get bit, get slapped, men call you names, men can spit on you. They don't tell you those things.

The types of violations Marie mentioned segue into increasingly severe violence. Gina agreed to go on a date with a customer at the strip club where she worked, and was raped:

Anyway, he invited himself in afterwards. And so he came downstairs to my area of the apartment at the time. And we were sitting on the couch, and he decided he wanted to have sex with me.... But I didn't really want to have sex with him, and I ended up having sex with him, because he wouldn't take no for an answer. I felt very disgusted, very out of control. He held me down. I mean, at the time I was using so many drugs.... Many times I tried to struggle against him, like no, I don't want this, come on, stop kissing me. And eventually I just gave up. I was like, alright, fine, whatever, do your job. I knew I was just a cheap little piece of ass to him.

Rape, sexual assault, and stalking occur at higher rates among women in the sex work industry, and the argument that sex work victimizes women identifies the extreme exposure to risk that is involves.

Overall, a sex worker's success depends on how well she can embody sex in performance, appearance, behavior, and activity. She exists for the sexual pleasure, visual and/or physical, of the customer. Since her living revolves around the limited and devalued objectification of her body, it is argued that she is a more likely target for exploitation and abuse.

Empowerment

Those who assert that sex work is empowering for women suggest that women are taking control over the objectified meanings of their bodies by cashing in on them. Sex work then becomes the ultimate expression of sexual freedom, as women use their bodies and sexuality for their own purposes and gain. By making customers pay for the sex and/or the sexual performance, the sex worker is empowered. As Ronai and Ellis (1989, 295) note, "Being the purveyors and gatekeepers of sexuality has always provided powerful control for women.... it serves this function even more for those women who make sexual turn-on into an occupation." Gina, a stripper, stated that

The power comes in when there's the money exchanging hands issue. There's the "I'm controlling you for the next three minutes"—a dance is three minutes long—"I'm controlling everything you're thinking, I'm making you want me. With everything. For the next three minutes." It's almost like they just kind of sit there and give it up to you. And I've had guys say to me, my god, that is better than some sex I've had. And it makes me feel very powerful.

Gina suggested that it was almost as if the customers surrendered their will when they handed their money over to her. In her description, the man supplicates, willingly abandoning power—both his money and his sexual desire—to her.

A sex worker who feels empowered by using her body as a moneymaker might identify this as a source of women's advantage over men. For example, Cory, an exotic dancer, likes being a woman because she can use her sexual objectification to her benefit. She said, "We can use our body and make good money, unlike guys. I mean, sometimes I go into a store, and I just give them this look while carrying on a conversation, and guys are like, do you want me to give that to you? I'm like, yeah, I want a discount!" Similarly, Marie stated, "I always felt like you could use your body to get men. 'Cause I remember even before I started dancing I could go into a bar and be watching a game and I knew any guy in the bar would buy me a beer. I knew I could use my body to get something from men." Seeing this as power allows for the construction of the customers as foolish or stupid, whereas the sex worker is savvy and sharp:

> I think men are mostly idiots. I didn't think they were that stupid until I started being a dancer. They will give their money away. And they actually think that the more money they spend, they're actually going to get the time of day. . . . I've seen men that come in [to the strip club] every single day. But she doesn't want them, she wants their money. And you'd think they'd be smart enough to know that. (Lana)

Another dancer, Rita, had a similar viewpoint:

> I like to think of it as I'm in charge, guys are paying to glorify me, and they're the ones getting ripped off. A lot of people are like, oh, that's so shameful, that girls have to stand up there, and do that, men paying for their bodies. . . . I'm the one making out here, in my mind. They're the stupid ones paying for this. Most of the time they're paying for my conversation, to stare at me. You're like, I cannot believe you pay for this, and they pay a lot. Like, this kid was dropping $1,000 a night to sit and be my friend. To stare at my tits, maybe?

There is some research that alludes to an additional component of the empowerment argument—namely, that many sex workers experienced a loss of power over their bodies due to childhood abuse, and sex work is a way to reclaim that power. To explore this idea, it is helpful to examine this relationship more closely. According to Raphael (2004), across 20 recent prostitution studies, the lowest percentage of women sexually abused as children was one-third, while the highest was 84 percent. In fact, rates of child sexual abuse (CSA) for women both as prostitutes and exotic dancers are higher than those in the general population (remembering that for both groups these rates are undoubtedly underestimated). Although there may be higher numbers of CSA survivors among sex workers, CSA certainly does not cause women to go into sex work. So what *is* the relevance of CSA?

The first issue is that of survival. It is estimated that 70 percent of teenage girls on the streets are running away to flee a violent home (Chesney-Lind 2001). Because these girls are desperate and have few resources at their disposal, sex work or survival sex become viable options for them. It is confirmed in prostitution samples from Los Angeles to Chicago that the overwhelming majority of prostitutes ran away from their childhood homes (Raphael 2004). Putting together this information, a study of jail detainees in Chicago found strong support for the hypothesis that "sexual abuse and having run away influence entry into prostitution" (McClanahan et al. 1999, 1611). Second, and more closely related to the empowerment argument, is the reality that the lessons taught by the sexual abuse have produced "traumatic sexualization" (Finkelhor 1988). CSA teaches children to use sexual behavior as a strategy for manipulating others in order to have their needs met. In addition, the sense of control, lost through early sexual assault, could feel reclaimed through adult sexual power over men. "Remaining in the sexual arena to grab the power back, women in prostitution, the majority of whom are incest victims, end up developing personal power only in relation to men and sex, or within sexually defined gender roles" (Raphael 2004, 26). Skye, a stripper, determined that feeling powerful was compensation for the way she was victimized by sexual abuse as a child. She described her attitude toward customers: "Because I lost that power as a child, I'm going to use it on your pocketbook." Many dancers described the ego boost they got from receiving the customer's money and adoration, and Paula also perceived this as reparation for her past:

> It's also kind of an ego thing....I had a guy actually bow down on stage and kiss my feet. As if I were a god. And I know these men are so enchanted by the idea of me. That they're going to go home smelling their shirts, laying in their beds next to their wives, thinking of me. There's something about...Being at all the foster homes I've been, something I've always wanted is to be remembered. Now it's my chance to get even.

For Paula, dancing ascribes to her a sex symbol status that burns her image into the minds of her customers; they are unable to forget her. The power seemingly regained tips the balance in a way that makes the women feel superior to their male customers.

The position that sex work is empowering for women thus focuses on women taking control of the meanings of their bodies and being rewarded monetarily for those meanings. Some argue this is the ultimate form of sexual freedom for the female sex worker, and that the customer is the one getting short shrift in the exchange. Sex workers may also feel as though the rewards they receive in return for their bodies are compensation for the loss of power over their bodies that they experienced in childhood. By capitalizing on their sexual objectification, they can be seen as more strongly in control of their sexual selves.

COMPLICATING THE DEBATE

There are policy implications for the sex work victimization/empowerment debate, so it is essential to take the debate seriously. If sex work only victimizes women, it makes sense to abolish it; if it is empowering for women, why not legalize it in all its forms? In reality, victimization and empowerment are opposite poles between which lie a range of complicated arguments. Above, it was noted that one way to challenge the victimization/empowerment dichotomy is to consider how the day-to-day lives and experiences of sex workers are located within broader social realities. An exploration of this complexity begins with the sex workers themselves, and the ways they negotiate their lived experiences.

Complex personhood means that "even those who live in the most dire circumstances possess a complex and oftentimes contradictory humanity and subjectivity that is never adequately glimpsed by viewing them as victims or, on the other hand, as superhuman agents" (Gordon 1997, 4). Accordingly, sex workers are not just passive recipients of objectification; nor are they unrestricted agents making choices about their bodies from a full array of options. Sex workers feel, simultaneously and often contradictorily, different combinations of power, powerlessness, and indifference. Gina, a stripper, described this as follows;

> Being on stage is another powerful time. When everyone's looking at you, you're putting on a good show, it's 4:00 on a Friday and you've got everyone's attention and people are hooting and hollering, and guys are coming up and throwing money on stage, yeah, you feel very *powerful*. 'Cause you have everybody's attention, right there, in your hand. But at the same time, when it's Friday at 4:00 and everybody's watching stage two because Pamela Anderson's on it, *that really destroys you*. (italics added)

The money and attention given to one dancer is thus easily diverted to another, and the power is lost. Marie also demonstrated a struggle regarding power:

> No, I didn't think I had control over my body. But you have control over how much you tease somebody and how much you don't. You have

---

COYOTE

COYOTE (Call Off Your Old Tired Ethics) was the first prostitutes' self-advocacy organization, founded in 1973 by former sex worker Margo St. James. With the exception of the early 1990s period, COYOTE was run by former prostitutes. The goals of organizations like COYOTE are to provide education and support. Other agencies take the approach that it is most important to help prostitutes find strategies to exit the industry. These are antiprostitution organizations, and include the Council for Prostitution Alternatives (CPA) in Portland, Oregon. CPA receives city and county funding and private grants and is run by social workers as well as former prostitutes.

control, you're in the driver's seat. You can break them or make them whenever you want. But you lose control of your body when you go in there. Because it's not yours, it's somebody else's. They decide what looks good and what doesn't.... So that's what I mean when I say you walk in the doors and lose control of who you are. But you do have control of the situation. You can search out a guy in the club and you know he's vulnerable, and you know he has a wallet full of money and you can get every dollar out of that wallet. And it's that knowing that you can do that that gives you power.

Marie's statement vacillated between assertions of power over the customers—"you have control over how much you tease somebody," "you're in the driver's seat," "you can break them," "you can get every dollar out of that wallet"—and her feelings of vulnerability at the hands of the customers—"you lose control of your body when you go in there," "they decide what looks good and what doesn't," "you...lose control of who you are." This negotiation revolves around an ongoing conflict for sex workers: although the women make money from their bodies, the bodies that are rewarded are determined by the male customers. This removes some aspects of control from the women's hands, and makes feelings of power, though present, seem fleeting and only skin deep.

Ronai and Ellis (1989) suggest that in a society that awards women little influence in larger spheres, women learn to obtain various needs through emphasizing and being rewarded for behaviors and appearance that focus on their objectification.

Interaction in the strip bar also reflects power dynamics in mainstream society. As a subordinate group, women in general have responded to men's macromanipulation of societal institutions by using micromanipulation—interpersonal behaviors and practices—to influence the power balance (Lipman-Blumen 1984). Women in the bar play a game that they know well; in some form, they have been forced to play it for years (Lipman-Blumen 1984, 295)

According to this statement, sex workers are engaging in and capitalizing on one of the few strategies available to women to achieve any power. This can also trap women in a system of disadvantage, since some argue that the attention paid to women's sexually objectified bodies translates into very little power in "legitimate" arenas, or those seen as culturally valuable. In other words, women's sexual objectification or the attention they receive for their sexualized bodies does not elevate their status or influence in the political, social, and economic realms that help shape or change society (Irigaray 1985). This creates contraction and struggles for sex workers, since their feelings of power are legitimate but impermanent and limited in influence and impact.

In conclusion, both poles of the sex work victimization/empowerment debate retain some integrity on the level of the individual sex worker. Because sex workers may at times *feel* empowered, there is power there. Because they may *feel* or *be* victimized, victimization exists. Just as legitimate are the sex workers' experiences of contradiction and struggle. Yet just as it is important to pay attention to the sex workers' individual experiences, their interpretations of power and victimization must be located within the larger social context in which they occur.

In short, as Wendy Chapkis (1997) points out, women working in the sex industry operate within the constraints of social prejudice and unequal privilege. Not surprisingly, these differences of location produce dramatically different experiences of sex work. As a consequence, reforms directed at the sex trade itself will only partially address the problems sex workers face. The far greater challenge lies in tackling the structural inequalities reflected in the industry but rooted in society at large (Chapkis 1997, 106).

Chapkis's (1997) statement points to the limitations of directing policy concerns about sex work at the industry only. Although individual sex workers have a range of experiences concerning power, victimization, and everything in between, no real positive changes will result for this group until the role of structural inequalities is linked directly to the reality of sex work.

See also Militarized Prostitution; Pornography; Work: Paid versus Unpaid.

Further Reading: Bartky, Sandra, *Femininity and Domination* (New York: Routledge, 1990); Bordo, Susan, *Unbearable Weight* (Berkeley, CA: University of California Press, 1993); Chapkis, Wendy, *Beauty Secrets: Women and the Politics of Appearance* (Boston, MA: South End Press, 1986); Chapkis, Wendy, *Live Sex Acts: Women Performing Erotic Labor* (New York: Routledge, 1997); Chapkis, Wendy, "Power and Control in the Commercial Sex Trade," in *Sex for Sale: Prostitution, Pornography and the Sex Industry,* ed. Ronald Weitzer, 181–201 (New York: Routledge, 2000); Chesney-Lind, Meda, "What about the Girls? Delinquency Programming as if Gender Mattered," *Corrections Today* 63 (2001): 38–45; Cotton, Ann, Melissa Farley, and Robert Baron, Robert, "Attitudes toward Prostitution and Acceptance of Rape Myths," *Journal of Applied Social Psychology* 32, no. 9 (2000): 1790–1796; Finkelhor, David, "The Trauma of Child Sexual Abuse," in *Lasting Effects of Child Sexual Abuse,* ed. G. Powell and G. Wyatt, 61–82 (Thousand Oaks, CA: Sage Publications, 1988); Gordon, Avery, *Ghostly Matters: Haunting and the Sociological Imagination* (Minneapolis, MN: University of Minnesota Press, 1997); Griffin, Susan, *Pornography and Silence* (Harper and Row, 1981); Irigaray, Luce, *This Sex Which Is Not One,* trans. C. Porter (Ithaca, NY: Cornell University Press, 1985); Lipman-Blumen, Jean, *Gender Roles and Power* (Englewood Cliffs, NY: Prentice Hall, 1984) Martin, Emily, *The Woman in the Body* (Boston, MA: Beacon Press, 1992); McClanahan, Susan F., Gary M. McClelland, Karen M. Abram, and Linda A. Teplin, "Pathways into Prostitution among Female Jail Detainees," *Psychiatric Services* 50 no. 12 (1999): 1606–1613; Miller, J., and M. D. Schwartz, "Rape Myths and Violence against Street Prostitutes," *Deviant Behavior* 16 (1995): 1–23; Monto, Martin, "Why Men Seek Out Prostitutes," in *Sex for Sale: Prostitution, Pornography, and the Sex Industry,* ed. Ronald Weitzer, 67–84 (New York: Routledge); Monto, M. and N. Hotaling, "Predictors of Rape Myth Acceptance among Male Clients of Female Street Prostitutes," *Violence against Women* 7 (2001): 275–293; Raphael, Jody, *Listening to Olivia: Violence, Poverty, and Prostitution* (Boston, MA: Northeastern University Press, 2004); Ronai, Carol Rambo, and Carolyn Ellis, "Turn-Ons for Money: Interactional Strategies of the Table Dancer," *Journal of Contemporary Ethnography* 18 (1989): 271–298; Weitzer, Ronald, ed., *Sex for Sale: Prostitution, Pornography, and the Sex Industry* (New York: Routledge, 2000); Wesely, Jennifer K., "Growing Up Sexualized: Issues of Power and Violence in the Childhood and Adult Lives of Female Exotic Dancers," *Violence against Women* 8 (2002): 1186–1211; Wesely, Jennifer K., "'Where am I Going To Stop?': Exotic Dancing, Fluid Body Boundaries, and the Effects on Identity," *Deviant Behavior* 24, no. 5 (2003): 483–503.

Jennifer Wesely

SEXISM IN LANGUAGE

Language gives meaning to and reflects components of all cultures, yet scholars disagree as to whether language itself creates gender biases or whether it merely reflects gender biases that already exist in society. Feminist scholars have debated whether language itself should be the focus of reform, or whether sexism should be addressed in other aspects of society such as the economy, the political process, or in educational institutions.

BACKGROUND

Simone de Beauvoir (1952) has said that "One is not born, but rather becomes, a woman." When children are born, they are given names that reflect their sex. Hospital nurseries provide *pink* caps for female infants and *blue* for males. Children grow up into *boys* and *girls* through socialization via gendered social cues and they learn to see other children as boys and girls. At all stages, language plays a vital role in defining how boys are different from girls, and how gender relations are perceived and give meaning to a given social order. Many scholars have analyzed the relationship between language and sexism, or discrimination on the basis of sex and/or gender, including the question of how or if language influences the socialization process. Some argue that language is merely a reflection of an already-existing sexist society; others argue that language itself is sexist and helps reproduce gender inequalities in society at large (Richardson 1997).

WHAT IS LANGUAGE?

Language is a system of signs. Sounds count as language only when they serve to express or communicate ideas; otherwise they are just noises. And in order to communicate ideas, noises must be part of a system of conventions, part of a system of signs (Culler 1988). The sign is the union of the *signifier* (a sound image or a written shape) and a *signified* (a concept). *Signifier* and *signified* exist as components of the sign. The signs of a language are deeply rooted in the culture that produces that language and therefore language is a social system.

Linguist Ferdinand de Saussure (1857–1913) revolutionized the study of language. In outlining a general science of signs, semiology, he provided the means of analyzing the systems of conventions that give significance to human behavior. His findings opened a new world of possibilities for the exploration of the relationship between language and social order. Post-Saussurean linguistics saw language as an important cultural tool that operates at various levels and takes varied forms. Feminist scholars have built on this scholarship and raised important questions about the question of women and sexism in language.

DEBATES ON GENDER AND SEXISM IN LANGUAGE

Language is available in verbal and visual forms. Verbal is that which is spoken or heard while visual is that which we read or see, as in literature of all kinds, or as in sign language used by people who are deaf or hearing impaired. Language can also be a set of images grouped together to generate meaning sometimes supported by words as in advertisements, or even graffiti and writings on the walls of public places such as trains, public toilets, and so forth. All these forms of expression are included in language and they are rooted in specific cultures and generate specific meanings when read. They express certain opinions about people and incorporate certain attitudes towards them.

Sexism in language has an important role to play when it comes to the construction of male and female stereotypes in a given literature and culture. French feminists such as Helene Cixous (1992) and Luce Irigaray (see Whitford 1991) have drawn from psychoanalytic and linguistic theory to analyze the uses and misuses of language for women. They argue that language is inherently phallocentric, or centered on a male view point, one that typically involves domination over women. In this view, language directs the understanding of the roles assigned to men and women in patriarchal societies. Language is not independent of its social connotations and cannot be seen in isolation. It signifies meanings and commands and controls the attitudes rooted in specific cultures. This, in turn, gives meaning to our understandings and perceptions. Literature is one component that clearly demonstrates the ideas proposed by language. And if one examines literary history for example, it exclusively refers back to the concept of man, to *his* torment, and *his* desire to be (at) the origin. The reference is always directed back to the male, particularly to the father figure. There is an intrinsic bond between the philosophical and the literary (to the extent that it signifies, literature is commanded by the philosophical) and phallocentrism. The philosophical construct itself starts with the abasement of woman, the subordination of the feminine to the masculine order that appears to be the condition for the functioning of the society (Cixous 1992). This is a *man-made* world where *mankind* thrives. Darwin's theory of evolution for example, suggests that *mankind* has evolved through time into our present form. History (*his-story*) documents facts and findings about mankind as if mankind is an all inclusive term.

Language also directs the logic of cultural thinking. Language loaded with sexist terms has typically looked down on womanhood or glorified and tailored it to suit to the needs of male-dominated societies. Women in literature, for example, have been represented by male writers as embodiments of tolerance, affection, love, and patience, they are also portrayed as belligerent, wicked, and gossipy. Both sacred and profane roles are assigned to women and language has served as an instrument in establishing inequality by defining social rankings and promoting social hierarchies.

The discourse of language is loaded with images and metaphors used time and again to gain a certain meaning in specific sociocultural contexts. These meanings define the qualities attributed to people and inscribe undertones in what is signified. Femininity for example is pitted against masculinity. Powerful, strong, and huge are considered as one set of images with beautiful, tender, and soft as their opposites. The opposite of masculinity (femininity) is viewed as inferior. Thought in literature, philosophy, and criticism are typically

MONIQUE WITTIG'S "THE LANGUAGE YOU SPEAK"

French author and feminist theorist Monique Wittig (1935–2003) played an important role in challenging phallocentrism in language. In her own writing, she struggled passionately for a woman's voice free of male domination, which she attempted by both writing about sexism in language and by utilizing nongendered signifiers in her own stories, which were often centered on utopian societies devoid of men (Wittig 1976 and 1985). Following is an excerpt from her writing.

> The women say, the language you speak poisons your glottis tongue palate lips. They say, the language you speak is made up of words that are killing you. They say, the language you speak is made up of signs that rightly speaking designate what men have appropriated. (Monique Wittig in Showalter 1992, 341)

understood by opposition, by dual hierarchical opposition (Cixous 1992). The binary oppositions used in language unfortunately subscribe to a hierarchy that consciously or unconsciously control women's lives and writings; this is the view held by scholars who believe that language produces social reality. This view, which emerged through de Saussure's revolutionary thinking, continues to be put to the test in academic studies. Laurel Richardson (1997) provides a helpful list of six ways to think about how sexism is embedded in the English language.

1. By including *women* under the generic *man*.
2. By attributing different personality traits and career aspirations to men and women—"Nurses, secretaries, and school teachers are almost invariably referred to as 'she;' doctors, engineers, electricians, and presidents as 'he'" (Richardson 1997, 116).
3. By defining women as immature, incompetent, and incapable and males as mature, complete, and competent.
4. By defining women in terms of their sexual desirability (to men) and men in terms of their sexual prowess.
5. By defining women in terms of their relations to others (e.g., men, children, families) and men in terms of their relations to the world at large.
6. By using pejorative or demeaning language that is gendered (e.g., "lady," "mistress," "girlie," "hussy").

SEXISM IN LANGUAGE: THE CONSTRUCTION OF WOMANHOOD

According to Laurel Richardson (1997) and other feminist linguistic and literary scholars, language serves to reinforce gender difference in part by invoking specific notions of womanhood and domesticity. Patriarchal societies consider motherhood as one of the most important functions of womanhood. Motherhood is given a very special place and an ideal mother is portrayed and understood as an embodiment of womanhood. Through language, chastity is valorized and chastity takes a prime place in the role-modeling of "a good woman." If a woman does not embody the role of the good woman she may be humiliated through insults to her body and sexuality. This is illustrated by proverbs from around the world:

> "Women are saints in the church, angels in the street, devils in the kitchen, and apes in bed." (English)
> "Women have got long hair and short sense." (Maltese)
> "Women have their brains below their knees." (Indian)
> "Of women and horses there are none without defects." (French)

Language contributes abundantly to the construction of domesticity as a domain for women. Susan Brownmiller (1984) speaks of "setting the table," the household game played by girls in the United States and elsewhere. Forks were placed to the left of the plate, knives and spoons to the right. When a knife or a fork dropped to the floor, it meant a man was unexpectedly coming for dinner. When a spoon dropped to the floor, it announced the surprise arrival of a female guest. Despite the fact that these visitors never arrived on cue, girls learned the rule of gender identification. Men were straight edged, sharply pronged, and

---

GENDER STEREOTYPING IN LANGUAGE

Take a look at the following sentences.

- *Man* gives birth to *mankind.*
- "One small step for man, one giant step for mankind."
- "Man overboard!"
- We are so different from the *early man.*
- We (*men*) represent *mankind* and enjoy this land left behind for us by our *forefathers.*
- You need proper *manpower* to execute this plan.
- Our language should be so simple that even a *layman* can understand what is said.
- Students of fine arts should be familiar with the works of the *old masters*; only then can they be *masterful* enough to develop their own skills and have *one man shows.*

These are expressions that deny female existence altogether. Some feminist scholars have attempted to counter this usage of language by creating new words that do not invoke a traditional gender hierarchy, such as *womyn* (instead of women), *herstory* (instead of history), *chairperson* (instead of chairman), *Ms.* (instead of Mrs. or Miss), and *flight attendant* (instead of steward or stewardess). By contrasting these terms used for the same subject, we can see that there is a range of attitudes and feelings in society toward that subject. The use of these terms heavily influences how we think about men's and women's identities and societal roles.

Source: Richardson 1997.

formidable. Women were softly curved and held their food in a rounded well (Brownmiller 1984).

The idea of domesticity is generally associated with the state of being tamed and conditioned. Domesticity is related to the idea of home and all that it stands for. Domesticity gives security, shelter, and protection. Concepts such as family and children lead to the above conditioning. The socially constructed notions of motherhood, marriage, the duties of a wife or a daughter, and other icons of femininity and womanhood, all work as tools for fostering domesticity.

Concepts such as home, family, workplace, tradition, and other social constructs participate in the formation of domesticity. Language actively promotes the idea of domesticity through the meanings associated with these concepts. Women's space, for example, is often associated with metaphors of home and kitchen, and with jobs like cooking, washing, cleaning, and homemaking. These metaphors are associated with the notion of the feminine and in turn understood as nonmasculine and therefore nonintellectual. While women in literature have been represented by male writers as embodiments of tolerance, affection, love, and patience, they are also portrayed as belligerent, wicked, and gossipy. Both sacred and profane roles are assigned to women.

LANGUAGE: NATURE AND THE NATURAL

Elements of nature are exaggerated and beautified in literature. The beautification of nature is carried out by invoking the female body. The female body is brought to the forefront and nature is perceived in the form of a woman. The woman is appropriated to nature and a certain persona is sketched out for her. The femininity imposed on her in this manner is seen as natural to her.

For example, expressions such as *woman's heart* (a tender heart), *woman's natural expression, naturalness in her expression, purely feminine consciousness,* and so forth, are often used to characterize poems by women poets. If one looks carefully, these uses of language try to restrain women's poetic expression within traditional patriarchal frameworks (Sagar 2004).

Feminist critics have argued that it is important to "embark on a revisionist re-reading of our entire literary inheritance" (Hawkes 1985). While arguing the case for women's writing, Dale Spender (1989) criticizes Ian Watt (1963), author of *The Rise of the Novel,* and comments that the only reason why writings by women do not count in the histories of literature is the fact that they are written by women. Spender points out that the worth of women writers is not based on any consideration of their writing; it is a worth determined by their gender.

CONCLUSION

As feminist scholars have pointed out (Cixous 1992; Whitford 1991), because women use language in which the embedded metaphors and meanings are often molded to suit patriarchal interests, it becomes difficult to express opinions. Language itself reinscribes oppressive structures. Women in general, feminist critics and women writers in particular, have shown resistance to the varied aspects of sexism in language in their own ways.

American, French, and British feminist critics have all drawn attention to the philosophical, linguistic, and practical problems of women's use of language and the debate over language is one of the most exciting areas in linguistic and literary criticism. Poets and writers have led the critiques of language, arguing that while it often appears to be abstract and void of social consequences, it is in fact through the medium of language that we define and categorize areas of difference and similarity, which in turn allows us to comprehend the world around us (Showalter 1992). Male-centered categorizations dominate American English and subtly shape our understanding and perception of reality; this is why attention has been increasingly directed to the inherently oppressive aspects of a male-constructed language system (Furnam in Showalter 1992).

The debate on sexism in language demonstrates the importance of language as a strong component of patriarchy. It reveals the role played by language in supporting women's lower status in society based on gender. Sexism in language recreates restricted social spaces for women and speaks as if these spaces are natural to them. However, feminist scholars disagree as to whether language should be prioritized as the primary source of critique or whether other factors such as culture, religion, or political economy should be viewed as "outside" language and as sources of sexism or gender inequalities themselves.

See also Education; Gender Socialization; Nature versus Nurture.

Further Reading: Brownmiller, Susan, *Femininity* (New York: Linden Press/Simon and Schuster, 1984); Cixous, Helen, "Sorties," in *Modern Criticism and Theory*, ed. David Lodge, 287–293 (London: Longman, 1992); Crowley, Tony, Alan Girvin, and Lucy Burke, eds., *The Routledge Language and Cultural Theory Reader* (New York: Routledge, 2000); Culler, Jonathan, *Saussure* (London: Fontana Press, 1988); de Beauvoir, Simone, *The Second Sex* (New York: Vintage, 1952); Eckert, Penelope, and Sally McConnel-Ginet, eds., *Language and Gender* (Cambridge: Cambridge University Press, 2003); Hawkes, Terence, "Introduction," in *Making a Difference: Feminist Literary Criticism,* ed. Gayle Greene and Coppelia Kahn, 22–35 (London: Routledge, 1985); Kali for Women Proverb Resource, available at: http://cogweb.ucla.edu/Discourse/Proverbs/; Munn, Jessica, and Gita Rajan, eds., *A Cultural Studies Reader: History, Theory Practice* (New York: Longman Group Ltd., 1995); Richardson, Laurel, "Gender Stereotyping in the English Language," in *Feminist Frontiers IV,* ed. Laurel Richardson, Verta Taylor, and Nancy Whittier, 115–121 (New York: McGraw Hill, 1997 [1981]); Sagar, Mamta, *Gender, Patriarchy and Resistance: Contemporary Women's Poetry in Kannada and Hindi (1980–2000),* PhD diss., University of Hyderabad, India, 2004; Sagar, Mamta, *MahiLa Vishaya: Essays in Kannada and English on Gender, Language, Literature and Culture* (Bangalore, India: Ila Prakashana, 2007); Showalter, Elaine, "Feminist Criticism in the Wilderness," in *Modern Criticism and Theory,* ed. David Lodge, 339–341 (London: Longman, 1992); Spender, Dale, "Women and Literary History," in *The Feminist Reader: Essays in Gender and the Politics of Literary Criticism,* ed. Catherine Belsey and Jane Moore, 25 (London: The Macmillan Press Ltd., 1989); Tax, Meredith, and Womens's World, eds., *The Power of the Word: Culture, Censorship, and Voice* (New York: Women's World, 1995); "Turkish Proverbs," Ottoman Souvenir, available at: http://www.ottomansouvenir.com/index.html; Watt, Ian, *The Rise of the Novel* (New York: Penguin, 1963) Whitford, Margaret, ed., *The Irigaray Reader* (Malden, MA: Blackwell, 1991);

Wittig, Monique, *The Lesbian Body* (New York: Avon, 1976; [1973 in French]); Wittig, Monique, *Les Guérilleres* (Boston: Beacon Press, 1985 [1969 in French]).

Mamta Sagar

SEXUAL ASSAULT AND SEXUAL HARASSMENT

The gendered nature of sexual violence is well documented in academic research, organizational and policy studies, and government documents. Viewpoints on why men are responsible for the vast majority of rapes and cases of sexual harassment, with the victims being largely women and girls, often clash in the social, political, and advocacy arenas. Battles between nature and nurture, social construction and biology, and feminism and conservatism contribute to divergent views on both the causes and the consequences of these behaviors.

BACKGROUND

While men are sexually assaulted by women, and same-gender sexual assault does occur (for example, a man sexually assaults a man), statistics indicate that the majority of sexual violence perpetrators are men, and the majority of victims are women. In fact, 91 percent of the victims of sexual assault are women and 9 percent are men, and nearly 99 percent of offenders in single-victim assaults are men (BJS 1997). However, not all men who commit acts that meet the legal definition of sexual assault identify their behavior as such. For example, 1 in 12 male college students surveyed report engaging in acts that meet the legal definition of rape or attempted rape, but 84 percent of them report that what they did was "definitely not rape" (Warshaw 1994). The debate about the gendered nature of sexual violence exists in multiple contexts in society. Some argue that it is men's nature to sexually dominate and control women. Driven by a biological need to procreate, men sexually dominate women to ensure the continuation of the species and of their own biological line. Thus, when presented with a situation that imposes a barrier to reaching this goal, such as a woman who does not want to have sex, a man's biological predisposition takes the driver's seat, resulting in a disregard for the woman's wishes and leading to sexual assault. However, others argue that it is the patriarchal U.S. society and systemic oppression by men of women that explains the prevalence of men's sexual violence. In what is called a culture of violence, dominance and control are presented as positive attributes of masculinity in society. According to this argument, men and women's socialization begins in childhood, where toughness is valued in boys and submissiveness is valued in girls. Observers and advocates point out that these messages, paired with a society where men's sexual violence is tacitly accepted, lead to rampant sexual violence with minimal consequences.

THE SEXUAL VIOLENCE CONTINUUM

Regardless of their ideological perspectives on sexual violence, most observers would agree that the phenomenon of sexual violence in the United States has grown into an epidemic. With statistics indicating that a rape occurs every 2.5 minutes in the United States and that one in every six women in the U.S. is a victim of rape or attempted rape (RAINN 2006), sexual violence causes increasing alarm and commands increasing attention. When viewed as a systematic form of violence, sexual violence is not seen as a single act; rather, sexual violence refers to a range of behaviors commonly described as a sexual violence continuum. These behaviors include stranger rape, date/acquaintance rape, intimate partner rape, and sexual harassment, as well as incest, child sexual abuse, voyeurism, and unwanted sexual touching. The concept of a sexual violence continuum is used as an explanatory model by rape crisis centers and sexual assault coalitions nationwide. While various versions of the model use slightly different stages, they generally refer to a range of behaviors beginning with socially accepted behavior and ending with sexually violent death.

This continuum serves as a road map for exploring the many facets of sexual violence in a larger, societal context.

SOCIAL NORMS VERSUS CRIMINALIZATION

While violent crimes such as stranger rape are criminalized in our society, the social norms, that is, the attitudes, behaviors, and beliefs that are considered acceptable in a society, about violence against women often contradict or undermine laws and policies. Thus, while institutional policies and laws may specifically denounce and sometimes criminalize a behavior, social norms may contradict this by allowing, or failing to respond to, certain behaviors. For example, in most states it is illegal to initiate sexual activity with someone who is asleep, as that person is unable to give consent to the activity. However, many fairy tales tell of a prince kissing a princess who is asleep as a result of a wicked spell. The kiss is the only thing that can break the spell, and it is seen as loving and romantic. In fact, many young girls wait for their "prince" to carry them off to a castle to live happily ever after. The idea, or social norm, that kissing a sleeping princess is romantic is both powerful and pervasive in U.S. culture, and strongly contradicts legal definitions of nonconsensual sexual behavior. Social norms create an atmosphere in which behaviors are accepted and even socially rewarded based on responses from peers. Imagine a situation in which a number of college-age young adults are attending a party. Most guests are drinking alcohol, there is music, and plenty of people are dancing and kissing. In this situation, there may be peer pressure for young women and men to behave in certain ways. Young men receive messages that they are supposed to "get a girl," and they receive positive peer reinforcement for initiating and maintaining intimate contact with one or more young women. In fact, the more the man encourages a woman to drink alcohol and engage in intimate behavior, the more social messages the man receives from his peers, praising him as a "stud." At the same time, the young woman receives messages that she should feel flattered by the sexual attention and that she should do as the man encourages or wants. The social norms of this situation send messages to the woman that she should not assert her own feelings or desires if it will cause a scene or embarrass the man, and the man receives messages that he should continue to push the woman, regardless of her wishes. These messages create an environment where unwanted sexual behavior can occur with little or no intervention from bystanders. This has important consequences for the way observers of rape and sexual harassment patterns assign blame and design policies and laws to address these behaviors.

INDIVIDUAL BELIEF SYSTEMS

Despite existing social norms, sexual violence can occur only when the perpetrator holds individual belief systems that allow him to engage in sexually intrusive behavior. These belief systems include the ideas that men have ownership or control over women, that a woman owes a man sexual behavior in exchange for some interaction (for example, "If I buy you dinner, you owe me sex"), and that men have earned or have the right to sexual activity regardless of a woman's wishes. These belief systems are reinforced by the larger societal context of systemic oppression and sexism, which sends messages about gender roles, power, and control though the media and social norms. No amount of alcohol or peer pressure can "make" a person force sexual behavior on an unwilling participant if his/her individual belief system does not already support such action to some extent. The controversy lies in people's support for or opposition to individual belief systems that view rape as consensual ("even if she says 'no,' she means 'yes'") and in the belief that sexual harassment is natural and simply part of a man's natural sex drive, rather than an unjustifiable act of aggression toward a woman.

RAPE AND SEXUAL ASSAULT

While there are many legal definitions of *sexual assault* and *rape,* in general the terms refer to oral sexual contact or intercourse without consent. While stranger rape is the most publicized type of rape, it is one of the least often committed. Among female victims of sexual assault, 67 percent reported they were assaulted by intimate partners, relatives, friends, or acquaintances (Catalano 2005). In addition, only 8 percent of sexual assaults involve weapons, again in contradiction to the stereotypical idea of stranger rape. This is important, because societal myths about rape and sexual assault affect offenders, victims, bystanders, and those responding to the crimes through law enforcement and social service systems. In struggling with these myths, many victims either believe that the rape was their fault or fail to identify what happened to them as rape. According to one study, only approximately 35 percent of sexual assaults were reported to the police in 2004, an increase in recent years but still a rate substantially lower than the rates for non-interpersonal crimes (Catalano 2005). Many victims choose not to report because of shame, fear, guilt, or concern about others' perceptions. The responses of varying social systems, and in particular of law enforcement, can reinforce these feelings if the victim feels blamed by first responders. While on one hand the judicial system is set up to address charges of rape, based on the societal view that rape is wrong, in practice, many people find it difficult to address the issue, and there

RAPE MYTHS AND FACTS

Myth #1: If I am careful, I will never be raped.

Fact #1: Anyone can be raped. While there are steps people can take to protect themselves, such as going out with a friend or meeting dates in a public place, it is the rapist who chooses to assault the victim. Only the rapist can prevent the crime.

Myth #2: Rape is about sexual desire.

Fact #2: Rape is about power and control. Sex becomes the weapon of humiliation, not the goal.

Myth #3: Most rapists are strangers.

Fact #3: Approximately 60–80 percent of rape victims know their attacker, and for women 15–25 years old, 70 percent of sexual assaults happen during dates (Kanel 2007).

Myth #4: Women who are drinking or wearing revealing clothes are asking to be raped.

Fact #4: No one asks to be raped, and the rapist holds sole responsibility for the crime. Women should be able to wear anything and drink alcohol without fear of being sexually victimized.

Myth #5: Once men get turned on, they can't stop.

Fact #5: Could he stop if his mother walked in? (Kanel 2007, 233). There is no "point of no return." Both men and women can choose to stop sexual behavior at any point, even if the result may be discomfort or embarrassment.

Source: Adapted from Kanel 2007.

---

is often great silence and shame experienced by victims as well as by perpetrators, families, law enforcement officials, and other people involved in the process.

SEXUAL HARASSMENT

Sexual harassment is even more difficult than rape to legally define and document; observers disagree as to when an act actually constitutes harassment. According to law, sexual harassment is an illegal form of sex discrimination that violates two federal laws: Title VII of the Civil Rights Act of 1964, and Title IX of the Education Amendments of 1972. Both laws address sexism and gender discrimination; the Civil Rights Act focuses on nondiscrimination in the workplace, while the Education Amendments focus on nondiscrimination in educational settings. As defined by the U.S. Equal Opportunity Commission (USEEOC), "unwelcome sexual advances, requests for sexual favors, or other verbal or physical conduct of a sexual nature constitute sexual harassment when submission to or rejection of this conduct explicitly or implicitly affects an individual's employment, unreasonably interferes with an individual's work performance or creates an intimidating, hostile or offensive work environment" (USEEOC 2002, 1). In an educational environment, this sexual harassment can "threaten a student's physical or emotional well-being, influence how well a student does in school, and make it difficult for a student to achieve his or her career goals" (U.S. Department of Education [ED] 2005, 1). There are two types of sexual harassment as defined by law: quid pro quo and hostile environment.

Quid pro quo, which means "something for something," is a type of sexual harassment that occurs when "an employee [or student] is required to choose between submitting to sexual advances or losing a tangible job [or educational] benefit" (Rubin 1995, 2). Examples may include a boss harassing an employee, a teacher harassing a student, or a coach harassing an athlete. In quid pro quo sexual harassment there must be a power differential between the target and the harasser. The harasser must be able to exercise control over the threatened job or educational benefit. Sexual harassment occurs regardless of whether the target chooses to accept the sexual behavior, as long as the conduct is unwelcome.

Hostile environment harassment is "unwelcome conduct that is so severe or pervasive as to change the conditions of the claimant's employment [or education] and create an intimidating, hostile, or offensive work environment" (Rubin 1995). Hostile environment harassment can include gender- or sexual orientation–based jokes or comments, calling people by derogatory gender-related names (for example, "slut"), threats, touching of a sexual nature, offensive email or Web site messages, talking about one's sexual behaviors in front of others, spreading rumors about co-workers' or other students' sexual performance, and negative graffiti (for example, in a bathroom stall).

In general, the standard for sexual harassment is what a "reasonable person" would find offensive. However, a decision by a 1991 circuit court allowed for a "reasonable woman" standard, allowing for differences in perception of offensiveness across gender lines (Rubin 1995). Some argue that jokes, comments, and sexual innuendos are actually compliments to women, and are men's natural way of bringing their biological drive toward sexual behavior to the

---

NORTH COUNTRY

North Country, a Hollywood film starring Academy Award winner Charlize Theron, is based on the nonfiction bestseller *Class Action*. The film and book are based on the true story of Lois Jensen, one of the first women hired to work in a northern Michigan mine in 1975. As one of a handful of female miners in the company, Jensen was subjected to repeated incidents of harassment including derogatory language, pornographic graffiti, stalking, and physical assaults. In 1984, she decided to file a complaint against the company. Although at first other female miners were afraid to become plaintiffs in the case, eventually many of them joined Jensen and, with a strong team of lawyers, they won their case in court, making this case the first successful sexual harassment class action lawsuit in the United States.

---

forefront. However, men and women often report different perspectives on whether behavior is flattering or offensive.

Additional issues related to the legal criminalization of sexual harassment and rape concern encroachment on a person's sense of sexual safety and invasion of a person's space. This type of behavior may include a physical intrusion, such as "accidentally" brushing against someone in a sexual manner, but often does not involve actual touch. Sexual jokes, catcalls and whistles, leering at a sexual body part, and making sexual comments are all invasions of sexual space. Some argue that such behavior by men is actually complimentary to women, and frequently those who speak up by identifying such behavior as degrading and disrespectful are labeled as vindictive feminists, jealous, or too serious. Comments such as "Lighten up, it's just a joke" reflect this view. Sexual assault activists argue that this type of commentary sends a message condoning harassment and also contributes to silencing bystanders who seek to intervene. According to some activists, unwanted sexual touch is the first point on the sexual violence continuum. This is a point at which gender role messages conflict with sexual safety. In most social settings, men receive positive messages with regard to engaging in such behavior in a public setting, and women are often acutely aware of the message that it is not acceptable to embarrass a man. Often, if a woman rebuffs the initial stages of sexual touching, this results in both the woman and the man being viewed negatively in a social context.

SEXUAL ASSAULT PREVENTION: RESPONSES TO VIOLENCE AGAINST WOMEN

Traditional sexual assault prevention programs focus on risk reduction strategies for women and girls, teaching them how to avoid situations in which sexual assault is likely to occur, based on knowledge of risk factors. However, some argue that risk reduction programs inherently carry a biased view, namely, that victims can prevent sexual assault if they simply learn to behave in the "right way." Therefore, more recent strategies involve addressing men's socialization processes as well. Literature on engaging men in rape prevention activities focuses clearly on how essential it is to appeal to men as bystanders, not as perpetrators or potential perpetrators (Katz 2001). In order for bystanders to intervene, they must understand the dynamics and risks of sexual violence, have empathy for the devastating impact of sexual violence on victims, and have the skills and confidence to intervene. In social situations, many young people report feeling uncomfortable when they notice a woman who is the target of sexual attention that appears to be unwanted, but they also report feeling embarrassed at the reaction of their peers if they intervene (Warshaw 1994). Men's love and care for the women in their lives can be a powerful tool in building empathy. And it is men who are "embedded in peer culture" with other men and who are in the most influential position to intervene (Katz 2001, 7). Additionally, activists point out that we cannot challenge the systemic oppression of patriarchy, men's entitlement and privilege, and violence as acceptable without engaging men. According to Katz, "as empowered bystanders, men can interrupt attitudes in other men that may lead to violence. They can respond to incidents of violence or harassment before, during or after the fact. They can model healthy relationships and peaceful conflict resolution" (2001, 7). Teaching men to intervene at the earlier stages of the sexual violence continuum, especially at the social norms and individual belief systems stages, will result in preventing sexual assaults from occurring.

CONCLUSION

When viewed through the lens of the sexual violence continuum, it can be seen that there is a clear connection between sexism, social norms that condone violence and the transgression of sexual boundaries, gender role socialization messages to men and women, and sexual harassment, abuse, and assault. According to this model, intervening at the initial stages will prevent the later stages (sexual violence). Ultimately, though, sexual assault activists argue that sexual violence will end only when it becomes completely intolerable in society. Due to long-held beliefs in men's innate sex drive and women's innate desire to be protected, conquered, or gazed upon, debates on how to address rape and sexual harassment will surely continue. Whereas some observers believe that the federal government should support sexual assault initiatives, others believe that only state or local governments or the private sector should be held responsible for addressing these behaviors. This reveals how difficult it is to legally address behaviors that we are socialized to see as naturally emanating from biology rather than from our social environments, although of course sexual assault activists have worked hard to change these beliefs.

See also Child Sexual Abuse; Sexual Assault and Sexual Harassment.

Further Reading: Bureau of Justice Statistics (BJS), *Violence against Women,* FBI Uniform Crime Reports (Washington, DC: U.S. Department of Justice, Bureau of Justice Statistics, 1997); Bureau of Justice Statistics (BJS), *Extended Homicide Report,* FBI Uniform Crime Reports (Washington, DC: U.S. Department of Justice, Bureau of Justice Statistics, 2005); Catalano, Shannan M., *Criminal Victimization, 2004* (Washington, DC: U.S. Department of Justice, Bureau of Justice Statistics, September 2005); Kanel, Kristi, *A Guide to Crisis Intervention,* 3rd ed. (Pacific Grove, CA: Brooks/Cole Publishing Company, 2007); Katz, J., *Building a "Big Tent" Approach to Ending Men's Violence,* report published through a grant from the Office on Violence Against Women, Office of Justice Programs (Washington, DC: U.S. Department of Justice, 2001); Kilpatrick, Dean G., and Ron Acierno, "Mental Health Needs of Crime Victims: Epidemiology and Outcomes," *Journal of Traumatic Stress* 16, no. 2 (2003): 119–132; Rape, Abuse and Incest National Network (RAINN), 2006, available at: http://www.rainn.org/statistics/index.html, accessed August 31, 2006; Rennison, Callie Marie, *Rape and Sexual Assault: Reporting to the Police and Medical Attention, 1992–2000* (Washington, DC: U.S. Department of Justice, Bureau of Justice Statistics, 2002); Rubin, Paula N., *Civil Rights and Criminal Justice: Primer on Sexual Harassment,* National Institute of Justice: Research in Action (Washington, DC: U.S. Department of Justice, Office of Justice Programs, 1995); Sidran Foundation, "Post-traumatic Stress Disorder Fact Sheet," 2005, available at: http://www.sidran.org/ptsdfacts.html, accessed August 31, 2005; U.S. Department of Education, *Sexual Harassment: It's Not Academic* (Washington, DC: U.S. Department of Education, 2005); U.S. Equal Employment

Opportunity Commission (US EEOC), "Facts about Sexual Harassment," 2002, available at: http://www.eeoc.gov/facts/fs-sex.html, accessed October 10, 2006; Warshaw, Robin, *I Never Called It Rape: The Ms. Report on Recognizing, Fighting, and Surviving Date and Acquaintance Rape* (New York: HarperCollins, 1994).

Kathryn Woods

SEXUAL IDENTITY AND ORIENTATION

The notion that every person has a sexual identity or a sexual orientation that can be described as lesbian, gay, bisexual, or heterosexual has become commonplace in modern industrialized Western nations. Controversies concerning sexual identity stem from debates on the causes of homosexuality and heterosexuality, the degree to which the environment shapes identity, the accuracy of the categories used to describe sexuality, and the question of which civil rights and forms of social justice should be extended or denied to people who define themselves according to sexual identity categories considered deviant by the majority.

BACKGROUND

Debates on sexual identity have tended to focus on the origins and meaning of homosexuality in modern society, obscuring until recently critical investigations of the causes and social implications of heterosexual behavior and the identities attached to it. Ethnographers and historians have documented a wide range of social and cultural contexts in which people we might describe today as gay, lesbian, or bisexual have been socially recognized, validated, and accepted. As early as 600 B.C., the first recorded laws mentioning homosexuality were found in ancient Crete and Sparta and encouraged men to engage in homoerotic relationships with one another. The late Yale historian John Boswell (1995) documented the Catholic Church's blessing of male same-sex unions over the course of several centuries leading up to the modern era, and ethnographer René Gremaux (1993) reported on a sizable number of cases of women, often called "sworn virgins," living as men in eastern European societies during the past century. The significant leadership roles of people of both sexes (two-spirit people) in North American Plains Indian tribes have been widely documented (Blackwood 1984; Roscoe 1993), as have the almost commonplace romantic friendships of women in the United States in the early twentieth century (Faderman 1998). In the broad sweep of history, people who express same-sex attractions have been valued and validated in a variety of ways across a wide range of contexts.

Laws against same-sex sexuality can also be dated back to the ancient world, particularly in cultures that adopted the Abrahamic religions of Judaism, Christianity, and Islam. In contemporary nation-states around the globe, men and women who define themselves as gay or lesbian "suffer from discrimination virtually everywhere," as Adam, Duyvendak, and Krouwel note in their 1999 essay, "Gay and Lesbian Movements beyond Borders: National Imprints of a Worldwide Movement." During the twentieth century, many of the world's countries formalized new laws oppressive of people whose sexual identities, desires, or actions centered on people of the same sex. In some instances, homosexuality has been considered an illness as well as a crime, and those accused of same-sex sexual behavior have been not only imprisoned as criminals but also institutionalized and "treated" for mental illness, using a variety of methods that have often resulted in bodily and emotional harm—including lobotomy, sex change surgery, sexual aversion therapy, and sexual identity "reprogramming."

In response to this intensive repression, people who identify themselves as gay, lesbian, and bisexual have formed groups around their common marginalization; they and their allies have engaged in much social movement activity over the last 125 years in efforts to end the oppression of people in sexual minority groups. Adam, Duyvendak, and Krouwel (1999) note that around the world, local lesbian and gay activism focuses on two general issues: (1) ending discrimination and (2) creating public spaces in which gay and lesbian people may gather for political and social purposes.

In the United States, the early-twentieth-century homophile movement and its mid-century successor, the gay and lesbian liberation movement, worked to decriminalize homosexuality by lobbying legislators to remove antisodomy laws from local and state statutes (D'Emilio 1998). In a related move, the movement worked to depathologize homosexuality by convincing the American Psychiatric Association to remove "homosexuality" as a diagnostic category from its *Diagnostic and Statistical Manual;* being able to diagnose homosexuality as a disease had allowed medical professionals to institutionalize lesbian and gay people and subject them to a range of horrifying "treatments" devised to "cure" people of homosexuality (D'Emilio 1998). After they won this victory, gay men and lesbians, who had collaborated to achieve this important goal, often saw themselves as having different interests and agendas, and developed somewhat segregated single-sex communities throughout the 1970s.

When the AIDS crisis began in the United States in the early 1980s, gay and lesbian activists began to collaborate more closely to end official government silence around AIDS, and to fight discrimination against those infected with the virus, as well as discrimination against the broader gay and lesbian population. The magnitude of the AIDS crisis in the United States and its devastating impact on the gay male population contributed to the politicization of many gay and lesbian people, as well as to the increased visibility of gay and lesbian people in the media, politics, art, education, religion, and other social institutions. In recent decades, in response to activist pressure, a number of countries (the Netherlands, Belgium, Canada, and Spain) have legalized same-sex marriage and created protections for gay and lesbian parents; still more have legalized same-sex unions (Denmark, Norway, Sweden, Iceland, France, Germany, Finland, Luxembourg, New Zealand, Britain). In other places, including the United States, debates rage on regarding whether same-sex couples should have rights equal to those of people in cross-sex relationships, including the right to marry, to legally protect their partnerships, to parent, and to be free from employment discrimination. Some states in the United States have legalized same-sex unions, while others have adopted amendments to their state constitutions precluding the possibility of establishing same-sex marriage within those states. In some countries, homosexual acts remain punishable by death (Nigeria, Somalia, Sudan, Iran, the Chechen Republic, Saudi Arabia), imprisonment, or censure, and lesbian and gay activists continue to be subject to harassment.

WHAT "CAUSES" HOMOSEXUALITY? ETHICAL, CULTURAL, AND BIOLOGICAL DEBATES

Most of the discrimination, oppression, conflict, debate, and conversation around homosexuality centers on fundamental questions about (1) whether same-sex sexuality is "natural"; (2) whether human beings may legitimately be categorized as gay/lesbian, heterosexual, and bisexual; and (3) whether some of these identities are more morally acceptable than others. While the system of sexual categorization on which this conversation turns (gay/straight) is taken for granted in most contexts in the United States today, it is not universal. It has been the working model in Western industrialized nations for only a short period of time, and has diffused from these countries, which have a disproportionate impact on global culture, to other cultural contexts. Without the assumption that it is meaningful to describe people as being lesbian, gay, bisexual, or heterosexual, it would be impossible to talk about gay people and straight people, let alone to debate whether gay marriage should be legalized. It would still be possible, however, to advocate for same-sex marriage rights and to describe sexual behavior in terms of same-sex and opposite sex sexuality and affection. In short, while same-sex sexuality appears to be universal, describing same-sex sexuality in terms of lesbian, gay, and bisexual identities, like describing cross-sex sexuality as attached to "straight" identity, is a product of scientific modernity in the Western industrialized world.

Just as racial categories are historically specific, culturally variable, and used by members of dominant racial groups to define "others" who may be deprived of rights and privileges, categories of sexual identity have been used by members of the dominant group to create sexual-social categories and to use their social, legal, and economic power to exclude members of "sexual minority" groups from full social rights and privileges. In the case of race, the social belief that members of each racialized category are biologically different from each other is contradicted by the scientific and social evidence that most people are multi-racial in background. In the case of sexual identity/orientation, research indicates that, as a species, humans possess a far more fluid sexuality than the presumptive categories of sexual identity/orientation would indicate.

Although more people identify as heterosexual than as gay, lesbian, or bisexual, conversations about sexual identity and orientation often focus on the minority, for a number of reasons. These categories came into circulation in the late nineteenth century, originated by a group of European physicians. Working as "sexologists," these thinkers, mostly physician-scholars, were interested in how we as human beings experience and organize our sexual lives. Because they regarded same-sex sexuality as unusual or atypical, it served as a topic of much interest for investigation and theorizing (Ellis 1897, [1915] 1923). The French philosopher Michel Foucault (1990) has noted that before Western society could talk about "the heterosexual," it first defined "the homosexual" as "a species." This conceptualization is consistent with that of the French sociologist Emile Durkheim (1963 [1893]), who had noted nearly a century earlier that in almost all domains, social groups define the deviant category first, as a way of establishing what is "normal" or "normative" in contrast to it; without the definition of which groups are " outgroups," we could not define which groups are "in" or "normal." As a result, conversations about sexual identity often focus on lesbian and gay identities instead of on straight or heterosexual identities; this allows heterosexual or straight identities to seem natural, normal, and right, instead of as deeply social in their invention and maintenance as every other sexual identity. Only recently have scholars begun to study heterosexual identity as a distinctive, culturally produced, identity form (Richardson 1996; Katz 1996).

WHAT IS SEXUAL ORIENTATION?

From a sociological perspective, the term *sexual orientation* connotes innate qualities of sexual attraction. Indeed, the term is used most commonly by people who make the assumption that people are born with some kind of sexual destiny or sexual constitution that is immutable. From this perspective, people are born with a predetermined or "hard-wired" sexuality that can technically be described as heterosexual (attracted to people of "the opposite" sex), homosexual (attracted to people of the same sex), or bisexual (attracted to people of both sexes). This particular assumption has an interesting political history. Sometimes it has been favored by those who oppose gay and lesbian rights, and sometimes it has been favored by the gay and lesbian movement, depending on the political climate and political goals of the period. For example, during the 1960s and 1970s, during the heyday of the radical gay liberation movement, many gay activists argued that human sexuality was not fixed but fluid, that all people had both heterosexual and homosexual potential, and that as a society we needed to adopt a less rigid notion of sexual identity categories. The conservative counterdiscourse during this period involved the argument that people were born gay, that gayness was either a disorder or a disease in need of treatment, and that gay people should simply choose not to act on their same-sex attractions. In recent decades, the rhetoric of these two movements has been inverted. Mainstream gay and lesbian movement activists have adopted the position that people are born gay and, therefore, must be granted civil rights because to be discriminated against on the basis of an innate characteristic is patently unjust; the conservative antigay movement now frequently argues that being gay is a "lifestyle," and that people who live it should simply choose a "straight lifestyle" or face what members of the antigay movement believe to be justifiable discrimination (Herman 1997).

Is the direction of any individual's sexual attraction biologically determined? We know more about same-sex and opposite-sex sexuality at the levels of populations and species than we do about the causes of sexual attraction for any particular individual. Among humans, same-sex sexuality and affection have been documented widely, both transhistorically and cross-culturally, although the meanings assigned to sexual or romantic relationships between people of the same sex have varied. For example, the anthropologist Gilbert Herdt documented male same-sex sexuality among the Sambia, a cultural group in New Guinea, in which boys are taught about sexuality by men who initiate them into sexual relationships over a period of years (Herdt 1987). Many of the boys go on to relationships with women, while some, as they come to maturity, prefer to assume the role of initiator. Among Plains Indian tribes in North America, women could take on male roles, marry women, and raise adopted children in these familial contexts; the women they married were seen as heterosexual women, while the "female-bodied men" were seen as men, not as women who loved women (Blackwood 1984; Roscoe 1993). In both instances, these forms of same-sex sexuality have been recognized and sanctioned by the community.

That there is much evidence of same-sex affection and sexuality among humans is not surprising, given its ubiquity among other species. In *Biological Exuberance: Animal Homosexuality and Natural Diversity,* biologist Bruce Bagemihl (1999) notes that homosexual behavior occurs in at least 450 animal species across the planet, in "every major geographic region and in every major animal group" (12). Far from being limited to the genital sexual contact that many imagine when they hear the word "sexuality," same-sex sexuality among animals, like same-sex and cross-sex sexuality among humans, involves a wide array of sensual, erotic, affectionate, and sexual behaviors. According to Bagemihl,

> On every continent, animals of the same sex seek each other out and have probably been doing so for millions of years. They court each other, using intricate and beautiful mating dances that are the result of eons of evolution. Males caress and kiss each other, showing tenderness and affection toward one another rather than just hostility and aggression.

SAME-SEX BONDING AMONG BOTTLENOSE DOLPHINS

In many species, same-sex pairs form lifelong bonds that include both sex and affection. One species in which this is common is the bottlenose dolphin. Adolescent male dolphins commonly travel in exclusively male groups, and within these groups they often initiate partnerships with other males that last the rest of their lives. These same-sex pairs, according to Bagemihl (1999), become "constant companions, often traveling widely; although sexual activity probably declines as they get older, it may continue to be a regular feature of such partnerships. Paired males sometimes take turns guarding or remaining vigilant while their partner rests. They also defend their mates against predators such as sharks and protect them while they are healing from wounds inflicted during predators' attacks. . . . On the death of his partner, a male may spend a long time searching for a new male companion—usually unsuccessfully, since most other males in the community are already paired and will not break their bonds. If, however, he can find another 'widower' whose male partner has died, the two may become a couple" (344).

Females form long-lasting pair bonds—or maybe meet just briefly for sex, rolling in passionate embraces or mounting one another. Animals of the same sex build nests and homes together, and many homosexual pairs raise young without members of the opposite sex. Other animals regularly have partners of both sexes, and some even live in communal groups where sexual activity is common among all members, male and female. Many creatures are "transgendered," crossing or combining characteristics of both males and females in their appearance or behavior. Amid this incredible variety of different patterns, one thing is certain: the animal kingdom is not just heterosexual. (11–12)

While there is much evidence that same-sex affection and sexuality are natural among the species living on Earth, the scientific evidence on the biological bases of sexual attraction/orientation/identity itself is both scant and weak, although many researchers have been interested in this question. In her research on "lesbians under the medical gaze," cultural theorist Jennifer Terry (1995) reviews the lengths to which the American physicians and scientists who succeeded the European sexologists in this line of enquiry went in their efforts to locate biological bases of difference between lesbians and heterosexual women. For instance, they mapped lesbians' heights and weights, tracked their facial features, and measured and sketched their genitals, expecting to discover physical differences that would explain differences in sexual interests and attraction. Although such efforts resulted in no determination of the bases for differentiating women into sexuality categories using gross anatomy, researchers have continued to pursue questions about biological differences between "gays" and "straights," investigating a wide range of possibilities, including differences in fetal exposure to sex hormones, genetic differences, and differences in brain development. Most of these studies have sought to establish people who consider themselves gay or lesbian as people of one sex who are somehow more like members of the opposite sex—thus, the researchers in Terry's study sought to establish lesbians as women with a sexual anatomy more like men's, while brain studies have investigated whether gay males' brains are "more like women's." By using a model of presumptive heterosexuality, such research ironically consistently positions gay and lesbian people as transgendered or proto-transsexual, instead of as people of one sex who are attracted to members of the same sex.

WHAT IS SEXUAL IDENTITY?

Setting aside the question of the causes of heterosexuality, homosexuality, and bisexuality allows us to turn to the question of sexual identity. In sociological terms, identity involves individuals' or groups' senses of themselves. In the last 150 years in North America and Europe, and more recently in Africa, Latin America, and Asia, people have begun to think of themselves as having the sexual identities "lesbian," "gay," "bisexual," and "straight" or "heterosexual." Reflecting the work of the sexologists who defined these categories in the late nineteenth and early twentieth centuries, these categories have undergirded the

THE CONTINUING SEARCH FOR BIOLOGICAL DIFFERENTIATION BETWEEN STRAIGHTS AND GAYS

During the late nineteenth century and through the first quarter of the twentieth century, scientific theorizing on the nature of homosexuality centered on the body; sexologists assumed that individuals who were sexually attracted to the same sex were somehow biologically or constitutionally different from those attracted to the opposite sex. Around the turn of the century, Sigmund Freud began to question biologically based theories of homosexuality, positing that homosexuality reflected psychological processes, not biological ones. A study in New York City conducted from 1935 to 1941 by the Committee for the Study of Sex Variants (Terry 1995) combined both theoretical models, asking homosexuals for details about their personal histories and relationship practices, and describing their bodies in painstaking detail, including the size, shape, and coloring of the genitalia. Such studies give evidence of the long-standing desire to define gay men and lesbians as biologically different from heterosexuals. Although such studies, conducted over nearly a century and a half, failed to identify biological sources of sexual differences between people, scientists continue to ask this question. Ethicists need to ask the related question: what difference would such a discovery make?

efforts of dominant groups to pathologize and discriminate against those they consider deviant. In response, those oppressed by heterosexism in culture, society, and the law have challenged the limitations imposed upon them. As the dominant group wrote and enacted laws against gays and lesbians and same-sex sexuality, it actually helped to institutionalize the idea that people might define themselves as gay or lesbian. As more people came to define themselves in these terms, there emerged more visible lesbian and gay populations (D'Emilio 1998), and this, in turn, helped to establish the concept that everyone has a sexual identity that can be described in the terms mentioned above.

While the phrase "sexual identity" immediately draws our attention to sexuality, sexual identity often refers to more than sexual attraction or behavior. Because of the emergence of visible and politically active gay and lesbian movements and communities over the course of the last century, to have a gay or lesbian identity often means to have a sense of connection to those movements or those communities, whether one is sexually active or not, single or partnered, young or old, a member of a dominant racialized group or a member of a minority ethnic community. Recently, with the emergence of programs to support gay and lesbian youth in high schools, many people have been "coming out" in their teen years, developing a sense of identity as gay or lesbian before they have opportunities to date members of the same sex, just as heterosexual people often express their sexual identities in their adolescent years even before they become sexually active. Because heterosexuality is assumed to be the normative category, it has been undertheorized, compared with gay, lesbian, and other marginalized identities.

Sexual identity is often different from sexual behavior. In the United States, the same-sex behavior of men who are married and heterosexually identified was documented by the sociologist Laud Humphries in the 1960s. The AIDS crisis made it even clearer that many whose social identities are rooted in one category engage in sexual behavior associated with other categories—for example, "straight" men who engage in sex with men, "gay" men who have sexual contact with women. Paula Rust's (2000) research on lesbian and bisexual women notes that many women with strong lesbian identities occasionally have sex with men without a disruption in their sense of self as lesbians.

THE POLITICAL IMPLICATIONS OF SEXUAL IDENTITY VERSUS SEXUAL ORIENTATION

Sexual identities and orientations might be codified in terms other than those provided by the current nomenclature, which focuses on what psychologists once called "object choice"—that is, the sex of the people to whom we are attracted. For example, we might conceptualize sexual proclivities along the lines of the sexual or affectionate activities people enjoy, the ways they express their sexuality in social spaces, or how they relate to others, regardless of sex, in sexual encounters. Within the current paradigm, which requires that we describe our own sexualities in terms of others—that is, the sexed bodies of those to whom we are attracted—debate continues to center on whether we are born straight, lesbian/gay, or bisexual; when we use the term *sexual orientation,* we signal our comfort with the idea that people have innate, immutable sexualities; when we use the term *sexual identity,* we situate identities in a broader context made up of communities, movements, politics, and the social world.

The significance of the biological determinist or biological essentialist view in political conversations on the status in society of people in the sexual minority cannot be underestimated. If we were to explore further the socially constructed qualities of heterosexuality, we would likely expand our understanding of the impact of both biology and social life on sexualities of all kinds. The recent ten-

TWO-SPIRIT PEOPLE

Plains Indian tribes in North America commonly recognized and valued "two-spirit people," who were called *berdache* by the Europeans who encountered and were reviled by them. Two-spirit people were/are commonly thought of as people with a spirit that is both masculine and feminine residing in one body, which may be biologically male or female. Historically, specific highly visible and important roles—such as spiritual leadership—were assigned to two-spirit people, who were often thought to have special powers and abilities because of their integration of the masculine and feminine. Two-spirit people were generally treated as members of their chosen sex, often enjoying special opportunities denied to other members of their biological sex—for example, male-bodied female two-spirits were often included in military expeditions from which female-bodied women would have been excluded. In many tribes, female-bodied two spirits married women and raised children with them, while being included in important tribal structures from which women historically were excluded.

dency within the lesbian and gay movement to promote an essentialist view of sexuality turns on the argument that if sexuality is a fixed feature of a person, gay and lesbian people cannot be expected either to change to comply with what feminist theorist Adrienne Rich (1980) has famously called "compulsory heterosexuality" or to live lives devoid of love, affection, sexual bonding, or the opportunities in civil society enjoyed by those in opposite-sex pairings. The essentialist view also promotes the drive to "prove" biological differences between gay/lesbian and straight people. Somewhat ironically, other oppressed groups—for example, women and people of color—have worked in the last century to use science to disprove their purported biological differences from majority groups that have used the idea of biological difference to justify discrimination. The risk for the gay and lesbian movement of promoting an essentialist view of sexuality is the risk of reestablishing the homosexuality as disease model, a model that may promote efforts to "cure" those seen as afflicted, whether through abortion, gene or hormone therapy, or surgery.

The concept of sexual identity puts aside questions of the etiology of sexuality as either innate or chosen and emphasizes instead a sense of self in relation to others, whether those others are romantic or sexual partners, members of a community or population, or participants in a social movement for change. Unlike the concept of sexual preference, which is currently out of vogue both in the lesbian, gay, and bisexual movement and among its antagonists, the concept of identity signifies a sense of a person in context. Nonetheless, because one's sexual identity and one's sexual behavior may not be perfectly correlated, epidemiologists, researchers, and sexual health advocates have recently begun to adopt language that simply conveys behavioral concepts, for example, by advising "women who have sex with men" "men who have sex with men" and "women who have sex with women" to take specific precautions against sexually transmitted diseases.

CONCLUSION

Cross-sex and opposite-sex bonds of affection and sexuality occur in a wide variety of species on our planet, including our own. Because we have limited understandings of the meaning of same-sex bonds among other animals, we may speak of their behaviors as heterosexual or homosexual or offer descriptions of their dyads as cross-sex or same-sex pairings. Among humans, the "meaning-making" species, contemporary Western interpretations of sexual affection, attraction, and behavior allow us to describe not only behaviors but also the identities that both reflect and inspire those behaviors. Although "lesbian," "gay," "bisexual," and "heterosexual" by no means constitute the only possible ways of constructing identities around sexuality, these categories have come to dominate Western thinking and popular discourse in the last century and a half. In the political sphere, activists for and against full civil rights for people defined as lesbian and gay continue to engage in debates around whether sexuality is innate or a function of culture and choice, assigning various meanings and implications to its origins, depending on their political goals. Although science has made repeated attempts to demonstrate essential differences between gays and straights, no credible evidence has yet emerged indicating that sexual orientation/identity differences are a function of biology. Should such evidence emerge, those opposed to gay rights may well recommend altering the biological factors that produce same-sex desire, while advocates of gay rights will continue to argue that members of sexual minority groups should be accepted for who they are, without oppressive restrictions on their rights. Gay rights advocates might do well to consider changing the terms of this particular debate by emphasizing sexual identity over sexual orientation, since biological difference from a dominant group has almost universally worked against the interests of minority groups in U.S. history. By emphasizing instead the rights of all people in a democratic society to equal rights regardless of sex, gender, sexual identity, marital and parental status, partner choice, health status, sexual orientation, and race, no matter how individuals may have come to be defined in terms of these categories, activists in the lesbian and gay movement may create the foundation for a more thoughtful conversation oriented toward wider principles of social justice.

See also Heterosexism and Homophobia; Homosexual Reparative Therapy; Lesbian, Gay, Bisexual, Transgender, and Queer Movements; Queer; Sex versus Gender.

Further Reading: Adam, Barry, Jan Willem Duyvendak, and Andre Krouwel, "Gay and Lesbian Movements beyond Borders," in *The Global Emergence of Gay and Lesbian Politics: National Imprints of a Worldwide Movement,* ed. Barry Adam, Jan Willem Duyvendak, and Andre Krouwel (Philadelphia: Temple University Press, 1999); Bagemihl, Bruce, *Biological Exuberance: Animal Homosexuality and Natural Diversity* (New York: St. Martin's Press, 1999); Blackwood, Evelyn, "Sexuality and Gender in Certain North American Indian Tribes: The Case of Cross-Gender Females," *Signs* 10, no. 1 (1984): 27–44; Boswell, John, *Same Sex Unions in Pre-Modern Europe* (New York: Vintage, 1995); D'Emilio, John, *Sexual Politics, Sexual Communities: The Making of a Gay and Lesbian Movement* (Chicago: University of Chicago Press, 1998); Durkheim, E., *The Rules of Sociological Method* (New York: Free Press, 1963 [1893]); Ellis, H. H., *Studies in the Psychology of Sex,* vol. 1 (London: University of London Press, 1897); Ellis, Havelock, H., *Studies in the Psychology of Sex,* vol. 2 (Philadelphia: F. A. Davis. 1923; orig. pub. 1915); Faderman, Lillian, *Surpassing the Love of Men* (New York: Harper, 1998); Foucault, Michel, *The History of Sexuality: An Introduction* (New York: Vintage, 1990); Gremaux, René, "Woman Becomes Man in the Balkans," in *Third Sex, Third Gender: Beyond Sexual Dimorphism in Culture and History,* ed. Gilbert Herdt, 214–281 (New York: Zone Books, 1993); Herdt, Gil, *The Sambia: Ritual and Gender in New Guinea,* Case Studies in Cultural Anthropology (Boston: Wadsworth, 1987); Herman, Didi, *The Antigay Agenda: Orthodox Vision and the Christian Right* (Chicago: University of Chicago Press, 1997); Humphries, Laud, *Tearoom Trade: Impersonal Sex in Public Places* (New York: Aldine Transaction, 1970); Katz, Jonathan Ned, *The Invention of Heterosexuality* (New York: Plume Press, 1996); Rich, Adrienne, "Compulsory Heterosexuality and Lesbian Existence," *Signs* 5, no. 4 (1980): 631–660; Richardson, Diane, ed., *Theorizing Heterosexuality: Telling It Straight* (New York: Open University Press, 1996); Roscoe, Will, "How to Become a Berdache: Toward a Unified Analysis of Gender Diversity," in *Third Sex, Third Gender: Beyond Sexual Dimorphism in Culture and History,* ed. Gilbert Herdt, 329–372 (New York: Zone Books, 1994); Rust, Paula C. Rodriguez, "'Coming Out' in the Age of Social Constructionism: Sexual Identity Formation among Lesbian and Bisexual Women," in *Bisexuality* *in the United States,* ed. Paula C. Rodriguez Rust, 512–534 (New York: Columbia University Press, 2000); Terry, Jennifer, "Anxious Slippages Between 'Us' and 'Them': A Brief History of the Scientific Search for Homosexual Bodies," in *Deviant Bodies,* ed. Jennifer Terry and Jacqueline Urla, 129–169 (Bloomington: Indiana University Press, 1995).

Amber Ault

SEXUAL ORIENTATION AND THE LAW

Debates concerning individual rights to sexual liberty and autonomy are rooted in the legal doctrines of economic due process, substantive due process, equal protection, and free speech, and in divergent views on what constitutes a legal minority group. While the Supreme Court has developed a framework that includes the decriminalization of sodomy, it has not yet recognized lesbian, gay, and bisexual people as a discrete and insular minority for purposes of strict review under equal protection, including in regard to harassment and hate crimes.

BACKGROUND

Sexual orientation has been understood in a variety of ways in legal arenas. Some argue that lesbian, gay, bisexual, and transgender (LGBT) people should be protected by the law; others argue that they do not merit the status of a protected class in the same way as groups exploited due to their race, creed, religion, or sex. In legal terms, a group of people that has been found in the court of law to be exploited is called a "discrete and insular minority." The Supreme Court has defined a discrete and insular minority as a group that shares an immutable characteristic, a history of discrimination, and a current state of political powerlessness. Courts have granted various levels of legal scrutiny for groups depending upon how they are viewed in the eyes of the law. For example, courts have granted strict scrutiny for groups defined by race or national origin, intermediate scrutiny for groups defined by gender, and low-level review for groups defined by sexual orientation, class, age, and disability. Future cases will continue to determine how each of these groups, including sexual minorities, will be legally treated.

LEGAL DOCTRINES THAT INFLUENCE HOW SEXUAL ORIENTATION IS LEGALLY UNDERSTOOD

To fully understand the intersection of sexual orientation and the law, it is important to address the four legal doctrines that have laid the groundwork for sexual liberty and autonomy: economic due process, equal protection, substantive due process, and freedom of speech. These legal doctrines stem from the Fourteenth Amendment, which was one of three Reconstruction amendments made to the U.S. Constitution following the Civil War and the abolition of slavery. The amendment is commonly considered to be the guarantor of individual liberties. Three clauses are significant: the privileges and immunities clause, the due process clause, and the equal protection clause. The privileges and immunities clause

LAMBDA LEGAL DEFENSE FUND

The Lambda Legal Defense Fund is the oldest national legal advocacy group working in the United States on behalf of lesbian, gay, bisexual, and transgender people, and people living with HIV. Lambda selects the cases it will represent based on their potential impact on their target communities.

In the 1990s, much of the work done by Lambda had to do specifically with fighting attempts to prohibit antidiscrimination laws for LGBT people. This battle was largely won when the Supreme Court handed down its landmark decision in *Romer v. Evans*. Currently, the work done by Lambda focuses largely on national efforts to ensure that LGBT people enjoy the right to marry.

---

was found by the Supreme Court in 1873 not to apply to laws made by the states. Therefore, this clause has been largely ineffective in guaranteeing the preservation of individual liberties. The due process clause, instead, has been the language from which the Court has determined what individual rights people may not be deprived of. Similarly, the equal protection clause is enforced by courts to prevent discrimination against discrete and insular minorities. Each of these clauses is significant for understanding how LGBT people are understood (or not) as discrete and insular minorities in the law.

The due process clause allows citizens to petition the U.S. courts to determine whether laws passed by the legislature are constitutional. Economic due process is the courts' practice of reviewing laws that regulate an individual's rights to own property or to contract. Substantive due process is the courts' practice of reviewing laws that regulate a person's private activities and relationships. The historical development of individual rights to sexual autonomy and liberty is grounded in the relationship between these two practices.

Contemporary interpretations of the equal protection clause stem from a 1938 case, when the Supreme Court handed down a decision in *United States v. Carolene Products*. In the "filled milk" case, it was argued that filled milk or milk with additives was sold more cheaply than products sold by other merchants, giving it an unfair comparative advantage in the market. Critics argue that the law was passed under pressure from special interest groups that had an investment in the profit from milk that was not filled. During the case, Justice Stone wrote that a more exacting and focused review might have been warranted if the filled-milk regulation was pointed at "discrete and insular minorities," implying that economic regulations are appropriate except if the regulation discriminates against a discrete and insular minority in violation of the equal protection clause.

The doctrine of substantive due process developed as the doctrine of economic due process declined and has important implications for contemporary legal debates on sexual privacy. Historically, the doctrine is substantiated by a series of decisions that debate the fundamental concept of "liberty" as guaranteed by the Fourteenth Amendment. In 1923, the Supreme Court in *Meyer v. Nebraska* directed that the right to education was a fundamental component of "liberty."

Again in 1925, the Court affirmed that education was fundamental to individual liberty and held in *Pierce v. Society of Sisters* that parents have the liberty to choose a private education for their children.

Until its decision in *Griswold v. Connecticut* (1965), the Supreme Court had interpreted "liberty" to include rights that are expressly implied in the Bill of Rights. Yet, in *Griswold*, the Court found unconstitutional a state law that prohibited the use of contraception. Critics of the decision argue that the Framers of the Constitution took special care to enumerate which individual rights were protected; modern courts should not read beyond those rights to recognize new rights unintended by the Framers. On the other hand, supporters of the decision in *Griswold* argue a functionalist interpretation: the Constitution is a living document and was meant by the Framers to be a flexible and adaptable blueprint for individual liberties. The expansion of substantive due process is largely built upon this functionalist philosophy, which in *Griswold* was used to argue that a penumbra of implied rights emanated from each express right. The Court referred to these emanations as "zones of privacy."

SEXUAL PRIVACY AND THE LAW

Many of the Supreme Court's most controversial decisions have granted rights that exist in the zones of privacy, namely, abortion, marriage, and contraception, but the Supreme Court has only recently recognized sexual autonomy as a fundamental component of liberty. In 1986, the Supreme Court in *Bowers v. Hardwick* upheld a Georgia law that criminalized sodomy (sexual activity that is not intended for the purpose of reproduction) based on the rationale that states have the power to regulate the public health, safety, and welfare. This decision was criticized on grounds both of substantive due process (sexual activity is an individual liberty) and of equal protection (because the sodomy law was applied only to acts of sodomy between same-sex participants rather than to acts between participants of the opposite sex).

AMERICAN CIVIL LIBERTIES UNION (ACLU)

Since 1920, the American Civil Liberties Union (ACLU) has been leading the battle to protect the civil liberties of citizens of the United States, particularly in regard to the right to free speech. The ACLU also works specifically with the LGBT community to ensure the installation of their constitutional rights. In this way, the ACLU often bridges the divide that sometimes exists between protecting the LGBT community and upholding civil liberties.

The ACLU has traditionally opposed cases that stripped students of their rights to free speech. The ACLU has recently supported the plaintiff in *Morse v. Frederick*, who was suspended in 2002 for displaying a sign saying "Bong Hits 4 Jesus" at a rally for the Olympic torch relay. The ACLU hopes that the Supreme Court will use the case to reaffirm its decision in *Tinker v. Bell*, which held that students retain their constitutional right to free speech while at school.

The Court's decision in *Bowers* was overruled in 2003 by its landmark decision in *Lawrence v. Texas*. Three justices dissented on grounds of stare decisis, the principle that laws should not be overturned, because people rely on laws for order and plan their lives accordingly. Justice Scalia further argued that the decision would result in the repeal of laws regulating bigamy, incest, same-sex marriage, and prostitution. The majority of justices, however, reasoned that consensual sex between adults is distinguishable from other sexual activities and ordered that the criminalization of these consensual, adult activities is a violation of the liberty guaranteed by the Fourteenth Amendment.

The Court's decision in *Lawrence* has been the high-water mark for sexual liberties under the doctrine of substantive due process. Many gay rights advocates hope that the decision will be used to further convince courts that there is a constitutional right to marry. Under substantive due process, this achievement would require courts to find the right to same-sex marriage within the penumbras emanating from the Bill of Rights. If the right is to be found under the equal protection clause, then it will require an application of strict scrutiny and, as discussed, this application would be given only if same-sex couples were proven to be a discrete and insular minority.

SEXUAL ORIENTATION AND HARASSMENT IN SCHOOLS

Gay harassment in schools is another issue that has been raised in the courts. In 1996, in *James Nabozny v. Mary Podlesny et al.,* the Seventh Circuit Court of Appeals ruled that a gay student's constitutional rights were violated when his school did not protect him from being harassed and attacked for being gay. James had been "mock raped" by two other male students in front of 20 other students. On another day, male students took James into the restroom and pushed his head into the toilet. And finally, on yet another day, James was beaten so badly by other students in the hallway that he collapsed from internal bleeding. The school administrator, Mary Podlesny, told James and his parents that "boys will be boys" and that James should be prepared to accept such treatment because he was gay. When the harassment did not stop, school officials suggested that James should take a break from school. After nearly two weeks away, James returned; the harassment continued and James eventually attempted suicide.

James Nabozny filed his claim on grounds of equal protection, arguing that he had been discriminated against because of his sex and because of his sexual orientation. As to the claim for sex discrimination, the court found that it had occurred, because the school district admitted that it would have treated the case differently if James had been a female student attacked by a male student. As to the claim for sexual orientation, the court found that homosexuals are a discrete and insular minority for purposes of equal protection and accordingly found that there was no rational basis for allowing James to be harassed and attacked for being gay.

In response to the increased reporting of circumstances like those of James Nabozny, legislatures have begun to consider laws that prohibit harassment and

GAY LESBIAN STRAIGHT EDUCATION NETWORK (GLSEN)

The Gay Lesbian Straight Education Network (GLSEN) began as a local group in 1990 and has since become a national group composed of chapters all around the country. GLSEN focuses its mission on creating a world in which every child learns to accept and respect all people, regardless of their sexual orientation and gender expression.

One area in which GLSEN has been most productive is in its registering of gay-straight alliance (GSA) organizations in high schools and middle schools all over the country. A GSA organization functions in a school as a safe place for LGBT students and their allies. In its biannual report detailing the harassment and violence that LGBT students endure, GLSEN notes that schools that have a GSA organization are considerably more safe for LGBT students.

A second area in which GLSEN has been active has been the legislative lobbying for antiharassment statutes that prevent bullying based on sexual orientation and transgender identity. While only a handful of states currently have such laws, GLSEN hopes that the groundwork it lays by its annual reporting and continuous lobbying efforts will create change in the near future.

---

bullying in schools. The Gay Lesbian Straight Education Network (GLSEN) defines this as one of their key objectives. Since 2001, GLSEN has published a biannual national report on the severity and pervasiveness of the harassment suffered in schools by lesbian, gay, bisexual, and transgender (LGBT) students. In 2004, GLSEN reported that 75 percent of students surveyed frequently heard the derogatory terms "faggot" or "dyke" at school and more than one-third of students surveyed reported experiencing physical harassment because of their sexual orientation or gender identity (Kosicw 2004).

The resistance to laws prohibiting harassment comes in many forms. Many policy makers are simply resistant to adding sexual orientation or transgender identity to any law that grants protections, for fear of strengthening the precedent for treating LGBT people as a discrete and insular minority. More interesting, however, are those legal advocates who are resistant to the antiharassment laws because of what they perceive as a conflict of interest between protecting the youth and protecting the values of free speech.

For example, this conflict was discussed by the Third Circuit Court of Appeals in *David Warren Saxe et al. v. State College Area School District et al.* The plaintiff had brought a challenge to the defendant's implementation of a harassment policy that included the typical prohibitions of harassment based on sex, race, color, national origin, age, and disability but went further to include a "catch-all category of 'other personal characteristics'" including clothing, appearance, hobbies, values, or social skills. The Third Circuit, in an opinion written by current Supreme Court Justice Samuel Alito, found the policy to be over-broad because it prohibited speech that was not vulgar and not sponsored by the school. The Court went on to state that the primary function of a public school is to educate its students and that unless speech is proven to be disruptive of this function, then it cannot be constitutionally prohibited.

The court's opinion in *Saxe* attempts to draw a line at which a student's right to free speech and expression overcomes another student's right to be free of harassment. On one side of the line, advocates for policies like the one implemented by the State College Area School District (SCAD) argue that language is a form of violence. An analogy might be drawn between verbal harassment and the violence suffered by James Nabozny: words, like physical violence, can be emotionally and psychically traumatizing to a student. Furthermore, harassment of any kind is an impediment to a student's right to education.

On the other side of the line, advocates for free speech argue that a person's substantive due process right to education and liberty does not extend to being free of any form of harassment at school. The danger in teaching children to be silent and not to acknowledge difference among individuals is more dangerous to democracy than is allowing students to be verbally taunted or even harassed. The speech that is prohibited by a policy such as SCAD's is distinguishable from the harassment endured by James Nabozny because that harassment clearly escalated to violence and inhibited Nabozny's ability to learn.

CONCLUSION

Today, while courts have incrementally protected lesbians, gays, and bisexuals, for the most part they continue to be seen as an unprotected group. The decriminalization of sodomy is one example of a federal legal protection; further successes have been limited to individual cases, as in the case of student James Nabozny, or to specific states, as in the case of the same-sex marriage law in Massachusetts.

In the case of school harassment, very few states have adopted laws that prevent bullying based on sexual orientation, gender identity, or other classes unrecognized by federal laws; but the debates that are occurring in statehouses regarding the principles of such legislation are debates that are grounded in the constitutional doctrines discussed above. The challenge of lawyers and advocates for LGBT people is to work within these complex frameworks of substantive due process and equal protection to find a balancing point of liberty that is also consistent with the values concerning free speech. More broadly, the legal framing of these debates will depend upon how the deeply entrenched values concerning privacy and the free expression of sexuality and gender evolve in the courts.

See also Lesbian, Gay, Bisexual, Transgender, and Queer Movements; Lesbians and Gays in the Military; Same-Sex Marriage; Sexual Identity and Orientation.

Further Reading: *Abrams v. United States,* 250 U.S. 616 (1919); Anderson, Ellen Ann, *Out of the Closets and into the Courts: Legal Opportunity Structure and Gay Rights Litigation* (Ann Arbor: University of Michigan Press. 2006); *Bowers v. Hardwick,* 478 U.S. 186 (1986); *David Warren Saxe et al. v. State College Area School District et al,* 240 F.3d 200 (3d Cir. 2001); Gerstmann, Evan, *The Constitutional Underclass: Gays, Lesbians, and the Failure of Class-Based Equal Protection* (Chicago: University of Chicago Press, 1999); GLSEN (Gay Lesbian Straight Education Network), "From Teasing to Torment: School Climate in America," October 2005, available at: http://www.glsen.org/cgi-bin/ iowa/all/library/record/1859.html, accessed June 9, 2007; Goldstein, Stephen, "Reflections on Developing Trends in the Law of Student Rights," 118 *U.Pa.L.Rev.* 612 (1970);

Griswold v. Connecticut, 381 U.S. 479 (1965); Ingber, Stanley, "Socialization, Indoctrination, or the 'Pall of Orthodoxy': Value Training in the Public Schools," *U.Ill.L.Rev.* 15 (1987); *James Nabozny v. Mary Podlesny et al.*, 92 F.3d 446 (7th Cir. 1996); Kosciw, J. G., *The 2003 National School Climate Survey: The School-Related Experience of Our Nation's Lesbian, Gay, Bisexual, and Transgender Youth* (New York: GLSEN, 2004); *Lawrence v. Texas*, 539 U.S. 558 (2003); *Lochner v. New York*, 198 U.S. 45 (1905); *Meyer v. Nebraska*, 262 U.S. 390 (1923); *Morse v. Frederick*, (06-278) U.S. Supreme Court slip opinion, October term 2006, decided June 25, 2007; *Pierce v. Society of Sisters*, 268 U.S. 510 (1925); *Romer v. Evans*, 517 U.S. 620 (1996); Rubenstein, William B., *Lesbians, Gay Men, and the Law* (New York: New Press, 1993); *The Slaughterhouse Cases*, 83 U.S. 36 (1873); *Sexual Harassment Guidance: Harassment of Students by School Employees, Other Students or Third Parties*, 62 Federal.Reg. 12034–50 (March 13, 1997); *Tinker v. Des Moines Independent Community School District (Tinker v. Bell)*, 393 U.S. 503 (1969); *United States v. Carolene Products*, 304 U.S. 144 (1938); Wright, R. George, "Free Speech Values, Public Schools, and the Role of Judicial Deference," *New England Law Review* 22, no. 59 (1987).

Derek Mize

SPORTS: PROFESSIONAL

Although women's participation in professional sports has historically been discouraged, their increased participation in professional sports, including basketball, soccer, golf, and tennis, has been debated on the grounds of whether women's athleticism is an appropriate expression of femininity and whether women deserve equity in pay, media coverage, and treatment within the male-dominated sporting industry.

BACKGROUND

Because of political pressure, opportunities for women in professional sports are increasing. In the United States there are new participatory sporting leagues and women are working as coaches, commentators, media broadcasters, referees, sports writers, and trainers in both men's and women's sports. The Women's National Basketball Association (WNBA) was successfully launched in 1997, albeit amid controversy; and several female tennis players, including sisters Venus and Serena Williams, have become media sensations, as have female golfers such as Korean American Michelle Wie (born 1989), who has also played on the male professional golf circuit. These openings, however, must be placed in social context and mediated by a discussion of cultural gender ideologies, patriarchal heteronormativity, social class and consumerism, postfeminism, and the politics of the women's movement as they have shaped the role of women in sports today.

WOMEN'S SPORTS AND GENDER EQUITY

Today, girls and women owe their opportunities for participation in professional sports to persistent and organized political pressure from members of the women's movement. For most of modern Western history, sporting activities were characterized as exclusively male pursuits, effectively excluding half the population from participating. To counter the notion that women are physically unable to play or are uninterested in sports, activist groups have had to engage in sustained and creative confrontations to challenge firmly entrenched gender ideologies. They have also worked to reconstruct family obligations, in order to garner the time and resources necessary for women's active involvement in sports. These efforts have occurred at the global, national, and local levels.

In the United States, the most famous and no doubt most influential formal challenge to men's dominance over sports resources occurred in 1972. After activists had for decades engaged in lobbying the United States Congress, legislation in the form of Title IX of the Educational Amendments was passed. Although it took five years before the government enforced the law proclaiming that sex could not be used to exclude persons from participation in educational programs funded by federal dollars, it had an immediate impact on the everyday lives of girls and women and helped to create many professional opportunities in sports. It is interesting to note that this law did not even mention athletics. As many scholars of gender will argue, this lacuna speaks to the reality that sports are a crucial site for the contestation of gender politics in (post)modern times.

Internationally, activists have argued that sports are important arenas for enriching the lives of individual women through self-knowledge and expression, social interaction, body awareness, improved long-term health, skill development, and sheer enjoyment. Further, some groups contend that women's sports participation enriches communities, as sports are vehicles for social integration. When women are active in their communities, more responsible development occurs.

Those convictions underlie the International Working Group on Women and Sport (IWG), an activist group that promotes the development of physical activity and sport involvement for girls and women globally. The IWG's influence and efforts are vast and range from grassroots support to lobbying governments to fund international sports programs for women. The IWG was first formed in 1994 at an internationally diverse conference held in England. Concerned delegates from over 85 countries met to develop global equity standards that were initially known as the "Brighton Declaration." The unanimously signed document is used internationally by activists as they press for equal access to sports resources and opportunities. The IWG meets every four years to reaffirm its commitment to physical activity for women and to assess progress. These efforts and other pressures represent the now globally established goal of guaranteeing women and girls the right to sports participation, inspired and motivated by the women's movement.

"YOU THROW LIKE A GIRL!" GENDER IDEOLOGIES AND SPORTS

In almost all societies and throughout history, women have been limited by gender ideologies claiming that athleticism is a male characteristic. Activities involving coordination coupled with physical and emotional strength, control, and skill were reserved for men. Women's supposed inferiority in sports has long been seen as natural and the narratives surrounding sports support this notion. As dominant ideology paints women as the opposite of men; taunting a boy by saying "he throws like a girl" is a common critical remark rhetorically framing girls' performance as the opposite of the performance of good (presumably male) athletes.

As social constructions, gender categories must be continually reified by people "doing" gender. "Doing gender involves a complex of socially guided perceptual, interactional, and micropolitical activities that cast particular pursuits as expressions of masculine and feminine 'natures'" (West and Zimmerman 1987, 126). Because gender ideologies become embodied, they are built into kinesthetic awareness of the way people move and experience the world with and through their bodies. This is one distinctive way in which sports, including athletics, matter in theorizing the implications of gender. Many feminist scholars argue that through sports, women tap into and utilize the power of their bodies and that this may have the transformative effect of empowering them. When society sees girls and women participate in a myriad of physical activities, it is challenging to the gender order, and this is why sports have been important sites for negotiating ideology.

Gender is powerfully displayed through sporting bodies, and institutionally sports, including athletics, are a primary site for the ideological construction of women and men as biologically different and as opposites. Physical activities are based on expectations and values that vary according to whether we are dealing with informal group recreation or inflexible, bureaucratically controlled sports organized for maximum individual competition. Sport sociologist Jay Coakley (2004) effectively contends that in the United States today, athletic activities are best understood as privileging a "power and performance" model. Here, sports that emphasize domination, competition, risk taking, quantitative record keeping, exclusive participation, hierarchy, and lifestyle-dominating commitment are prized, to the disadvantage of other ways of "doing" sports. These ideals are

BABE DIDRIKSON ZAHARIAS, A WOMAN AHEAD OF HER TIME?

Babe Didrikson Zaharias, more commonly known as Babe Didrikson or simply "Babe" (1911–1956), grew up as a tomboy and played many sports traditionally viewed as belonging to the male domain, including basketball, track, golf, baseball, tennis, swimming, diving, boxing, volleyball, handball, bowling, billiards, skating, and cycling (Schwartz 2007). At a time when women were viewed as freakish or inappropriate, Babe qualified for five events in the track competition at the 1932 Olympics. She went on to become a golf star, winning 55 tournament victories, including three U.S. Women's Open tournaments. With her husband, George Zaharias, Patty Berg, and Fred Corcoran, she founded the Ladies Professional Golf Association (LPGA) in 1949. Babe was once voted the "Greatest Female Athlete" by the Associated Press. Despite criticism aimed at her from the media and from sports fans, she overcame great obstacles in order to pursue her athletic goals and passions. Biographer Susan E. Cayleff (1995, 1) says of Babe: "Her name, image, and impact transcended her deeds. She was like Muhammad Ali, whose magnetic presence overshadowed not only his competitors, but his era." Didrikson died of cancer at the age of 45.

located in traditional masculine social constructions and are the standard by which sports forms are evaluated today. Football is now considered "America's pastime," as it epitomizes hegemonic masculinity, and although women have organized football leagues, they are not highly visible. When women play football organized for them by dominant groups it is called "powder puff football." Power and performance sports highlight powerful bodily performances and have been used as evidence of men's aggressive nature, their superiority over women, and their right to claim social and physical space as their own.

Prior to the mid 1970s, most people in society believed that women were too fragile to play sports. Traditional definitions of femininity relegated women to sports that could demonstrate their "natural" inclinations to grace and beauty, such as figure skating and gymnastics. Some women participated in swimming, tennis, and golf, but the power, strength, and speed aspects of those sports were downplayed. When organizers of professional tennis tournaments realized that women were competing "like men," they reduced the number of sets that women were required to play, justifying women's smaller earnings and alleging women's limited fitness.

Women athletes have demonstrated that claims to female fragility are rooted in ideology, not nature. In 1973, the famous match between female tennis pro Billie Jean King and former male tennis pro Bobby Riggs caught the eyes of the nation. At the height of the second wave women's movement, Riggs challenged King to play him in a "Battle of the Sexes" match on national television, which ended in King's victory. While clearly this match involved as much spectacle and sensationalism as actual sporting expertise, it nonetheless marked a historical moment in which a female athlete demonstrated that women are not always the "weaker sex."

PROFESSIONAL SPORTING LEAGUES

Historically, women's sporting leagues have ebbed and flowed, often reflecting the broader demand of U.S. culture to highlight women's athleticism when there has been a shortage of men, as in the case of the women's softball leagues established during World War II. As soon as the war ended, most of these women, many of whom had become excellent players, were asked to "return to their homes" so that men's sports could continue "as usual." This course of events, which was depicted in the 1992 Hollywood film, *A League of Their Own,* has occurred in other sports as well.

More recently, in the 1990s, an attempt was made for women to gain control over a women's professional sport, with the inauguration of the American Basketball League (ABL) in 1996 and the Women's National Basketball Association (WNBA) in 1997. The ABL played from October until March; players had salaries in the $40,000–$150,000 range; and the league was totally independent and self-supporting. The players had stock options in their organizations, played with the same size ball as men, used the same type of shots and shot clock, had timeouts and quarters, and played 44 games per season (Kampfner 2001, cited in Costa 2003, 156). Yet despite their tremendous start, ultimately they failed and had to dismantle the ABL the following year. Why did they fail? To begin with, there was scant media attention: the media knew that the WNBA, the "sister" league of the NBA, was about to be launched. As a result, the media paid little attention to the ABL. Second, the ABL did not have sufficient financial backing. Whereas the WNBA had 11 sponsors and full financial backing from the corresponding NBA franchises, the ABL had little sponsor support and remained largely marginalized in mainstream press coverage of sports. Also, whereas the ABL season took place during the traditional basketball winter months with the men's NBA games, the WNBA season was arranged to take place during the summer months so as not to compete with the men's games.

To date, the teams of the WNBA and the NBA are the only professional teams that are close to gender and racial equity. This equality is the direct result of the way in which the WNBA was established. The commissioner of the NBA insisted that the women's teams be equal partners with their counterpart organizations in the NBA. They were given equal access to the same facilities for practices and games; equal access to coaching, media representation, officiating, and medical facilities; and most importantly, equal access to revenue dollars (Costa 2003). A total of 27 percent of WNBA players are from outside the United States, and many players spend the off-season playing for European teams.

In other sports, including golf and tennis, women's earnings have never equaled those of men, although the gender gap is closing in some sports and/or tournaments. For example, from 1996 to 2000, the annual LPGA prizes rose from $26.5 million to $38.5 million, a positive step, although men's prizes in the PGA range from $70 million to $167 million. Among the four Grand Slam tennis tournaments, held each year in Australia, France, Britain, and the United States, only Wimbledon continues to pay men more in winnings. According to one observer (Associated Press 2006), the All England Club argues that it is being fair to the men, while women tennis players call the practice a relic of the "Victorian Era." Additional sports that have been extremely supportive of women's leagues include soccer and volleyball, two sports that are played by women around the world. Despite the lack of support for male soccer teams in the United States, the women's national soccer team has won two Olympic gold medals (1996 and 2004), two Women's World Cups (1991 and 1999), and five Algarve Cups (2000, 2003, 2004, 2005, and 2007), attracting new forms of support and new respect for women's soccer in a country where the media and sporting industries have traditionally downplayed this sport because it represents cultures from which new Americans emigrated rather than the "new country" (Hartmann and Pfister 2003).

GENDER INEQUITIES IN SPORTS

While women have acquired some rights within professional sports, gender inequities in sports continue at institutional levels, both within the United States and globally. Simply counting the number of prospects for women in sports demonstrates the unequal distribution of resources and chances to play. For example, the 2004 Olympics in Athens had 125 medal events for women and 166 for men—of the 10,568 athletes, 41 percent were women. Women's groups are currently challenging the International Olympic Committee's decision to eliminate softball as an event for women in the 2012 games. Included in the basic demand for gender equity and fairness is the recognition that softball can be played in "discreet" dress, which is particularly important for increasing the opportunities of Olympic participation for Muslim women (Feminist Majority Foundation 2007).

Prior to the 1980s, the longest distance women were permitted to run in track and field events was 1,500 meters. The Olympic Games' most famous race, the marathon, was reserved for men; organizers argued that women's health would be negatively affected if they ran such a distance. Several women runners, activists, and legislators demonstrated marathon success and then demanded that women have the right to run marathons. Seeing the opportunity to link their products with healthy active women, a number of corporations sponsored women's marathons in the 1980s and the event became almost mainstream (Lovett 1997).

MEDIA COVERAGE OF WOMEN IN SPORTS

The increased presence of women in professional sports has led to their increased coverage in the media. For the first time in history, beginning in the early 1990s, women have been able to see their exploits in sports consistently covered by the media. Although the amount and level of detail pales in com-

---

BEND IT LIKE BECKHAM: FILM PORTRAYALS OF WOMEN'S SOCCER

Recent film productions from around the world have positively portrayed women entering the traditionally male domain of sports. The British film *Bend It like Beckham* (2002) depicts the clash of cultural ideologies present in two girls' lives as they explore their passion for soccer. One girl, Jess, is from an immigrant Punjabi family and her parents must contend with their daughter's dreams of becoming a soccer star like male soccer superstar David Beckham; the other, a white British girl, Jules, must contend with her mother's concern about her "becoming a lesbian." In Jess's case, because her parents prohibit her from playing soccer, she must sneak out to continue playing with her team, not always successfully hiding her passion. In the end, Jess's father comes to appreciate his daughter's talent, and her parents end up supporting her decision to attend college in the United States on a soccer scholarship.

Offside, a 2006 Iranian film, documents persistent gender biases in Iranian law that do not allow women or girls to attend public soccer matches. The film takes place during the 2005 World Cup qualifying match between Iran and Bahrain, and depicts several young women who each, for a variety of reasons, attempt to sneak into the game disguised as men. Discovered by the stadium police, they spend most of the game "offside," in a makeshift enclosed area outside the stadium walls, awaiting their transfer to jail. As with *Bend It like Beckham,* *Offside* highlights the contradictions experienced by family members and observers as they themselves must come to grips with their own reasons for barring women from either playing or viewing sports.

---

parison with men's sports, there are increasing outlets for information. The media are a major force behind crafting the messages and meanings of women in professional sports. The Ladies Professional Golf Association (LPGA) tour is consistently televised, as are many WNBA events and women's tennis matches that were previously viewed only on select channels or given sideline coverage. However, women's ice skating competitions receive the highest viewer ratings and many scholars attribute this popularity to the ideology of women in grace-and-beauty sports reifying gender expectations (Coakley 2004).

While the amount of coverage is modestly increasing, the form that the coverage takes is rather stereotypical. Women athletes feel as much pressure to look pretty (in that traditional, heterosexually seductive manner) as to hone their sporting skills. Many of the 2004 Olympic athletes posed for *Sports Illustrated* magazine in stages of undress, rather than in action photographs of their involvement in their respective sports, as most men are depicted. In 1999, after scoring the winning goal in the World Cup, soccer star Brandi Chastain peeled off her jersey revealing a discreet sports bra. This image of sheer joy and exuberance was translated into what the media referred to as a "strip tease" and she was offered endorsement deals for lingerie and later posed naked for a men's magazine (Messner, Duncan, and Cooky et al. 2003). Players in the WNBA are most often photographed in street clothes and with their children in an effort to frame this league as offering wholesome family entertainment. Many observers have pointed out that homophobia and women's sports have a long history and that the media most often objectify women athletes in a way that has historically pleased men (Kane 1998).

CONCLUSION

Because of political pressure and strongly motivated athletes, opportunities for women in professional sports are increasing. However, these openings must be placed in their social context and mediated by a discussion of social class and consumerism, the politics of gender roles, and gender equity advocates' demands in the shaping of modern sports industries. As many women have shown that they can play, perform, and succeed while maintaining their health and even raising families, historical arguments against women playing professional sports on the basis of their health are waning. However, female athletes are still portrayed by the media as graceful rather than strong, and as beautiful rather than powerful. An entire cosmetic fitness industry has surfaced, focusing on women as consumers of athletic products, with the idea of maintaining bodies that are attractive, rather than bodies that are active in sports. As many feminist and sports scholars continue to point out, in order for equity to be achieved in sports, such traditional gender ideologies must be challenged.

See also Affirmative Action; Equal Rights Amendment; Title IX and Women's Sports.

Further Reading: Associated Press, "Men's Winner Will Still Earn More than Women's," April 26, 2006; Cayleff, Susan E., *Babe Didrikson: The Greatest Female Athlete of All Time* (Urbana: University of Illinois Press, 1995); Coakley, Jay, *Sports in Society: Issues and Controversies,* 4th ed. (New York: McGraw Hill, 2005); Costa, Margaret D., "Social

Issues in American Women's Sports," in *Sport and Women: Social Issues in International Perspective,* ed. Ilse Hartmann-Tews and Gertrude Pfister, 145–160 (New York: Routledge, 2003); Feminist Majority Foundation, "Gender Equality in Athletics and Sports," 2007, available at: http://www.feminist.org/sports/olympics.asp/, accessed August 28, 2007; Griffin, Pat, *Strong Women, Deep Closets: Lesbians and Homophobia in Sport* (Champaign, IL: Human Kinetics, 1998); Hartmann-Twes, Ilse, and Gertrude Pfister, eds., *Sport and Women: Social Issues in International Perspective* (New York: Routledge, 2003); Heywood, Leslie, and Shari L. Dworkin, *Built to Win: The Female Athlete as Cultural Icon* (Minneapolis: University of Minnesota Press, 2003); Kampfner, Judith, "The End of the American Basketball League," *Sportsjanes Newsletter,* August 2001, 1–4; Kane, M., and H. Lensky, "Media Treatment of Female Athletes: Issues of Gender and Sexualities," in *Media Sport: Cultural Sensibilities and Sports in the Media Age,* 186–201 (New York: Routledge, 1998); Lovett, Charles, *Olympic Marathon: A Centennial History of the Games' Most Storied Race* (London: Praeger, 1997); Messner, Michael A., Margaret Carlisle Duncan, and Cheryl Cooky, "Silence, Sports Bras, and Wrestling Porn: Women in Televised Sports News and Highlights Shows," *Journal of Sport and Social Issues* 27, no. 1 (2003): 38–51; Schwartz, Larry, "Babe Didrikson Was a Woman ahead of Her Time," ESPN.Com News, 2007, available at: http://espn.go.com/sportscentury/features/00014147.html, accessed: May 29, 2007; West Candace, and Don H. Zimmerman, "Doing Gender," *Gender and Society* 1 (1987): 125–151.

Carla Corroto

TERRORISM AND NATIONAL SECURITY

Debates on what constitutes terrorism and responses to it in the form of national security involve historical and cultural perceptions of nationality, gender, family life, and citizenship. The debate about who is a terrorist and what should be national policy regarding terrorism is a contentious discourse with significant ramifications for women. Often, organized violence against women, such as rape, has not been considered a form of terrorism. Similarly, violent acts that prevent women from carrying out their caregiving roles have been left unexamined.

BACKGROUND

Terrorism, like nationalism, is related to political legitimacy. Global terrorism encompasses any collectively planned and systematically implemented injurious acts by a group against another group for political and economic goals (Gerami and Lehnerer, 2007). The gendered nature of terrorism and nationalism is revealed in the manipulation of biological sex and the cultural role expectations that accompany it. Consequently, global terrorism and national security become interrelated processes that affect women in many ways, from bodily injury including sexual assault to deliberate disruption of their social roles as caregivers.

Systematic sexual assault is a strategy of terrorizing a population, destabilizing a community, and challenging its national security. It is uniquely directed at women's bodies and at women's ability to reproduce. Rape is more than humiliation of the female victim and an attack on her (presumably male) partner; it is used to annihilate an ethnic group through forced impregnation and childbearing (Allen 1996). The cases of Bosnia-Herzegovina and Rwanda serve as examples of the ways in which women's bodies and social roles can be used to construct ethnic unity, territorial integrity, and national security. The relationship of Iraqi women to American women illustrates a more subtle effect of fighting, or conversely, using terrorism to secure national security. In this case the social roles of women as nurturers and caregivers are used to create and defend political policies that pit women against each other based on nationality and ethnicity.

BOSNIA-HERZEGOVINA: MASS RAPE FOR THE SAKE OF ETHNIC HOMOGENEITY

The UN Commission on Human Rights in 1993 recognized systematic rape, forced slavery, forced pregnancy, and forced prostitution of women as war crimes (Barstow 2000, 237). In 1996, eight Bosnian Serb military and police officers were indicted on charges of raping Bosnian Muslim women (Enloe 2000, 135). It has become evident from the proceedings of the War Crimes Tribunal in The Hague, Netherlands, that Serbia is the modern exemplar for the use of women's bodies through rape as a weapon of war. The actions of the Serbian military (1991–1995) were directed at women's bodies and their reproductive capabilities with the goal of terrorism and ethnic cleansing.

Ethnic cleansing is accomplished through the use of "concentration camps, torture, sexual violence, mass killings, forced deportations, destruction of private and cultural property, pillage and theft, and the blocking of humanitarian aid" (Bassiouni and McCormick 1996, 5). Although all of these tactics were utilized by the Serbs, it was the use of rape and forced pregnancy that was most significant in regard to the construction of national security. It is estimated that twenty thousand women were tortured and raped during this conflict. The goal of this policy was to create a "greater Serbia" that would be a religiously, culturally, and linguistically homogenous Serbian nation (Bassiouni and McCormick 1996). This policy was planned and implemented by Serbian political and military leaders with the support of Serbian and Bosnian Serb armies and paramilitary groups.

The history of this policy begins in 1992 with the release of a Serbian ruling party document entitled "Warning" (Salzman 2000). This document, focusing on demographic issues, highlighted the fact that Albanians, Muslims, and Roman Catholics had much higher birthrates than Serbian women. A resolution was drafted that mandated a program of "population renewal." This program outlined a policy that was intended to stimulate birthrates in Serbian parts of the country and to deliberately lower birthrates in non-Serbian parts of the country. The Serbian Orthodox Church identified the low birthrate of Serbian women as the "White Plague" (Papic 1995). With the combination of political and religious forces, the cultural stage was set for the use of women's bodies to destroy the enemy's community, forge nationalism, and achieve security. Serbian women's bodies were to produce soldiers for themselves, Serbia, and God. Non-Serbian women's bodies were targeted for rape that ended in either death or impregnation.

Referring to the Serbian military policy of genocidal rape to achieve ethnic cleansing, Allen (1996) identifies three practices making it clear that the use of rape had as its endpoint ethnic cleansing. First, prior to the arrival of the Serbian military, locals who supported Serbian policy would publicly rape the women in their community. The women and other members of the community would flee and be unlikely to return, knowing that their assailants were there. Second, within Serb concentration camps, Bosnian-Herzegovinian and Croatian women were raped and then murdered. Third, at the "rape/death camps," the Serbians practiced forced impregnation through rape. As Allen (1996) points out, this last practice does not seem like a logical way to achieve ethnic cleansing. But, if we turn to the dialectical relationship between terrorism and national security we find logic behind this practice.

The reproduction of a "desirable" population as a means of achieving national security can only be understood if we recognize that the Serbs accepted the patriarchal myth that the father determines the ethnic identity of the child. What makes this belief even more powerful is the fact that it was also accepted by the victims, their families, and their communities (Salzman 2000, 79). As women from the rape/death camps have reported, their attackers would say they intended to have the women produce "Chetnik" or Serbian babies (Stiglmayer 1994). The intended outcome of ethnic cleansing is to remove the undesirables that are perceived as a threat to ethnic domination and national security. Fear of the "other" is the strong cord that links terrorism, national security, and gender. Fear of the other can be triggered internally as in the Serbian case or externally as in the Rwandan case.

DID YOU KNOW?

- The first International Tribunal on Crimes Against Women took place in 1976. It was attended by over 2,000 activists, policy-makers, and advocates from over 40 countries. This and later conferences addressing systematic patterns of rape in war-torn countries such as the former Yugoslavia and Rwanda led to the establishment of institutional mechanisms for addressing rape as a war crime, as a crime against humanity, and/or as an act of genocide; the three areas covered in the jurisdiction of the International Criminal Court, which took force in 2002.

- The Rome Statute, the treaty that established the International Criminal Court in 2002, includes as rape those situations where the victim is deprived of her ability to consent to sex, including providing sex to avoid harm or to obtain basic necessities.

- The Rome Statute states that when rape and sexual violence are committed as part of a widespread or systematic attack directed against any civilian population, they are considered crimes against humanity, and in some cases may constitute an element of genocide.

Source: Amnesty International, "Rape As a Tool of War: A Fact Sheet," available at: http://www.amnestyusa. org/women/pdf/rapeinwartime.pdf.

RWANDA: RAPE AS A MEANS TO TERRORIZE

The civil war in Rwanda (1993–1994) must be placed in historical context to appreciate the influence of colonization. The Banyarwandans, as they were known before colonialism, were composed of social strata defined by their relation to property, power, and the sharing of a language (Flanders 2000). The crossing of lines between groups was practiced, yielding a flexible and productive state in the middle of Africa. Belgium colonialists, applying nineteenth-century race theory, took over this state and began to classify groups according to "race." The Tutsis were identified as the "superior" race because of a mythologized connection to European roots. Tutsi women were idealized as being more beautiful than Hutu women. This idealization eventually set the stage for the events of 1994.

In addition, colonists backed the Tutsi leadership in their suppression of the Hutu. Most significant is the fact that the Belgium colonialists instituted a policy that not only grouped people according to "race" but issued identity cards that placed all Rwandans in groups. These groups were given more or less political power dependent upon Belgium backing. When independence was achieved in 1959, the members of the Tutsi minority not only lost power but were the recipients of a deadly backlash against past aggression. Over time and through many waves of violence between the Tutsis and the Hutus, Tutsi women were singled out by propagandists as "seductress spies" or female "serpents." Propagandists promoted a stereotype of Tutsi women as "arrogant, deceptive, and sexually special" (Flanders 2000, 97). When the genocide of 1994 began, Hutus were culturally prepared to wreak havoc on the bodies of Tutsi women. The "European" physiology of these women, including noses, necks, and fingers as well as genitals, was attacked symbolically and physically. As one survivor states, it was as if her rapist wanted to "see what Tutsis look like inside" (Flanders 2000, 97).

Between April and July of 1994, it is estimated that between 500,000 and one million men, women, and children were murdered in Rwanda. This genocide was perpetrated by the ruling Hutu government against the Tutsi minority and moderate Hutus. Women were systematically raped and often killed, with the intent of (1) dishonoring the women, and (2) making them unable to have Tutsi children. In contrast to the Serbian intent to produce more Serbians, the Hutus' intent was to ensure there would be no more Tutsis. This strategy was driven by the fact that the Tutsis, by cultural practice, would not marry a woman who had been raped by a Hutu (Barstow 2000, 238). The mark of the other on a woman's body made her a threat to ethnic unity and national security.

THE WAR ON TERROR: THE BOND THAT BINDS IRAQI AND AMERICAN WOMEN

The United States' War on Terror, culminating in the 2003 invasion of Iraq, connects Iraqi and American women across international borders in the name of national security. Iraqi women and girls pay for America's definition of national security in many ways: they are victims of car bombings and random killings by insurgents or raids by U.S. forces. They lose children and other family members and are becoming heads of households as men are killed, imprisoned, or leave to find work in neighboring countries. They are harassed by extremist forces on all sides as a convenient target of factional fights. Many are forced to leave their homes and become internally displaced persons or refugees outside the country.

For Iraqi women, Saddam Hussein's regime was a double-edged sword of socialist gender equality and cruel suppression of ethnic minorities. Iraqi women had one of the highest levels of legal protection among Arab countries. But Saddam Hussein's desire for regional control and his manipulation by the superpowers exposed Iraqi women to the hardship of three wars (war with Iran, 1980–1988; war with Kuwait, 1991; and war with America, 2003), the longest recorded embargo, and foreign invasions. Kurdish, Shiite, and now Sunni women continue to pay the double price of gender and ethnicity.

From 1991 to 2003, Iraqi women suffered the physical and social consequences of a long and difficult scarcity, planned presumably to stifle Hussein's plans for global terrorism and guarantee the national security of the Western powers. The effects of sanctions on the population were more severe than the effects of the eight-year war with Iran. After the Iran/Iraq war, Iraq was 50th out of 130 countries on the UNDP Human Development Index, with 97 percent of urban and 78 percent of rural population receiving primary healthcare and a school attendance rate of 83 percent. By 1995, Iraq had descended to 106th out of 174 countries and by 2000 to 126th. Between 1995 and 2000, infant mortality, which had declined during the two wars to about 60 per 1,000 live births, skyrocketed to 107 per 1,000 live births. The effects of this process of *de-development* are 10 times greater than the effects of the civil strife in Rwanda or of HIV/AIDS in South Africa (UNICEF 2003).

Since the start of the U.S./Iraq war in 2003, the conflict has seen over 3,000 American soldiers killed and an estimated 54,000 Iraqi civilians becoming casualties (Iraq Body Count Project January 2007). More than one million people have been internally displaced due to the 1991 war, Saddam Hussein's policies, and the current war. The fate of Iraqi women goes beyond death and the loss of loved ones. The current Iraqi government does not have the budget or the bureaucratic machinery to care for the families of dead soldiers or civilians. Amnesty International warns of the hazards of insecurity for women, including a potential rise in domestic violence (2005). Women who have lost husbands or family members to random car bombings or shootings fare badly when attempting to care for children. A report issued in November 2004 documented a 7 percent increase in malnutrition among children under the age of five since the current war began (Vick 2004). Since women are socially responsible for the care of children, caring for their families under the conditions of war is an often invisible burden that they have to bear.

American women have two interlocking functions in the post-9/11 War on Terror. Their role in the military campaign in Iraq is used to gender the war and make it inclusive. Politicians, speakers, and the media often use variations on the theme of "our men and women" in Iraq, "our men and women soldiers," and "our young men and women in uniform." This challenges the soldier-as-masculine notion, makes the war inclusive and more humane, and elicits a supportive response. While it is true that women make up approximately 10 percent (17,000 members) of the forces conducting the military operation in Iraq (Ginty 2005), what is left unsaid is the high concentration of working class and racial minorities in the troops.

Similarly, variations on the words "military families" are intended to make the War on Terror part of the "family values" campaign of the conservative right in America. Another aspect of women's roles in the campaign is the use of military families against the antiwar/peace movement. During the past five years, whenever there is a sign declaring "Peace," or "Stop the War," there is an opposition sign, not expressing support for the war but saying "Support Our Troops."

Those with family members involved in the war pay a psychological, financial, and emotional price of government policy. The physical cost to women is less severe than the psychological and financial hardships they endure. They struggle with anxiety for family members' safety, and those who have lost loved ones always carry the emotional pain of the question, "Was it worth it?"

The roles of American and Iraqi women collide when we consider that a declared message of the war on terrorism is the liberation of Muslim women from the tyranny of their culture. According to Mrs. Laura Bush in a radio address of November 17, 2001, "The fight against terrorism is also a fight for the rights and dignity of women." By constructing Arab and Muslim women as victims in need of U.S. liberation, American policy makes violence against women an essential element in any definition of terrorism and national security. Hatem refers to this as "condescending" (2005, 39); and Cooke points out that "Politics in the era of U.S. empire disappears behind the veil of women's victimization" (2002, 469); that is, that political motives hide behind a humanitarian screen. Ironically, when fighting Soviet expansionism, the same imperialist notion of national security ignored the terrorizing of Afghan women by the Mojahidin and later by the Taliban, and dismissed women's calls for action against these groups.

CONCLUSION

An act of violence becomes terrorism when it is so defined, first, by those with the power of definition, and, second, by the victims. For the victims' definition to become accepted, ultimately it needs the powerful group's blessing, otherwise it will remain a marginal definition. In the cases covered, manipulating women's ability to reproduce and their social obligation to care for others became the cornerstone of terrorist as well as national security strategies. Therefore, any comprehensive discussion of terrorism and national security must include recognition and an examination of the various forms of violence directed at women and their dependents.

See also Colonialism and Imperialism; Leftist Armed Struggle; Nationalism; Sexual Assault and Sexual Harassment.

Further Reading: Allen, B., *Rape Warfare: The Hidden Genocide in Bosnia-Herzegovina and Croatia* (Minneapolis: University of Minnesota Press, 1996); Amnesty International, "Iraq: Iraqi Women—The Need for Protective Measures," 2005, available at: http://web.amnesty.org/library/index/engmde140042005; Barstow, A. L., ed., *War's Dirty Secret: Rape, Prostitution, and Other Crimes against Women* (Cleveland, OH: Pilgrim Press,

2000); Bassiouni, C., and M. McCormick, *Sexual Violence: An Invisible Weapon of War in the Former Yugoslavia* (Chicago: International Human Rights Law Institute, 1996); Cooke, M., "Saving Brown Women," *Signs* 28, no. 1 (2002): 468–470; Enloe, C., *Maneuvers: The International Politics of Militarizing Women's Lives* (Berkeley: University of California Press, 2000); Flanders, L., "Rwanda's Living Casualties," in *War's Dirty Secret: Rape, Prostitution, and Other Crimes against Women,* ed. A. L. Barstow, 95–100 (Cleveland, OH: Pilgrim Press, 2000); Gerami, S., and M. Lehnerer, "Gendered Aspects of War and International Violence," in *Blackwell Encyclopedia of Sociology,* ed. G. Ritzer, vol. 5, 1885–1888 (Oxford: Blackwell, 2007); Ginty, M., "Record Number of Female Soldiers Fall," 2005, available at: http://www.womensenews.org/article.cfm/dyn/aid/2226/context/cover/; Hatem, M., "Arab Americans and Arab American Feminisms after September 11, 2001: Meeting External and Internal Challenges Facing Our Communities," *MIT Electronic Journal of Middle East Studies* 5 (Spring 2005): 37–49; Iraq Body Count Project 2007, available at: http://www.iraqbodycount.net/background.htm, accessed January 2007; Papic, Z., "How to Become a 'Real' Serbian Woman?" *War Report,* no. 36 (1995): 41; Salzman, T., "Rape Camps, Forced Impregnation, and Ethnic Cleansing," in *War's Dirty Secret: Rape, Prostitution, and Other Crimes against Women,* ed. A. L. Barstow, 63–92 (Cleveland, OH: Pilgrim Press, 2000); Stiglmayer, A., "The War in the Former Yugoslavia," in *Mass Rape: The War against Women in Bosnia-Herzegovina,* ed. A. Stiglmayer, 1–34 (Lincoln: University of Nebraska Press, 1994); UNICEF, "The Situation of Children in Iraq: An Assessment Based on the UN's Convention on the Right of the Child," March 2003, available at: http://www.unicef.org/pubsgen/situation-children-iraq/children-of-iraq.pdf; Vick, K., "Children Pay Cost of Iraq's Chaos: Malnutrition Nearly Double What It Was before Invasion," *Washington Post,* November 21, 2004, A1, available at: http://washingtonpost.com/wp-dyn/artcles/A809–2004Nov20.html.

Shahin Gerami and Melodye Lehnerer

THIRD GENDERS

"Third gender" is a concept that loosely refers to those individuals whose identities fall outside the Western binary of traditional male and female gender identities, roles, and forms of expression. Western scholars disagree as to whether third genders are simply deviant expressions of the traditional male versus female gender binary, or whether they represent a broader range of gender identity and expression that is simply limited by Western philosophical and medical understandings of identity.

BACKGROUND

There is inconsistency in the terminology that is used for third gender individuals across historical time periods and in different cultures. The clearest distinctions are between those individuals who assume a gender role not usually associated with their sex type due to cultural needs of inheritance and family leadership but are *not* seen as third genders; those who are seen as not-men and not-women, who fulfill occupational or spiritual roles in their communities, and *are* accepted as third genders; and finally, those who defy the connection between biology and gender and display alternative gender conceptions but are *denied* third gender recognition. While perhaps a matter of semantics, these differences tell us quite a lot about a particular culture's understandings of gender and level of patriarchal control.

Whereas in Western culture, biology is the primary means by which gender is understood, in other cultures around the world one's occupation, social role, or spiritual role may predominate in terms of how gender is understood and how familial and community gender relations are organized. The *hijras* of northern India, for example, are among the most visible and culturally accepted third genders in the world (Nanda 1998). In Hindu traditions, multiple sexes and genders among humans and deities are often celebrated. *Hijras,* typically young boys who either choose to become *hijra* or are offered by their families to a *hijra* community, undergo ritual castration and dress as women. The name is sometimes translated as *eunich,* although in modern times some *hijra* may identify as transgender, cross-dressers, or gay men. After their operation and bodily transformation, they become agents of the Mother Goddess and acquire a spiritual status in traditional Hindu communities. They perform at weddings, births, and festivals, bestowing good fortune upon the participants. While sometimes viewed as objects of scorn, especially in contemporary society with its increasingly Westernized attitudes, this scorn is sometimes limited by the fact that their powers can also be used to bring misfortune upon a newly married couple or a newborn.

Another example concerns the *mahu* ("half-man, half-woman") of Tahiti and contemporary Hawaii. *Mahu* are males (as defined at birth) who take on feminine traits. In Samoa, males who take on feminine characteristics are called *fa'afafine* ("like a woman"); in Tonga they are called *fakaleiti* ("lady"). In Polynesia, these gender variants are not associated with a specific ideology, sacred meaning, or cultural role. The main signifier is that they engage in women's work. Other feminine gender markers include dress, speech, and dance.

The *acault* of Southeast Asia are men who take on feminine behaviors and traits due to spirit possession by the goddess Manguedon. They act as shamans and seers and are valued for the good fortune and success they bring as agents of the goddess.

ALBANIAN SWORN VIRGINS

Albanian "sworn virgins" are honorary men living mostly in remote areas of the northern part of the country. Their existence is a response to the need for a male head of household in a strict patriarchal society. If a family is without a son, there is no one to inherit the house, head the family, take care of the parents' souls after death, or defend the family. The "sworn virgins" wear men's clothing and take on men's roles, for example, taking up arms in blood feuds to defend the family's honor and representing the family in village meetings. In all cases, sworn virgins are celibate and can never marry or have children. Sworn virgins are not men because they identify as men in terms of biology or gender identification; rather, they become social men due to the specific social and economic needs of their culture.

In many African societies, women may become social males with all the privileges men enjoy; these women have been called "female husbands" by Western anthropologists. They own property and participate in community politics. The social male pays bridewealth for a wife and becomes the legal and social father of the wife's children. This is the case, for instance, among the Nandi of Kenya, where the female husband is an older woman who has not produced a male heir.

NATIVE AMERICAN THIRD AND FOURTH GENDERS/TWO SPIRITS

As elsewhere, third genders exist in North America, although scholars disagree as to how to conceptualize their identities. Historically, alternative gender roles were a distinctive aspect of some native societies throughout North America. They were originally known as *berdache* (a term meaning "male prostitute"), but today many of them self-identify as " two-spirit" people, a term also reclaimed by gay and lesbian Native Americans in recent decades. Will Roscoe has documented third genders (male-bodied two spirits) and fourth genders (female-bodied two spirits) in numerous North American tribes. According to Roscoe's accounts, the specifics of their gender behaviors were quite variable. Some cross-dressed, while others did not; some performed the work of both males and females, others the work of only one gender. In fact, the range of terms used for third and fourth gender people in different tribal languages demonstrates the adaptation of tribal cultures to the reality of two-spirit people. By the late 1800s, Native Americans were a conquered people and two-spirit people particularly suffered. As a consequence of the colonizers' rejection of two-spirit people, they were jailed, killed, or forced to use clothes and hair cuts different from those they wanted (Roscoe 1998).

THIRD GENDERS IN THE CONTEMPORARY UNITED STATES

Gender is viewed as an incontrovertible biological fact in the United States; this is a cultural assumption that makes the idea of third gender impossible to understand for most people. If someone identifies as a transsexual (a person whose gender identity does not match the body), that person is often pathologized with the psychological diagnosis of gender identity disorder. Sex reassignment surgery is then considered as a treatment option. The surgical focus on the genitals shows how solid is the acceptance of genitals as the determinants of sex and gender in the United States. There are no ritual roles for third gender people in the United States. However, there is a political movement advocating for the acceptance of fluid or alternative gender behaviors, types, and roles.

Alternative conceptions of gender include those of androgynous people who do not identify as men or as women and/or who want ambiguous gender presentations; butch women who view butch as a gender of its own, not just being masculine women; genderqueers who reject the sex and gender binaries and want to look and act according to different gender combinations or alter their gender based on their feelings; drag kings and drag queens who perform gender for entertainment; male cross-dressers who are content to be men but want to express their femininity by presenting as females at times; transsexuals who go through varying stages of transition to live as the gender they feel they are, which is contrary to the body type with which they were born; and transgender individuals. The distinctions between some of these categories are often unclear, but there are some shared characteristics—no one in these categories feels completely at home with the traditional masculine/feminine binary and all of these individuals are stigmatized and lack civil rights.

CONCLUSION

The treatment of third gender individuals varies historically and geographically. In countries and regions where gender is defined less by biology than by occupational or spiritual status, the connection between the literal physical body and gender is less rigid than in Western societies. Where there is a religious or spiritual paradigm for mixed roles and genders and where individuals can occupy spiritual roles regardless of their biological sex, as in Hinduism, the idea of a third gender has been historically accepted. However, these individuals may not be literally called members of a third gender. Rather, they are integrated into the culture to varying degrees, recognized as not-men and not-women, feminine men, or female husbands.

In parts of the world where there are individuals who defy a gender binary and the culture relies primarily on biology to determine gender, third genders tend not to be socially accepted. In the United States, for example, there is no concept of third gender, even though there is a variety of people who reject strict gender roles. These people tend to experience discrimination and stigmatization as a result of these rigid gender categories.

See also Femininities and Masculinities; Queer; Transgender and Transsexual Identities.

Further Reading: Connell, Robert W., *Masculinities* (Berkeley: University of California Press, 2005 [1995]); Jacobs, Sue-Ellen, *Two Spirit People: Native American Gender Identity, Sexuality and Spirituality* (Champaign: University of Illinois Press, 1997); Herdt, Gilbert, *Third Sex/Third Gender* (New York: Zone Books, 1994); Lang, Sabine, *Men as Women, Women as Men: Changing Genders in Native American Cultures* (Austin: University of Texas Press, 1998); Nanda, Serena, *Gender Diversity: Crosscultural Variations* (Prospect Heights, IL: Waveland Press, 2000); Nanda, Serena, *Neither Man Nor Woman: The Hijras of India* (Beverly, MA: Wadsworth, 1998); Roscoe, Will, *Changing Ones: Third and Fourth Genders in Native North America* (New York: St. Martin's Griffin, 1998); Roscoe, Will, and Stephen Murray, *Boy-Wives and Female Husbands: Studies of African Homosexualities* (New York: Palgrave Macmillan, 2001); Young, Antonio, *Women Who Become Men: Albanian Sworn Virgins* (New York: Berg, 2000).

Lori Girshick

THIRD WORLD AND WOMEN OF COLOR FEMINISMS

Third world feminisms critique white privilege, stereotyping, and indifference to race in multiple social arenas. Third world feminist scholars argue that white feminists have achieved certain forms of equality through excluding women of color and poor women. Some white feminists disagree, and believe that equality-based feminism is accessible to all women, regardless of their class, racial background, or ethnic background.

BACKGROUND

Western feminism has long been understood as the standard feminist method of discussing and writing about issues of race and gender and advocating for the right of women to control their bodies and gain equality within the workplace. Third world feminism has emerged from women in third world countries and from women of color in the United States who have introduced new ways of understanding and critiquing Western feminism. Some women of color in the United States have called themselves third world feminists to describe their positions as members of groups colonized by the United States or by European countries. Thus, the concept of "third world feminism" has been adopted by women of color in Western countries, and the concept is also used in analyses of feminisms and women's movements in non-Western countries.

Since third world women belong to the lowest level of the social, economic, and feminist hierarchy, third world feminists provide an analysis and critique of "living under the Western gaze" (that is, under the gaze of the Western world, which includes industrialized countries). Third world feminists such as Chandra Talpade Mohanty (1991) critique Western feminism for examining women in non-Western contexts through an exclusively Western understanding of gender, racial, and class relations. Mohanty, who was born and raised in India and came to the United States to attend graduate school and work as a professor, argues that Western feminist perspectives on non-Western women's lives are part and parcel of the Western tendency to reduce all women in third world countries to the categories of "poor, illiterate, downtrodden and backward." Theorists of third world feminisms, such as African studies scholar Patricia McFadden, characterize African feminist thinking as committed to removing the monolithic view of African women as victims of sexual and imperial exploitation and oppression. For example, McFadden elaborates on the increased educational advancement of Zimbabwean women during the latter part of the twentieth century: they have "the most educated [female] population in the Southern African region" (McFadden 2005, 6). In summary, third world feminist scholars seek to examine non-Western women's lives in more complex, realistic terms than those, purportedly, of liberal Western feminists.

U.S.-based third world feminism refers to those U.S.-based feminist women who provide a counterargument to dominant theories within U.S. feminism regarding race, class, and national identity. Their analyses parallel those of scholars such as Mohanty, because women of color in the United States have also been viewed as racially inferior to white women. Women of color have criticized and stood in opposition to the liberal feminist notion that gender issues and concerns are more important than racial and class issues and concerns. Women of color see gender, racial, and economic inequalities as interchangeable and intimately tied to white male dominance. In her book, *Feminist Theory: From Margin to Center* (2000), bell hooks argues that women of color think differently about gender than white women. Women of color, a term used by some feminist scholars to mark their political visibility or collective empowerment as nonwhite women, often see race first and gender second. For example, hooks notes that when black babies are born, skin color is the first thing that is noticed. In other words, black babies' skin color as well as their gender determines their fate in society.

Third world feminists also challenge the notion that "sisterhood is global"; that is, they call into question the liberal feminist idea that all women throughout the world share similar forms of oppression. Chicana feminist Chela Sandoval (2000), for example, rejects feminist attempts to assert a universal sisterhood among all women, since not all women experience sexism in the same way, and some women are privileged because of their color and class in ways that actually work to disempower or exploit women of color. Third world feminists typically utilize an intersectional approach to understanding oppression, an approach that emphasizes the intersection of gender, race, and class, along with other factors such as religion, nationality, or sexuality. In contrast, liberal feminists tend to emphasize gender over all other forms of oppression. These different views on women's roles in society stem from women's diverse historical experiences.

For example, African American feminism came into existence during the 1950s and 1960s, in the context of civil rights struggles and African American mobilization to end racist laws in the South. In 1975, black lesbian feminist Barbara Smith organized the Combahee River Collective, a group that called for a black feminist movement and spoke out against acts of racial, gender, and class discrimination and exploitation experienced by black women within their communities and the larger society. In a powerful and widely circulated statement originally published in April 1977 (CRC 2003), the Combahee River Collective critiqued the mainstream feminist movement for refusing to admit blatant and self-righteous forms of racism within their movement and for failing to account for the herstory and experiences of black women. They critiqued feminism for operating from within a "color-blind perspective"; that is, for refusing to see race as a factor in discussing issues relating to sexism. Whereas many white middle-class women identified with Betty Friedan's *The Feminine Mystique* (1963), in which she argued that housewives were oppressed as a result of being household bound and personally unfulfilled because they could not pursue careers, many black women and other women of color pointed out that they had always been working, not necessarily to achieve personal fulfillment but because they had no other choice. Furthermore, they argued, in many cases, middle-class women could advance in traditionally male-based occupations such as law and medicine only because they hired poor women of color to clean their houses and care for their children. Thus, from this view, middle-class women's liberation even came at the expense of poor women of color. As a result of this type of bias in white middle-class feminist thought, women of color began to create their own theories by drawing from their own experiences of oppression and empowerment. Today, a large amount of research has been done in the area of black feminist thought, including the important work of sociologist Patricia Hill Collins (2000, 2005). Black feminist thought calls for black-female-centered scholarship, referred to by Hill Collins and others as Afrocentric feminist epistemology and knowledge, that challenges and critiques both male and white biases in the Western production of knowledge about women's lives and experiences. Rather than placing black women on the margins of the scholarship, these scholars place them at the center, thereby creating an entirely different version of history from the dominant version published and disseminated in U.S. society.

Black feminists have also utilized the notion of "womanism" to describe their forms of thought and activism. In her book, *In Search of Our Mothers' Gardens,* originally published in 1974, Alice Walker coined the phrase "womanism" to describe black feminism and black feminist spirituality. She defines a "womanist" as a woman who loves being a woman and enjoys the company of other women (Walker 2003). Walker's work has been used by a wide variety of scholars and practitioners, including writers, theologians, policy makers, and academics.

In similar fashion, Native American feminists have addressed their own forms of oppression, which are related to the continued colonization of their communities, through the lens of multiracial or third world feminisms. In "Speaking to Survival" (2001), Diane R. Schulz discusses some of the primary issues for Native American feminists: petitioning for their democratic rights and advocating for land, water, and fishing rights and usages. Many Native American women activists strive to preserve the languages, histories, and experiences of Native American women as a necessary field of study and activism in feminism. Andrea Smith's important research on the historically high rates of sexual abuse among Native American women underscores the importance of linking domestic or sexual violence with larger processes of cultural genocide. According to Smith (2002), the cofounder of the country's largest women of color antiviolence network, Incite! Women of Color against Violence, Native American women continue to face high rates of sexual abuse due to the colonial legacy, the legacy of colonizers using sexual abuse as a form of control in native communities. Thus from a native feminist perspective, violence against women is not just about men's power over women; it also concerns issues of colonization, national sovereignty, and wars among cultures and nations (Smith 2002). Like Chicana and Latina women, Native American, Asian American, African American, Muslim American, and Jewish American women have also organized and written extensively on the intersecting nature of their particular experiences of oppression, a topic often overlooked by white middle-class scholars who continue to give primacy to gender as a category of analysis.

Multiracial feminism is another term utilized by some scholars and activists as a means to create a political stance by women of color with regard to their shared experiences of racial and ethnic oppression. This perspective emerged during the 1960s, in the context of the civil rights movement, and through newly created ethnic studies and women's studies departments in universities. Japanese American civil rights activist Yuri Koshiyama, for example, used an antiracist feminist perspective to deal with issues of racism in New York's Harlem district.

During the 1960s, Koshiyama worked with black political organizations in order to change the racist and sexist climate in Harlem and in Asian American communities. She attended classes in the Harlem freedom schools in order to learn more about black history and culture and she also worked for equality, better healthcare, and an end to job discrimination for Asian Americans. Her antiracist agenda became an important political statement about the need for a multiracial perspective (Hoshino 2004). Likewise, Maxine Baca Zinn and Bonnie Thornton Dill (1996) have written extensively about the need for a multiracial approach to addressing the lives of men and women, in both historical and contemporary perspectives. Baca Zinn and Thornton Dill argue that this type of framework "does not offer a singular or unified feminism but a body of knowledge situating women and men in multiple systems of domination" (1996, 322).

DEBATES AND ISSUES WITHIN THIRD WORLD FEMINISM

Third world feminism addresses issues pertaining to the lives of women of color. Often, these issues differ from those presented by white middle-class feminists. In recent scholarship, women of color have addressed a wide range of issues pertaining to their experiences with sexism, racism, and class exploitation. Some have also addressed the current context of immigrant women's lives as a way to understand the impact of citizenship and immigration laws on poor immigrant women, many of whom end up working at the lowest levels of the U.S. economy. While these issues span a broad range of topics, regions, and identities, together they shape the contemporary field of third world feminist scholarship in the United States.

RETHINKING THE GENDER GAP AND WOMEN'S MARRIAGEABILITY IN COMMUNITIES OF COLOR

In order to escape the problems associated with women being in the home, mainstream Western feminists have advocated for women to seek educational and marital improvements and advancements. Often they advocate for these types of women's rights based on the idea that women should have personal freedom to decide how to live their lives. Betty Friedan, for example, rejected altogether the idea of the housewife and called for housewives to enter the workplace and fulfill their career aspirations. She referred to housewives' boredom and depression, resulting from feeling useless, as "the problem that has no name," a now famous phrase (Friedan 1963, 3). During the period when Friedan wrote *The Feminist Mystique* and helped found the National Organization for Women (NOW), white middle-class feminists began pushing for women to demand pay and advancements equal to those of men. Friedan and other white, middle class feminists assumed that women would be able to maintain housekeeping and childcare duties, while also becoming committed workers in the labor force.

However, women of color and third world women challenge and problematize mainstream feminist views on woman's place in the home and society. To begin with, women of color with low socioeconomic status were already working outside the home. They had to endure low pay and overwork at their jobs, while maintaining household and childrearing duties. In many families of color, women were the heads of their families and breadwinners for their families.

Third world women working in the United States as maids in white suburban families also challenge and problematize the gender gap existing between white middle-class women and women of color. White middle-class women experience a gender gap because they can't achieve the same professional goals as their husbands do; "migrant maids" are taking care of middle-class women's children and cleaning their houses for low pay. Migrant maids are unable to remain heads of their families since many of these women travel alone to the United States to work as maids. Instead they balance continuous child-care supervision and other household duties that they perform for white women. Thus, the gender gap" is much broader and more complicated than Friedan and other liberal feminists would argue.

Moreover, women of color from wealthy social and academic backgrounds struggle to maintain equal success within the workplace, marriage, and motherhood. Middle- to upper-class African Americans face a "double marriage squeeze" when they postpone marriage to secure educational and social advancements. Many successful black men have already married black women at an "appropriate" marriage age. Moreover, there is a shortage of emotionally available and financially secure black men to marry, because a disproportionate number of men are incarcerated. According to Harrison, Paige, and Beck, Bureau of Justice Statistics, "among males age 25 to 29, 12.6% of blacks were in prison or jail....the percentage of black males age 45 to 54 in prison or jail in 2004 was an estimated 4.5%—more than twice the highest rate (1.7%) among white males (age 30 to 34)" (2005, 11). Many black women choose to remain single or date and marry interracially. According to a 2001 census, 41.9 percent of black women never marry (McKinnon 2003). The issues we have discussed significantly affect how black women (and men) view their gender identities, including the opportunities or possible ways for them to advance in society. Thus, their career and marriage trajectories do not conform to a white middle-class analysis of women as married housewives, a point made by many third world feminist scholars.

In third world countries, educated women also face the "double marriage squeeze." One study points out that, like African American women, "highly educated" Vietnamese women postpone marriage with local men until after their educational goals are achieved; some never marry (Thai 2002). In choosing to postpone marriage or never marry, these Vietnamese women are choosing to disregard traditional Asian and Confucian notions of marrying as early as 20. As a result, they are unable to find equal partners, because traditionally, educated and successful Vietnamese men marry "traditional" women who are younger than themselves and hence have lower socioeconomic status. Thus, educated Vietnamese women become "unmarriageable" and "unmarketable." Some seek transnational husbands because of the promise of equal partnership. Others seek transnational husbands with low socioeconomic status, in the hope that such men will respect them more than Vietnamese men; this contributes to the growing trend toward international marriages among upper-class Vietnamese women and working-class Vietnamese American men (Thai 2002).

DOMESTIC ABUSE AND ITS RELATION TO RACISM

Like marriage practices, issues of violence against women are quite distinct in communities of color. A third world feminist perspective on domestic abuse is different from a white middle-class Western perspective. Mainstream feminism notes that men oppress women due to male views that see men as controllers of the public sphere and male arguments labeling women as inferior to men in mind and body. Western notions of womanhood are defined by the ability to control one's sexuality and reproductive system and to make one's own decisions (Mohanty 1991, 493). As a result, Western feminists tend to view higher rates of domestic violence against nonwhite women as a sign of their victimhood at the hands of sexist nonwhite men. In contrast, third world feminists link the prevalence of domestic abuse against nonwhite women to their socioeconomic conditions, to racial stratification, and to definitions of masculinity within particular traditions and cultures. Native American feminist scholars often identify the main source of domestic abuse as their colonization as a people. According to this view, Native American men have adopted masculine traits from their oppressors (that is, white colonizers); these traits were not necessarily indigenous to their communities prior to their contact with European colonizers. Nonetheless, today, some Native American men practice European models of male dominance and aggression within marriage, which increases the likelihood of spousal abuse within native communities. According to a 2001 article in the *National NOW Times,* violence against Native American women is the highest in any racial group (Bhungalia 2001). Some Native American women risk losing custody of their children if they decide to leave their spouses or escape to domestic abuse shelters. In other cases, Native American women stay in abusive relationships because of their fear of communal rejection as well as Native Americans' historical mistrust of the American legal system. These structural factors greatly exacerbate and complicate the experiences of Native American women who are victims of domestic violence, a point often overlooked by white middle-class feminist scholars who attribute domestic violence only to men, rather than to broader structural inequalities and forms of stratification.

WOMEN OF COLOR AND THE LABOR FORCE

Scholars have long noted the fact that the most marginalized groups in society tend to have access to low-paying, often insecure jobs. Women of color are often at the bottom of the economic hierarchy, thereby creating a unique set of issues often overlooked in mainstream feminist scholarship. For example, during the Jim Crow period, African American women were often unable to find jobs except in low-paying fields such as housecleaning and childcare. Eventually, as African American women found work in better-paying occupations, immigrant women from Latin America and Asia began to fill those roles.

In "America's Dirty Work: Migrant Maids and Modern-Day Slavery," Joy M. Zarembka (2002) notes that the recent increase in demand for migrant house-hold workers (for example, nannies, housecleaners) in the United States has also given rise to increased violence against these workers. Often working without legal protection, many of these women face verbal and physical abuse and ex-ploitation by their employers due to their status as migrant workers. They are sometimes paid less than the minimum wage and are forced to work longer hours than stated in their contracts. Some of their employers take away their pass-ports, contracts, and other important legal documentation; also they are often denied health and dental insurance and social security (Zarembka 2002, 146). Other scholars have documented physical abuse against migrant care workers (Anderson 2002). Third world feminist scholars such as Pierrette Hondagneu-Sotelo (2001), a sociologist who studies the lives of immigrant domestic care workers in Los Angeles, point out that white middle-class feminist scholarship often overlooks the experiences of the most oppressed women. Migrant female workers enter the United States from the Caribbean, Central America, Africa, and parts of Asia with the hope of securing better-paying jobs by working in the homes of predominately white Americans. Though they sign contracts to work as domestic servants, nannies, or personal attendants, many simply become cheap labor. Third world feminists note that race, class, and gender inform the reasons why their employment opportunities are limited to the bottom rung of the economy, as well as the ways in which they are treated by their employers.

CULTURAL REPRESENTATIONS OF WOMEN OF COLOR IN THE MEDIA

In addition to pointing out the economic or material problems faced by women of color, third world feminists have focused a great deal of attention on the ways in which women of color are portrayed, often in negative and stereotyp-ical ways, in popular culture and the media. Generally speaking, representations of women of color in the media are major issues debated within mainstream Western feminist circles. Many feminists have drawn from John Berger's influ-ential 1972 publication, *Ways of Seeing*, in which he forcefully argues that in the visual world, men act while women appear (Berger [1972] 1990). In Berger's analysis, men look (or gaze) at women and women in turn merely react to the looking. In this way of looking, women are transformed into passive beings and objects that are pleasing to men's sight. The male gaze transforms women's bod-ies into sexual objects. Mainstream feminists criticize the media for represent-ing women and women's bodies according to such traditional ways of looking. A feminist critique of representations of black females in music videos illustrates this point. Contemporary hip-hop artists such as Chingy, Nelly, Ludacris, Lil' Jon, and Cash Money, for example, refer to black women in derogatory terms in their lyrics and show them in sexually degrading ways in their music videos. The Big Tymers' song "Number One Stunner" (2000) celebrates the group's ability to wield so much sexual power (referred to as "stunning power"), so much that they can cause physical harm during sexual relations with black women.

But black feminists also argue that race must be taken into consideration when examining representations of black women in hip-hop lyrics and videos. Black feminists note that the soft-pornographic and misogynist messages found in contemporary hip-hop represent black women as they were represented in American slavery: as sexual servants. Black women's bodies are degraded in order for black rappers to feel powerful, just as white male slaveholders degraded black female slaves in order to feel powerful and in control. The degradation of black women's bodies helps to sustain black male notions of masculinity and reinforces and condones sexual violence within black communities. While statistics show that rape occurs every six minutes in the United States, according to third world feminist scholars, black women are raped in both the symbolic and the literal sense during the rotations of these music videos (Cole and Guy-Sheftall 2003).

Black feminists are also quick to note that contemporary female rappers such as Salt, Trina, and Eve offer a response that counters representations of black females in their male counterparts' videos. In contrast to misogynist rappers, female rappers choose to rap about black female sexual and social empowerment. They celebrate women's bodies and their ability to offer gratification within a loving and healthy relationship. Black female rappers such as Eve and Trina exemplify aspects of womanism. They celebrate black female agency, respect, and empowerment through verbal speech and through positive representations of black female sexuality and identity.

Another example involving stereotypical representations of black women in the music industry involves the hit VH1 reality show, *Flavor of Love*. In this show, which debuted in January 2006 and is one of the "most watched non-sports programs on cable," Flavor Flav, former "hype man" member of Public Enemy, invites women to live in his mansion and participate in a series of challenges in the hope of winning his heart. Flav judges them and then decides to either eliminate or keep them, after each challenge. The winner becomes his main interest. The show represents women of color and their bodies as sexual objects that are pleasing to the male gaze within stereotypical racist associations. These women's gender identities are redefined according to racist codes and ascriptions that deem them hypersexual (Hill Collins 2005). According to a third world feminist viewpoint, in this show, race determines gender, and black women are viewed through the lens of white producers and consumers rather than through their own eyes.

OPRAH'S LEADERSHIP ACADEMY FOR GIRLS

Oprah's Leadership Academy for Girls in South Africa, founded by business and entertainer mogul Oprah Winfrey, opened in January 2007 and promises to be an academic institution that will decrease the stigma associated with disadvantaged South African girls. South African girls in the school declare that they are being prepared to "take over the world." The school serves as a safe space for young South African women to develop the academic, social, and leadership skills needed to advance South African politics and to become leaders within their communities.

CONCLUSION

Women of color and third world women have addressed cultural representations of women of color in the media; the gender gap and women's marriageability in communities of color; domestic abuse and its relation to racism, economic exploitation, and colonization; and women's limited opportunities in the U.S. labor market, using an intersectional approach that takes into account the racial, class, and gendered locations of women of color. In the process, the issues facing nonwhite women are revealed to be multidimensional and the notion of shared experiences, in which white feminists once believed, is forever debunked.

Black feminists such as Barbara Smith (1993) have called for white feminists to address not only issues pertaining to women of color and third world women but also issues pertaining to white women's experiences of racial privilege. Smith sees this as crucial to removing the wall dividing white women and nonwhite women within feminist circles and debates; other third world feminist scholars point out that because white women "also have a raced, classed and gendered position in society" (Uttal 1990, 43), they too should begin to examine their lives using an intersectional approach that accounts for the forms of oppression they experience as much as it does for their forms of privilege.

Some scholars have begun to do just that: Anne Braden, for example, has described the effects of racism on white women trying to challenge white male dominance in the United States. In her 1999 book, *The Wall Between,* she notes that racism, which she refers to as the "disease of segregation," poisons and affects whites as well, perhaps more "terribly" than blacks. Braden argues that "Racial bars build a wall around the white people as well, cramping their spirits and causing them to grow in distorted shapes" (1999, 24–25). She asserts that the disease of segregation contributes to "death in the heart and soul of gentle white[s]" (29). Though some white feminists advocate for women of color and their experiences, much work has to be done to rethink whiteness in feminist studies scholarship and to better document and understand the lives of women through the lens of third world feminist scholarship.

On July 13, 1848, Elizabeth Cady Stanton (ca. 1815–1902), a pioneer advocate for women's rights in the United States, planned the Seneca Falls Convention for women to express their grievances and demands for voting rights, leadership roles within the church, marriage rights, custody rights, property rights, and educational opportunities and advancements. These rights were compiled and read from a list called the Seneca Sentiments. In 1851, Sojourner Truth (ca. 1792–1883), a former slave, echoed these grievances in her speech at the Women's Rights Convention in Akron, Ohio, "Ain't I a Woman?" Truth's speech also draws attention to the problems facing black women in their fight to secure rights. Truth had been forced to watch as several of her 13 children were sold into slavery. She was unable to protect and care for her own children. As a black mother, she could not demand custody rights. Truth destabilized the term *woman.* She revealed that racism differentiates women and limits the ability of women from a particular racial group to petition successfully for equal rights.

Lora Jo Foo dedicates her time to raising awareness of the issues affecting Asian American females. Foo is president of Sweatshop Watch, a coalition committed to eliminating inhumane sweatshop conditions in the United States and globally. In October 2000, the Ford Foundation commissioned her to write a report on the issues facing Asian American females. Foo reported that Asian American females often face problems with homelessness, sex trafficking, sexual harassment, increased suicide rates, increased rates of hepatitis B and cervical cancer, and sweatshop abuse, among others. Foo calls into question the notion that Asian Americans are "model minorities." The model minority designation refers to the belief that particular nonwhite groups, in this case Asian Americans, achieve sociopolitical and socioeconomic advancement through hard work and the tireless pursuit of the American dream. Their model minority status serves as a model for other racial groups to follow. However, cultural stereotypes that portray Asian American women as exotic, passive, and studious cause some of them to become easy targets of sexual harassment and exploitation, mainly because men believe they will be passive and not fight back. Foo asserts that attention must be paid both to Asian American successes and to their problems due to racism, sexism, classism, and discrimination within the workplace and educational institutions. Foo's text, *Asian American Women: Issues, Concerns, and Responsive Human and Civil Rights Advocacy* (2007) remains important to Asian American feminist scholarship because it provides an in-depth examination of the ways in which groups of Asian American females are changing the sexist climate within the United States.

See also Affirmative Action; Race and Racism: Social Stratification in the United States; Second and Third Wave Feminisms.

Further Reading: Alexander, M. Jacqui, Lisa Albrecht, Sharon Day, and Mab Segrest, eds., *Sing, Whisper, Shout, Pray: Feminist Visions for a Just World* (Boulder, CO: Edge Works, 2003); Anderson, Bridget, "Just Another Job? The Commodification of Domestic Labor," in *Global Women: Nannies, Maids, and Sex Workers in the New Economy,* ed. Barbara Ehrenreich and Arlie Russell Holhschild, 104–114 (New York: Henry Holt and Co., 2002); Anzaldúa, Gloria E., *Borderlands/La frontera: The New Mestiza* (San Francisco, CA: Aunt Lute Books, 1999); Anzaldúa, Gloria E., and Analouise Keating, eds., *This Bridge We Call Home: Radical Visions for Transformation* (New York: Routledge, 2002); Baca Zinn, Maxine, and Bonnie Thornton Dill, "Theorizing Difference from Multiracial Feminism," *Feminist Studies* 22, no. 2 (1996): 321–331; Berger, John, *Ways of Seeing,* reprint ed. (New York: Penguin Classics, 1990 [1972]); Bhavnani, Kum-Kum, ed., *Feminism and "Race"* (Oxford, UK: Oxford University Press, 2001); Bhungalia, Lisa, "Native American Women and Violence," *National NOW Times,* Spring 2001, available at: http://www.now.org/nnt/spring-2001/nativeamerican.html; Braden, Anne, *The Wall Between* (Louisville: University of Tennessee Press, 1999); Cole, Johnnetta B., and Beverly Guy-Sheftall, *Gender Talk: The Struggle for Women's Equality in African-American Communities* (New York: One World/Ballantine, 2003); Combahee River Coalition (CRC), "A Black Feminist Statement," in *Feminist Theory Reader,* ed. Carole R. McCann and Seung-Kyung Kim, 164–171 (New York: Routledge, 2003 [1977]); DuBois, Ellen Carol, and Lynn Dumenil, eds., *Through Women's Eyes: An American History* (Bedford/St. Martin's Press,

2004); Foo, Lora Jo, *Asian American Women: Issues, Concerns, and Responsive Human and Civil Rights Advocacy,* 2nd ed. (Lincoln, NE: Universe, Inc., 2007 [2003]); Friedan, Betty, *The Feminine Mystique* (New York: W. W. Norton, 1963); Harrison, Paige M., and Allen J. Beck, *Prison and Jail Inmates at Midyear 2004,* Bureau of Justice Statistics (Washington, DC: U.S. Department of Justice, April 2005); Hill Collins, Patricia, *Black Feminist Thought: Knowledge, Consciousness, and the Politics of Empowerment,* 2nd ed. (New York: Routledge, 2000); Hill Collins, Patricia, *Black Sexual Politics: African Americans, Gender, and the New Racism* (New York: Routledge, 2005); Hondagneu-Sotelo, Pierrette, *Doméstica: Immigrant Workers Cleaning and Caring in the Shadows of Affluence* (Berkeley: University of California Press, 2001); hooks, bell, *Feminist Theory: From Margin to Center,* 2nd ed. (Boston, MA: South End Press, 2000); Hoshino, Lina, dir., *Caught in Between: What to Call Home in Times of War* (videocassette, Progressive Film Productions, 25 min., 2004); McFadden, Patricia, "Becoming Postcolonial: African Women Changing the Meaning of Citizenship," *Meridians: Feminism, Race, Transnationalism* 6, no. 1 (2005): 1–18; McKinnon, Jesse, "The Black Population in the United States," in *Current Population Reports* (Washington, DC: U.S. Census Bureau, 2003); Mohanty, Chandra Talpade, "Under Western Eyes: Feminist Scholarship and Colonial Discourses," in *Third World Women and the Politics of Feminism,* ed. Chandra Talpade Mohanty, Anne Russo, and Lourdes Torres, 51–80 (Bloomington: Indiana University Press, 1991); Moraga, Cherríe L., and Gloria E. Anzaldúa, eds., *This Bridge Called My Back: Writings By Radical Women of Color,* expanded and revised 3rd ed. (Berkeley: Third Woman Press, 2002); Sandoval, Chela, *Methodology of the Oppressed* (Minneapolis: University of Minnesota Press, 2000); Schulz, Diane, "Speaking to Survival," *Awakened Woman E Magazine,* August 19, 2001, available at: http://www.awakenedwoman.com/native_women.htm; Segal, Marcia Texler, and Theresa A. Martinez, eds., *Intersections of Gender, Race and Class: Readings for a Changing Landscape* (Los Angeles: Roxbury, 2007); Smith, Andrea, *Conquest: Sexual Violence and American Indian Genocide* (Boston, MA: South End Press, 2002); Smith, Barbara, *Home Girls: A Black Feminist Anthology* (New York: Kitchen Table, Women of Color Press, 1983); Thai, Hung Cam, "Clashing Dreams: Highly Educated Overseas Brides and Low-Wage US Husbands," in *Global Woman: Nannies, Maids, and Sex Workers in the New Economy,* ed. Barbara Ehrenreich and Arlie Russell Hochschild, 230–253 (New York: Metropolitan/Owl Books, 2002); Uttal, Lynne, "Inclusion without Influence: The Continuing Tokenism of Women of Color," in *Making Face/Making Soul: Creative and Critical Perspectives by Feminists of Color,* ed. Gloria Anzaldúa, 42–45 (San Francisco: Aunt Lute Books, 1990); Walker, Alice, *In Search of Our Mothers' Gardens: Womanist Prose,* reprint ed. (New York: Harvest Books, 2003); Women of South Asian Decent Collective, ed., *Our Feet Walk the Sky: Women of the South Asian Diaspora* (San Francisco: Aunt Lute Books, 1993); Zarembka, Joy M., "America's Dirty Work: Migrant Maids and Modern-Day Slavery," in *Global Woman: Nannies, Maids, and Sex Workers in the New Economy,* ed. Barbara Ehrenreich and Arlie Russell Hochschild, 142–153 (New York: Metropolitan/Owl Books, 2002).

Patrice Natalie Delevante

TITLE IX AND WOMEN'S SPORTS

Title IX is a federal law that was enacted to provide girls and women with equal access to educational opportunities in elementary, secondary, and postsecondary institutions. Since Title IX's enactment in 1972, there has been a controversy over the need to provide equality in sports programs for women and girls. To date, there has been an increase in female participation in sport; however, men's teams have been cut due to budgetary constraints and male participation in sport has decreased, a situation that some have blamed on Title IX.

BACKGROUND

"Title IX of the Education Amendments of 1972 is a federal law that prohibits sex discrimination in any educational program or activity at any educational institution that is a recipient of federal funds" (Women's Sports Foundation 2002). Title IX addresses a wide variety of issues including educational programs for medicine and law. In addition, female athletes benefit from this legislation, even though it was not specifically directed toward them. Title IX also suggests that a federally funded educational institution cannot discriminate by gender. In essence, if a high school or college receives any money from the government, all students, men and women, must have equal opportunity in educational programs including sport.

There are three ways of fulfilling the Title IX requirements. First, proportionally, they can be fulfilled by having the same percentage of female athletes as in the student body; for example, a school with a 50 percent female student body would be required to have the same percentage of female athletes in its athletic programs. Second, they can be fulfilled by showing that there is a conscious effort to increase women's sport; in other words, if an institution is gradually expanding women's programs or if the concerns of the female student body are being addressed, the institution does not have to worry about making sure that the programs have the same percentage of male/female participants as does the student body. Third, the requirements can be fulfilled by making sure that women's interest in a sport is being satisfied. Title IX also requires that male and female athletes receive the same treatment and benefits, including access to equipment, training, facilities, coaching, scholarships, and awards.

DID YOU KNOW?

- The modern founder of the Olympics, Baron Pierre Coubertin, never intended that women should participate in the Olympics.
- In 1942, the formation of the All-American Girls Baseball League was announced. These baseball players were talented but had to make sure that they showed they were women by wearing skirts, lipstick, and nail polish.
- In 1973, Billie Jean King, a female tennis player, played an exhibition match against Bobby Riggs and won. Riggs did not support female athletes; this event gave momentum to female athletes.

CONTACT SPORTS AND TITLE IX

The language of Title IX suggests that physical education classes need to be coeducational, with both sexes in the same class, unless students are engaged in a contact sport. Contact sports can include, but are not limited to, wrestling, boxing, rugby, ice hockey, football, and basketball. For example, a school must offer a coeducational physical education class if students are playing volleyball, but schools have the option to offer single-sex classes if students are engaged in wrestling, because it is deemed a contact sport under Title IX. There are also debates centered on coaching, facilities, scholarship, and the elimination of men's programs.

Opponents of Title IX suggest that Title IX encourages not equality but special treatment, in that Title IX's ability to create athletic opportunities for women places women in a special category and as a result leaves no room for men's sport (Walton 2003). The opportunity to participate in sport increases for women and in turn decreases for men. This suggests that Title IX encourages reverse discrimination. Some would imply that Title IX has created a "war on boys" (Walton 2003, 11). This goes back to the idea of reverse discrimination.

A 30TH-ANNIVERSARY CHALLENGE

In 2002, Title IX celebrated its 30th anniversary, but not without controversy. The main debate centered on the decline in men's sport. The National Wrestling Coaches Association suggested that Title IX was being used to eliminate men's varsity sports teams and that it caused men's sport to decline (Staurowsky 2003; Walton 2003). Supporters of Title IX suggested that other factors have affected men's minor sports, including increased costs (Walton 2003). In a study conducted by Anderson and Cheslock (2004), it is suggested that schools are more likely to add female participation than to cut male teams as they move closer to Title IX compliance. These authors acknowledge that there will be both intended and unintended effects on men's teams and on men's participation in sports.

As a result of this debate, in 2002, on the recommendation of George W. Bush, the U.S. Department of Education appointed the Commission on Opportunities in Athletics to gather information, analyze the issues, and obtain public input on Title IX (Staurowsky 2003). The commission seemed to respond to several men's minor sport constituencies, like the National Wrestling Coaches Association, which believed that Title IX encouraged an illegal quota system and was being used to eliminate men's varsity sports programs. The final decision by the Department of Education was in favor of upholding Title IX (Yiamouyiannis 2003).

TITLE IX'S INTERPRETATION AND THE COURTS

Title IX has been repeatedly challenged in the courts over the last 25 years. One of the more recent cases was *Cohen v. Brown University* (1997). Brown University was facing budget restrictions and cut two women's and two men's teams; this, however, did not ensure compliance with the Title IX requirements of equal participation (Carpenter and Acosta 2005). The female team members sued. The courts concluded that the actual participants need to be counted to avoid any misrepresentation of participation, and that surveys or ratios cannot be used to determine compliance (Carpenter and Acosta 2005). Another recent case, *Pederson v. Louisiana State University* (2000), centered on female athletes' interest in soccer and softball. The courts ruled that ignorance on the part of the institution, where the institution appears not to take adequate account of the interests and abilities of the female student body, is not a reason for noncompliance, and the intent to treat the sexes differently is sufficient to trigger monetary damages (Carpenter and Acosta 2005). Even though Title IX continues to be challenged in the courts, in practice there still exists gender inequities in sports in educational institutions and every federal appellate court that has considered the validity of Title IX has upheld it as constitutional.

See also Affirmative Action; Equal Rights Amendment; Sports: Professional.

Further Reading: Anderson, Deborah J., and John J. Cheslock, "Institutional Strategies to Achieve Gender Equity in Intercollegiate Athletics: Does Title IX Harm Male Athletes?" *American Economic Review* 94, no. 2 (2004): 307–311; Carpenter, Linda Jean, and R. Vivian Acosta, *Title IX* (Champaign, IL: Human Kinetics, 2005); Dowling, Colette, *The Frailty Myth: Women Approaching Equality* (New York: Random House, 2000); Johnson, Anne Janette, *Great Women in Sports* (New York: Visible Ink, 1996); Messner, Michael, *Taking the Field: Women, Men and Sports* (Minneapolis: University of Minnesota Press, 2002); Priest, Laurie, "The Whole IX Yards: The Impact of Title IX: The Good, the Bad and the Ugly," *Women in Sport and Physical Activity Journal* 12, no. 2 (2003): 27–44; Rhoads, Steven E., "Sports, Sex and Title IX," *Public Interest* 154 (2004): 86–98; Staurowsky, Ellen J., "Introduction to Title IX Theme; Title IX in the Aftermath of President George W. Bush's Commission on Opportunities in Athletics," *Women in Sport and Physical Activity Journal* 12, no. 2 (2003): 1–4; Walton, Theresa A., "Title IX: Forced to Wrestle up the Backside," *Women in Sport and Physical Activity Journal* 12, no. 2 (2003): 5–26; Women's Sports Foundation, *Mythbusting: What Every Female Athlete Should Know!*, July 1, 2002, available at: http://www.womensportsfoundation.org/cgi bin/iowa/issues/rights/article.html?record=34; Women's Sports Foundation, *Title IX: The Most Commonly Asked Questions about Title IX and Athletics Answered by Women's Sports Foundation Executive Director, Donna Lopiano*, April 19, 2002, available at: http://www.womensportsfoundation.org/cgi-bin/iowa/issues/rights/article.html?record=888; Yiamouyiannis, Athena, "The Future of Title IX: Ensuring Success through Proactive Approaches," *Women in Sport and Physical Activity Journal* 12, no. 2 (2003): 45–54.

Giovanna Follo

TRANSGENDER AND TRANSSEXUAL IDENTITIES

While conflict and controversy around trans issues occur in conversations among non-trans people, transsexual and transgendered people also often find themselves in conflict with one another around issues regarding trans identities, the politics of "passing" as the "opposite" sex, and whether gender crossing coded in trans terms reflects personal pathology or a form of social protest. In both their transgenderism and their transsexuality, however, trans people challenge the notions that sex and gender are always related in particular, predictable ways and that both sex and gender are innate and immutable.

BACKGROUND

The phenomenon of people of one sex taking on the social characteristics of the other—biological males assuming women's roles or biological females assuming the status of men—is documented across a wide range of cultures and historical periods. From Native North American two-spirit people of both sexes to the *hijra* of India, to women of various sexual identities passing as men in order to participate in politics, the military, male-dominated professions, and working-class wage economies, the practice of persons of one sex "becoming" the other, or at least assuming the gendered behaviors of the other sex, is fairly common. In premodern Europe, among alchemists, hermeticists, and the general public, there seems to have been a common understanding that under certain conditions females could become males, and that in other circumstances, people could be born as members of both sexes. There remain a number of records from the colonial period in the United States of individuals of one sex—usually male—identifying as female or being identified by others as women, despite their biological sex.

Among these examples, the meaning assigned to cross-gendered behavior, by both those who engage in it and those who observe it, varies widely. In the contemporary context, transsexuality and transgenderism have become common concepts in which to frame extreme cross-sex and cross-gender behavior; although it is possible to discern differences between transsexuality and transgenderism, debates about their origins, their meanings, and their relationships to broader social institutions continue to be lively. As anthropologist Ann Bolin (1993, 447) puts it, "the Berdache traditions documented globally have captured the anthropological imagination, offering serious challenges to scientific paradigms that conflate sex and gender. This complexity is reiterated in Euro-American gender variance among those who have come to identify themselves as preoperative, postoperative and nonsurgical transsexuals as well as male and female cross dressers and transvestites."

Transsexuality may be defined most narrowly as the process of transforming a body of one biological sex into a body that has the physical features of the other—as in the surgical and hormonal modification of a biologically male body so that it has the characteristics that define a body as female, and vice versa. Transgenderism may be most narrowly defined as the practice of a person of one biological sex engaging in the social presentation of the gender of the other sex, without medical modification of the body—as in a biologically female person adopting the mannerisms, speech patterns, and physical postures associated with masculinity in a particular culture, and vice versa. In the narrowest, most technical sense, while both transsexual and transgendered people modify the presentation of their genders, transsexual people acquire or seek to obtain surgery to modify their bodies in ways that are consistent with the gender they present, while transgender people engage in "gender bending" without surgical or hormonal intervention. Differences among and between transsexual and transgendered people are, however, often in reality far broader than this technical distinction, and often center on differences in philosophy, interpretation, and identity. For instance, a preoperative male-to-female transsexual may engage in a gendered presentation of self very similar to that of a male-to-female transgendered person; but while these two people may seem very much alike to observers, the meanings they attach to their choices may be very different and, perhaps, even contradictory or contentious. While most transsexually identified people seek sex reassignment surgery (also known as SRS), many do not obtain it but use other forms of medical intervention, such as hormone therapy, to produce changes in their bodies, while some transgender people uninterested in surgical changes sometimes take feminizing or masculinizing hormones as well.

As Bolin (1993) documents, the widespread availability of the concept of transsexual identity in the United States may effectively be traced to the late 1960s, during which "gender clinics" began to appear on the American cultural landscape. By the early 1980s, more than 40 such clinics offering sex reassignment surgery were in operation, many affiliated with university hospitals and medical schools. In such clinics, biological males could undergo surgical and hormonal treatments that would modify their bodies, effectively reconstructing them in ways that reflect dominant notions of both normative female sexual characteristics and conventions of feminine gender presentation. Sex reassignment surgery for male-to-female transsexuals often involves a reconstruction of the genitals, resulting in the absence of a penis and the presence of a vagina, breast enlargement, and sometimes facial contouring and other procedures designed to give a more feminine appearance to the face and neck. Biological females could also seek SRS in gender clinics. Female-to-male SRS, which is less common in the United States (though some countries report equal ratios), involves mastectomy and chest reconstruction, and can involve phalloplasty, although this procedure has yielded mostly cosmetic results and many female-to-male trans people elect not to undergo the procedure.

As with most surgical procedures, considerable expense is attached to sex reassignment surgery. While people with wealth can afford to undergo these procedures as elective processes, others are dependent upon insurance companies to underwrite sex reassignment surgery and the associated hormone therapies, should they seek SRS. In both instances, physicians and surgeons need to justify their prescription of hormones and their surgical modification of healthy bodies. As a result, in order for those seeking sex reassignment surgery to be seen as legitimately eligible for these interventions, the medical establishment has required that they be diagnosed with an illness. Because there is as yet no documentation of any physical pathology that would justify sex reassignment surgery, the medical establishment has required that those seeking the procedures be diagnosed with a mental disorder, gender identity disorder (GID) of adulthood.

No other diagnosis in the *Diagnostic and Statistical Manual of Mental Disorders (DSM)* advocates surgery, let alone genital surgery, as a legitimate treatment for physically healthy individuals, as is done in order for people seeking sex reassignment to be considered qualified for the procedure. Equally ironically, in order to be diagnosed with this disorder, applicants for SRS must demonstrate the emotional stability necessary to accept the results of the surgery. As Ault and Brzuzy (n.d.) note, this diagnosis, tied to transsexualism and its medicalization, has become the most contested diagnosis at present in the *DSM*. Starting in the 1990s, many gender clinics have closed their doors, and fewer insurance companies have been willing to pay for sex reassignment as a treatment for gender identity disorder. Bolin (1993) argues that this change has spurred the appearance of larger numbers of people identifying as transgender; there have also emerged debates both within and around transsexuality and transgenderism and the status of both within lesbian, gay, and bisexual (LGB) communities, the feminist movement, and our broader society.

THE DESIRE FOR CHANGE: PEOPLE WITH DISORDERS OR A DISORDERED SOCIETY?

Although, as Ann Bolin says, anthropologists, sociologists, and historians have documented gender-crossing behavior in a wide variety of social, geographic, and historical locations, the interpretations of these behaviors and the identities attached to them vary widely. In some societies, those of one sex who wish to be treated as members of the other are seamlessly integrated into the structure of the societies in which they live. In other contexts, including the present-day United States, the bodies of those who wish to live as gender variants from their sex face challenges that range from social ostracism and contempt to loss of employment, violence, and numerous health risks associated with the medicalization of trans bodies and desires. Among trans people themselves, scholars and practitioners who study or support them, and the general public, the ultimate source of the difficulties faced by trans people is the subject of contention and debate.

One perspective on the desire to transform one's body in such a way that it has the characteristics of the opposite sex is that those with this desire suffer from a disorder or illness. This perspective, articulated in the GID diagnosis and connected closely with the standards for sex reassignment surgery as they were articulated in 1966 by Harry Benjamin, a pioneering physician in the field of sex reassignment, holds that those seeking sex reassignment suffer from what sociologist C. Wright Mills calls a "private trouble," analogous to other random illnesses or disorders suffered by individuals (1976, 226). Trans people who adopt this perspective often report the sensation of being a person of one sex "trapped" in the body of the other—that is, being a man trapped in a woman's body or a woman trapped in a man's body. Although there is as yet no medical evidence that most people seeking sex reassignment are *physiologically* different from other biological males or females, the solution to this problem offered by medical science and often sought by trans people has been addressed to the bodily processes of the person: sex reassignment surgery and related hormonal therapies designed to bring a person's body in line with his or her sense of self.

An alternative perspective on the desire for sex reassignment surgery, one often articulated by feminist and queer theorists as well as by other scholars across a range of disciplines, is that it represents not a personal trouble, in Mills' vernacular, but, instead, a social problem—that is, a phenomenon that affects a large number of people and reflects broader patterns within a social context. From this perspective, transsexuality might be read as a function of a society with gender roles so rigid that a person of one sex experience feels gender dysphoric (the disjuncture between ones self-perception and one's assigned gender identity) when experiencing the feelings associated with the opposite sex or when enjoying activities associated with the opposite sex. For example, because of the rigid gender coding of this society, boys who play with dolls, as in the gender identity disorder of childhood diagnosis, may be seen by others as gender deviants and may come to regard themselves in this way, even though playing adult roles, such as parenting, is regarded by many as a healthy form of childhood socialization. From this perspective, trans identities reflect a rigid binary

"INDIAN TOWN ELECTS TRANS MAYOR"

On November 26, 2000, a town in northern India best known as a publishing site for Hindu scriptures made a *hijra* its mayor by a large margin. Although the name is often translated as "eunuch," most *hijra* are transgenders, cross-dressers, and gay men; after a long period living a marginal or even outlaw existence as entertainers and bringers of blessings and curses, they have only recently begun to win any official recognition as a minority group.

Asha Devi, 45, running as an independent on a platform of clean government and improved infrastructure, was elected by the more than 500,000 residents of Gorakhpur in the state of Uttar Pradesh by a margin of 65,304 votes. Devi's campaign was actively supported by another *hijra*, Shabnam Mausi, who was elected to the legislative assembly of the neighboring state of Madhya Pradhesh in a special election a year earlier.

Some contested Devi's victory because the state election commission allowed her to run for a seat reserved for women after she changed her name from the masculine Amarhaht Yadav. However, she was legally considered a female and her election was upheld. In contrast, *hijra* Kamla Jaan was elected and sworn in as mayor of the Madhya Pradesh town of Katni in January 2000, only to be deposed on gender grounds by a state appellate court in 2003. The court ruled that Jaan is legally male. This ruling continues to place pressure on *hijra* politicians such as Devi, and the gender status of elected *hijras* continue to be challenged in the courts.

"Now I am going to prove to the people that all you need to excel as the first citizen is sheer love for people," Devi told reporters. Illiterate herself, she said her priorities would include "the uplift of women, encouraging literacy, building homes for the homeless and leaving no stones unturned to see the city spick and span." Her other infrastructural concerns include improving local roads, drainage, and drinking water.

Source: Planet Out (2000).

sex/gender structure: if the gender structure of the society were more porous, malleable, or fluid, individuals of both sexes could comfortably express their genders along a broader continuum; "crossing over" in such a context would be unnecessary, if not impossible, because it depends on sex/gender polarization.

IDENTITIES CROSSING OVER: NEWLY MINTED MEN AND WOMEN OR TRANSPEOPLE?

Although trans communities may include transsexuals, transgender people, transvestites, and their partners, children, and family members, conflicts often occur within these communities over interpretations of the origins and meaning of trans behaviors and identities. For those most comfortable with the medical model holding that trans people are individuals of one sex trapped in the bodies of the other, sex reassignment surgery is seen as a desirable medical treatment because it should provide relief from the constant sense of incoherence between the person's sex and his or her gender. For individuals most comfortable with this perspective, expectations for a life after sex reassignment surgery center on being able to move in the world and to be accepted as a member of the sex consistent with their sense of gender. Such individuals do not aspire to or espouse a trans identity; their perspective is that their sex/gender dysphoria has been treated and they now may live as fully functioning members of one sex. Their goal is to "pass" in mainstream society without calling attention to the history of their change in sexual status. Ann Bolin (1993) reports, based on her fieldwork, that within the trans community, such individuals see themselves as superior to other trans people who do not seek sex reassignment; indeed, those seeking or having obtained sex reassignment see those who do not pursue it as "sick" or just playing around.

For their part, transgendered people and transvestites often see themselves on a continuum with transsexuals, not as qualitatively different from them. Within the trans communities, however, the emergence of trans identities has been a cause of tension and anxiety, as well as a source of difficulty in creating a social movement strategy that supports the interests of all trans people. For those more comfortable with a social-constructionist approach to trans issues, the approach that sees the desire to cross gender lines as a reflection of the intractability of those lines, the goal of gender crossing, whether surgical or nonsurgical, is not necessarily to "pass" as members of the opposite sex. Individuals espousing a social-constructionist approach have argued that to do so, indeed, is not only unrealistic but also hypocritical. Kate Bornstein, for example, a postoperative male-to-female trans person, takes the position that because she was raised as a boy and lived much of her life as a male, albeit uncomfortably, she should not represent herself postoperatively as a woman but as something else, not a man, not a woman. For any number of post-op trans thinkers (Wilchins, Bornstein, Stone), as well as many non-op transgendered people, the desirable alternative is to lay claim to a trans identity. Sandy Stone (1991), for example, makes use of the concept *mestiza,* developed by Gloría Anzaldua, to characterize a posttranssexual or transgender identity that is neither male nor female.

When activists hoping to make a better world for trans people meet to explore strategies for achieving that goal, conflicts between those comfortable with the dual-sex model and those espousing a multiple-sex model arise. For those whose goal is simply to live as members of the sex opposite that of their birth, their political goals include the legal recognition of their new sex in employment and legal contexts, the solution of healthcare insurance issues, the acceptance of legal rights to children born before their transitions, and a range of other concerns associated with being able to integrate themselves as members of their new sex into existing social structures. Theoretical discussions must meet the real hostility encountered from those who think one is using the wrong restroom.

Those more comfortable with a social constructionist approach, who are less concerned with passing, are often more concerned with challenging existing

THE COST OF SEX REASSIGNMENT SURGERY

The price range for SRS varies widely. Often those seeking SRS travel to Bangkok, Thailand, where costs are lower. In the United States, according to the *New York Times*, the cost of male-to-female (MTF) surgery is $37,000; and for female-to-male (FTM) surgery $77,000 ("San Francisco Workers Get Sex Change Coverage" 2001). These figures likely include a full range of procedures and follow-up care, including corrective surgery if necessary. For MTF transsexuals, SRS surgery could include breast augmentation if hormones have not produced acceptable breast growth, penectomy, and vaginaplasty. Frequently a series of operations is required to achieve desirable results. FTM surgery includes mastectomy, hysterectomy, and oophorectomy. Further procedures, such as penoplasty, are rarer, since results are less than satisfactory. The gender disparity in research, costs, and effectiveness of procedures is significant. Far more attention has been given to enabling successful male-to-female transitions than to enabling female-to-male transitions.

Healthcare coverage: some health management organizations (HMOs) cover hormones as treatment for GID. Though the costs of surgery are high for an individual, the cost per person in a large pool is relatively insignificant. Nevertheless, coverage for surgery is rare. Coverage may distinguish between "medically necessary" operations such as vaginaplasty or phalloplasty and "cosmetic" operations such as facial surgeries.

Many transsexuals save for years or spend their life savings to pay for surgery. For others, the prohibitive costs make surgery out of the question. MTF facial feminizing surgeries could include 15 separate procedures, from forehead/brow contouring to chin and jaw contouring. The number of surgeons, the range of procedures available, and the information on the results of FTM surgery are much more limited than for MTF surgery.

The process of transitioning can take two years if one follows standard protocols, including a year of "real-life" experience. Many transsexuals pursue hormones and surgery without this—circumventing the institutional barriers but taking health risks, such as injecting hormones from reused needles, at unregulated doses, with little or no education about the side effects, such as increased risk of heart disease in FTMs.

social structures and the existing institutional patterns of gender organization. While they, too, want job security and health insurance for their partners, they may see these as liberal or even conservative goals that simply reinforce the status quo. Whereas traditional transsexuals, to coin a phrase, are not interested in using their sexual transition to disrupt the conventions of sex and gender, less traditional transgendered people often see challenging the sex/gender system as a fundamental goal of social action among trans people.

THE POLITICAL IMPLICATIONS OF TRANSSEXUALITY VERSUS TRANSGENDERISM

As a number of scholars have noted (Bolin 1993; Nestle, Wilkins, and Howell 2002; Stone 1991), transsexuality is both regressive and transgressive. On one hand, the idea that an individual's gender can vary from his or her sex challenges patriarchal and scientific thinking about an essentialist relationship between these two qualities of individuals. On the other hand, the idea that one might simply transition from being a member of one sex into being a member of the other leaves in place the fundamental notion that there are two mutually exclusive genders, and that in order to enact one or the other, a person must have a particular configuration of genitals. Feminists have criticized the medicalization of transsexuality on a number of fronts as a result.

Acknowledging the history of sex reassignment surgery as initially oriented toward "curing" gay men of homosexuality by turning them into women, feminists have argued that this practice is rooted in both homophobia and heterosexism, and have wondered whether many male-to-female transsexuals opt for sex reassignment surgery in lieu of accepting their homosexuality. Others have resisted the inclusion of male-to-female transsexuals in feminist political and social spaces (Raymond 1979), arguing that although such people have modified their physical bodies, their socialization as boys and men continues to result in their using male privilege in women's spaces. Heated conflicts have taken place around the inclusion of trans people at the Michigan Women's Music Festival, a predominantly lesbian space, as more transgendered and male-to-female transsexuals have requested admission and more "woman-born women" have expressed unease over sharing "women's space" with people initially socialized as men.

The inclusion of trans issues in the lesbian and gay movement has also been a cause of conflict within LGBT spaces. Although many formerly gay and lesbian organizations now bill themselves as serving lesbian, gay, bisexual, and transgendered people, the interests of lesbian, gay, and bisexual people often differ from those of transsexual and transgendered people. Lesbian, gay, and bisexual identities center on sexual attraction, whereas trans identities center on gender presentation. Early in the lesbian and gay movement in the United States, activists focused on convincing psychiatrists, policy makers, and the general public that they did not suffer from gender confusion but were, indeed, people of each sex comfortable in their masculinity or femininity and attracted to members of the same sex. While some transsexual people are lesbian, gay, or bisexual, many wish to live mainstream heterosexual lives after their transition, and many may experience the benefits of heterosexual privilege, which are denied to gay and lesbian people. While many trans people feel allied with lesbian and gay people as cultural outsiders, lesbian and gay people may wonder whether precious movement resources should be devoted to trans concerns that do not seem directly related to lesbian and gay issues.

In addition to asking whether transsexuality and transgenderism reinforce or disrupt dominant systems of sex, gender, and sexuality, exploring the politics of these identities also requires that we examine who benefits from the practices involved in them. In the case of transsexuality, it is clear that several healthcare industries profit from the diagnosis and treatment of gender identity disorder through sex reassignment and/or hormonal therapy. In order to receive the diagnosis that qualifies a person for SRS, an individual must become a patient of a social worker, psychiatrist, or psychologist and establish a long-term relationship with that care provider; once a GID diagnosis is established, the person seeking SRS begins hormonal therapy that she or he will continue for the remainder of his or her life; eventually, if the person undergoes SRS, a team of surgeons and nurses and a hospital facility will all receive financial benefit from the patient who receives services. In the case of transsexual people seeking sex reassignment, therefore, a host of care providers stand to benefit from an individual's transition from one sex to the other. Regarding transgendered people, who may chose either to live with trans identities or to live as the opposite sex/gender

SEX REASSIGNMENT SURGERY IS NOT THE ONLY HEALTH ISSUE TRANS PEOPLE FACE

For poor or economically disadvantaged trans people, especially people of color (POC), sex reassignment surgery and hormone therapy are simply unaffordable. Meeting basic healthcare needs is a struggle. The barriers to adequate healthcare include lack of access to health services in the community, lack of education, and lack of training for healthcare providers.

Healthcare services for communities of color are often lacking. For example, a district of 200,000 people in Los Angeles has no hospital in the community (Tamuno-Koko 2007). Information about healthcare available to trans people may be available in locations to which many trans folks in poor communities and communities of color have little access, such as colleges. "According to the Los Angeles Transgender Health Community Report (2001), of the 244 GV [Gender Variant] persons interviewed 47% reported being high school dropouts, 22% completed high school, and only 31% have more than 12 years of education. In addition, 50% reported they were sex workers" (Tamuno-Koko 2007). Furthermore, lack of education makes it difficult to navigate a healthcare system that is outside one's neighborhood and inattentive or even hostile to the specific healthcare needs of transgender folks.

Finally, barriers to medical care exist across class and race. Since GID disorder is characterized as a psychological disorder rather than a medical disorder, medical schools do not address the health issues faced by transsexuals and transgendered persons (Xavier et al. 2004). The lack of appropriate medical training means that even well-intentioned healthcare providers are simply uninformed about transgender/transsexual healthcare needs.

without the impact of hormones or surgery, the financial gain for care providers is reduced.

CONCLUSION

Although many societies have integrated into their social systems people born one sex who desire (or are required) to live as the other, contemporary Western society offers limited legitimate options for integrating both masculinity and femininity into one personality or lifestyle. Because of the continuing rigidity of our sex/gender structure, some individuals who feel constrained by the expectations put on their assigned sex adopt either transsexual or transgendered identities. For transsexual people, the availability of both sex reassignment surgery and a medical discourse that posits the possibility of an essential discordance between the gendered self and the sexed body allows sexual body modification to appear a good and reasonable solution to the problem of how to appropriately and fully express one's sense of self. For others, the idea of transgendered identities that make transparent the integration of qualities of both genders and sometimes both sexes presents an alternative that does not involve passing but, instead, presenting new and alternative forms of gender presentation. While both strategies challenge the essentialist notion that the sexed body always results in a consistent gender, both also depend on a recognition of a binary gender structure; in order to "cross" categories, a perception of a clearly defined division must first be in place.

See also Gender Identity Disorder; Sex Reassignment Surgery; Sex versus Gender; Third Genders.

Further Reading: American Psychiatric Association, *Diagnostic and Statistical Manual of Mental Disorders,* 4th ed. (Washington, DC: American Psychiatric Association, 2000); Ault, Amber, and Stephanie Brzuzy, "Eliminating Gender Identity Disorder (GID) from the Diagnostic and Statistical Manual of Mental Disorders: A Role for Social Work," unpublished paper, n.d.; Benjamin, H., *The Transsexual Phenomenon* (New York: Julian Press, 1966); Blackwood, Evelyn, "Sexuality and Gender in Certain North American Indian Tribes: The Case of Cross-Gender Females," *Signs* 10, no. 1 (1984): 27–42; Bolin, Anne, "Transcending and Transgendering: Male to Female Transsexuals, Dichotomy, and Diversity," in *Third Sex, Third Gender: Beyond Sexual Dimorphism in Culture and History,* ed. Gilbert Herdt, 447–486 (New York: Zone Books, 1994); Bornstein, K., *Gender Outlaw: On Men, Women, and the Rest of Us* (New York: Routledge, 1994); Butler, J., *Gender Trouble: Feminism and the Subversion of Identity* (New York: Routledge, 1994 [1999]); Butler, J., *Undoing Gender* (New York: Routledge, 2004); Califia, P., *Sex Changes: The Politics of Transgenderism* (San Francisco: Cleis Press, 1997); Conn, C., *Canary: The Story of a Transsexual* (New York: Bantam, 1977); Currah, P., R. Juang, and S. Minter, eds., *Transgender Rights* (Minneapolis: University of Minnesota Press, 2006); Doctor, R. F., *Transvestites and Transsexuals: Toward a Theory of Cross-Gender Behavior* (New York: Plenum Press, 1988); Elbe, L., *Man into Woman: An Authentic Record of a Change of Sex. The True Story of the Miraculous Transformation of the Danish Painter, Einar Wegener* [Andreas Sparre], ed. Niels Hoyer [Ernst Ludwig Harthern Jacobsen], trans. H. J. Stenning (New York: E. P. Dutton, 1933); Feinberg, L., *Stone Butch Blues: A Novel* (Los Angeles: Alyson Books, 2004; orig. pub. Ann Arbor: Firebrand Books, 1993); Foucault, Michel,

The History of Sexuality: An Introduction (New York: Vintage, 1990); Green, J., *Becoming a Visible Man* (Nashville, TN: Vanderbilt University Press, 2004); Gremaux, René, "Woman Becomes Man in the Balkans," in *Third Sex, Third Gender: Beyond Sexual Dimorphism in Culture and History,* ed. Gilbert Herdt, 214–281 (New York: Zone Books, 1994); Halberstam, J., *In a Queer Time and Place: Transgender Bodies, Subcultural Lives* (New York: New York University Press, 2005); Mills, C. Wright, *The Sociological Imagination* (New York: Oxford University Press, 1976 [1959]); Nestle, J., R. Wilkins, and C. Howell, eds., *GenderQueer: Voices from beyond the Sexual Binary* (Los Angeles: Alyson Press, 2002); Nettick, G., and B. Elliot, *Mirrors: Portrait of a Lesbian Transsexual* (New York: Masquerade, 1996); Morriss, J., *Conundrum* (New York: Harcourt Brace Jovanovich, 1974); Namaste, V., *Invisible Lives: The Erasure of Transsexual and Transgendered People* (Chicago: University of Chicago Press, 2000); Planet Out, "Indian Town Elects Trans Mayor," Planet Out, November 27, 2000, available at: http://www.planetout.com/news/article.html?2000/11/27/3; Raymond, J., *The Transsexual Empire: The Making of the She Male* (Boston: Beacon Press, 1979); Rich, Adrienne, "Compulsory Heterosexuality and Lesbian Existence," *Signs* 5, no. 4 (1980): 631–660; Riddell, C., *Divided Sisterhood: A Critical Review of Janice Raymond's "The Transsexual Empire"* (Liverpool, UK: News from Nowhere, 1980); Roscoe, Will, "How to Become a Berdache: Toward a Unified Analysis of Gender Diversity," in *Third Sex, Third Gender: Beyond Sexual Dimorphism in Culture and History,* ed. Gilbert Herdt, 329–372 (New York: Zone Books, 1994); Rubin, H., "Reading Like a (Transsexual) Man," in *Men Doing Feminism,* ed. Tom Digby, 305–324 (New York: Routledge, 1988); "San Francisco Workers Get Sex Change Coverage," *New York Times,* February 18, 2001, available at: http://www.nytimes.com/gst/fullpage.html?res=9801EOD71130F93BA25751COA; Stone, S., "The Empire Strikes Back: A Posttranssexual Manifesto," in *Body Guards: The Cultural Politics of Gender Ambiguity,* ed. J. Epstein and K. Staub, 280–304 (New York: Routledge, 1991); Stryker S., and S. Whittle, eds., *The Transgender Reader* (New York: Routledge, 2006); Straub, K., and J. Epstein, eds., *Body Guards: The Cultural Politics of Gender Ambiguity* (New York: Routledge, 1991); Tamuno–Koko, A., "Gendering and the Role It Plays in Healthcare Access of Gender Variant People of Color," available at: FTMI.org, accessed February 25, 2007; Xavier, J., D. Hitchcock, S. Hollinshead, M. Keisling, Y. Lewis, E. Lombardi, S. Lurie, D. Sanchez, B. Singer, R. Stone, et al., "An Overview of U.S. Trans Health Priorities: A Report by the Eliminating Disparities Working Group," August 2004 update, available at: http://www.nctequality.org/HealthPriorities.pdf, accessed February 26, 2007.

Crista Lebens and Amber Ault

WELFARE REFORM

Providing welfare assistance to poor women has always been controversial, although the dramatic overhaul of the United States' social welfare system in the early 1990s brought on a new set of debates. Controversies concerning women and welfare reform involve the questions of what the role of the state should be in providing for citizens in need; whether childcare and economic job security should be the mother's, the father's, or the government's responsibility; whether women are disproportionately affected by poverty or not; and how poverty and unemployment can best be eradicated.

BACKGROUND

The U.S. government has provided public assistance to poor women with children since the 1930s, with the passage of the federal Social Security Act of 1935. This marked the beginning of an era in which it was believed that the national government should provide for its most needy; women were often targeted in their roles as mothers of children and, by extension, as mothers of future generations and of the nation (Hill Collins 2006). The original federal program was called Aid to Dependent Children (ADC). It provided cash assistance to women and children who were in need, including poor, unemployed female heads of households and their dependents. The program changed in the 1960s and became known as Aid to Families with Dependent Children (AFDC). It still provided cash assistance to poor families but now this was extended to families with fathers present in the home, although the majority of families receiving assistance were still headed by women and the typical family receiving

TIMELINE

1935: The Social Security Act of 1995 is passed. Included in it is the first federal program for public assistance, known as Aid to Dependent Children (ADC).

1962: The name of the program changes to Aid to Families with Dependent Children (AFDC) to reflect the fact that government assistance would include both unemployed parents (mothers and fathers) as well as children.

1964: President Lyndon Johnson launches the War on Poverty as a part of his Great Society Program amid growing awareness of the poor in the United States.

1996: AFDC ends and is replaced with the Temporary Assistance to Needy Families Program (TANF), a much more restricted public assistance program.

2005: TANF is reauthorized by Congress.

2006: The 10-year anniversary of TANF is marked by a decline in public assistance recipients, but still great controversy over the "success" of the program exists.

assistance was a mother with two children, utilizing services for two years or less. This program operated under the premise that government assistance was an entitlement. Entitlement in this context means that every person who could demonstrate need could receive government assistance. The federal government in conjunction with states would provide enough money to ensure that all families who qualified would receive services. AFDC also included job training and job placement programs (Trattner 1999). The AFDC program existed until 1996, when it was overhauled amid controversy. Opponents of the program argued that the accessibility of public assistance encouraged laziness and dependence on the federal and state governments. Supporters of the program argued that it was working exactly as it was designed to work and that most women and their children did not need services beyond a two- to three-year period. At the time, President Bill Clinton (1992–2000) wanted to end "welfare as we know it" and to create an assistance program that would support not "dependency" but rather "opportunity," two notions that have been heavily debated since they gained salience in public policy debates during this period (Fraser and Gordon 1994).

The result of the overhaul was the Personal Responsibility and Work Opportunity Reconciliation Act of 1996, which ended AFDC and replaced it with the Temporary Assistance for Needy Families (TANF) program, which ended the guarantee of benefits for poor families. As the replacement program for AFDC, TANF still provides cash assistance to poor families; however, it includes several new restrictions. In particular, it mandates that recipients work in order to be eligible for temporary benefits. Generally, states were given more latitude in defining eligibility and length of benefits, although the federal cap is five years. TANF is funded through block grants to individual states. The federal government now gives only a capped amount of money to states to provide assistance. When the money runs out, there is no guarantee of providing additional families with assistance. Supporters of the reforms believed this would finally end dependency on public assistance. Opponents of the reforms saw this as a major breach in the federal safety net that had supported poor women and children for the previous 60 years.

THE GOALS OF TANF

There are four main goals associated with TANF. These are assisting needy families so that children can be cared for in their own homes; reducing the dependency of needy parents by promoting job preparation, work, and marriage; preventing out-of-wedlock pregnancies; and encouraging the formation and maintenance of two-parent families. TANF imposes a five-year lifetime limit on the receipt of cash assistance for individuals and families. In addition, TANF also requires that almost all TANF recipients engage in a work activity within two years of receiving assistance. Failure to gain employment within two years can result in a denial of assistance. Also, TANF requires that child support be collected from the fathers of children. In addition to the requirements, incentives are given to women who are married. TANF also promotes certain lifestyles deemed to be healthy and stable. The new requirements and restrictions of TANF carry with them many implications for women, because women with children are most likely to need and receive public assistance.

WORK REQUIREMENTS

The work requirements of TANF are extensive. The law stipulates that recipients (with few exceptions) must work as soon as they are job ready or no later than two years after beginning to receive assistance. Single parents are required to participate in work activities for at least 30 hours per week. Two-parent families must participate in work activities for 35 or 55 hours a week, depending upon circumstances. Failure to participate in work requirements can result in a reduction or termination of benefits to the family. However, on a more positive note, states cannot penalize single parents with a child under six for failing to meet the work requirements if they cannot find adequate childcare. It is assumed the child will be in school at the age of six, thereby solving the issue of childcare. States have to ensure that 50 percent of all families and 90 percent of two-parent families are participating in work activities. If a state does not follow specific guidelines such as this, its funding could be revoked. Activities that are considered to be work include the following: unsubsidized or subsidized employment, on-the-job training, work experience, community service, job-skills training related to work, satisfactory secondary school attendance, and the provision of childcare services to individuals who are participating in community service. Searching for a job can be included as a work activity. However, the length of time allowed for this activity is not to exceed six weeks in total and can include no more than four consecutive weeks. Vocational training is also included as work activity, which can be beneficial to women, for it will allow them to learn a specific job skill. However, vocational training cannot exceed 12 months in length. It should be noted, however, that attending a college or university is *not* considered a work activity. This is a real detriment to recipients. It is well established that many higher-paying jobs that provide opportunities for advancement require a college degree.

The requirements pose a major problem for single mothers. They are forced both to work outside the home and to care for their children in order to receive benefits. And if a single mother wanted to receive a college degree, she would have to do so in addition to working at least 30 hours a week, which is required of single mothers. This is virtually impossible. However, without a college degree, a woman will often be relegated to working a job that offers little pay and little room for advancement. This makes it much more difficult to escape poverty and earn a living wage. In addition, although single mothers are forced to work outside of the home, good-quality, low-cost childcare is extremely difficult to obtain (Fineman 2001). In fact, the lack of adequate childcare is a reason why many women are not able to fulfill the work requirements of TANF, and as a result they lose their benefits. Single mothers are forced to work at least 30 hours per week outside the home in order to maintain their benefits, which does not allow them to care for their children at home. However, two-parent families need engage in only 35 or 55 hours of work activity a week in total, allowing one parent to stay at home with the children.

Many would consider employment outside the home a means to enable women to participate fully in society and become self-sufficient. After all, women have fought to be accepted and respected in the workplace. Requiring work is also seen as beneficial because work is believed to be a much better alternative than receiving public assistance. Steady employment is believed to be a way for women and their children to get out of poverty. In fact, many TANF recipients want to work. They too see it as a way to a better life for themselves and their children. Many women work to repudiate the stereotype that welfare recipients are lazy and dependent on the government. However, the reality is that mothers who need public assistance lack the means necessary to work full-time and care for children on their own.

PROMOTION OF MARRIAGE AND TWO-PARENT FAMILIES

Under the new law, states are also given incentives if they are able to decrease the number of children born "out of wedlock" without increasing the number of abortions. There are incentives for women receiving assistance as well, should they choose to marry. Marriage was seen as especially important for proponents of the Personal Responsibility and Work Opportunity Reconciliation Act (PRWORA), of 1996, because it was often thought that the increase in recipients of public assistance was directly correlated with the increase in the numbers of single mothers since the 1960s (Jimenez 1999). In 1996, congressional hearings supported the idea that marriage is the foundation of a successful society and an essential institution in a society that successfully promotes the interests of children. In addition, the following ideas were put forward: a successful marriage is one that is financially stable; and marriage is key not only to reducing poverty but to reducing the characteristics said to be associated with it, such as laziness, immorality, and bad decision making. Marriage was also promoted because the two-parent family is the "ideal" and the "healthiest" situation for all involved. The law promotes marriage by requiring two-parent families to spend less time per week in the workforce so that children can be cared for in the home. The negative impact on women can include being forced into relationships with men and feeling pressured to get married in order to receive needed benefits. One underlying assumption is that poverty is caused by single motherhood. But this ignores many structural inequalities that contribute to poverty. There is also the assumption that two-parent families are healthier and more stable than single-parent families. Such laws do not support alternative family formations such as poor lesbian and gay households with children. The promotion of marriage is a promotion of heterosexuality and heteronormativity. In addition, the law does not take cognizance of the fact that marriage is a personal choice and many women may choose to raise children on their own. Two-parent families in which the mother and father are married are seen as healthy environments, but this may not necessarily be the case. Previously harmful relationships may cause future harm for women who are forced back into such relationships to obtain better support options.

CHILD SUPPORT ENFORCEMENT

In addition to providing marriage incentives, TANF also requires child support to be paid by the father of the child if possible. Before any benefits can be obtained, there must be disclosure of paternity for all children. Orders for child support are required by the states, by order of the federal government. Forcing men to pay child support is the states' method of forcing fathers to take responsibility for their children, at least, to take financial responsibility. This was seen as one of the more positive aspects of the reforms and was embraced by many on both sides of the debate. There was general agreement that fathers should take responsibility for their children, and that responsibility for childcare should not rest squarely on the mothers' shoulders. Some believe that if more men paid child support, as they are required to do by law, then there would be less reliance on government assistance. This provision fits in with the work requirements and the promotion of marriage. All are viewed as necessary and viable methods for moving from government assistance to "self-sufficiency." Some feminists supported the child support provision of TANF. They argued that poverty among women and children is caused by irresponsible fathers and not immoral mothers, and that often, mothers are blamed for making poor choices that lead them to public assistance. Feminists supported child support enforcement because they recognized that the fathers of the children should be forced to provide support to the mothers.

However, as other feminist observers have noted (Mink 1998, 1999), this provision can place a burden on many mothers. As a result of the reforms, women may be forced into a relationship with the fathers of their children. Whereas incentives to marriage are highly encouraged but still optional, the provision regarding child support by fathers is mandatory. Women are required to reveal personal details in order to receive assistance. This is indicative of the transition from a program of entitlement to one rife with restrictions and obstacles. It is also seen as an invasion of privacy. Women who are not receiving government assistance are never required to disclose the paternity of their children, unless they are seeking child support from the father. Also for such women, the decision to seek child support is personal. This highlights one way in which the government treats women who seek assistance differently from other women. Finally, there was a perception that mothers would be able to keep child support monies for the benefit of their children, but the monies collected actually go to the state to repay public assistance, although states provide a very small "pass-through" amount that goes directly to mothers for the benefit of children.

CONCLUSION: WELFARE REFORM TODAY

It has been 11 years since TANF was created with the goal of "ending welfare as we know it." Since 1996, the number of people receiving public assistance has decreased significantly. On the surface, this may be seen a positive result, and welfare reform supporters argue that it demonstrates success. However, though there are fewer people receiving welfare, some observers point out that this does not mean there are fewer people needing services (Coven 2005). For example, due to the five-year limit, many families lose their benefits. The numbers of people receiving benefit have decreased, the analysis goes, because of the time limits and also because of the strict requirements of the program. Many women, for example, are removed from the program for failing to find work within two years. Critics also point out that there are many issues associated with poverty other than government assistance and that many of these other issues make it difficult to meet the expected work requirements. These include mental and physical impairments; substance abuse; domestic violence; low literacy or skill levels; learning disabilities; having a child with a disability; and problems with housing, childcare, transportation, and low-paying jobs (Coven 2005).

In 1996, according to the Department of Health and Human Services (2006), there were 12,156,000 public assistance recipients. In 2003, the number had dropped to 5,432,000. This statistic is often thought to be proof of the success of TANF and social welfare reform efforts. However, as most scholars of women and welfare observe, this does not translate into fewer poor and impoverished families. It does not necessarily mean that millions of families have successfully ended their need for public assistance and are employed in higher-paying jobs. On the contrary, most people who leave public assistance due to the time limits, the sanctions, or a "successful" transition to work are in low-paying hourly paid jobs that lack benefits (Morgen 2006). Women, and especially single mothers, are often unduly burdened by the requirements and restrictions specified by the law and they have the most to lose, as has been documented by sociologists and journalists who have spent considerable time documenting women's experiences with the new welfare system (Ehrenreich 2001; Hays 2003).

See also Feminization of Poverty; Work: Paid versus Unpaid.

Further Reading: Adair, Vivyan, "Class Absences: Cutting Class in Feminist Studies," *Feminist Studies* 31, no. 3 (2005): 575–603; Coven, Martha, *An Introduction to TANF* (Washington, DC: Center on Budget and Policy Priorities, 2005); Department of Health and

Human Services, "Office of Family Assistance," 2006, available at: www.acf.hhs.gov/programs/ofa, accessed May 7, 2007; Ehrenreich, Barbara, *Nickel and Dimed: On (Not) Getting By in America* (New York: Metropolitan, 2001); Fineman, Martha Albertson, "Dependencies," in *Women and Welfare: Theory and Practice in the United States and Europe,* ed. Nancy J. Hirschmann and Ulrike Leibert, 23–38 (New Brunswick, NJ: Rutgers University Press, 2001); Fraser, Nancy, and Linda Gordon, "A Genealogy of Dependency: Tracing a Keyword of the U.S. Welfare State," *Signs* 19, no. 2 (1994): 303–337; Gordon, Linda, *Pitied but Not Entitled: Single Mothers and the History of Welfare* (Cambridge, MA: Harvard University Press, 1994); Hays, Sharon, *Flat Broke with Children: Women in the Age of Welfare Reform* (New York: Oxford University Press, 2003); Hill Collins, Patricia, *From Black Power to Hip Hop: Racism, Nationalism and Feminism* (Philadelphia: Temple University Press, 2006), especially chapters 1–2; Jimenez, Mary Ann, "A Feminist Analysis of Welfare Reform: The Personal Responsibility Act of 1996," *Affilia: Journal of Women and Social Work* 14, no. 3 (1999): 278–293; Mink, Gwendolyn, *Welfare's End* (Ithaca, NY: Cornell University Press, 1998); Mink, Gwendolyn, ed., *Whose Welfare?* (Ithaca, NY: Cornell University Press, 1999); Morgan, Sandra, et al., "Living Economic Restructuring at the Bottom: Welfare Restructuring and Low Wage Work," in *The Promise of Welfare Reform,* ed. Keith Kilty and Elizabeth A. Segal (New York: Haworth Press, 2006); Piven, Frances Fox, Joan Acker, Margaret Hallock, and Sandra Morgen, eds., *Work, Welfare and Politics: Confronting Poverty in the Wake of Welfare Reform* (Eugene: University of Oregon Press, 2002); Trattner, Walter, *From Poor Law to Welfare State: A History of Social Welfare in America* (New York: Free Press, 1999).

Katie Weber

WORK: PAID VERSUS UNPAID

Economic debates continue with regard to women's productive (paid) labor and women's reproductive (unpaid) labor, which includes their culturally ascribed gender roles in childrearing and managing households. Critics of women's "double burden" of paid and unpaid labor contend that it is exploitative, rooted in sexism rather than biology, and therefore changeable. In contrast, defenders of women's dual workload argue that women's gender roles are normal, natural, and help sustain a balanced household.

BACKGROUND

Studies from around the world reveal that women continue to face on average lower wages than men in occupations of comparable worth, as well as sex segregation within industries, barriers in hiring and promotion (the glass ceiling), discrimination due to pregnancy and maternity, and sexual harassment in the workplace. Although women have made significant progress in entering the labor force in manufacturing, service, and agricultural sectors around the world, they continue to perform the bulk of work in the household, including unpaid domestic labor and childrearing.

A key concept in understanding women's position in the economy is the concept of work. *The Oxford English Dictionary* (2nd ed.) defines work as "an activity involving mental or/and physical effort done in order to achieve a result." In agricultural and feudal societies, work was performed by all members of the household including non-blood kin, children, serfs, slaves, and other laborers, all of whom had a role in producing for consumption or for the market. Different gender, class, and racial-ethnic groups were involved in and controlled different dimensions of this economy, according to rigid hierarchical structures. Economic activities (including small farms, large plantations, communal production in rural areas, and artesan, retailing, and service activities in villages) varied according to geographical location and historical period. With the development of capitalist industrialized societies, a split occurred between work performed within the household and work performed outside it, in the labor market. On the one hand, *wage work* in the labor market is demanded for the production of commodities and services for the market and directly generates surplus value for the accumulation of capital. On the other hand, *unpaid work* in the household is demanded for the production of use values for direct consumption and is necessary for the maintenance and reproduction of the labor force. Even though home work contributes to the process of capital accumulation by socializing, maintaining, and reproducing the labor force, it has been ignored as part of the economic process and unrecognized and undervalued in classical studies of economic theory (Armstrong and Armstrong 1990).

In addition to the division of labor between the home and the workplace, feminist scholars have pointed out that patriarchal structures play an important role in the division of labor among genders. In this view, *patriarchy* predates capitalism and is a separate, fundamental and autonomous social, historical, and power structure; a set of societal relations that generates a system for the division of labor and power between genders, in which men control the economic and political public spheres as well as the sexuality, reproduction capacity, and work of women. Patriarchy informs two realms: the *public sphere,* traditionally associated with men (the economy of paid work, institutionalized religion, and political institutions), and the *private sphere,* traditionally associated with women (the economy of unpaid work that produces use values for direct consumption in the household, unpaid work that includes home chores, reproduction, child care, and sexual services). In capitalist economies, women's relegation to the private sphere and the invisibility and devaluation of their work in this sphere, together with occupational segregation by sex in the public sphere, are the result of gender inequities in the realm of work (Armstrong and Armstrong 1990).

THE NEOCLASSICAL ECONOMIC MODEL OF WOMEN'S WORK

According to Francine Blau and Marianne Ferber (2005), at a microeconomic level, neoclassical economic models explain the traditional division of labor between genders in society and within the household as a result of informed and rational decisions that result in maximizing the utility or well-being of the family. The production of commodities from which the family derives the greatest possible amount of utility and satisfaction results from a combination of time at home with family members and goods and services purchased in the market. Time spent on paid work produces the income necessary to purchase market goods and services, which are needed, together with home work, to produce commodities for consumption by the family. A crucial question for the family is that of how time should be allocated between home and market most efficiently in order to maximize satisfaction.

Accordingly to a neoclassical understanding, the division of labor and allocation of time are accomplished by specialization, exchange, and comparative advantage. Commodity production is carried out more efficiently if one member of the family specializes in market production while others specialize in home production. They may then exchange their output or pool the fruits of their labor to achieve a utility-maximizing combination of goods and services produced in the market and in the home. In order for this system to be efficient, it is necessary for the members of the family to have different comparative advantages with regard to home and market production. According to this view, the traditional division of labor between women and men tends to make women relatively more productive at home and men relatively more productive in the market. The traditional division of labor is socially determined, but at present, according to this model, the reality is that women are better in work at home because they have been educated to specialize in it. According to this theory, there are economic gains and efficiency when a couple joins efforts and divides the benefits. If the two people do not have different comparative advantages, the conclusion no longer follows and their pooled income will presumably be no greater than the sum of their separate incomes (Blau and Ferber 2005).

At a macroeconomic level, the development of the women's labor force participation rate (WLFPR) has traditionally been explained by neoclassical economics as a consequence of economic development and the industrialization process. The classical perspective gives great emphasis to the impact of the technological change and the reorganization of the production process brought about by the rise of capitalism on the social position of women in the productive apparatus. Proponents of the classical model argue that the process of transformation of women in the labor force occurs in accordance with historical stages that resemble a "U" curve (Aguiar 1983).

In the initial stage of the industrial process, according to the "U" curve model, agriculture still constitutes the principal productive activity, coexisting with at-home manufacturing and small-scale commerce. These activities enable a high women's labor force participation rate, since housework activities can easily be coupled with agricultural, commercial, and manufacturing activities. In the second stage, the agrarian economy turns capitalist, a large segment of the population starts to migrate to urban areas, and the WLFPR tends to decline. In the third stage, the development of the productive forces reaches a point that allows the liberation of women from domestic settings, and an increase in the WLFPR is observed, principally in the service sector, which grows as a consequence of industrial expansion. At this stage, women's incorporation in the labor force goes hand in hand with economic growth.

FEMINIST CRITIQUES OF THE NEOCLASSICAL ECONOMIC MODEL

Feminist scholars have questioned the microeconomic and macroeconomic neoclassical explanations of the traditional gender division of labor as it affects women's labor force participation on various levels. For example, feminist economists such as Julie Nelson (1996) and Pamela Sparr (1994) note that neoclassical economics is a theory that is not value neutral but rather is grounded in culturally and historically specific interpretations of human behavior seen through the lenses of the particular race, ethnicity, class, and gender of the creators of the discipline. The theory universalizes the experience of a handful of fairly industrialized economies at a certain point of time and it assumes that these experiences do not fundamentally vary among different societies. Therefore, it neglects the cultural, historical, geographic, and political characteristics of different societies and the relations among nations; and it ignores the interaction between gender, class, race, and sexuality structures within communities (Sparr 1994).

Drawing upon the average expected performance of the white, middle-class, Western economic male in the capitalist market world, neoclassical economic theory is constructed around the notion of a "rational economic man." The theory assumes that all human behavior is primarily individualistic, selfish, competitive, and money oriented, and that individuals' decisions are the outcome of the free, informed, and rational choices of economic agents, specializing according to their innate comparative advantage. By assuming that "rational economic man" behavior applies to all human beings, the theory ignores or obscures important aspects of social and political life (Nelson 1996). It ignores the structural relations of domination (such as international core-periphery relations, class, race, and gender) and dependent relations (such as those of children and the elderly) that define access to resources (who controls income and property, how these are managed, how decisions are made to allocate income, and who gets what), roles (who does what), and responsibilities (who makes the decisions). It also ignores human networks in which by cultural conviction, religious or otherwise, collectivism (a system that emphasizes collective sharing and exchange, in contrast to individualism) is an accepted mode of behavior and the accumulation of material goods is not the priority. As a consequence, the theory cannot deal with situations where conflictive or cooperative behaviors are present, and equally it cannot infer the possibility of better results where cooperative behaviors are present. The definition of the neoclassical family is similar to the Eurocentric ideal notion of the nuclear patriarchal family, although, cross-cultural studies of kinship systems reveal a great variety of family forms. The formations of family life and structures, like many other social experiences, are nested within the class, race, and gender relations of a given historical period and geographical location, and these factors are overlooked and simplified in economic theory.

LINKING PRODUCTIVE AND REPRODUCTIVE LABOR

Diane Elson (1995) and other feminist scholars such as Marilyn Waring (1990) argue that the economic structure and all the institutions that accompany it are gendered. Specifically, they argue that neoclassical macroeconomics analyses, which focus on the productive economy and on national aggregates such as gross national product (GNP), are incomplete because they neglect a whole area of production, the unpaid production of human resources, which is largely women's work. There is interdependence between the economy of profit-oriented production and the non-profit-oriented "reproductive economy," a term now widely used by economists interested in how unpaid work helps to support the economy. Equally, feminist political-economists such as Pat Armstrong and Hugh Armstrong (1990) argue that the ability of capital to mobilize labor power for "productive work" (wage work) depends on the operation of non-profit-oriented sets of social relations that mobilize labor power for "reproductive work." Specifically, the unpaid labor of women who work in their households, raising children and taking care of relatives, in addition to performing volunteer labor such as involving themselves in community organizations, all contribute significantly to the economy despite the fact that they are not officially included in national income accounts. The monetary economy cannot sustain itself without an input of unpaid labor, an input shaped by the structure of gender relations. The way in which these relations exist in a given society influences the forms of structural discrimination in the labor market and in the realm of reproductive labor (Elson 1994).

Ignoring the interdependence of the reproduction of human resources with paid areas of production (the interdependence between meeting people's needs and making a profit), macroeconomic policies tend to assume that the reproductive economy can adapt itself to whatever changes these policies introduce and that the reproductive economy can continue to function adequately no matter how it is disrupted by the productive economy. In practice, this has meant that poor women, in particular, have had to work harder and have essentially served as buffers during times of economic crisis (Benería and Feldman, 1992). As Elson (1994) argues, the process of production of human resources differs from the processes of production of goods, services, and capital. Once human resource production is undertaken, women tend not to abandon this process, even if it is not economically sound. Ignoring women's contribution to the economy means macroeconomic policies are able to assume that women's capacity to undertake unpaid work is infinitely elastic and does not diminish women's ability to undertake other forms of production.

Women perform many kinds of labor that fall within the realm of paid and unpaid work. For example, in Latin America, Africa, and Asia, many studies show that women, rather than disappearing from the economy during the transition from agrarian to capitalist modes of production, continue to engage in traditional subsistence farming and/or work in informal, domestic, home-based manufacturing, small-scale commerce, paid domestic service, or sexual service sectors, in addition to continuing their traditional unpaid work at home (Waring 1990). Most of these activities are not accounted for in official economic statistics, and they are commonly treated as noncapitalist and/or nonmonetary labor, despite the fact that women earn incomes through many of these forms of labor.

Neuma Aguiar (1983) also argues that classical economics makes assumptions about women's labor in the Latin American context, assumptions that devalue traditional forms of production. These forms of production in Latin America are analyzed through the use of categories such as informal labor markets, underemployment, hidden employment, and marginality. Work that is done outside the hegemonic capitalist structure (wage work) is automatically devalued as "traditional," stagnant, backward, and deviant in relation to the "progressive" Western capitalist model. The narrow concept of paid work under capitalism devalues or ignores the existence of traditional modes of production under which people have lived for centuries, especially in the realm of women's unpaid labor as well as in subsistence agriculture and indigenous economies. Whereas prior to industrial capitalism, men's work and women's work were arguably valued in more equal terms, with the historical rise of capitalism women continue to work in the traditional, informal, and/or unpaid economies but their work is invisible and undervalued in monetary terms.

At the microeconomic level (which focuses on the decision-making behavior of individual economic units such as the family and the firm), feminists have also contested assumptions made by neoclassical economics. As noted above, neoclassical economists argue that the division of labor in the household is based on each individual's maximizing of his or her skills in the household economy. In contrast, feminist economists believe that households involve interactions of "cooperative conflict" rather than merely altruism or selfishness (Sen 1987). According to this view, cooperative conflicts are situations in which individuals stand to make gains from cooperating but have different and conflicting interests in the distribution of benefits. The microlevel institutions are characterized by cooperation in both the reproduction process and the production process, but there is also conflict in the distribution of the benefits. Relations within the family and the firm are not necessarily mediated by harmonious rational interests or by a joint utility function that maximizes the well-being of each member of the institution. Rather, a profoundly unequal accommodation is often reached between individuals (men and women) who occupy very different social positions and enjoy very different degrees of social and economic power. Social norms constrain people's choices about the division of labor and income in the family and the firm (Elson 1994). A good example of this involves communities that provide greater investment in boys than in girls in areas such as education, health, and other assets, a problem that the United Nations has documented in studies of countries as diverse as India, China, and the United States.

Following this line of thinking about women's and men's participation in the household economy, the amount of power men and women have is highly dependent on the relative material resources at their disposal. Wives who are not employed, or whose potential market wage rate is diminished while they bear and raise children or simply because of the general discrimination and wage differentiation faced by women in the labor market, are less likely to influence family decision making. The asymmetry of control over income between genders decreases women's bargaining position within the household. The vulnerability of women to violence, now widely documented, is also an indication of their relative powerlessness within the context of the family. The specialization of women in the unpaid production of goods for family consumption and reproductive work often places them at a disadvantage in the labor market.

In the work of some economists, "rational economic man" analysis has also been applied to the fundamental characterization of human beings as economic agents and to questions of gender, race, and class as they shape people's opportunities (or lack thereof). One example concerns African American households in the United States. According to Andersen (2005), the experience of African American households is rooted in a system of racism, sexism, and class inequality. In the early twentieth century, racial discrimination in the labor force denied African Americans employment using the very skills they had acquired in slavery. As a result, men could only find unskilled employment, often seasonal and always underpaid. Women were more likely to find steady, although also severely underpaid, employment, most commonly as domestic servants or nannies. Discrimination denied men the possibility of becoming steady breadwinners, even if they wanted it. Black women's labor thus made them steady providers for their families, as well as reproductive workers. As the twentieth century developed, continuing discrimination and unemployment encouraged the formation of female-centered households.

CONCLUSION

Women's labor force participation rates are directly linked to definitions of work. In the U.S. capitalist economy, work is more often than not defined as activities engaged in through salaried relations of production. Official statistics associate production with the capitalist market and labor with wage work. Since part of women's work is associated with the traditional economy and/or the unpaid reproductive economy, it remains unrecognized as an important source of labor in the modern economy. As long as people view women's roles in child-rearing and domestic work as natural extensions of their culturally prescribed gender roles, and as long as their paid work is viewed as "secondary" to men's participation, the debates about gender inequalities in the realm of productive and reproductive work will continue.

See also Comparable Worth; Gender and Globalization: Trends and Debates; Welfare Reform.

Further Reading: Aguiar, Neuma, "Women in the Labor Force in Latin America: A Review of the Literature," in *Women and Work in the Third World: The Impact of Industrialization and Global Economic Interdependence,* ed. N. M. El-Sanabary (Berkeley: Center for the Study, Education and Advancement of Women, University of California, Berkeley, 1983); Andersen, Margaret L., *Thinking about Women: Sociological Perspectives on Sex and Gender,* 7th ed. (Boston: Allyn and Bacon, 2005); Armstrong, Pat, and Hugh Armstrong, eds., *Theorizing Women's Work* (Toronto: Garamond Press, 1990); Benería, Lourdes, and Shelley Feldman, eds., *Unequal Burden: Economic Crises, Women's Work and Persistent Poverty* (Boulder, CO: Westview Press, 1992); Blau, Francine, and Marianne Ferber, *The Economics of Women, Men and Work,* 5th ed. (Upper Saddle River, NJ: Prentice-Hall, 2005); Elson, Diane, "Micro-Meso-Macro: Gender and Economic Analysis in the Context of Policy Reform," in *The Strategic Silence: Gender and Economic*

Policy, ed. Isabella Bakker (London: Zed Books, 1994); International Labour Organization, *Gender Equality around the World: Articles from "World of Work" Magazine 1999–2006* (Geneva: International Labour Organization, 2007); Nelson, Julie, *Feminism, Objectivity and Economics* (New York: Routledge, 1996); Sen, Amartya Kumar, *Gender and Cooperative Conflicts,* WIDER working papers, WP 18 (Helsinki: WIDER, 1987); Sparr, Pamela, *Mortgaging Women's Lives: Feminist Critiques of Structural Adjustment* (London: Zed Books, 1994); Waring, Marilyn, *If Women Counted: A New Feminist Economics* (San Francisco: HarperCollins, 1990).

Olga Sanmiguel-Valderrama

BIBLIOGRAPHY

Abelove, Henry. 1993. *The Lesbian and Gay Studies Reader.* New York: Routledge.

Albelda, Randy, and Chris Tilly. 1997. *Glass Ceilings and Bottomless Pits: Women's Work, Women's Poverty.* Boston: South End Press.

Alexander, M. Jacqui, and Chandra Talpade Mohanty, eds. *Feminist Genealogies, Colonial Legacies, Democratic Futures.* New York: Routledge.

Bacchetta, Paola, and Margaret Power, eds. 2002. *Right-Wing Women: From Conservatives to Extremists around the World.* New York: Routledge.

Baumgardner, Jennifer, and Amy Richards, eds. 2000. *Manifesta: Young Women, Feminism, and the Future.* New York: Farrar, Straus and Giroux.

Bornstein, Kate. 1998. *My Gender Workbook.* New York: Routledge.

Boston Women's Health Book Collective. *Our Bodies, Ourselves.* New York: Simon and Schuster, 2005; originally published in 1970.

Brumberg, Joan Jacob. 1998. *The Body Project: An Intimate History of American Girls.* New York: Vintage.

Butler, Judith. 1990. *Gender Trouble: Feminism and the Subversion of Identity.* New York: Routledge.

Castelli, Elizabeth A., with Rosamond C. Rodman. 2001. *Women, Gender, Religion: A Reader.* New York: Palgrave.

De Beauvoir, Simone. [1952] 1989. *The Second Sex.* New York: Vintage.

Edut, Ophira, ed. *Adiós, Barbie: Young Women Write about Body Image and Identity.* Seattle: Seal Press.

Ehrenreich, Barbara. 2001. *Nickel and Dimed: On (Not) Getting By in America.* New York: Metropolitan/Owl Books.

Ehrenreich, Barbara, and Arlie Russell Hochschild, eds. 2003. *Global Woman: Nannies, Maids, and Sex Workers in the New Economy.* New York: Henry Holt.

Faludi, Susan. 1992. *Backlash: The Undeclared War against American Women.* New York: Anchor.

Fausto-Sterling, Anne. 2000. *Sexing the Body: Gender Politics and the Construction of Sexuality.* New York: Basic Books.

Frankenberg, Ruth. 1993. *White Women, Race Matters: The Social Construction of Whiteness.* Minneapolis: University of Minnesota Press.

Friedan, Betty. [1963] 2001. *The Feminine Mystique.* New York: W. W. Norton.

Gamble, Sarah. 2000. *The Routledge Critical Dictionary of Feminism and Postfeminism,* New York: Routledge.

Gordon, Linda. 1994. *Pitied but Not Entitled: Single Mothers and the History of Welfare.* Cambridge, MA: Harvard University Press.

Grewal, Inderpal, and Caren Kaplan, eds. 2006. *An Introduction to Women's Studies: Gender in a Transnational World.* 2nd ed. New York: McGraw Hill.

Halberstam, Judith. 1998. *Female Masculinity.* Durham, NC: Duke University Press.

Hartmann, Betsy. 1995. *Reproductive Rights and Wrongs: The Global Politics of Population Control.* Boston: South End Press.

Heasley, Robert, and Betsy Crane, eds. 2003. *Sexual Lives: A Reader on the Theories and Realities of Human Sexualities.* Boston: McGraw Hill.

Hermann, Anne C., and Abigail J. Stewart, eds. 2001. *Theorizing Feminism: Parallel Trends in the Humanities and Social Sciences.* 2nd ed. Boulder, CO: Westview Press.

Hill Collins, Patricia. 2005. *Black Sexual Politics: African Americans, Gender, and the New Racism.* New York: Routledge.

Hoff-Sommers, Christina. 1995. *Who Stole Feminism? How Women Have Betrayed Women.* New York: Simon & Schuster.

hooks, bell. [1984] 2000. *Feminist Theory: From Margin to Center.* Boston: South End Press.

Jetter, Alexis, Annelise Orleck, and Diana Taylor, eds. 1997. *The Politics of Motherhood: Activist Voices from Left and Right.* Hanover, NH: University Press of New England.

Katz, Jonathan Ned. 2007. *The Invention of Heterosexuality.* Chicago: University of Chicago Press.

Kempadoo, Kamala. 1998. *Global Sex Workers: Rights, Resistance, and Redefinition.* New York: Routledge.

Kessler, Suzanne J. 2000. *Lessons from the Intersexed.* New Brunswick, NJ: Rutgers University Press.

Kleindeinst, Kris, ed. 1999. *This Is What Lesbian Looks Like,* Ithaca, NY: Firebrand Books.

McCann, Carole R., and Seung-Kyung Kim, eds. 2003. *Feminist Theory Reader: Local and Global Perspectives.* New York: Routledge.

Moraga, Cherríe L., and Gloria E. Anzaldúa, eds. 2002. *This Bridge Called My Back: Writings by Radical Women of Color.* Berkeley, CA: Third Woman Press.

Narayan, Uma. 1997. *Dislocating Cultures: Identities, Traditions, and Third World Feminism.* New York: Routledge.

Peterson, V. Spike, and Anne Sisson Runyan. 1993. *Global Gender Issues.* Boulder, CO: Westview Press.

Roth, Benita. 2003. *Separate Roads to Feminism: Black, Chicana and White Feminist Movements in America's Second Wave.* Cambridge: Cambridge University Press.

Roughgarden, Joan. 2005. *Evolution's Rainbow: Diversity, Gender and Sexuality in Nature and People.* Berkeley: University of California Press.

Ruiz, Vicki L., and Virginia Sánchez Korrol. 2005. *Latina Legacies: Identity, Biography, and Community.* Oxford: Oxford University Press.

Schiebinger, Londa, ed. 2000. *Feminism and the Body.* Oxford: Oxford University Press.

Smith, Bonnie G., and Beth Hutchinson, eds. 2004. *Gendering Disability.* New Brunswick, NJ: Rutgers University Press.

Springer, Kimberly. 2005. *Living for the Revolution: Black Feminist Organizations, 1968–1980.* Durham, NC: Duke University Press.

Stryker, Susan, and Stephen Whittle, eds. *The Transgender Studies Reader.* New York: Routledge.

Sullivan, Nikki. 2003. *A Critical Introduction to Queer Theory.* New York: New York University Press.

Walter, Lynn, ed. 2001. *Women's Rights: A Global View.* Westport, CT: Greenwood Press.

Whitehead, Stephen M., and Frank J. Barrett, eds. 2001. *The Masculinities Reader.* London: Polity Press.

Wilchins, Riki. 2004. *Queer Theory, Gender Theory.* Los Angeles: Alyson Books.

Wolf, Naomi. 2002. *The Beauty Myth: How Images of Beauty Are Used against Women.* New York: Harper Perennial.

Worcester, Nancy, and Mariamne H. Whatley, eds. 2004. *Women's Health: Readings on Social, Economic, and Political Issues.* Dubuque, IA: Kendall Hunt.

ABOUT THE EDITORS AND CONTRIBUTORS

Amy Lind is Mary Ellen Heintz Associate Professor of Women's Studies and faculty affiliate of planning and Latin American studies at the University of Cincinnati. She is the author of *Gendered Paradoxes: Women's Movements, State Restructuring and Global Development in Ecuador* (2005) and the editor of *Development, Sexual Rights, and Global Governance* (forthcoming) and has published several articles and book chapters on gender and sexual politics in the Americas.

Stephanie Brzuzy, PhD, is chair and associate professor of social work at Xavier University. She is the coauthor of *Social Welfare Policy and Practice* (with E. Segal, 1998) and has published articles on the impact of social welfare policies on women, people with disabilities, and economically disadvantaged populations.

Amber Ault, PhD, is director of diversity in the School of Pharmacy at the University of Wisconsin, Madison.

Medora Barnes is a PhD candidate in the Department of Sociology at the University of Connecticut.

Wonda Baugh is an undergraduate student in interdisciplinary studies, with an emphasis on women and gender studies and history, at Arizona State University.

Suzanne Bergeron, PhD, is director of the Women's and Gender Studies Program and associate professor of women's studies and social sciences at the University of Michigan, Dearborn.

Darla Bowen is an MA student in women's studies at the University of Cincinnati.

Aimee Burke is a PhD candidate in the School of Social Work at Arizona State University.

Samantha Casne received her MA in women's studies at the University of Cincinnati in 2007.

Karma R. Chávez recently finished her PhD in intercultural communication and rhetoric at Arizona State University. Her current research centers on the intersections between sexuality and migration and on coalitional politics. She is guest editing a forthcoming issue of *Women's Studies in Communication,* on power feminism.

Cynthia Childress is a PhD candidate in the Department of English at the University of Louisiana at Lafayette, specializing in women's literature and feminist theory.

Sara Collins is a senior at Gallaudet University, majoring in sociology and minoring in government and women's studies. She has maintained a 4.0 throughout her years of study at Gallaudet, while engaging in extensive service and lobbying work. She plans to pursue law or graduate school after graduating in spring 2008.

Lynn Comerford is assistant professor of human development and women's studies at California State University, East Bay.

Carla Corroto is assistant professor of sociology at the University of Wisconsin, Whitewater.

Damaris Del Valle is an MA student in women's studies and a JD student in the College of Law at the University of Cincinnati.

Patrice Natalie Delevante is currently a PhD student in American studies at the University of Maryland, College Park. She received her MA in gender/cultural studies at Simmons College. Her research and teaching interests include twentieth-century African American literature and culture, transnational studies, and popular culture. She is a contributing author to the *Oxford Encyclopedia of Women in World History* (2007).

Nadia Dropkin is an undergraduate student in women's studies at the State University of New York, Oswego.

Breanne Fahs, PhD, is assistant professor of women's studies at Arizona State University.

Giovanna Follo is a PhD candidate in sociology at Wayne State University. Her research interests include studies of gender, sport, and inequality. Her current research focuses on women's experiences when participating in contact sport.

Jan Marie Fritz, PhD, is professor of planning and faculty affiliate of women's studies at the University of Cincinnati.

Marcella Gemelli is a PhD candidate in sociology at Arizona State University in 2007.

Federica Gentile received her MA in women's studies at the University of Cincinnati in 2007.

Kathryn Gentzke received her MA in humanities at the International University of Bremen, Germany.

Shahin Gerami, PhD, is director and associate professor of women's studies at San Jose State University.

Michelle Gibson, PhD, is an associate professor of women's studies at the University of Cincinnati. She is coauthor, with Deborah T. Meem, of *Femme/Butch: New Considerations of the Way We Want to Go* (2002) and *Lesbian Academic Couples* (2006).

Lori Girshick, PhD, is program coordinator at the Intergroup Relations Center at Arizona State University.

Dustin Goltz is a PhD student in the Hugh Downs School of Human Communication at Arizona State University. His interests include performance studies, queer theory, and popular culture criticism.

LaKresha Graham is a PhD student in the Hugh Downs School of Human Communication at Arizona State University.

Lanai Greenhalgh, MA, MS, LCSW, received her MS in communication from Utah State University and her MA in social service administration at the University of Chicago.

Jennifer Heller is lecturer in humanities and Western civilization at the University of Kansas.

Sabine Henrichsen-Schrembs is a PhD candidate in social sciences at the International University of Bremen, Germany. She has taught in the Department of Humanities at Dominican University of California.

Yetta Howard is a PhD candidate in the Department of English at the University of Southern California.

Jeni Jenkins is an MA student in women's studies at the University of Cincinnati.

Elizabeth Jenner, PhD, is an assistant professor of sociology at Gustavus Adolphus College.

Jessica Jennrich, MA, is associate chair of women's and gender studies and a PhD student in educational leadership and policy analysis at the University of Missouri, Columbia.

Marc J. W. de Jong is a PhD candidate in sociology at the University of Southern California.

Emily Joy received her BA in art and women's studies at the University of Cincinnati in 2007.

Marjon Kamrani is a PhD candidate in the Department of Political Science at the University of Cincinnati.

Wendy Kline is associate professor of history and faculty affiliate of women's studies at the University of Cincinnati. She is the author of *Building a Better Race: Gender, Sexuality and Eugenics from the Turn of the Century to the Baby Boom* (2005).

Kai Kohlsdorf received his MA in women's studies at the University of Cincinnati in 2007.

Jeanette Koncikowski, MEd, is an adjunct psychology instructor at Trocaire College and a child welfare education specialist at Buffalo State College. She is also cofounder of Prevention Educators, a consulting agency dedicated to violence prevention through community education and empowerment.

Suzanne Goodney Lea, PhD, is director of the Criminal Justice Program at Trinity University, where she focuses her research and teaching efforts on juvenile delinquency, the social psychology of crime, and the nexus of race, gender, and crime. Her recent book, *Delinquency and Animal Cruelty: Myths and Realities about Social Pathology* (2007), challenges the idea that animal cruelty enacted by children leads to adult violence.

Margaret Leaf is a PhD candidate in sociology at Florida State University.

Crista Lebens, PhD, is associate professor of philosophy and religious studies at the University of Wisconsin, Whitewater.

Melodye Lehnerer, PhD, teaches sociology in the Department of Human Behavior at the Community College of Southern Nevada.

Anne McDaniel is a PhD student in sociology at Ohio State University.

Sara McKinnon is a PhD student in the Hugh Downs School of Human Communication at Arizona State University.

Lori McNeil, PhD, is an assistant professor of sociology in the Department of Sociology and Anthropology at Long Island University, C. W. Post Campus.

Andrea Bertotti Metoyer, PhD, is assistant professor of sociology at Gonzaga University.

Derek Mize received his MA in women's studies and is a JD student in the College of Law at the University of Cincinnati.

Christine H. Morton, PhD, is a research sociologist, examining maternity care roles and women's experiences of birth and breastfeeding. She founded ReproNetwork, a social networking resource for reproductive advocates and academics.

Craig Nagoshi, PhD, is associate professor of psychology at Arizona State University.

Julie Nagoshi is a PhD student in the School of Social Work at Arizona State University.

Meredith Nash is a PhD candidate in gender studies and development at the University of Melbourne, Australia.

Lisa Nicolosi is an MA student in women's studies and a JD student in the College of Law at the University of Cincinnati.

Arlyn Penaranda is a senior, majoring in sociology and government with a minor in women's studies, at Gallaudet University. In the summer of 2007, she completed an internship in the Philippines, where she worked with an organization that is trying to curtail the amount of human trafficking and sex slavery that goes on in the country by providing better options for women and strengthening the laws that prevent these abuses.

Heidi Pitzer received her MA in women's studies at the University of Cincinnati in 2007.

Carrie Anne Platt is a PhD candidate and Walter R. Fisher Fellow in the Annenberg School for Communication at the University of Southern California.

Margaret Power, PhD, is associate professor of history at the Illinois Institute of Technology. She is the author of *Right-Wing Women in Chile: Feminine Power and the Struggle against Allende, 1964–1973* (2002).

Sarvani Prasad is an MA student in women's studies and a JD student in the College of Law at the University of Cincinnati.

Martha Woodson Rees, PhD, is head of anthropology and associate professor of anthropology and women's studies at the University of Cincinnati.

Mamta Sagar, PhD, is based in Mehdipatnam, Hyderabad, India.

Olga Sanmiguel-Valderrama, PhD, is assistant professor of women's studies at the University of Cincinnati.

Jessica Share, PhD, received her doctorate in women's studies at the University of Iowa, where she focused on studies of queer identities and space.

Danielle Smith, PhD, is assistant professor of sociology at the Rochester Institute of Technology.

Dewi Susilastuti, PhD, is visiting assistant professor of sociology at the University of Kentucky.

Farha Ternikar, PhD, is assistant professor of sociology at Le Moyne College.

Laura Turner received her BA in women's studies at the University of Cincinnati in 2007.

Andrew S. Valeras, DO, is a Family Practice Resident at Concord Hospital in Concord, New Hampshire. He received his BA in biology from Boston College and graduated from Arizona College of Osteopathic Medicine in 2007.

Katie Weber is an MA student in women's studies and a JD student in the College of Law at the University of Cincinnati.

Jennifer Wesely, PhD, is assistant professor of criminal justice at the University of North Florida.

Jill Williams is an MA student in women's studies at the University of Cincinnati.

Trish Wilson is an independent writer and a graduate of Hood College.

Julie Winterich, PhD, is research assistant professor of Family and Community Medicine at Wake Forest University.

Chana Wolfson is a senior, majoring in women's studies and minoring in Latin American studies, at the University of Cincinnati.

Kathryn Woods (MSW, Arizona State University) is assistant director of the Office of Women's Programs and Studies at Colorado State University, Fort Collins.

Laura J. Zilney is completing her PhD in human sexuality at the Institute for Advanced Study of Human Sexuality, San Francisco. She has authored several articles on sexuality and is the coauthor of two forthcoming books on sexual offending. She has a private practice as a clinical sexologist in Brampton, Ontario, Canada.

Jason Zingsheim is a PhD candidate in the Hugh Downs School of Human Communication at Arizona State University.

INDEX

Bisexuality, 54–60; biphobia and, 239–40; connotations of, 55; dominant culture threat of, 58; marginalized culture threatened, 58–59; as sexual liberation, 59; stress and, 56
Bivans, Ann-Marie, 35
Black, Julia, 196
Black Panthers, 179
Blackwell, Susana, 311
Black widowhood, 100
Blau, Francine, 628
Blum, Linda, 98
Body dysmorphic disorder (BDD), 394
Body image, 521–26
Body modification, 390, 392–95
Bolin, Ann, 611–13, 615
Bolotin, Susan, 436
Borden, Lizzie, 100, 101
Borger, Julian, 421
Bornstein, Kate, 615
Born to Brothels, 530
Boserup, Ester, 218–19
Boswell, John, 563
Botox revolution, 392
Bottlenose dolphins, 567
Bowers v. Hardwick, 243, 575
Bowlby, John, 82
Boyden, John S., 418
Braden, Anne, 605
Brasher, Brenda, 491
Braun, Carol Moseley, 397, 473
Breast cancer, 60–63
Breastfeeding, 63–66, 343–44
Breedlove, Marc, 385
Brewer, Lucy, 368
Brink, Judy, 492
Briski, Zana, 530
Brock, Deborah, 102
Broverman, I., 176
Broverman, J., 176
Brown, Antoinette, 484–86
Browne, Cheryl, 33
Brown, Lyn Mikel, 525
Brownmiller, Susan, 176, 553
Bruce, Steve, 488
Bruch, Hilda, 128
Brumberg, Joan, 127
Bryant, Anita, 296, 410, 412
Buchanan, James, 417
Buck, Linda, 142
Buddhism, 485–86
Buder, Madonna, 16
Buffy the Vampire Slayer, 331
Bulimia, 127
Bush, George W., 4, 157, 160, 164, 198, 311, 363, 506, 510, 609
Bush, Laura, 95, 510, 592
Bussee, Michael, 250
Butler, Judith, 177, 386, 446, 456
Butler, Richard G., 379

Cachen, Raymond, 84
Cady Stanton, Elizabeth, 605
CAH. *See* Congenital adrenal hyperplasia
California Institute of the Arts, 182–83
Cancer, 61
Capitalist society, 17–18, 403
Caraway, Hattie, 396
Carder, Angela, 195
Carpenter, Karen, 128
Carr, Marilyn, 207
Carroll, Diahann, 330
Carter, Jimmy, 410
Casket girls, 308
Caste system, 14
The Catcher in the Rye (Salinger), 431
Catholic church, 480
CAWP. *See* Center for American Women in Politics
Cayleff, Susan E., 581
CDC. *See* Centers for Disease Control
CEDAW. *See* Convention on the Elimination of All Forms of Discrimination Against Women
Center for American Women in Politics (CAWP), 397
Centers for Disease Control (CDC), 247
Cesarean childbirth, 50
Chapkis, Wendy, 366, 549
Chase, Cheryl, 272
Chase, Margaret, 396
Chastity, 166
Chaudhry, Neena, 16
Chaung, 531
Chen, Martha, 207
Chernin, Kim, 130
Cheslock, John J., 609
Chesney-Lind, Meda, 103
Chicago, Judy, 182–84
Childbirth, 45–54; alternative approaches to, 50–52; best practices for, 53–54; cesarean, 50; history of, 46–47; home, 51–52; information on, 47; lotus, 51; medical intervention in, 48–49; medicalization of, 341–42; pain relief for, 52–54
Childcare, 80–86; defining, 81–82; medical influence in, 83–84; private/collective responsibility in, 82–83; public opinion on, 84; stay-at-home parental, 83, 86; wages/turnover in, 85–86
Child custody, 67–73; citizens impacted by, 67–68; federal/state interventions on, 70–71; gender-neutral, 68; solutions debate on, 69–70; types of, 68–69
Children, 83, 190
Child sexual abuse, 73–79, 545; coping skills in, 78; defining, 74; impact of, 76–79; intimacy/sexuality difficulties in, 77–78; PTSD in, 78–79; resiliency in, 76–77; shame/self-blame in, 77
Child support, enforcing, 162–63, 625–26